cover, *20 West, Sloansville, New York*, Laurie Searl
page i, *20 West, New York*, Laurie Searl

PUBLISHED BY STATE UNIVERSITY OF NEW YORK PRESS, ALBANY

© 2008 State University of New York

For information, contact State University of New York Press, Albany, NY
www.sunypress.edu

Production and book design, Laurie Searl
Marketing, Susan M. Petrie

Library of Congress Cataloging-in-Publication Data

Nelson, Mac.
 Twenty west : the great road across America / Mac Nelson.
    p. cm.
 Includes bibliographical references and index.
 ISBN 978-0-7914-7469-3 (hardcover : alk. paper) 1. United States —
Description and travel. 2. United States Highway 20 — Description and
travel. 3. West (U.S.) — Description and travel. 4. United States —
History — Anecdotes. 5. United States Highway 20 — History —
Anecdotes. 6. West (U.S.) — History — Anecdotes. 7. United States
— History, Local. 8. United States — Biography. 9. Nelson, Mac —
Travel — United States. I. Title. II. Title: 20 West.
 E169.Z83N46 2008
 973–dc22   2007035524

10   9   8   7   6   5   4   3   2   1

Mac Nelson

20 WEST

ACROSS AMERICA

state university of new york press

... the crooked roads without improvement
are the roads of genius.

WILLIAM BLAKE, *The Marriage of Heaven and Hell,* 1793

contents

Acknowledgments   ix

Introduction: The Road and Us   xi

1   The Power of the Word along the Great Road   1

2   The Great Road to Justice and Freedom:
God, Man, and Woman   27

3   Power and Empire on the Great Road:
Six Presidents and a Plutocrat   71

4   Westering: Prairies and Plains,
the Big Empty and the Sandhills   99

5   Soldiers and Indians:
The Struggle for a Continent   139

6   The Best Idea:
Yellowstone, the Peaceable Kingdom   167

7   The Great Road to Wilderness   219

8   "Ocian in View! O! The Joy!"   261

Notes   293

List of Works Cited (and Other Important Books)   309

Index   313

acknowledgments

Nobody writes a book like this without a lot of help from a lot of great people. My deepest thanks are due to:

Fellow travellers:
The Nelson family I rode with as a kid. The friends—Andy, Mike, Ralph, Stan—whom I drove with as a teenager. And another Nelson family, my late wife Jeanne and our children, Michael, David, Laurie, and Julie. We did a lot of great miles and wet tents together.

Thanks to all my canoe partners, from Jim O'Brien through Jack Berkley, Tom Loughlin, Ted Sharon, Stan Kessler ("the Marine"), Terry Klaaren, Ralph Wanger, and Bernie George.

Sources of knowledge and inspiration:
From Henry David Thoreau and Aldo Leopold through many knowledgeable friends, named in the text. The Yellowstone Loons (members of a benign chatroom cult) have taught me much, especially about getting into the wilderness. The staffs of Daniel Reed Library, SUNY-Fredonia, and the University of Nebraska Love Library, Lincoln, have been unfailingly helpful. Caroline Sandoz Pifer was invaluable for Sandoz material and lore.

Helpful associates and critics:
Joyce Haines, Elizabeth Hoffman Nelson, and Diana Hume George traveled with me while I researched parts of this book, helped me see things more clearly, and helped collect information. Bob Schweik, bless him, read the entire manuscript in its cruder stages and provided stiff but supportive and extensive criticism. Ted Sharon did the same with the Yellowstone

sections. Terry and Howard Mosher made helpful suggestions. My computer guru, Matthew Warren, steered "Mac's book" through digital minefields. My colleagues and the administration at SUNY-Fredonia have been generous in supporting and granting leave time, without which this book would never have been finished. Thank you, President Dennis Hefner, and all your associates. The staff of SUNY Press has been great, including the anonymous readers, who helped make this a better book. Laurie Searl and Susan Petrie have been patient, smart, and creative.

And, for at least 111 K hard miles:
Three canoes, many tents, and a mythic host of cars: "Oh, my Bert and my Tingy long ago," and my current great rides, Lilley and Loopy.

Thank you all.
Mac Nelson
Brocton, New York, on the Great Road

Mac at Mud Volcano, Yellowstone National Park, circa 1982
Photo by Diana Hume George

introduction

the road and us

◆ Most Americans have strong relationships to and feelings about The Road—to one special road, or just to the idea of The Road—from "The Arkansas Traveler" and *Huckleberry Finn* to *On the Road* and *Thelma and Louise*. Ours is such a vast country that travel is a major topic of American history, literature, legend, and art. Coming to the New World in the sixteenth century, the Spaniards shortened its vast distances with horses, which they unwittingly bequeathed to the Plains Indians, changing and enriching their lives forever.

Some great early American roads were on water, some on rails. Voyageurs paddled canoes on the lakes and rivers. John Chapman ("Johnny Appleseed") carried his bountiful cargo down the Ohio in a double canoe. (See Michael Pollan's wonderful book *The Botany of Desire*, which paints him as an "American Bacchus.") After the completion of the Erie Canal in 1825, shallow draft boats towed by mules or horses hauled "lumber, coal, and hay" from Albany to Buffalo. The Erie Canal was 363 miles long and four feet deep (soon enlarged to seven feet, to take much heavier loads): quite boring and immensely practical. Hence the grand old comic song about bogus maritime peril:

> Oh, the Ee-ri-ee was a risin',
>> And the gin was a-gettin' low,
> And I scarcely think we'll get a drink
>> 'Til we get to Buffalo-o-o, 'til we get to Buffalo.

The historic Erie Canal route is now part of a National Heritage Corridor, much of it paralleling the route of US 20 in New York State.

You can see a stone lock from the old canal, one of what were once eighty-three such, dry now, near milepost 308.3 on the New York Thruway, a modern version of old US 20.

The author circa 1939, riding a stationary vehicle near the the Great Road.

early American travel

Lewis and Clark planned more river travel than they could accomplish. Their main aim, to find a water route to the Pacific, was unsuccessful, as there wasn't one.[1] The Missouri River is not nearly so deep or navigable as the Mississippi or the Ohio, so the Corps of Discovery walked or rode much more than they floated, towed, or sailed. The decaying skeleton of their unwieldy iron-framed river boat is still buried somewhere in the West, a treasure for some fortunate future archaeologist to find. The first successful steamboat, Robert Fulton's Clermont, went up the Hudson from New York City to Albany in 1807 at the brisk speed of five miles per hour. Abe Lincoln, like Huck Finn and Jim, rafted on the Mississippi; Mark Twain and his fellows piloted riverboats there. Clipper ships connected the otherwise separate American coasts by laboriously rounding stormy Cape Horn at the southern tip of South America. Some Gold Rush '49ers tried to get to the California gold fields more quickly by crossing the Isthmus of Panama by land. This arduous route was not a success.

The Pony Express had a brief and unsuccessful history in fact, being rendered irrelevant by the telegraph in 1852, after less than two years of service. Its riders—"young skinny wiry . . . orphans preferred"—survive as heroes of legend, as they should. One of them, Buffalo Bill Cody, became the archetypal Western scout and showman. The transcontinental railroad, completed in 1869, made another revolution and made possible the unification of the nation, the settling of the plains, and international markets for American livestock and crops. See Walt Whitman's

US 20 in Brocton, NY, looking west. My town, my car, my road, my title.

"To A Locomotive in Winter," "unpent, and glad, and strong;" and Emily Dickinson's "I Like To See It Lap The Miles." I think her "neigh like Boanerges" (a locomotive shrieking like a Biblical monster) is one of the weirdest, finest phrases in American poetry.

the Model T and the need for good roads

Then, a century ago, came the mass-produced automobile—with few decent roads to drive it on. In the mid-nineteenth century, the federal government had built the National Road, from the East (Washington, D.C.) to the then far West: Vandalia, Illinois. But the National Road was not intended or built for heavy vehicular traffic. Not until the development of the internal combustion engine did road traffic approach water or rail in efficiency or bulk volume.

The Ford Model T, which began production in 1907, wrought a social revolution. The movement for good roads took off when more than a few rich people had autos. In 1913, Henry Ford inaugurated the assembly line process for manufacturing autos in ever larger numbers at an affordable price. Nineteen thirteen also saw the beginning of the commercial construct known as The Lincoln Highway. Nineteen twenty-seven saw the first comprehensive, systematic federal road planning and numbering.

A twenty-nine-year-old U.S. Army lieutenant colonel from Abilene, Kansas, participated in the Army's Trans-Continental Convoy in 1919, as an observer from the Tank Corps. He had a great, boyish time, camping out along the way, seeing, experiencing, learning his country. It took the convoy sixty-two days to reach the Pacific, at an average speed of six miles an hour. That's a very small gain over the pace of the steamboat *Clermont*, one hundred and twelve years earlier (*Automobile*, December 2006, 88–89). That lieutenant colonel never forgot how tough it was to slog through the mud of the early roads, even the best of them, that would become parts of the Lincoln Highway, the convoy's main route from the Zero Milepost in Washington, D.C., to San Francisco. Nearly forty years later, when former Lieutenant Colonel Dwight D. Eisenhower had planned and ordered the largest attack in the history of warfare, won a world war, and become President of the United States, the Interstate Highway system was mandated and begun. President Eisenhower signed the legislation in 1956, and the system is now named for him. That system was first planned, promoted, and financed, as were Hitler's autobahns, as military infrastructure for moving troops rapidly about the country.

road trip!

The Road is so fundamental and mythic for modern Americans that we almost don't notice its poetic power. A most persistent media topic is Road Rage; some states post special emergency numbers on road signs to report it. So auto-oriented are we that even "parking rage" has become an issue in San Francisco (New York Times, January 6, 2007). Politicians tremble and scurry for cover whenever gasoline gets near four dollars a gallon, half what it costs Italians or Brits. If it stays that high for long, metaphorical heads will roll.

Americans were restless, nudgy, from the beginning. Old song: "I get a toothache in my heel / When I try to settle down." In the 1830s, Alexis de Tocqueville wrote that the American was ever eager for travel, to "whirl away his happiness." Remembering some difficult trips, I agree. When a pre-motorized 1850s American got "the hypos," "the spleen" (the blues, funk, depression), or started following funeral processions, or "methodically knocking peoples' hats off," "whenever it is a damp, drizzly November in my soul," he might escape by going to sea on a whaling ship, as Herman Melville's Ishmael did. The place where Melville completed that wonderfully funny opening page of *Moby Dick*, Arrowhead Farm in the Berkshires, is just off US 20, hence part of my itinerary for this book.

Our ancestors might also walk, as Henry David Thoreau so famously did: "Eastward I go only by force; westward I go free." Not that Thoreau much liked roads: "Roads are made for horses and men of business." Later in the same essay ("Walking") he says, "There are a few old roads that may be trodden with profit . . . if . . . they are nearly discontinued." "I frequently tramped eight or ten miles through the deepest snow to keep an appointment with a beech tree, or a yellow birch, or an old aquaintance among the pines" (*Walden*, "Former Inhabitants; & Winter Visitors").

But in the century since the Model T Revolution, most Americans go for a Sunday drive, or on a Road Trip, go "On the Road again," take *Main-Travelled Roads*, or travel *Blue Highways*. When we go *On The Road*, we can learn about our remarkable country and its history. We can also, as Jack Kerouac did, learn a great deal about ourselves. We all have stories about exploits on and relationships to The Road. This book will deal with some of mine, and trace some relationships to the roads I have known, traveled, lived on, dreamt about. If it has value, it will remind others of their experiences, and perhaps enrich them.

mythic American roads

Why US 20? Why not another road?

The American roads that have become important parts of our public consciousness are The Lincoln Highway, most of it now subsumed in the Interstate Highway system and US 30; parts of US 40, once known as the National Road; and what little is left of US 66, the Mother Road of the Dust Bowl. They all deserve their celebrity: for important firsts, scenic merit, or historic diasporas. Much has been said, written, and sung about them. My bibliography refers you to some of this fine stuff.

These historic roads run east-west, suited to the "westering" American soul. Henry David Thoreau agreed: "I must walk toward Oregon, and not toward Europe. And that way the nation is moving, and I may say that mankind progress from east to west. . . . We go westward as into the future, with a spirit of enterprise and adventure" ("Walking," in *The Heath Anthology of American Literature*, Volume One, Second Edition, New York, 1994, 2086, 2089.) There are some fabled roads that run other ways. There are great north to south roads, too: US 1 in the east, 2,400 miles, Maine to Key West, Florida; US 101 and California 1 in the west. The Natchez Trace angles southwest to New Orleans. I know 'em and like 'em all. But the mythic American roads head west.

the roads in my life: north / south

Before I was conscious of having a consciousness, some great roads began to speak to me, to impress their characters on my life. US 41 was the first. After some typically restless American questing, eight domiciles throughout the Midwest in my first ten years, my family moved in 1943 to the North Shore Chicago suburb of Highland Park. For the first year, we rented a big house on the high lateral moraine that gives the western Lake Michigan shoreline its bluffs. Our house was half a block up the hill from the lake, half a block from sternly fenced Fort Sheridan, sited there in the late nineteenth century to give a comforting military presence for Chicagoans nervous about Haymarket bombs, Pullman strikes, labor unions, and socialist agitation. I watched AT-6 trainer planes towing sleeve targets above the lake to train ("pom-pom-pom!" "ack-ack-ack-ack!") World War II antiaircraft gunners. I was a very patriotic ten-year-old plane spotter. If a Zero or a Messerschmidt 109 were to attack Highland Park, Illinois, I was prepared to identify and report it. The Japs and the Nazis must have known I was ready for them, because they never came. Fort Sheridan has since been decommissioned and has become a posh real estate development.

Our next house—where I grew up—was down and west from the lake, in a different physiographic province, on the northeastern swath of the great prairie that sweeps west to Nebraska. To the east was Lake Michigan, Elm Place School and Highland Park High School, and the center of town. The mayor owned Garnett's department store, Earl Gsell ran the drug store, Anton Fraunhofer trimmed me in Tony's Barber Shop. Meyer's and Baum's were the bakeries, Shelton's was for hamburgers, Larson's for magazines, Neill's for baseball gloves. Town centers still mattered then, though the shopping mall was a-borning, in Kansas City, in Washington, D.C., in the Chicago exurbs.

South was Chicago: radio (no TV yet, though Kukla, Fran, and Ollie would arrive soon, bless them), politics, excitement, gangsters, culture, the *Trib*, the *Daily News*, the Cubs and Sox and Hawks and Bears. On clear nights we would watch the sweeping light of the Lindbergh Beacon

Kukla, Mac, and Ollie. Chicago Historical Society Museum, Chicago

atop the Palmolive Building, later the Playboy Building (*o tempora, o mores*), twenty miles to the south on the city's lakefront. The building survives, but the beacon has been turned off—it bothered the moneyed occupants of the newer high-rises. North was, briefly, summer among the cool lakes and pinelands and mosquitos of Northern Wisconsin.

We didn't look or think west much, except to visit family in DeKalb County. West seemed the least interesting direction. But it did boast US 41, Skokie Boulevard, a very high-tech road for its time: Four Lanes of Traffic! Speed Limit 45 mph! 45! Skokie also had frequent stoplights and cross streets, no median, and a high accident rate. Superhighways were still on the horizon, realized only minimally in the distant marvel of the Pennsylvania Turnpike, which I had not yet seen. On sweltering summer Sunday nights, trying to get to sleep before there were home air conditioners, I heard the distant hum of traffic and horns on Skokie and saw the faint glow of the lights, mostly, I fancied, people coming back from the lake country after a cool weekend in southern Wisconsin.

41 was the road my family would take, later in the summer, for *our* week among the fir trees, *our* week to catch the northerns, *our* road trip to the land of Schlitz and Blatz and cheese shops and polkas and white margarine. (Wisconsin's politically potent dairy farmers pushed the butterfat by forbidding the sale of artificially colored oleomargarine until well into the 1960s. Wisconsin's license plate slogan is *not* "Eat Cheese or Die," but it oughta be.)

41 was the road to the North Woods, the great American wilderness: camps, canoe trips, Indian reservations, muskellunge so big the fishing guides carried little revolvers to kill them. Was that just hype? Did they ever *use* them? 41 took us to the richest ice cream in the world, butterscotch ripple from the Iron River Creamery, outhouses, funny old mildewed books—Chick Sale, *Bab Ballads*, Robert W. Service. 41 took us to spiderwebs in the musty cabins, songs and stories and boats and campfires, walleyes and cribbage and too much breakfast.

41 was our teenage Jornada del Muerto, where we drove too fast in the hot summer dark. "We hit a hundred!," at least by the hyped-up speedometer in Stan's father's black whale of a '49 Lincoln convertible, four doors, no top, no seat belts, no sense, "wild to be wreckage forever," in James Dickey's wonderful phrase.

41 was a boundary, political, geographical, developmental. Just one mile west, on the west side of 41, you could, with connections, get beer. No alcohol could be bought or sold in our smug suburb, a dry town like

most of the others along the North Shore. Consumption, on the other hand, was quite legal and very popular.

41 was the road north in the fall. Once there was even a miss school/play hookey/go fishin' October week that turned into a blaze of sugar maples and birches and pines, purple and orange and red and white and green, reflected in chilly bright blue water. Those days stunned me—a twelve-year-old lout—with their beauty.

41 was the glamour road that became elegant Lake Shore Drive and ran past the Gold Coast in Chicago. There at the Oak Street beach curve is where Bertha Palmer, wife of Potter Palmer of Marshall Field wealth, ruled her vast Victorian mansion. My grandmother Blanche Hutton

The old house, looking something like it did in 1834.

went to a ball there as a girl in the 1890s. Fifty years later she was still in awe that the house had had no external doorknobs: one had to be admitted. Once and once only, she was. The Potter Palmer house is long gone, replaced by minimalist high-rises, but I remember it brooding over the great lakefront curve of 41.

41 was the way south in the winter for some people, though not for us. It was years before I connected the dots and realized that our 41 was the same 41 I later drove near Miami, years more before I discovered it ran all the way from northern Michigan (the Keewenaw Peninsula, jutting into Lake Superior) to Miami, ending with that glorious American coinage, the Tamiami Trail (Tampa to Miami). Chicago and Miami, North and South. Keewenaw to Tamiami—wonderful names, for the termini of the same beckoning road.

Connections: the road made them, and I was slowly making mine. Later, this road, US 41, conjoined with US 12 and US 20, would be the road I would take around the southern tip of Lake Michigan to leave home, to go east to college. In September 1951, the Chicago and Milwaukee area Williams College contingents traveled to college on three connecting passenger trains, in the last year that the Boston & Maine, the railroad that Thoreau wrote "rides on us," took passengers to Williamstown, Massachusetts. Always thereafter in a car, always starting on 41 and 20. US 41, a great road, might have been the subject of this book.

the roads in my life : east / west

But Americans think mostly east-west, not north-south. Robert Frost saw the mythic direction of the land as "vaguely realizing westward." At the age of seven or eight, before I had heard of Lewis and Clark, before I knew how to read a map, I would often go across the road from my house at 4015 Gladstone Boulevard to a steep bluff in the north end of Kansas City, Missouri, overlooking the road part way down, appropriately named "Cliff Drive." I loved to stand and look off across the Missouri River, beyond the railroad roundhouse and freightyard way below the cliff, into the blue haze of distance.

I know now that I was, in a way, looking West, "Across the Wide Missouri," looking into both the past and the future of America. Never mind that the view was, at that particular bend in the great river, more north than west. Never mind that I couldn't see the river from the overlooks along the bluff. I knew it was Westward, and I knew the Missouri was there somewhere.

I didn't have the language for it then, but, though it wasn't the Grand Canyon, I'd say that that overlook was my first brush with The Sublime. It sure as hell gave me a sense of scope, immensity, unimaginable distance, though I had no idea I was in contact with the Louisiana Purchase, with the drainage system of the mightiest river in North America.

Partisans of the Mississippi may take issue with this last statement. I think of the Missouri as the greater of the two, and consider the Mississippi's primacy a trick of water volume and Eurocentric east-west history. White men knew the Mississippi long before they traced the Missouri to its source, so in their minds they subjugated the greater to the lesser, the longer to the shorter.[2] Kindly do not confuse the author with hydrological facts. The Missouri River drains one-sixth of the North American continent, more than half a million square miles. Wallace Stegner called the Missouri "the mightiest river on the continent." I agree.

What about other east-west roads? One that speaks powerfully to me is US 6. 6 was once the longest coast-to-coast highway of all, from Long Beach, south of Los Angeles, all the way to the northern tip of Cape Cod, 3,652 miles (Federal Highway Administration Web-site). In its current bobtailed form, it's still 3,249 miles, and it traverses fourteen states. Indeed, there seems no good reason why it shouldn't still go cross-country. But in a reorganization of highway routes in 1963, The Lords of the Numbers decreed that US 6 should poop out in Bishop, just over the California border from Nevada, that it should not share the historic, water-plundered Owens Valley route with US 395 and William Mulholland's aqueduct, on its way to flush the toilets of L.A. Pity. (I hear the Owens Valley may soon be getting back some of its water, for sixty-two miles, at least. Good for everyone involved, especially the mayor of L.A., Antonio Villaraigosa. Cf. *High Country News*, December 25, 2006, 3).

US 6, coast-to-coast: I've done most of it, including all the western sections. What a trip it is, as rich and diverse as any east-west road. From Provincetown, Massachusetts, off whose coast the Pilgrims signed the Mayflower compact, to Disneyland; from First Encounter Beach, in Eastham, Mass, where Pilgrims and Indians first fought each other, across the Appalachians to the prairies and the plains and the Rockies to Deseret (the Mormons' name for their haven), to the Great Basin and down along the Sierra past glorious Yosemite to the Pacific at L.A. and Long Beach. Wow. What a long, strange trip it's been.

Jack Kerouac was drawn to US 6, even drew a line along it on a map from coast to coast, the same way I plan routes. He made his first, comically abortive, attempt to hitch across the country on 6. He got no farther than one very rainy day On The Road in New York state, rethought it, and hitched home to wait for better weather. Later, he bought a bus ticket to Chicago and hitched across Iowa on US 6, though I like to fancy that he might have done some of his hitchhiking on Twenty.

Iowa's US 6 was the very street I once lived on ("Sixth Street") in Grinnell, Iowa. East on US 6 was the road to the Amanas and great German food. 6 is where microprocessors began, sorta, even before there was a Silicon Valley. Bob Noyce, inventor of the integrated chip, was born in Burlington, Iowa, and raised and schooled in Grinnell. He saw his first transistors as a Grinnell College physics student. I talked with him there in 1967, just before he helped found Intel, though I had no clue at the time what a microchip was, or how it would change the world. US 6 is where I sat in the sunroom windows, looking south on 6th and Broad, and watched John Stoops, then a spry ninety-four, James Norman Hall's philosophy professor, cut his lawn. There we planned the family camping trips we loved, and that always began, east or west, on US 6.

US 6 is a highway that has drawn me and mine for forty years, as we crossed the Sagamore Bridge and the Cape Cod Canal, hurrying to East Brewster to get a good campsite at Nickerson State Park—on 6, though it's been demoted to 6A by the superhighway that took its number. US 6 is the road I still take to Cape Cod in the spring, to a cottage I've rented for twenty-five years. The cottage is on Cape Cod Bay, two miles west of 6. The last forty miles of US 6 are known as

"Suicide 6" to the Capers who see it fill with frenzied vacationers every summer, and avoid it as much as possible 'til after Labor Day. I lost a dear friend to its traffic. Farewell, Dingy.

US 6, in short, was and is a big part of my life, and I may write more about it. But this is not a book about 6, or 2 (Larry McMurtry's ideal, Howard Mosher's route), or 40 (George Stewart's choice), or 50 (which William Least Heat Moon favors), great roads all. This is a book about Twenty. Why?

coast-to-coast highways

Numbers are part of the reason. Great coast-to-coast designations have shrunk over the years, mostly under the pressure of the Interstates. These superhighways have superseded and nearly destroyed US 66—as road, though not as myth. They have also undermined the remaining major US highways. In many places, the old US highway exists only as a black and white sign along an Interstate right of way. There are really only two coast-to-coast highways left: US 30 and US 20.

Neither goes quite ocean-to-ocean. Astoria, Oregon, though on a tidal river mouth, is five miles from the Pacific. That's where US 30 ends; it begins in Atlantic City, New Jersey. US 20 starts at Boston's Kenmore Square, three miles from Boston Harbor, Massachusetts Bay, and the Atlantic, and ends a mile from and in sight of the Pacific. These qualifications are piffle. I hereby declare both roads coast-to-coast.

What about US 30, then? When the official, regularized numbers were applied in 1927, the old route known as the Lincoln Highway—originally plotted out and promoted by a combine of businessmen and tourism-hungry cities—was split up among several cross-country routes. US 30 retained most of the Lincoln Highway's eastern mileage.[3] Thirty now runs from Atlantic City, New Jersey, to Astoria, Oregon: just over three thousand miles, through eleven states. It was a great road, especially in the West. It paralleled the Oregon trail for a thousand miles, starting with the mighty Platte River in Nebraska ("an inch deep and a mile wide"), then joining with the Snake and the still mightier Columbia on the way to the Pacific, to the Ultima Thule of Lewis and Clark, their farthest point northwest, where they built Fort Clatsop, Oregon. There's a good book in US 30, but it's not this book.

US 30 has limitations. It begins much farther west than US 20, and is shorter. Atlantic City is not Boston. US 20 stretches across almost fifty-three degrees of latitude (71.07W to 124.05W), four more than US 30. US 20, by my count more than 3,300 miles, is much longer. "This is the big one," says George Cantor of Twenty (*Where the Old Roads Go*, New York: Harper Collins, 1989, 235), and I agree. More important, US 30 has lost much of its historic character. In Wyoming, Idaho, and Oregon, it rarely has an independent right-of-way, being subsumed into Interstates 80 and 84 for about a thousand miles, a third of its length. US 20 has two such sections, but Twenty disappears into interstates for only seventy-five miles, in Wyoming and Idaho. In short, US 20 is still a real cross-country road, really the only one left.

US 20 : the last great road

George Stewart, in his amiable book about US 40, accepts the scope of 20 (and 60 and 70) but says that they "dwindle into insignificance disappointingly in their western sections." (George Stewart, *US 40: Cross Section of the United States of America*, Boston: Houghton Mifflin, 1953, 8) Again, piffle. See what follows for a fuller refutation. Stewart apparently had no eye for Yellowstone or the Snake plains or the Oregon mountains and deserts. Too bad for him.

William Least Heat Moon makes a brief but good case for US 50 as the best road across the middle of the United States (*PrairyErth*, Boston: Houghton Mifflin, 1991, 4). Fine, but 50 begins even farther west than 30 (in Ocean City, Maryland), and craps out near Sacramento. That's not coast-to-coast. In *River Horse, A Voyage Across America* (New York: Houghton Mifflin, 1999, 405) Least Heat Moon calls US 20 "one of the formerly great transcontinental routes." Well, yes—but why "formerly?" It's still there and it's still great. In *Blue Highways*, Least Heat Moon anticipates the end of my journey. He describes Twenty in Oregon as twisty and rural, through mountains to the ocean: yup, sounds good, and is.

Finally: I know US 20, live on it, grew up near it, commute to work on it, and have run on it most mornings for twenty-five years. It has become the Main Street of my life. I am fond of it, and I want to tell its very American story. Hence this book.

twenty and me

Many people in western New York, where I live, date events with reference to The Blizzard of '77, a brutal storm that shut Buffalo down for days and contributed greatly to the city's unenviable and undeserved reputation as the Igloo, the Winter Armpit, of the Northeast. The most entertaining aspect of that harsh blizzard time was listening daily to an old-time AM radio morning drivetime personality, beloved in Buffalo for thirty years, going irascibly, embarrassingly, undeniably bonkers right on the air under the pressure of weather and danger and announcements and closings. He was forcibly retired after the spring thaw. People in Buffalo still hold winter balls based on a Blizzard theme. The big Thirtieth Anniversary is coming up. That's Buffalo humor: ironic, self-deprecatory, surviving.[4]

I lived on the fringes of the Blizzard of '77, hampered but not greatly discommoded by it. I missed one day of work, in my college town, Fredonia, New York, which is bisected by US 20. I had moved out of a house three blocks from Twenty. I needed a place to live. I had very little money. With my then significant other, Diana, I saw every hovel on the Chautauqua County real estate market and found only one I could think of buying and living in, a house that was empty, abandoned, old, drafty, sagging, patched, ugly—and on US 20. It's where I'm writing this. We borrowed some money (thanks, Nancy) and a truck, assembled some helpers, and moved thirty miles from our rental, in January, during that historic blizzard. It was a chilly move and a chillier winter.

The aged house had no insulation or storm windows. When the winter wind was southwest, its prevailing direction, snow blew through the cracks onto the living room floor. The house was (and is) plank style, post and beam, not balloon frame—older, heavier, looser. The huge main beams bore (and bear) adze marks. For many years in this house, winters were genuinely frightening. The winds would howl and the house would shake, the cars would be buried in piles of blown and drifted snow and often wouldn't start, the pipes would freeze and burst unless trickled all night and sometimes even then, toilet bowls *inside* the house twice froze and cracked.

I came to feel a close kinship to Tom Nashe and those other Elizabethans who wrote dippy sweet songs about the beauty of birdsong and the spring—"Cuckoo, jug-jug, pu-we, to-witta-woo! / Spring, the sweet Spring!"—because they were so goddam glad they'd survived another winter much less long and harsh than ours. It gave me a new understanding of pastoral poetry, and of the joy of warmth and spring.

But warmth and spring did come, and with them a chance to begin to know and appreciate this place. The two and a half acres turned green and we put in a half-acre garden, grateful for a bit of land to grow things and eat our own fresh produce, grateful for a big yard, for having our neighbors—a church, the American Legion—at a modest distance. We shored up the saggiest corner of the foundation (thanks, Mark) and turned the plywood and tar paper back wall, crudely patched after a fire, into siding and a door, a porch and a deck. Even in high summer, we could see, through the deep green of the maples, oaks, and horse chestnuts, the blue of Lake Erie, the North Coast of America, from our north windows. To the south, we saw the hills that are the first wrinkle of the Appalachians. It was fine to have a Great Lake in my life again.

The house was old, very old, no doubt about that; but how old? Local histories and historians helped a bit, but the biggest break was meeting Ella Dean, a bright-blue-eyed retired art teacher in her late seventies who lived in the big beautiful Victorian stick-style white house just a few hundred yards west across Main Street—US 20, of course. When I introduced myself, she smiled and took me into her kitchen. "This used to be your kitchen," she said, pointing at the arched tops of the windows in the room, exactly like those in most of my house, which we had taken to calling, deprecatingly, Falling Arches. These arches seemed our house's only nod in the direction of grace or beauty.

Ella told me a story that I later investigated and confirmed, and, at her death, she left me a photo of my house sited where hers now stands, with the same large barns in the background. Yes, it was our house, all right— but with barns, handsome chimneys, shutters, a cupola, and graceful, beautiful porches. There *had* been beauty and grace, but it had not been possible to move beauty and grace and grand sweeping porches on an oxcart.

When Stuart Dean, Ella's father, had wanted to build his new house, he had the front square of the old house jacked up and hauled on a wagon a quarter mile east, and put on the stone foundation it still occupies.[5] The old porches fell into scrap and dust, the old kitchen stayed where it was, and a new backroom kitchen was added to the old house on its new site. All this took place around 1888, the date the new house was built on the old site.

the house and the road

This house had been a hotel—"tavern" or "roadhouse" would probably be more accurate—built as a waystation for the coach traffic on the

The old house, sited where it was a road house. photo circa 1880

main road between Cleveland and Buffalo. Hence the oversized barns, still at the old site today, for relay teams of horses. The interurban railway had come through in 1852 (I found a rail spike from that time), so the house had to be older than that. A house answering this description was built in 1834 by Timothy Judson, who had moved from Connecticut to this frontier and bought property in that year.

> *And this, your house, was frontier . . .*
> STEPHEN VINCENT BENÉT, *Western Star*

In 1834, the United States had twenty-four states. Andrew Jackson, the seventh president, was in the first year of his second term. There were fewer than fifteen million Americans. The northwesternmost point of the nation was Missouri, where I would one day discover my West. In just one hundred years, I would be born. In 1888, when this house was moved, Grover Cleveland, from up the road on US 20, where he had been mayor of Buffalo and governor in Albany, was the twenty-second president. There were thirty-eight states, and the nation's population was close to sixty million.

The search was over. It all fit. I owned a house that had been built on a great road that subsequently became US 20, built there precisely because of the road, to serve and profit from its traffic. I lived in a roadhouse. Neat. What stories these great beams might tell; but they are silent.[6]

South Pass City, population about 7.

Oregon Trail, Wyoming ruts

another house, another road

I later learned more about my house in a most improbable place—the ghost town of South Pass City, Wyoming, near South Pass, a convenient low point (7,550 feet) where the Continental Divide could easily be crossed by wagon trains, and where the Oregon, California, and Mormon trails went west. An estimated 350,000 emigrants passed through South Pass in the 1840s and '50s. It was an American diaspora equalled only by

South Pass City Hotel, South Pass City, Wyoming

the less well chronicled movement of African Americans from the deep South to the industrial North in the first half of the twentieth century. This old mining town has become a grand state historic site, with dirt streets, wooden sidewalks, a visitor center, and (by 2005) thirty buildings stabilized and open to tourists. South Pass City only just escaped Knott's Berryfication in 1965; the buildings were almost sold and moved to the amusement park in Buena Park, California, in suburban Los Angeles.

As I stepped up onto the front porch of the South Pass City Hotel and walked in the front door, I was suddenly, immediately, unsettlingly, 1,700 miles east, going into my own front hall. Stairs and hall much the same, windows and door almost identical, side parlors and dimensions the same, upstairs, the rooms very similar. It was instructive and it was spooky. I had never before understood what Freud meant when he defined "the uncanny" as "the unexpected return of the familiar."

There was a hotel desk in what is my living room, there was a further stack of rooms at the back on both floors, and the attic and roof were lower, but it was otherwise almost identical. On a later visit I noted some significant alterations, but the main point remained. My house was built in 1834, as a roadhouse, to a common plan. Thirty-plus years later, in Wyoming, another builder made a similar structure for a similar reason—he built a roadhouse, to serve and profit from the traffic of another great road.

"oh what was your name in the states?"

Our ancestors went west for many reasons, mostly economic. No doubt some were driven from the states to the western territories by something even stronger than a desire for personal betterment, as this wonderful old American song, collected by Carl Sandburg, suggests:

> Oh what was your name in the states?
> Was it Johnson or Thompson or Bates?
> Did you murder your wife,
> And fly for your life,
> Tell me, what was your name in the states?

The first wagon train went through South Pass in 1824; Narcissa Whitman, the first white woman to make the journey, passed by in 1836. The hotel is later and almost elegant, probably built in 1867 or 1868, when the town became "the center of the Sweetwater gold rush. . . . The following year Main St. was lined with business buildings and the population had grown to nearly 2,000" (Alice Cromie, *Restored America*, American Legacy Press, 1979, 1984, 334). A handout at the site states that the hotel had many distinguished guests, including Robert Todd Lincoln and General Phil Sheridan. There is more continuity in American history, more east meets west, than we are aware of. Exploring and delighting in these connections, these remarkable synchronicities, is one of the pleasures of writing this book.

roads and porches

I have also relearned what Frank Lloyd Wright knew a century ago. Instructed by Ella Dean's photograph, I put new, old-looking porches on the house, and I love to sit on them and watch Lake Erie, as do my neighbors and friends. But US 20 is no longer a dirt road for people and oxen and coaches; it's a busy, noisy highway with lots of traffic, big trucks, people driving by fast, only a few walking by slowly. It proved impossible to do a TV interview on my front porch. It was undeniably scenic, but it required audio retakes indoors. Bucolic it ain't. Wright knew that the automobile was changing the towns and the old roads, so he turned his

Above : the old house loses its tacky siding.
Below : putting porches back on the old house, 2001.

Prairie Houses at right angles to, away from, the street. Porches are won-derful, but they're not as quiet, neighborly, and communal as they used to be. Yet, as I was writing this, I heard a common summer sound from Twenty—the clip-clop of hooves, the trotting buggy horses of my Amish neighbors. Some old things have remarkable life spans: buggies, horses, houses, roads.

While doing the preliminary planning for this book, I scanned a 1927 Road Atlas, enjoying the poetry of the names of the Old Highways: "Dixie," "Spanish Trail,"and the like. I discovered that the road I live and work on was once designated part of "The Yellowstone Trail," an early commercial construct like The Lincoln Highway. I first went to Yellow-stone National Park in 1955; I have since returned twenty-seven times. (At least I think it's twenty-seven; I have truly lost count.) It is still my favorite part of magical America, and it features largely in this book. If I had blundered into a life on "The Yellowstone Trail," even 1,900 road miles east of Yellowstone National Park, I had to write about it. There's a nice movement afoot to restore the nation's consciousness of The Yel-lowstone Trail, and I'm proud to be a tiny part of it (cf. www. yellow-stonetrail.org).

how great is the great road?

There are many ways, none of them perfect, to compute the mileage of a long road. Some standard sources, including the Federal Highway Administration, say 3,365 miles. I counted with three different road atlases, made some arbitrary decisions, and came up with a precise, sus-piciously round number: 3,300 miles, Boston to Newport, Oregon.

My mileages are: MA: 155; NY: 387; PA: 47; OH: 261; IN: 150; IL: 141; IA: 320; NE: 436; WY: 433 plus 91 (34 of which are Interstate); MT: 8, the shortest; ID: 408 (41 are Interstate); OR: 463, the longest, unless Wyoming is. The "plus 91" in Wyoming is my arbitrary decision to count ninety-one miles of Yellowstone National Park's road system as part of the Great Road. Officially, the US 20 designation stops dead at the park's east entrance, as a result of a decison made in 1926. It picks up again just as abruptly at the west entrance. So sue me. I agree with *The American Guide* (New York: Hastings House, 1949, 1109), which says that here "US 20 becomes part of Pk. hy. System." Sure. Common sense. Number or no number, it's the same road. Twenty is indeed "The Big One."

   This great road was heavily traveled very early because it was an easy, level way west, north of the barrier of the Appalachians. Parts of what was designated US 20 in 1926 have had other names. It was the "Old Mass Pike" in Massachusetts, and the "Genesee Turnpike" in western New York. A section from Albany to Cherry Valley was called "The Great Western Turnpike." In 1803 the road went west to Cazenovia, New York, as "The Third Great Western Turnpike." It has been part of several commercially linked Trails, including "The Yellowstone Trail." Recent attempts to stimulate tourist interest have brought names such as "The Concord Grape Trail," for the grapes grown here, or "The Chautauqua Wine Trail," or "The Seaway Trail." It's "The Jewel Road" in parts of Nebraska. George Cantor, in *Where the Old Roads Go*, calls US 20 "The longest road of all," and "The Great Western Road." I will adopt and adapt these terms. For me and for this book, US 20 will be simply "the Great Road."[7]

coverage : thematic outline

This book is not a mile-by-mile guidebook, though I discuss many roadside attractions. I have focused each chapter, moving from east to west, on one major emphasis. I describe everything along the road that relates to that emphasis, such as forts and fights and bison in the west, and poets, religions, and presidents' homes in the east. My aim is to tell the story of the Great Road, its landscapes and peoples, their triumphs and sorrows, its history and its present. In so doing, I move westward along US 20 as follows:

Chapter 1 deals with the eastern beginning of the Road near the Atlantic, and its relationship to American arts and letters, in early New England and in our time.

Chapter 2 studies the remarkable creative relationship of the Great Road to religion and social dynamics in nineteenth-century New York state and elsewhere.

Chapter 3 deals with the bygone age—chiefly the second half of the nineteenth century—when men from the Great Road dominated American politics, business, and society.

Chapter 4 moves past the Great Lakes across the prairies and plains to a series of new frontiers, new Wests, and deals with the lives of some immigrants along the Great Road.

Chapter 5 tells of some key events in the terrible struggle of the young nation against its indigenous peoples, and the nation's consequent movement westward.

Chapters 6 deals with the origins of the national park idea in Yellowstone National Park, and discusses that park's history, its wonders, its environs, and the practicalities of a trip to Yellowstone.

Chapter 7 discusses Yellowstone as an exemplar of wilderness, and deals with the significance and importance of wilderness to twenty-first century Americans.

Chapter 8 concludes the book downslope from the Rockies, traversing and discussing forests, deserts, and mountains, to the Pacific Ocean.

the power of the word along the Great Road

Boston : in the beginning

♦ William Bradford's *Of Plymouth Plantation* was written near the Great Road long before there was such a road, and published in 1630. It's still a fascinating read. The first American to publish a book of poems was Ann Bradstreet, in 1650. Born in Northamptonshire, England, she emigrated to Boston in 1630, as a founder of the Massachusetts Bay Colony. Phyllis Wheatley was born in Africa and brought to America as a slave. Freed and living in Boston, she published a book of poems in 1773; she was the first African American to do so. The Word—the American English written word, in poems, sermons, memoirs, histories—began in and near Boston, and swept west.

Today, US 20 begins three miles west of Massachusetts Bay, in Kenmore Square, under the shadow of Fenway Park's fabled left field wall, the "Green Monster." In the 1950s, US 20 began two miles farther east, almost at the sea; at the west end of Boston's Public Garden, next to Boston Common, the heart of the old city. It is tempting to deal with these historic places and their associations, but Boston is too big a subject for a book about a highway that simply starts west from there. Dozens of major American writers have significant connections to Boston or Cambridge, often through Harvard University: Cotton Mather, Edgar Allan Poe, Oliver Wendell Holmes, Henry Wadsworth Longfellow, T. S. Eliot, e. e. cummings, Elizabeth Bishop, Robert Lowell, Charles Olson, John Berryman (whose poem pays "Homage to Mistress Bradstreet"), Robert Creeley, John Ashberry, Frank O'Hara, Robert Bly, Kenneth Koch, George Plimpton, Donald Hall, Adrienne Rich, and so

1

on and on. I must leave most of Boston's literary and political history for others, and pick up the Great Road west of Boston, selecting a few writers to represent its creativity.

"I have traveled a good deal in Concord"

No one can write the history of any great American road without quoting Henry David Thoreau. His rich Concord world was on a parallel great westering road, Massachusetts 2, nine miles north of US 20; it is the main northern road from the coast to Berkshire county and the New York state boundary. It is geographically defensible to claim it as a northern branch of the Great Road. Soon after it enters New York state in the Albany area, it disappears into US 20 in the Mohawk Valley.

Thoreau enunciated, in a short life, ideas about nature and travel that we're still assimilating. In the essay "Walking," he anticipates the western impulse of the American spirit, and the plan of this book. If we would go west, we need to travel roads to the West, which, to Thoreau, was more than a region or a destination—it was healing, it was salvation, it was Eden, Zion, Jerusalem: "The West of which I speak is but another name for the Wild, and what I have been preparing to say is, that in Wildness is the preservation of the world. . . . I wish to speak a word for Nature, for absolute freedom and wildness . . . to regard man as an inhabitant, or a part and parcel of nature."

"Walking" ends thus: "So we saunter toward the Holy Land, till one day the sun shall shine more brightly than ever he has done, shall perchance shine into our minds and hearts, and light up our whole lives with a great awakening light, as warm and serene and golden as on a bank side in autumn" ("Walking," *The Heath Anthology of American Literature*, Second Edition, Volume One, Lexington MA: Heath, 1994, 2089, 2100). Such loopy, inspired flights of language and thought have made "Walking" a basic text for modern environmentalists like me.

west of Boston

US 20 leaves Boston through the inner suburbs, Brookline to Watertown to Weston and out. Brookline is the site of the home and, from 1884, the working space, of America's premier landscape architect, Frederick Law Olmsted. The Arnold Arboretum, all of Boston's "green necklace" of urban parks, Buffalo's 1,200 acres of Olmsted parks, Brooklyn's grand parks, all are the work of this remarkable, visionary man, of his partner, Calvert Vaux, and their studio. Indeed, he created the specialty he came to dominate, and also created much of the American taste for the pastoral and the picturesque in artificial landscapes. His work is striking and important in Manhattan's Central Park, in Yosemite Valley, in Riverside, Illinois, and many other beautiful green American places.

The Frederick Law Olmsted National Historic Site is two miles south of US 20. The landscape architecture firm that Olmsted and Vaux had founded dwindled and failed during the Great Depression. By the 1940s, the grand old house and grounds, which he punningly named "Fairsted," was no longer the thriving center of American landscape design. The Olmsted family arranged for it to be purchased by the federal government, and today the National Park Service runs excellent tours there. The house is sited on only two acres, but the site feels large, picturesque, almost rural. (Making much of little space is a characteristic Olmsted skill.) The little tour includes what the Rangers wryly call "the shortest hike in the National Park system"—a walk of thirty or forty yards among shrubs and trees on the south lawn. A million documents are preserved and stored here, a treasure trove for historians of landscape architecture.

Brookline is the birthplace of two distinguished Americans. John Fitzgerald Kennedy was born in Brookline in 1917 and lived there for four childhood years, though he's more closely associated with Boston, Cambridge, and Hyannis. The John F. Kennedy Birthplace National Historic Site is a handsome, modest house at 83 Beals Street, owned and occupied by the senior Kennedys until 1921, when they moved to a larger home nearby. It is a few blocks north of US 20. John Kennedy and three of his siblings were born here, reminding us how very recent is the practice of birthing babies in hospitals. The National Park Service gives excellent tours of the house, and of other Kennedy sites in the neighborhood.

The poet Amy Lowell (1874–1925) was born in Brookline into the New England aristocracy, not, like JFK, into a rising Irish political family. She was, with H.D. (Hilda Doolittle) and Ezra Pound, a founder of a major movement in American poetry called "imagism." It emphasized brief, sharp, disconnected images in poetry, of the sort that eventually made William Carlos Williams's "red wheelbarrow" ubiquitous. Lowell's best poem is "Patterns," a powerful dramatic monologue spoken by a woman whose lover has been killed "in a pattern called war," and it's not especially imagistic. She lives on that, and on her priority among modern

New England authors—one of the best female poets in a region justly famed for them. Her distant cousin, Robert Lowell (1917–1977) was a major midcentury poet and a founder of another important poetic school, called the "confessional."

Brookline is an older, inner suburb. Newton and Weston are younger, farther out. They are associated with another remarkable so-called confessional poet. Newton is the birthplace of Anne Sexton, and it is where Sexton often met and workshopped and talked poetry and people with her best friend, the estimable poet Maxine Kumin. (Kumin, who lives in New Hampshire, also lived near US 20 while she did teaching stints at Boston area universities.) Weston, on US 20, is very posh: it has the priciest housing of any city in the Commonwealth of Massachusetts (based on tax figures for houses, *Boston Globe*, June 2002). It is where Anne Sexton lived and worked until her suicide in 1974.

Sylvia Plath is the most flamboyantly famous of the confessional poets, for her short life as well as for her poems. She was born in Boston, in Jamaica Plain, the site of Olmsted's Arnold Arboretum. After her father's untimely and portentous death when Sylvia was eight, the family made its home in west suburban Winthrop. Though Plath's home at the time of her suicide in 1963 was a flat in Primrose Hill in London, suburban Boston was in her bones, as was Smith College, just north of US 20 in Northampton, Massachusetts.

twenty west :
an artistic overview of US 20 in Massachusetts

Smith is just one educational jewel of several in a region once known to geologists as "The Educational Lowlands," north along the Connecticut River. This region, a valley settled early, closely connected to the Great Road, is rich in associations with poets. Born in San Francisco, Robert Frost became farmer, poet, and sage in New Hampshire and Vermont, and was for a time poet-in-residence at Amherst College, in Massachusetts. Emily Dickinson lived almost her entire life in the pretty college town of Amherst, and is buried there.

Farther west in Massachusetts is Berkshire County, where William Cullen Bryant went to college. It has become a summer paradise for the arts—dance, music, art, and theatre. Just off US 20, in Lenox, is The Mount, the home of one of America's greatest novelists, Edith Wharton. Just off of US 20, in Pittsfield, is Arrowhead, the farm where Herman

Melville completed *Moby Dick*. His friend, Nathaniel Hawthorne, wrote *The House of the Seven Gables* (with a Boston area setting) in nearby Stockbridge.

Bradford, Mather, Bradstreet, Wheatley, Bryant, Thoreau, Dickinson, Longfellow, Melville, Hawthorne, Lowell, and Wharton. What a list! The Great Road can't claim Walt Whitman, but most of the other pillars of early Anglo-American religion, history, poetry, and fiction are here. If we curve just a bit north, to Route 2 and Concord, we can include Emerson, Margaret Fuller, and the Alcotts, too. In our own time, Sylvia Plath and Anne Sexton come from the Great Road.

"this is my letter to the world"

Modern American poetry is sometimes seen as a dialogue, or a tussle, between two utterly different poetic styles, those of Emily Dickinson and Walt Whitman. The prim New England spinster takes off the tops of her readers' heads very quietly, and the boisterous Brooklynite does similar creative damage at a higher, more explosive level. Since this is not a book about the history of American poetry, I will discuss only Dickinson, the one who lived and worked near the Great Road.

Emily Dickinson was born in 1830 to a prosperous family in a pretty college town. Amherst College had been founded just nine years before. Emily Dickinson's Amherst was a small but prosperous village in the Connecticut Valley, fifteen miles north of US 20. Noah Webster spent ten productive, impecunious years there (1812–1822), reading and defining for what would become his great *American Dictionary of the English Language* (1828).[1] Amherst's connections to the great world of Massachusetts and the nation went along the corridor of what is now US 20. When Emily made her rare visits to the capital of her state, it was along the route of the Great Road, the "Boston Post Road," from Springfield to Worcester to Boston. This was the road on which she sent her "letter[s] to the world." Most of the nine Dickinson poems that were published in her lifetime appeared in *The Springfield Republican*.

Though Emily Dickinson's family endured sorrows, deaths, losses, and one juicy sex scandal, her public life was fairly unruffled. Her youth was marred by her mother's mental problems. She spent most of a year nearby at Miss Lyons' Female Seminary, which would become Mount Holyoke College. Except for that year, and brief visits to Washington, Philadelphia (for medical treatment), and Boston, she spent her life entirely in Amherst. In this, she was like Henry David Thoreau, who mostly stayed home, yet famously "travelled a good deal in Concord." As the years went by, she went out less and less. Unmoved by the Second Great Awakening, she resisted accepting Jesus as her savior, and soon stopped going to church. After 1860, she spent her life entirely on the grounds of her family's houses, and then entirely in her house, the house her dominating father had built. That house is a shrine to her today.

Though she eventually became a social recluse, she maintained sprightly contact with friends and family, often through the notes and poems she scattered freely among them. She once described herself in a letter to an important editor as "small, like the wren," with "eyes, like the sherry in the glass that the guest leaves." Imaginative, self-deprecating, elusive, daring, cryptic, funny, passionate, dazzling: that's Emily Dickinson. She did *not* scatter her poems freely to the world, that world that "never wrote to [her]." She had contact with the big literary world largely through correspondence and reading, and the occasional visitor from the Great Road.

I don't much like the term *confessional* as it is applied to poets and poems. It has a negative, regurgitative, artless connotation: spill your guts and call it a poem. Despite the term's use to describe eminent male poets such as W. D. Snodgrass and Robert Lowell, it also often seems somewhat sexist. It implies that there is something unseemly about menstruation (Sexton) or a sliced thumb (Plath) or "my uterus" (Sexton again) as a poetic subject. In a sense, all lyric poetry is confessional, in that it is based on deep feelings from the author's experience, mediated into artful language. Emily Dickinson's poems are often about the most private and intensely moving things—erotic passion, agony, death, God, faith, and loss of faith. She begins a prim little stanza with the eye-popping lines "I like a look of agony / Because I know it's true." Is that "confessional"? It certainly sounds real and personal. Or is it just astonishingly powerful poetry about strong feelings?

belle of Amherst or Marquise de Sade?

Emily Dickinson's poems were in print for sixty-five years before they were published in an edition (Thomas Johnson's, in 1955) that did them justice. Her first editors censored and eliminated some, and regularized and diminished most, when her work was first published. It was thus just possible to see her as sweet and quaint and adorable and maidenly and harmless, writing of railroad trains and buggy rides, delight in birds, awe of snakes, sorrow at family deaths. This "Belle of Amherst," "I'm nobody—who are you?" Emily is undeniably part of her truth, but only part. She can be coy and cute, but she is much more.

Postmodern critics have corrected this patronizing distortion, though often excessively, e.g., that she was an intellectual kin of the Marquis de Sade. Nonsense. What she was was a great poet, the diversity and daring of her thought somewhat obscured by her elliptical language, and by the tight little verse form she used for almost all her poems. It is "common meter," or "ballad measure," usually alternating four beat and three beat iambic lines. She probably learned the form from the Protestant hymns of her childhood. Their authors in their turn had learned it from the old English ballads, where John Keats had found it (see "La Belle Dame Sans Merci"). She stretches and teases this simple form into stanzas of great subtlety and power. See especially "The Soul selects her own society," in which the soul shuts out unwanted visitors as a bivalve shuts its hard shell: "Like stone." Clang. Thud. So o-ver.

"tell all the truth but tell it slant"

She knew how unusual and perceptive she was, and knew it behooved her not to make that too plain, not to be too free with dangerous truths:

>Tell all the truth but tell it slant,
>   Success in circuit lies . . .

Otherwise, one might be avoided, discounted, or even put in a madhouse:

>Much madness is divinest sense,
>   To the discerning eye;
>Much sense the starkest madness,
>   Tis the majority
>
>In this, as all, prevails,
>   Assent, and you are sane.
>Demur, you're straightway dangerous,
>   And handled with a chain.

That is, treated as a lunatic in an asylum.

She wrote much of nature, clearly enjoying the little world around her family's houses. In one poem, a male speaker tells of feeling "a tighter breathing, / And zero at the bone" upon encountering a snake. She described another visitor thus:

> A route of evanescence,
>   With a revolving wheel,
> A resonance of emerald,
>   A rush of cochineal,
>
> And every blossom on the bush
>   Adjusts its tumbled head,
> The mail from Tunis, probably,
>   An easy morning's ride.

Fortunately for an otherwise hopelessly puzzled posterity, she appended a note to this when she sent it to a friend: "The Humming Bird." The ruby-throated hummingbird lives in eastern North America.

Emily Dickinson's house, Amherst, Massachusetts
Courtesy of the Emily Dickinson Museum ©2008

With this note, the red and green flashing light of the poem come clear, as does the joke in the last two lines—it wouldn't be a long ride from North Africa for such a swift and busy creature.

"he kindly stopped for me"

She wrote much of Death, of course. Death was a regular guest at the banquet of New England life, and the women of the house were expected to perform those final sacred cleansing duties that we now leave to undertakers. "I heard a fly buzz when I died" is written from the point of view of the dying person. (Many of her other speakers are already dead.) When her eyes grow dim, she sees the failure as outside her:

> And then the windows failed and then
> I could not see to see.

Her description of a house on the morning after death says that it "oppresses like the heft / Of cathedral tunes."

Her most famous poem about death is "Because I could not stop for Death." It presents the female speaker as too busy to go with Death, until that Gentleman Caller civilly comes to ask her out for a carriage ride on quite another Great Road. A proper New England spinster might be unwilling to go with him if they were to be alone, but there is a chaperone—"Immortality." She agrees to the ride, passing the earlier aspects of her life as they head toward what the reader comes to know is her grave, though the woman calls it "a house" that was but "a swelling in the ground."

> Since then, 'tis centuries, but each
> Feels shorter than the day
> I first surmised the horses' heads
> Were towards eternity.

Quietly terrifying, this wonderful poet: "zero at the bone."

There are many other rich aspects of Dickinson's poetry. She contained multitudes, like Walt Whitman, though in smaller, tidier packages. Her few erotic poems—"Wild nights, wild nights!!"—are dazzling, though there is no solid evidence of her having had sexual experiences with either men or women. I will leave her in Amherst, her physical and spiritual home, at her own grave. The day before she died, Emily Dickinson wrote her last letter to two relatives, the Norcross sisters. Here it is in full:

> Little Cousins,
> —Called back.
> —Emily.

Her tall marble gravestone in the iron-fenced family plot in Amherst reads:

> Emily Dickinson
> 1830–1886
> Called back

Sturbridge

For a good look at Emily Dickinson's immediate world, visit her house in Amherst. For a broader physical sense of how her age lived, a visit to Old Sturbridge Village, on US 20 between Springfield[2] and Worcester, is a must. It is an assemblage of authentic eighteenth and nineteenth-century buildings moved here from other sites. It aims to portray New England village life in the 1830s, when Emily Dickinson was a child nearby. It has no historic authenticity as a whole, but its mill and its chapel, its school, bank, and stores, are real enough. There's even a bogus graveyard with real old gravestones. (You can't help but think of Marianne Moore's wonderful description of poems as "imaginary gardens with real toads in them.") Staffed by docents in period dress, Old Sturbridge Village is instructive and compelling. "Living history" can be unbearably cutesy, but here it is well done, understated, and appealing.

"and I eat men like air"

Emily Dickinson's poetry would be a supreme landmark on the Great Road even if it did not lead to the work of two other Massachusetts poets whose great subject and grand passion was Death: Sylvia Plath and Anne Sexton. Though she was the younger of the two by six years, Sylvia Plath (1932–1963) gained fame and died before Sexton. A golden girl, beautiful and smart, she blazed her way from genteel poverty to a scholarship at Smith College in 1950 and a heady, prestigious summer stint in New York in 1953 as a student editor at the magazine *Mademoiselle*. In 1951–1952, my friend John Hall earned himself a feminist sainthood by becoming Plath's first serious boyfriend, someone who made that troubled soul feel good about herself. He tells me he saw her playing tennis in their Boston suburb, Wellesley, and asked a mutual friend for an introduction. "Who's that?" he asked. "That's Sylvia Plath," their friend said. "She doesn't get a lot of dates—she's so smart the boys are afraid of her." "Doesn't scare me," said John, and it didn't. He tells me that I partied with them during their time together. (John and I were at Williams, she at Smith, fifty-five miles away. Sadly, I didn't know her by name then.) John tells me that his granddaughter, doing a book report on Plath, came upon his name and called him to ask "Grandpa—is that you!?" It was and is.

Plath was excelling academically at Smith and writing poems of increasing power and distinction. In the midst of all this pressured achievement, her depression made her attempt suicide in 1953. Recovering after hospitalization and shock treatment, overachieving again, she graduated from Smith and won a Fulbright scholarship to attend Cambridge University in 1955. There she met another gorgeous and dazzling young poet, Yorkshireman Ted Hughes. At their first meeting at a party, she spoke one of his poems to him; she had memorized it for this moment. When he grabbed and kissed her, she bit him on the cheek, drawing blood. They were married four months later. Their relationship continued to be explosive and creative.

Mac with friend John Hall

They became the young uber-couple of Anglo-American letters, spending time in both countries. Two children followed quickly, as did Hughes's adultery and their breakup. Abandoned in a remote Devonshire cottage, Plath moved her very young children to London and rented a flat in Primrose Hill. There, in the coldest winter in a century, she wrote, at white heat, in a few months, most of the poems in the book that posthumously made her famous: *Ariel*.

It is full of stark statements about fathers ("Daddy, daddy, you bastard"), children ("Love set you going like a fat gold watch"), husbands ("A man in black with a *Mein Kampf* look"), and rage and revenge ("Beware, beware, / And I eat men like air"). She had taken the London flat on impulse because it had a blue London City Council plaque stating that William Butler Yeats had once lived in the building. I happened onto the place during a 1982 London walk after a visit to the nearby Regents' Park Zoo, and I noticed and recognized the same blue Yeats plaque. I took a brief, bizarre tour of the flat, courtesy of the very obliging student occupant who happened to come out while I was staring. It was the locus of her greatest work. She asphyxiated herself there in January 1963. Her two children survived. One, Frieda Hughes, has become a noteworthy poet.

Ironically, her husband became her literary executor. Hughes's judicious handling of the posthumous publication of her poems helped to make her famous, just as their story helped to make him a monster to some. He never responded to the criticism, and published in 1998, at the time of his death, some very tender early poems—*Birthday Letters*—about her and about their relationship (see chapter 6). Ted Hughes had by then become England's poet laureate, a sinecure held over the centuries by poets both great and piddling, from Dryden, Wordsworth, and Tennyson down to Colley Cibber. Its chief modern duties had been to write congratulatory poems on royal birthdays. The appointment of such a hard, dour writer to this piffling post seemed very strange, but it did signal Britain's acceptance of him and its admiration of his work, which had indeed been exemplary.

Sylvia Plath's late work was searing and uncompromising, lashing out at the men she thought had failed her, chiefly "Daddy" and the "model of you," to whom she said "I do"—Ted Hughes. Her poems are also often darkly funny. There is a story that, when Plath read "Daddy" to a woman friend, they rolled around on the floor laughing hysterically. The poem is indeed full of gloriously improbable comic words and sounds like "achoo" and "gobbledy-goo." Her whole oeuvre is broader than her late output would suggest, including a good series of poems on keeping bees, which she had done in Devonshire. It should be no surprise that her father had been an entomologist, specializing in bees.

Plath's work is not just intense and confessional; it is highly crafted. The insistently repeated "oo" sounds in "Daddy" make this angry poem ring with the sounds of a hurt child, afraid to "achoo." "Daddy, daddy, you bastard, I'm through" seems to me both angry rejection and plaintive call. But of course she wasn't really "through" with her problems. Death came to call for her when she was thirty.

her kind : the middle-aged witch

Sylvia Plath and Anne Sexton (1926–1974) met and studied together in Robert Lowell's poetry workshop at Boston University. They hit it off, these two smart, beautiful, wounded women. They and other work-shoppers would often unwind and share confidences and "3 or 4 or 2 martinis" ("clear as tears") at the Ritz in Boston. "[O]ften, very often, Sylvia and I would talk at length / about our first suicides. . . . Suicide is, after all, the opposite of the poem." "Intense, perceptive—strange, blonde, lovely Sylvia." (*Anne Sexton: A Self-Portrait in Letters*, Boston: Houghton Mifflin, 1977, 245–46). When Plath died, Sexton seemed to begrudge her having been the first to take "that ride home / with our boy" [Death]. Thus did Sexton acknowledge another influence, another priority—Emily Dickinson had got there before either of them, though not by suicide.

Sexton may have been the most wounded of the three. Her childhood was spent in uneasy luxury. Her parents had all the right friends and plenty of money, but there were family problems with alcohol and mental illness. Her idyllic summers at posh Squirrel Island, Maine, in one or another of the family's five "arking houses," were tainted by unhappiness or worse. Her mother, a poet herself, was jealous of Anne's early success. She accused her daughter of plagiarizing her stunningly original early poems. I met some older Squirrel Islanders on a boat to the island in the 1980s. When questioned, they remembered Sexton's mother, Mary Harvey, dancing gaily, indefatigably, at Squirrel Island parties in the '30s.

Skipping college, Anne Harvey eloped with Alfred ("Kayo") Sexton and soon gave birth to two daughters. After each birth, she went into deep postpartum depression, and spent long periods in a mental institution, where she began to write poetry as therapy. A therapist priest told her, "God is in your typewriter," and there was truth in that. Poetry seemed to have saved her for a time. ("My fans think I got well, but I didn't; I just became a poet.") She tried to believe, but God eluded her. As she wrote, "Need is not quite belief." She spoke of herself as magic, dangerous, other, a "middle-aged witch." A posthumous volume of her poems is entitled *The Awful Rowing Toward God*. In it, God plays cards with her, but He cheats.

She did a very successful series of books and poetry readings, including performances with a jazz group, "Her Kind," a reference to one of her poems. She was a powerful, gorgeous, theatrical presence, though she was often terrified in public situations. When I heard her, once she had got past nervously fluffing some lines, she was a compelling reader. She separated from Kayo, had affairs, drank too much, and took too many pills. She had lunch in October 1974 with her spiritual sister, her best friend, the poet Maxine Kumin,[3] revealing no dark plans. Anne Sexton then went home to Weston to take her last ride, almost literally, with "our boy," Death. She died of carbon monoxide poisoning in her car in her garage. Maxine Kumin was still publishing poems about this in 2006, trying to understand and accept it, trying, I think, to forgive her dear friend Anne.

Sexton's poetic legacy will outlive her sad biography. Like that of her poetic forebear, Emily Dickinson, her work is witty and often very funny. Her *Transformations* retells folk tales in strange, sharp, insightful modern ways. Her poems about suicide are tough and instructive. In "Wanting to Die," she says that suicides are different from the rest of us. Like carpenters, suicides never ask "Why build?," only "Which tools?" That is, what's the best way to do the inevitable? Like Sylvia Plath a former model, she was tall, beautiful and dazzling, and a fine and artful poet. "We must all eat beautiful women," she wrote. She wanted to die and she did. She loved language and fun and wordplay. Her poems are not simply emotional outcries; like Plath's, they are highly crafted. She loved palindromes, reversible aphorisms such as "Madam, I'm Adam." Her favorite was "Rats live on no evil star," which she had seen on the side of an Irish barn. She said she wanted that to be inscribed on her gravestone, as it "gave her a peculiar kind of hope" (*Anne Sexton*, 379). When I visited her grave in Jamaica Plain, Boston, I saw that an admirer had chalked that palindrome on her stone. It seemed wonderfully appropriate. Rest in peace.

the early Berkshires: Melville and Moby Dick

The Great Road takes us past the Connecticut Valley to the Berkshire Hills of Western Massachusetts. There three great American novelists lived and did some of their best work. Herman Melville bought a farm just east of US 20 in Pittsfield, in 1850. (When the 1956 film of *Moby Dick* played Pittsfield, it was billed on the theatre marquee as "By Pittsfield's own Herman Melville." If ya got it, flaunt it.) Melville named the farm "Arrowhead" for the neolithic points he found there while plowing. He farmed and wrote for thirteen years in this beautiful place. He is said to have loved the view of the Berkshires, of Mount Greylock, the state's highest peak, from his window. According to the Berkshire Historical Society, which now occupies the house, Melville wrote in 1851: "A great neighborhood for authors, you see, is Pittsfield."

Melville's family had long and deep connections to the Great Road. At its eastern terminus, his paternal grandfather, James Melvill [*sic*] dressed up as a Mohawk Indian and took part in the Boston Tea Party in 1773. His maternal grandfather, Philip Gansevoort, commanded the successful defense of Fort Stanwix against the British, near the Great Road in central New York, in 1777. (There's an impressive reconstruction of that fort in Rome, New York.) The young Melville was schooled for two years at the Albany Academy while he lived in Albany, New York, on the Great Road.

Melville sometimes eased his mental and financial troubles, treated his "hypos," by attending what he called his "Harvard and Yale": long voyages as a seaman on whaling ships. His early books—*Omoo* and *Typee*, romances of the sea and the South Pacific—had been popular and lucrative. His career slumped with the publication of *Mardi* and other increasingly difficult books. His work was very good, but he could not make a living from it.

He'd show them. He'd do fine work at Arrowhead, and he certainly did. There he completed *Moby Dick, or The Whale*, one of the two books most often put up for the honorific title of "The Great American Novel."[4] (*The Adventures of Huckleberry Finn* is the other. Both are.) *Moby Dick* is a long and difficult book, almost proverbially, even comically so, but it is rich, diverse, and funny as well as brooding, satanic, Shakespearean, and mythic. *Moby Dick* failed to make the great splash (pun intended) and the money its author hoped for. Defeated, he left Arrowhead in 1862 to move to New York City to work in obscurity as a customs officer. This would ironically echo another of his supreme Great Road fictions, "Bartleby The Scrivener" (1853), with Bartleby's portentous refrain, "I would prefer not to." Melville, like his creation Bartleby, would have preferred not to, but he had little choice, and he left. Here on the Great Road much of Melville's best work was done, including *Pierre, or The Ambiguities* and *Billy Budd*, which was not published until 1924, thirty-three years after

his death in obscurity. Arrowhead is open to visitors. It is a large, pleasant nineteenth-century farmhouse with the glorious Berkshire mountain
views that Melville loved.

Hawthorne and The House of the Seven Gables

After his early success with *The Scarlet Letter*, Nathaniel Hawthorne
left Salem, Massachusetts, and went west on the Great Road to Berkshire
County. He met Melville there in 1850, and they formed an important
personal and professional relationship. Hawthorne did not stay in the
Berkshires as long as Melville; but he stayed long enough to write another
major book there, his second masterpiece, *The House of the Seven Gables*.
Here he also wrote most of another important book, *The Blithedale
Romance*, based on his experience of the Utopian experiment called
Brook Farm. Using his political connections—better than Melville's—
Hawthorne soon left for an ambassadorship in England. He left the
Berkshires to Melville, who soldiered on alone. Hawthorne's Great Road
experience was brief but important.

chronicler and critic of the Gilded Age :
Edith Wharton and the Mount

Edith Wharton's story was the reverse of Herman Melville's. Melville
came to the Great Road to live and and earn a living by his writing, and
did not succeed. Wharton came as a wealthy woman and became a
hugely successful writer, though she did not need the considerable sums
her books earned. Melville was writing and working on a real farm.
Wharton was born rich, had made a very bad "good marriage," and had
all the money she needed. She built a grand showplace home called The
Mount just off the Great Road, and lived and worked there for much of
the period from 1902 to 1911. "The Mount was my first real home," she
said. There she once entertained another author with Great Road connections, her friend and mentor, Henry James. He is said to have been
surprised and delighted when she introduced him to the pleasures of
motoring—on the Great Road, of course.

Edith Wharton's main subject was the haughty, cruel, elegant world
of the super-rich of New York City. Like most of her female forebears,
she had had to struggle for personal and literary independence. Her first

book was about the design of houses and gardens, a proper subject (if she must write at all) for a wealthy society matron. The gardens at The Mount are indeed gorgeous. When her husband began to show signs of madness, she took up with a journalist, the love of her life.

Wharton divorced her husband in 1913, and thereafter spent most of her life in Paris; The Mount was her home for only ten years. Yet it was there that she wrote her two greatest works—*The House of Mirth* (1905), and *Ethan Frome* (1911). Emily Dickinson had had to break through the restrictions of mid-nineteenth-century gender roles to become a great poet. She did it by staying well under the radar and avoiding celebrity. A century later, Plath and Sexton rebelled against gender role conformity and limitation. Edith Wharton was a rebel and pioneer as well. If we except Harriet Beecher Stowe and Louisa May Alcott, and I might, she was the first great female American novelist. She had the toughness and independence to criticize her privileged world and find it crass and cruel and greedy. Her opinion of that world (and its response to that critique) partly explains her removal to Paris.

The Mount, Edith Wharton's home in Lenox, Massachusetts
Photo by Julia Schuyler

She also looked unflinchingly at another world that was neither Gilded Age nor wealthy, the hard world of the chilly New England hills she found around The Mount in Berkshire County. She says in her Introduction to *Ethan Frome*: "I had known something of New England village life long before I made my home in the same county as my imaginary Starkfield." She noted the "harsh and beautiful land" and said that she felt that "the outcropping granite . . . had been overlooked." She worked that stern outcropping for *Ethan Frome*, of all her works the one that is most often read today. Based on a tragic Berkshire County incident, the book is as flinty and unflinching as William Faulkner's best, in a stark New England setting on the Great Road. The Mount declined after Wharton sold it in 1911. It became a girls' school for a time, then served as a temporary home for a theatrical company. It is now being renovated and restored to recall her career and express her taste and personality. It is an elegant representation of The Gilded Age she meticulously and ironically chronicled.

muses in Arcadia : the Berkshires

Berkshire County was settled later than the rest of Massachusetts—the mountains were a natural barrier to settlement from the east. Berkshire County is roughly equidistant from Boston and New York City: close enough to be enriched and influenced by both, but distant enough to have maintained an independent character. Edith Wharton went there and took something of New York City and Paris with her. Oliver Wendell Holmes, from Boston, summered there. Hawthorne brought with him a whiff of Calvinist Salem. Melville came to it, then left it for New York City.

US 20 bisects Berkshire County. Within a few miles of its current route are all the literary sites mentioned above, and the rich artistic feast below. Nowadays, some of Boston's and New York City's best artistic endeavors take place in the Berkshires. The Berkshire County Travel Bureau calls the area "America's Premier Cultural Resort." That's local puffery, but it's not absurd. "The Muses in Arcadia" and "Culture in the Country" are other local slogans. Dance spends the summer at Jacob's Pillow, on US 20 near Becket. "The Pillow" was founded in the 1920s by famous dancers and teachers Ted Shawn and Ruth St. Denis. It takes its name from a rock that is thought to look a bit like a pillow, and from the conceit that US 20's switchbacks looked like the rungs of Jacob's Ladder. The Jacob's Ladder Trail, a National Scenic Byway, covers thirty-three beautiful miles of Twenty, from Russell to Lee.

Music is everywhere in a Berkshire summer, preeminently at Tanglewood, in Lenox. Music history was made there by musicians such as Serge Koussevitsky, Leonard Bernstein, Aaron Copland, Seiji Ozawa, John Williams, and James Levine. It is the summer home of the Boston Symphony Orchestra, and a nurturing ground for brilliant young musicians. Lennie Bernstein first went there from exurban Boston in 1940, aged twenty-one, and returned almost every summer of his life thereafter. The music is first-rate, and it is a glorious place to spend a summer evening, in the Koussevitsky Music Shed or on the lawn. Tanglewood's main entrance is just west of US 20, on the Lenox-Stockbridge border.

"lions, eagles, and quails"

Summer theatre is often trivial fun, and why not? Theatre should be fun. Summer theatres thrive in the Berkshires. For fun and much more than fun, there is Williamstown, Massachusetts, and the Adams Memorial Theatre and the Williamstown Theatre Festival. The local chamber of commerce calls Williamstown "The Village Beautiful," and it is. In the interest of full disclosure, I plead guilty to being a Williams alumnus, and to having sung and played on its concert and theatre stages. I heard Randall Jarrell, W. H. Auden, and the doomed, spellbinding Dylan Thomas there. A dear friend and I were inspired to do our honors theses on him—Anil on the prose, me on the poetry. After his superb reading, I checked his water glass, thinking it might be gin. It was water.

Williamstown is a lively college town during the academic year, and a center of art, theatre, and music in the summer. It is twenty miles north of Twenty, but it feeds off and contributes to the intellectual ferment of the Great Road. It is at the western end of the Mohawk Trail, the splendid old mountain road—Route 2—from Greenfield to North Adams. Poet and editor William Cullen Bryant went to Williams College. His astonishing Wordsworthian poem "Thanatopsis," written in the Berkshires when he was eighteen, amazed its readers, who could scarcely believe it was written on this side of the Atlantic.

In 1955, the Williamstown Theatre Festival took over the college's Adams Memorial Theatre, then largely unused in the summer, and made a humble start. Its charismatic director, the late Nikos Psacharopoulos, had a great vision which has since been amply fulfilled. Williamstown has become a venue where fine actors, major theatre people—Joanne Woodward, Edward Hermann, F. Murray Abraham, Blythe Danner, Christopher Reeve, Frank Langella, Roger Rees, Kathleen Turner—and

newer stars such as Kate Burton, Ethan Hawke, and Gwyneth Paltrow—take minimal pay to do serious work. Nick Psacharopoulos
directed a superb version of Chekhov's *The Seagull* there in the 1970s. It
was later filmed at the Berkshire cedar log summer house of my Williams
mentor and adviser, Clay Hunt, a legendary force in the Williams English Department. Gwyneth Paltrow was a toddler then; she grew up with
the Festival. Her mother, Blythe Danner, beautifully played the young,
doomed Nina. Toddler Gwyneth is said to have made a big hit at
rehearsals by lisping lines from her mother's first act soliloquy while
crawling nearly naked across the stage: "All men and beasts, lions, eagles,
and quails, horned stags, geese, spiders . . . all life . . . has died out at last."
In her turn, Gwyneth has played Nina there too. They do this every summer, and it's wonderful.

art new and old: Mass MoCA and the Clark

Five miles east is the huge new Mass MoCA—"Massachusetts
Museum of Contemporary Art"—in the old mill town of North Adams.
Handsome old brick mill buildings still stand on rivers throughout Massachusetts, though they no longer enclose poorly paid female operatives, or
use water power to turn spinning machines to make cloth. Here, several
mill buildings have been refitted to make enormous exhibit spaces—a
total of *thirteen acres* (*New York Times*, October 27, 2006)—for important
contemporary art. This museum-cum-rock concert venue in a once
obscure corner of the state is a must see.

Actually, this once obscure corner of the state has been a required stop
for art lovers since 1955, the year I graduated from Williams. With a family fortune made in manufacturing sewing machines, Robert Sterling
Clark built, endowed, and filled this large private museum with his and
his wife's vast personal collection. He is said to have chosen to build it in
Williamstown because he thought New York City was too likely to be the
target of atomic attack—this was the "Duck and Cover" era of the cold
war—and he wanted to preserve his treasures. The excellence of the midcentury Williams College Art Department was another major reason.

Loosely connected to Williams College, the Robert Sterling and
Francine Clark Art Institute is much more than just a splendid small
museum. It has become a major center for the study of display and conservation and art history. Indeed, American museum directors sometimes
refer darkly, if comically, to "The Williams Mafia," an alleged cabal

whose tentacles (pardon my mixed metaphor) have come to control major museums across the country. Well, maybe it's more than "alleged." "The college is famous for incubating future museum directors; the list includes Earl A. Powell III (the National Gallery), Thomas Krens (the Guggenheim), and Michael Gowan (the Los Angeles Museum of Art)," as well as Glenn Lowry of New York's Museum of Modern Art (*The New Yorker*, September 25, 2006, 130). In addition, Williams/Clark graduates have headed the Brooklyn Museum of Art (Robert Burk '61), the Art Institute of Chicago (James Wood '63), and the Dallas Museum of Art (John Lane '66). The troubled J. Paul Getty Trust has lured James Wood out of retirement to serve as its president and chief executive, and to use its five *billion* dollar endowment more judiciously and creatively ("At Getty Trust, a New Chief With Solid Art Credentials," *New York Times*, December 5, 2006).

The "Art Clark" is midsized, user-friendly, and gorgeous, and its stunning collection of Renoirs (thirty-eight!) is remarkable outside France. Eighteen Renoirs and a backup band of Pissaros, Monets, and Degas ballerina bronzes are exhibited in one grand room. About fifty by seventy-five feet, it is my favorite room in any museum in the world. Well, maybe it's a tie with the unicorn tapestry room at The Cloisters in New York City. The Clark's main emphases are turn-of-the-century French impressionist and nineteenth-century American, especially Winslow Homer and John Singer Sargent, but its collections are wide-ranging. Its traveling exhibits are strong—there was a wonderful late Turner show there in 2005, and a superb Alexandre Calame/ romantic Swiss landscape show in 2006. It's my favorite Berkshire institution, after Williams College. And it's free from November to May! Can't beat the price.

The Williams College Museum of Art, on the campus in Williamstown, is also very important. Its permanent collection—about twelve thousand items—is remarkable, from Assyrian and Egyptian antiquities to many moderns: Hopper, O'Keefe, Barlach, Picasso, Nevelson, Grant Wood, David Smith, and Andy Warhol. It is growing exponentially as successful alumni bequeath masterpieces to it. Both it and the Clark are a testimony to the lives and talents of outstanding Williams College art professors. I visited WCMA in November 2006, as Williams was gearing up to celebrate the ninety-ninth birthday of S. Lane Faison '29, known as "The Godfather" of the Williams Mafia, one of the "Holy Trinity" that included Whit Stoddard '35 and Bill Pierson.[5] Sad to say, Lane Faison died five days short of this milestone (*New York Times*, November 14, 2006), after a life of great accomplishments. He had been instrumental in helping the OSS, the predecessor of the CIA, recover art works looted by Nazis in World War II (*New York Times*, December 19, 2006). There is also an excellent collection of rare books in the Chapin Library at Williams College. As an undergraduate, I sang "The Angler's Catch" there with my friend Stran Stranahan from the first edition of *The Compleat Angler* (1653). The Chapin owns a Shakespeare First Folio (1623) that was famously stolen and surreptitiously recovered in 1940.

American visual icons

In Stockbridge is the imposing Norman Rockwell Museum. Is it finally time to accept this "illustrator" as a significant realist painter? The Norman Rockwell Museum thinks so, and so do I. So, apparently, does the art-biz world. His painting "Breaking Home Ties," bought for $900 in 1960, hidden for thirty years in a secret wall compartment, was sold recently for fifteen million dollars (*New York Times*, November 30, 2006). His many covers for *The Saturday Evening Post* were iconic and enormously popular, delineating and enshrining American life from the 1920s to the 1960s. They are often cute and sugary, and there is nothing progressive or modernist about them. Some have bite and social conscience, such as his late works on the subject of civil rights. It is as a supreme draftsman that Rockwell lives. His paintings are charming, sometimes powerful, and often very funny evocations of the human experience, and they're on display, as is his studio, in the town Rockwell came to live in and love for twenty-five years. I remember being impressed that a Williams classmate of mine had modeled for him in the early 1950s. "I showed the America I knew and observed to others who might not have noticed." Norman Rockwell made this modest claim, and it is true.

Less than a mile away in the same town are art works that are even more iconic. The place is Chesterwood, the former home and studio of the sculptor Daniel Chester French. He is known especially for two statues: One is "The Minute Man of 1775," "the embattled farmer" of the American Revolution and "the shot heard round the world," in Emerson's phrasing. In French's studio are three maquettes, different sized models, of the other, more famous icon: the somber seated Abraham Lincoln of the Lincoln Memorial in Washington, D.C., the prime backdrop for American cultural history from Marian Anderson to Martin Luther King Jr. and "I have a dream," from Solidarity Day to the Million Man March. The Berkshires in the summer are indeed "The Muses in Arcadia," the fruition of the artistic movement westward on Twenty from Boston.

the word heads west to Chicago along the great road

Though it's not about Massachusetts, the following discussion belongs here. The literary word maintained its primacy much farther west along the route of US 20. The epic migration of African Americans from the deep south to the industrial north spawned great writing as well as great music. Toni Morrison was born and grew up in Lorain, Ohio; her first novel, *The Bluest Eye,* is set there. Lucille Clifton came from DePew, New York, and attended my SUNY college in Fredonia. Born in Tennessee, Ishmael Reed grew up in Buffalo and attended the University of Buffalo.

At the south entrance to the tiny southwestern Ohio town of Camden, on US 127, there was for years a post bearing two signs. The first said "Camden Ohio / Birthplace of Sherwood Anderson." The second, beneath it, said "Famous Author." Just in case you wouldn't know who or what Sherwood Anderson was. It's a good bet that most Americans today wouldn't know who he was, though both Ernest Hemingway and William Faulkner acknowledged him as a powerful influence in their portrayal of the darker sides of the American character. A recent rereading of *Winesburg, Ohio* confirmed my memory of its power, and showed how important a stylistic influence he had been on Hemingway. Anderson's gritty stories influenced many American writers in the twenties and thirties. Faulkner's life and career were going nowhere special when he met Anderson, who advised him to write about his home town, as Anderson had. Faulkner's epic creation of Yoknapatawpha County was the result. Faulkner called Anderson "the father of my whole generation of writers."

Anderson had left Camden very young with his family and his feckless father, to live and grow up in Clyde, on US 20 in western Ohio. He left Clyde for Elyria, also on Twenty, where he prospered in the paint business. He grew dissatisfied with his narrow life, the pettiness of some of his neighbors, and the culture of his towns. He abandoned his business to write, both advertising copy and fiction (if there's a difference), winding up in Chicago during the richest years of the Chicago Literary Renaissance.

Like many towns with literary offspring, Clyde has a cautious, arms-length relationship with its famous adopted son. He is mentioned on the town's web site. A few associated sites remain and are acknowledged, including the house he lived in, but they are not, as of 2002, highlighted or signed. "Winesburg, Ohio," the fictional name of the grim town in Anderson's fiction, probably did not take kindly to his representation of it. The most honored son of Clyde, to judge by the tourist signs at its borders, is Private Rodger Young, the infantryman whose heroic, selfless death in the Solomons in World War II was immortalized in a beautiful patriotic anthem by Frank Loesser. Rodger Young is a hero in Clyde; Sherwood Anderson clearly is not, not yet, at least. But he was a great writer. And a "Famous Author."

US 20 heads west from Clyde, Ohio, to Chicago. Once it went right downtown, along the lake and right into the Loop, the heart of the city, and exited westward along Lake Street. Since 1938, it has been routed northwest from the southwest side, though it still runs briefly on West

Sherwood Anderson's home town—but he's not a hero there.

Lake Street. Twenty has always been a main road to the "City of the Big Shoulders." The Chicago that Anderson found his way to was a wonderfully yeasty city then, and it is still. Its glories are many, none grander than its literary heritage, as fine as its architecture and its sweeping lakefront parks.

That a city with such a corrupt political history should have preserved its precious lakefront for the use of its ordinary people is a great, improbable joy to me, and to millions of Chicagoans and their manic, ball-chasing dogs. I swim at North Avenue Beach every summer. Try to imagine twenty miles of beautiful public beaches on the Hudson or the East River in Manhattan. You can't, can you? Too bad. Hosannas to architect and planner Daniel Burnham, and to generations of civic-minded Chicagoans.

Chicago's literary heritage is the subject for another book, but, briefly: its early literary scene included L. Frank Baum, Carl Sandburg, Edgar Lee Masters, Vachel Lindsay, Floyd Dell, Harriet Monroe, Jane

Mac in Lincoln Park, Chicago

Addams, Ben Hecht, Upton Sinclair, Theodore Dreiser, Ring Lardner, and Ernest Hemingway, who grew up in suburban Oak Park. In later years, Chicago would nurture Richard Wright, James T. Farrell, Peter de Vries, Gwendolyn Brooks, Nelson Algren, Studs Terkel, Saul Bellow, Mike Royko, Ana Castillo, Sandra Cisneros, and Gary Paul Nabhan. Local boys like Frank Norris, Archibald MacLeish, John Dos Passos, William L. Shirer, Kenneth Rexroth, and David Mamet started here and flourished elsewhere. Ivan Doig left the rural Montana he so richly chronicles for the "east" and his college education at Chicagoland's Northwestern University, while I was in grad school there. Chicago theatre is strong, especially at the Goodman and Steppenwolf theatres. New, witty, verbal styles of American comedy began in Chicago: with Bob Newhart, Compass Players Mike Nichols and Elaine May, Barbara Harris, and Shelley Berman, and Second City performers Severn Darden, John Belushi, Alan Arkin, Bill Murray, and Stephen Colbert.

The Great Road is a Road of the Word from Boston to Chicago.

the great road to justice and freedom: god, man, and woman

burned-over New York

◆ Gods live in high places. Holy men thrive in caves. Religions bloom in deserts.

No such extreme physiographic conditions exist along the Great Road from western Massachusetts to eastern Ohio, essentially the central lateral slice of New York State with a small extension at each end. Yet this pleasant, fertile, well-watered, gently rolling trail has spawned beliefs and believers as though it were Judea or India. The Mohawk River ranks right up there with the Jordan and the Ganges. Why on earth? What mix of zeal, freedom, and energy made all this happen? First, an account of some of these religious visions and creations.

religious beginnings

Euro-American religion in New England began with a small group seeking religious freedom: the Pilgrims, who came to Plymouth in 1620. Then came a larger, very different group and faith, a theocracy. The people of the Massachusetts Bay Colony arrived in Boston in 1630, seeking to escape one religious orthodoxy and establish another—their own. When its tyranny lost credibility in the seventeenth century, partly due to the excesses and horrors of the Salem witch hunts, church and state in Massachusetts separated forever. One hopes.

Protestant Christianity spread westward from Boston along the Great Road, occasionally sparking into the flames of grim determinism

and evangelical enthusiasm, as in the influential life of Jonathan
Edwards. His most important pastorates were in Northampton, Massachusetts, just north of current US 20, and Stockbridge, on the Great
Road. His final flock in Stockbridge included Mohawk Indians. In his
poem "Jonathan Edwards in Western Massachusetts," Robert Lowell
refers to Edwards's last congregation, "a dozen Housatonic Indian children." Edwards's Hellfire sermons such as "Sinners in the Hands of an
Angry God" shook hearts and communities in western Massachusetts in
the 1740s and led to that powerful, amorphous movement throughout the
colonies now known as "The Great Awakening."

Flareups of such enthusiastic Christianity continued in the region
well into the nineteenth century, inspiring what is sometimes called "The
Second Great Awakening." This later movement affected, among others,
the eighteen-year-old Emily Dickinson. She resisted considerable
pressure, stood alone, and chose not to declare herself "saved," born
again, during her year (1848–1849) at the Female Seminary which would
become Mount Holyoke College. Clearly, the spiritual soil along this road
was fertile, and the time was right.

new ideas and a pattern

Religious creativity here was not exclusively Euro-American. In
about 1800, a Seneca Indian known to us as Handsome Lake had a vision
and began preaching a new religion. It has its own myth of origins, and
grows naturally from earlier Seneca beliefs, but it appears to have been
influenced by two new things: Indian losses and despair, and Christian
theology and ethics, by now well known from Christian missionary work
such as Jonathan Edwards's. In the late 1880s, a similar blend of American Indian mysticism and Christianity would culminate in the teaching
of the Paiute Indian Wovoka. From this came the Ghost Dance, and the
tragedy of Wounded Knee.

Despite strong disapproval from Handsome Lake's half-brother,
tribal leader Cornplanter, and another leading Seneca, Red Jacket, this
so-called Longhouse religion prospered. It met the needs of a dispirited
and diminished people. Today this religion is a major force on reservations in western New York, competing with Christian sects and displac-
ing or adapting old Seneca beliefs. Handsome Lake's home was in what
is now Irving, New York, on US 20, twenty-four miles east on Twenty
from my home.[1]

A pattern becomes clear. A man or a woman with a personal vision, often literally a visionary, and some awareness of orthodox beliefs, builds on and reshapes those beliefs, speaks out, and attracts followers—chiefly the poor and disenfranchised. That's not a bad description of the founding of Christianity by the Apostle Paul; and it is exactly what happened repeatedly along four hundred miles of the route of US 20 between 1770 and 1880. So intense and persistent was this pattern that the entire region, especially central and western New York along the Great Road, became known as "The Burned-Over District." This name refers to the flames of religious fervor that repeatedly heated, and sometimes singed or burned, the people of the region.

women and enthusiasm

The Shakers didn't launch their religion here, but, as refugees from England, like the Pilgrims, they found a free place for it to flourish. Their name for themselves was The United Society of Believers in Christ's Second Coming. Their faith was millennialist, expecting at any moment the end of this world, and preparing themselves for the next. Their popular name, "The Shaking Quakers," was said to be a description of the physical enthusiasm and movement in their services. They sang and danced a lot; next to their labor, it was their chief physical release. "To turn, turn, will be our delight, / Till by turning and turning we come round right." Dancing and singing, worship and theology, became one. Most modern Americans know the Shakers best through their music, especially through Aaron Copland's splendid use of this great song, "Simple Gifts," in his *Appalachian Spring* ballet music.

All the Shakers' major early sites are on or quite near the Great Road. Mother Ann Lee, a poor and ill-educated English Quaker girl, was their prophetess. There's a harbinger of female power in *that* term; and, indeed, she was considered by some of her followers to be divine. She brought them to America: to New York City in 1774, then to Watervliet, New York, in 1776, then to Niskayuna and other sites near Albany. Interesting original buildings and her grave can be found there today, on Albany-Shaker Road, very near US 20. Other Shaker sites on or near Twenty are a museum in Chatham, New York, and a large group of old buildings in New Lebanon, New York, thirty miles southeast of Albany near the Massachusetts border.

This was Mount Lebanon, the intellectual center of the Shaker movement in America from 1785 to 1947, when the last Shaker living in this community left. Some of these impressive buildings are open to visitors. The largest is a huge stabilized roofless ruin of the Great Stone Barn, built in 1859, when it was the largest such structure in the world. Mount Lebanon is now shared by the Darrow School and, since 1975, a Sufi retreat center, "The Abode of the Message Community." This American offshoot of early Islam is just one more religious plant to flourish in the fertile soil of the Great Road.

The Shakers' tools and buildings are a fitting memorial to their lives and beliefs. They were communal farmers and craftspeople. Their flat brooms (which they invented), their boxes, chairs, and quilts, are always simple and functional, and are often beautiful. They marketed excellent seeds and herbs. Their meeting houses had two entrances, one for each sex, as celibacy was their rule. Dancing was encouraged as an acceptable substitute for other, forbidden, physical activities.

If the world is ending soon, why not be ritually clean and free from physical sin, i.e., sex? That was the argument for celibacy among early Christians, some of whom had heard their Lord say they "should not see death before the Lord's Christ cometh" (Luke 2:26). Saint Paul grudgingly acknowledged to the Corinthians that it was "better to marry than to burn [with sexual passion]," but he clearly preferred abstinence (I Corinthians: 7, 9). Marriage was permitted to early Christians, but discouraged. Shaker theology taught that if we refrain from Adam's sin, sexuality, we can approach perfection here on earth. The Shakers took in overnight guests, but laid down seven rules for them, including: "Sixth. Married persons tarrying with us over night are respectfully notified that each sex occupy separate sleeping apartments while they remain. This rule will not be departed from under any circumstances."

With such rules, it is not surprising that there are very few Shakers left; there probably were never more than a few thousand at their peak in the 1850s. The wonder is that, without self-generated replacements, they have lasted so long. One reason is that they took in orphans. In times of Great Awakening, or of trouble, fear, and doubt, such groups flourish. Catholic religious orders were full to bursting during and after World War II; they are dwindling now. Failing the predicted Second Coming or Armageddon, such groups as the Shakers usually fade and diminish.

East of Albany on US 20 stands the best preserved physical example of all this, Hancock Shaker Village, a National Historic Landmark west of Pittsfield, Massachusetts. The Shakers called it their "City of Peace." It is a glorious restoration and presentation of Shakerism, but there are no Shakers here. It is a museum, not a living community. The huge round barn is especially interesting, beautiful and practical, form and function meeting as one, as did so many things in their lives. The Shakers' influence spread well beyond the Great Road, mostly into northern New England, where tiny communities such as Canterbury, New Hampshire, continue to this day. The name of Shaker Heights, a Cleveland suburb, marks their northwesternmost reach. Shaker communities also flourished briefly in Kentucky. Their chief legacy is in music and architecture, and, more subtly and profoundly, in this: it was the first significant American movement to be led by a woman.

native millenialism

Mother Ann's leadership was unprecedented, but it was not unnoticed. Other women, now little remembered, soon took positions of religious, hence social, leadership. Jemima Wilkinson, known as "The Public Universal Friend," was another former Quaker. She lived from 1752 to 1819, mostly in the Canandaigua area, on the Great Road. Like Mother Ann, she preached celibacy. Her public fame peaked and turned to notoriety when she declared herself the Second Coming of Christ. That seems to have been too much for even the Burned-Over District to swallow, and she was charged with blasphemy. The charges were dismissed in 1799, but her fame and her following dwindled. Twenty years later, her followers refused to accept the fact of her death until her body's decay made that fact irrefutable.

Another millennialist Christian-based religion soon grew out of this soil. William Miller was born in Pittsfield, Massachusetts, on the Great Road in 1782, and raised as a Baptist. He moved to northern New York to farm on the Vermont border, where tours of his house are available. It is east of the tourist mecca of Lake George, north of Whitehall, New York. Miller studied the Bible, particularly the Book of Daniel and the Book of Revelation. "Beware the man who has read only one book," says a wise Islamic proverb. Miller's study led him to believe that Bible prophecy had not yet begun to be fulfilled, and that it would soon unfold. Many adherents came to him and believed him when he predicted the Advent, the Second Coming of Christ, in "about the year 1843." When Christ failed to appear, some adherents fell away. Some went with another leader, yet another charismatic woman, Ellen Gould White. The schisms and upheavals that followed are too complicated to trace here. Ultimately, out of these "Millerite" beliefs came what has been known (since 1863) as the church of the Seventh Day Adventists. There are other, smaller Millerite groups.

Adventists, like Jews, celebrate the Sabbath on Saturday. They certainly have a point, since Genesis states that that was the seventh day of Creation, the day of rest. They do not smoke tobacco or drink alcohol. They expect the second coming of Christ, and they are a growing branch of modern Christianity, despite internal splits and controversy. There is a shiny new Adventist church two miles east of my house, on US 20. Is there no end to millennial belief, even in the face of hard contrary evidence? There seems no end to the reinterpretations of Biblical prophecy on the Great Road. Indeed, back in Boston at its eastern terminus, yet another religion would soon be founded by another charismatic woman: The Church of Christ, Scientist, by Mary Baker Eddy.

Mr. Splitfoot in Chautauqua County

The religious movements noted above may seem strange or marginal, but they pale in comparison with the story of the Fox sisters and their establishment of a religion which, despite widespread exposures and admissions of fraud, persists to this day: Spiritualism. This movement began in 1848 at a small cottage in Hydesville, near Newark, New York, about twenty miles from the Great Road. Two of the Fox sisters claimed to have contacted a spirit, and then to have communicated with the spirits of the dead. They reported (and probably produced) strange rapping sounds which they interpreted as communications from the spirit world. The accounts of the early sessions sound like teenage slumber party shockers. Their first respondent was "Mr. Splitfoot," surely a comic euphemism for the cloven-footed Devil.

At another time, in another place, this might have been dismissed as hysteria, nonsense, fraud, self-delusion, or just poltergeisty adolescent hormonal surges. At this time, from this fertile place, it swept the world, soon spinning far out of the control of the Fox sisters. It brought with it seances and rappings and mediums and psychics and floating trumpets and ghostly apparitions and automatic writing and spirits communicating in Morse code. Sadly, these talky spirits never seemed to have anything particularly interesting to say. Though the Fox sisters ultimately recanted and admitted fraud (and then recanted their recantation), nothing could stop the rush to believe.

If some people treated this simply as spooky entertainment, many did not. People as smart, eminent, and gifted as Arthur Conan Doyle, Alfred Russel Wallace, and William Butler Yeats became believers and practicers. This need to believe in and have evidence of the survival of the spirit after death was undoubtedly in part a reaction against the spread of Darwinian evolution and scientific materialism. Similar needs have convinced a twenty-first-century Kansas state school board to mandate the teaching of creationist religion as spurious science.

Harry Houdini, like The Amazing Randi in our time, was a professional magician and a vigorous debunker of fraud. He once visited Spiritualism's Vatican City, Lily Dale, New York, as many prominent people did. He knew that much of what passed for spiritualist miracles was cheap show biz trickery, and he ruthlessly exposed it. Unlike debunker James Randi in our time, he seemed to yearn that some of it should be true. Have people stopped trying to get Houdini's spirit to open padlocks? That was standard fare on Halloweens for years.

BREAKING NEWS: A definitive answer to my Houdini/padlock question appeared in the *New York Times*, November 1, 2006:

And the definitive answer is:

Sorta.

Though there seem to have been no padlocks involved, thirteen (of course; what else?) magicians and/or Houdini experts met on October 31 at Manhattan's Center for Jewish History in something like a séance. They invoked the spirit of the late magician, who died on Halloween in 1926. "We're waiting for a sign, Harry. . . . It's been eighty years, Harry." Twenty minutes of silence ensued. So people are still trying, and Houdini is still not talking, rapping, or unlocking. Yet one participant insisted, "I felt something in the room," so we can assume efforts will continue. Irrational belief is indestructible.

Spiritualism as a significant social force is largely history. What is left survives as an entertainment and a small formal religion, centered in Lily Dale, near Cassadaga, New York, a community just off US 20 in Chautauqua County, twelve miles from my house. Dozens of mediums live and hang out their shingles there. They are popular with tourists and local people. They are said to give good entertainment value for money in their "readings." There are quasi-Christian services on Sunday, involving contacting the spirits of the dead. Lily Dale gears up in the summer; it quiets down pretty quickly in the fall, with only about 120 permanent residents. For the snowbirds, there is Cassadaga, Florida, where the mediums (well, some of them) go in the winter. It bills itself as "Metaphysical Mecca" and "Home to Friendly Spirits." Aura photographs there (don't ask) are only twenty-five bucks, and there's a money back guarantee if you are not "satisfied with your reading."

A century ago, Lily Dale was as reputable and famous as its Methodist neighbor, The Chautauqua Institution. Distinguished people went there to lecture or study or play, not all of them believers. One delicious anecdote concerns Susan B. Anthony (born near the Great Road in Adams, MA). Told that the spirit of an aunt was trying to contact her, she is said to have responded that her aunt hadn't had anything interesting to say when she was alive; why couldn't she talk to the spirit of someone really interesting, like [her great friend and ally] Elizabeth Cady [Stanton]?

The National Congress of Spiritualist Assemblies describes itself thus: "Spiritualism is a Science, Philosophy, and Religion of continuous life based upon the demonstrated fact of communication by means of mediumship with those who live in the Spirit World. Spiritualism is a recognized religion and has been organized and functioning continuously since 1893" (NCSA President Rev. Barbara Thurman, news release, October 29, 1999, on the Web site "angelfire!!").

The Chautauqua Institution, of which more later, celebrated its 126th season in 2000. Not to be outdone by much, the Lily Dale Assembly claimed 2000 as its 121st season. An article promoting tourism in a local newspaper guide states that "it is a drawing card that cannot be denied" (Joan Josephson, *Dunkirk Observer Summer Supplement*, 2000). The Lily Dale Assembly's ad for one of its superstar lecturers gives the flavor of the summer program, and of the dogmas of the religion that organizes it:

> Death is a natural transition from one plane of existence to another. In this moving and profound workshop, Van Praagh will open your awareness to the energy fields that surround you. He will guide you through a meditation to bring you closer to the realms of the spirit. You will be invited to participate in a riveting and enlightening question and answer discussion imbued with compassion, depth and humor about the transition of death and various types of spirit communication . . . spontaneously reconnecting several audience members to loved ones who have passed on, conveying evidential, detailed messages from the other wide . . ." (ibid., back cover)

Like, wow, man.

There's a good little spiritualist/new age bookshop, a gazebo on the water, and a pleasantly creaky old wooden assembly hall. There's a magnificent grove of old growth hemlocks, Leolyn Woods, with an "Inspiration Stump," an outdoor locus for meetings and mediumship. Incongruously, there's a pet cemetery near it. The two lakes, connected by a channel, are very pretty; I've kayaked them. They are often frequented by a breeding pair of whistling swans, named, inevitably, Lily and Dale. Most of Lily Dale's architecture is somewhat down-at-heels Victorian Carpenter Gothic. The summer program is a melange of mediumship and American Indian dancing and New Age author/lecturers and therapists and self-helpers and crystals. There are sometimes good small theatre productions. But Lily Dale as a whole looks and feels run down, tatty.

The Fox sisters' cottage actually stood for a time on the grounds of Lily Dale, having been moved there from Hydesville in 1916. It was brought here as a kind of sacred object, something like the Bethlehem stable of the faith. Sadly, it burned to the ground not long after, perhaps torched by an arsonist. Some of the locals suspected its destruction was the result of religious persecution, and it may have been. In any event, Spiritualism is one more new religion, one more lively movement started by women, one more yeasty growth on the Great Road in a time of religious fervor. Lily Dale perfectly fills its tiny niche in the history of American religious life, though it is no longer an intellectually significant place.

Yet its influence is probably larger than its current importance suggests. Modern American society is obsessed with angels, aliens, area 51, Madam Chloe, astrology, the Psychic Network, runes, the Tarot, the I Ching, wicca, Left Behind, numerology, holy images on windows or trees or in cinnamon buns or pierogis or frying pans, weeping statues, soap scum Marys, any way to cut through hard thinking and get straight to the Really Big Stuff the quick and easy way. A piece of a grilled cheese sandwich with an alleged image of the Virgin Mary burned into the crust recently sold for $28,000 on eBay (*New York Times*, February 13, 2007). Astoundingly, some of the politicians who lead this country expect, even long for and work toward, Armageddon and The Rapture. It would be absurd to blame Spiritualism for all this nonsense, but its remarkable fad was a big step in this direction, and it all started on the Great Road.

giants in the earth : (well, one, anyway)

Excessive credulity in the Burned-Over District was not limited to religion. Cardiff, New York, then and now a tiny hamlet on US 20, became, in 1869, the site of the biggest hoax of the century. George Hull, a local promoter, had a large block of gypsum quarried in Iowa. He commissioned a humanoid statue to be cut from it, buried it, and later had it "found," dug up, near Cardiff. It became known as "The Cardiff

Giant," thought by some to be a petrified Indian, or a fossil of one of the "Giants in the earth in those days" (Genesis 6:4). Okay, religion *did* have something to do with it. George Hull, an atheist, was amusingly debunking belief in the literal truth of the Bible.

The hoax was soon exposed, even cheerfully admitted, but the ten-foot-tall "Giant"—obviously nothing more than a very big hunk of pale rock—continued to be a draw for the gullible well into the twentieth century. P. T. Barnum commissioned a plaster copy of the original and made big bucks off it. The Cardiff Giant competed successfully with all the progressive modern exhibits at the Pan American Exhibition in Buffalo in 1901—on US 20, of course. He has rested, since 1947, in the Farmers' Museum in the glorious village of Cooperstown, New York, just south of the Great Road. He was for a few years outside under a big tent in the summer, a deliciously appropriate reminder of his carny/show biz past. There are many better reasons—opera, baseball, architecture, history, art,

The Cardiff Giant

literature²—to visit this splendid museum-rich community; but don't miss the Giant if you go. And see chapter 4 below for an amusing afterthought to this silly story.

patriarchy reasserted : latter-day saints

Is there a pattern along the Great Road in New York, a pattern of strange new religions inspired and led by women? Yes, but it will have to withstand a huge exception, because, watch out, here comes a wholly patriarchal major new religion, from the same soil, at the same time. In 1805, in Palmyra, New York, Joseph Smith was born. That's six miles from the original site of the Fox cabin. Something in the water??

The Smiths were Connecticut Yankees, recent immigrants to the region. Joseph Smith had a troubled youth. He was arrested four times in the 1820s: for disorderly conduct, and for "glass looking," quasi-magical attempts (or perhaps just scams) to find buried treasure. In 1823, he announced that he had had a revelation from an angel named Moroni, who told him that Golden Plates were buried on Hill Cumorah, a local drumlin, a glacial remnant hill. Finding and translating them with the assistance of some mysterious magic stones (he said), he published them, in 1827, as *The Book of Mormon*. In 1830, he founded a church based on his mythology, but he was soon forced west to Kirtland, Ohio, by local hostility to his vision and his teachings, which already included polygamous marriage. Palmyra and Kirtland are both on the Great Road. He and his followers stayed six years in Kirtland (1831–1837) and built the first Mormon Temple there.

Pushed by local antipathy farther west to Illinois in 1839, he and his followers took over a young Illinois town on the Mississippi River, renamed it Nauvoo, and built a Mormon Temple there. Nauvoo's population soon swelled to more than ten thousand, making it the third largest town in Illinois at the time. But hostility to Mormon ways and beliefs, probably heightened by envy of their organization and prosperity, had followed them west. In 1844, the Smiths, Joseph and his brother Hyrum, were jailed and then murdered, lynched by a mob in Carthage, Illinois. The Nauvoo Temple soon burned and fell into disrepair. (It has recently been rebuilt by the historically minded parent church.) One might have expected the new faith to die, as had many before it.

Into this leadership crisis stepped an organizer of genius and iron will, Brigham Young, to take over what became the majority branch of the church. There are today two major LDS churches. The smaller "Reorganized" Church claims to have inherited the truth in a direct line from Joseph Smith. When Brigham Young took the majority west to Utah, the Reorganized Saints stayed in Missouri, where their central headquarters is today. Born in Vermont in 1801, Brigham Young grew up in—where else?—central New York. He did carpentry work, and he helped build and decorate (tradition says) one of the fireplaces in the William Seward house in Auburn, New York, on the Great Road.

polygamy lives

A smaller, more notorious branch of the original church is the Fundamentalist Church of Jesus Christ of Latter Day Saints. Because it still proclaims and promotes polygamy, it maintains its headquarters and its population in the "Arizona Strip," that narrow band of Arizona just south of Utah. Church leaders have often found it handy to be near borders, as Voltaire did at Ferney, ready to hop from repressive royalist France into safer, freer Switzerland. A 1953 Arizona raid on polygamists in the Strip is widely thought to have backfired, causing paranoia and a hardening of polygamist attitudes. There is rarely a paper trail proving plural marriage, so current law enforcement practices incline toward prosecution of the sexual exploitation of underage girls.

THIS JUST IN: Warren Jeffs, current leader of approximately six thousand Fundamentalist Mormons, lives an odd, schizoid life. He combines charismatic notoriety with lying low to avoid prosecution for arranging such plural ("spiritual") marriages between men and very young girls. On August 29, 2006, he was arrested while riding in a fire-engine red 2007 Cadillac Escalade near Las Vegas. In the SUV were wigs, shades, and $50,000 in cash. Big bucks, disguises, Vegas, a cherry 'Slade: sounds more like pimp or point guard than patriarch. This bids fair to become the supermarket tabloid titillation story to succeed the murder of poor little Jonbenet (New York Times, August 30, 2006). A court in St. George, Utah, has ruled that Jeffs should be tried as an accomplice to the rape of a fourteen-year old girl. The trial is scheduled to begin after this book goes to press. See more on LDS polygamy below.

"this is the right place"

This book cannot undertake even a brief retelling of the remarkable history of the main line Mormon Church; or, to give them the name they prefer, the Church of Jesus Christ of Latter Day Saints. Theirs is such a westering, continental, American story that it defies geographical localization, yet it all began here in the Burned-Over District. I admit that I find Joseph Smith's mythology, pseudohistory, anthropology, and theology bogus and unconvincing, and very much a product of mid-nineteenth-century central New York. There is no physical evidence for the stories of the Angel Moroni and the Golden Plates inscribed with *The Book of Mormon*. Though it has some creative individual features, Joseph Smith's wordy addendum to the Bible is absolutely typical of its time and place: visionary, millennialist, and culture-bound. Mark Twain, in *Roughing It*, called it "chloroform in print." I've never been able to slog through all of it.

Yet though these scriptures may fail as history or literature, they certainly succeeded as mythic inspiration. One must admire the Mormons' remarkable grit, planning, organization, and will. Many were from the disenfranchised peoples of northern Europe, coming from Britain and Scandinavia to the New World to find opportunity. In 1846–1847, thousands of them walked halfway across North America, pulling handcarts containing their belongings, to what Brigham Young called "the right place," their Zion, the Salt Lake Valley. That was remarkable enough. When they arrived, after great travail, in a not very hospitable place, their leader demanded and got unquestioned obedience from them. Some of their achievements still seem almost unbelievable, such as their arduous expansion through "Hole-in-the-Rock," across the Colorado River into southeastern Utah. It's an epic story, but I haven't time to tell it all here.

American communism : I have seen the future and it works

Their discipline enabled them to build what was essentially a communist state, a dictatorial organization and allocation of water and land and people. Without that, there would have been no "Deseret," their name for their new land. They labored hard and intelligently, and they made the desert, or at least the arable three percent of it, yield rich, communally irrigated crops. They were the first large, well-organized group of settlers to recognize the great truth of the American West: water is life, water is gold, water is everything, and whoever controls it controls the land. Though Mark Twain seems never to have written this, it is often attributed to him: In the West, whiskey is for drinking; water is for fighting over. The Mormons adopted, for the most part, the sensible but unusual policy of buying off the local natives, the Utes and Paiutes, instead of fighting them and trying to exterminate them. It was more practical as well as more humane. Brigham Young is reported to have said, "Feeding them is cheaper than fighting them." Couldn't other settlers have thought of that? And, of course, they also attempted to convert them, with some success.

The Saints' most flamboyant practice, polygamy, "celestial marriage," may have been less important than a century and a half of media titillation has made it seem. Yet *Big Love* is Big on HBO, and polygamy is still an issue even among main line Mormons in Utah, Idaho, and northern Arizona. It can still have a very negative impact on young women. The strange abduction of Elizabeth Smart, in Salt Lake City in 2004, shows that the idea still has destructive power. Polygamy is morally repugnant to most. It had to be repudiated, in 1890, in a pragmatic new "revelation," before Utah would finally be permitted to enter the union, late, in 1896. It helped that the mighty polygamist leader, twenty-seven-times-married Brigham Young, had died in 1877. Many faithful Mormons bitterly opposed this new idea as a terrible blow to the heart of the doctrine of the church. After another manifesto in 1904, church members who openly practised polygamy could be excommunicated. Officially at least, polygamy ended long ago, and most Utahns, Mormon or not, have more important things to think about.

Yet it's still something to squabble over, even in the main LDS church. In 2002, I saw battling billboards within two miles of each other on I-15 in Salt Lake City. One, with grand old black and white pictures of patriarchal Mormon familes, urged all to "HONOR YOUR LDS HERITAGE!" It didn't take a genius to realize that this meant *all* old LDS practices, not just consecrated underwear. The second billboard advertised a good local dark brew from nearby trendy Park City, clearly *not* brewed by Mormons:

> POLYGAMY PORTER
> Why have just one?
> Bring some home to the wives.

Badump bump. I bought the beer *and* the T-shirt—really—in Springdale, Utah, at the entrance to Zion National Park, whose Biblical nomenclature comes from LDS settlers.

The doctrine of polygamy won't quit. From the Associated Press, Salt Lake City, Utah, August 19, 2006: "Calling their lives blessed, more than a dozen young women and girls from polygamous families in Utah spoke at a rally Saturday, calling for a change in state laws and the right to live the life and religion they choose." About 250 showed up at the event, organized by Principle [*sic*] Voices of Polygamy. "We are not brainwashed, mistreated, neglected, malnourished, illiterate, defective or dysfunctional," seventeen-year-old Jessica said. "My brothers and sisters are freethinking, independent people . . ." Okay, I guess the issue hasn't gone away at all.

The LDS Church runs Utah, whatever its leaders may disingenuously say. Mormons are often charged with discriminating economically against non-Mormons, whom they call "Gentiles." (Utah is thus the only place in the world where Jews are Gentiles. Ya gotta love it.) The church is also doing very well in improbable corners of the world. Would you believe Samoa? Tonga? I was once approached by two young Mormon "Elders" on their mission, in good French, in the gardens of Versailles. Would I like to hear about "le religion Mormon"? Though I said, "Non, merci," many do not. Mike, a Utah LDS friend, confirms for me that some young Mormon women make missions, too. The young women are called "Sisters," not "Elders." As many as fifty thousand shiny-bright, idealistic, and energetic young people are out there right now, proselytizing. Thus do the people and ideas of the Great Road still powerfully impact the world.

The LDS Church is very media savvy, as anyone who has heard its Mormon Tabernacle Choir broadcasts or used its genealogical records will know. The Mormons do not neglect their creation myth, though they have come a long way, literally and figuratively, from Palmyra, New York. The Smith home there, which the prophet helped to build, is open for tours "every day of the year." I've not seen it, but I have been to the small museum at Hill Cumorah, which exhibits alleged replicas of Joseph Smith's golden tablets.

show biz on Hill Cumorah

Every summer, Hill Cumorah rings with amplified sound and blazes with light as the story of Joseph Smith's encounter with the Angel Moroni, and the mythic history of the church, are retold. The Great Road is crowded again with pilgrims and true believers, proselytizing and professing their truth for all to see. Jesus Christ recreates His prehistoric American appearance nightly: "Christ appears in the night sky, descends, teaches the people, then ascends into the night sky and disappears." With a laser show.

The Pageant, which I've not seen, promotes itself thus:

Since 1937, the Hill Cumorah Pageant, a uniquely American drama, has thrilled hundreds of thousands of visitors from all over the world. Today, it is presented in the tradition of the great religious pageants begun in the Middle Ages, but with the advantages of high-technology [sic]. Digital sound, state-of-the-art lighting, an erupting 37 foot volcano, water curtains [huh?], thunder and lightning and earthquakes all serve as a backdrop to the story. The Pageant is an account of the rise and fall of the ancient inhabitants of this continent and the visit of Jesus Christ. Don't miss this uplifting, family-oriented, free nighttime drama. (Source: a Handout at Hill Cumorah)

Whew.

Not shy, the pageant's Web site quotes the critics thus: "'Staging the Mormon Pageant on this holy site, with the statue of Moroni glittering atop the hill, roughly equals staging Oberammergau at Lourdes, except that this show has a distinctly American-style flash and grandeur'— *Rochester Democrat and Chronicle.*"

Not given to understatement, are they?

"'A pageant performed with the spirit of a George Lucas techno-dazzler and the scope of a Cecil B. DeMille Epic'—*The New York Times.*"

IT'S SHOWTIME!!! And right off US 20.

but wait! there's more!

Another Mormon sect, the Strangites, comes from the Great Road and my own Chautauqua County, although the group ultimately moved to Beaver Island in northern Lake Michigan. James Jesse Strang (1813–1856) was a small but charismatic man who, at age nineteen, lamented being just a farmer and yearned to be a king. Improbably, he got his wish.

James Strang moved to Chautauqua County from his native Scipio, New York, six miles south of Auburn and US 20. He read law, was called to the bar, and held a postmastership in Chautauqua County, in the town of Ellington. He became a Mormon, and, on the death of Joseph Smith, produced a letter that said Smith had chosen him as his successor. Brigham Young was already preparing to lead his group west, but Strang's claim appealed to many. Strang even had some plates dug up, and "translated them," passing them off as more divine Mormon revelations, to support his assertions. True, his plates were only brass—but at least he showed them to other people.

Ultimately, Strang led his group to southeastern Wisconsin, and then to Lake Michigan and Beaver Island, where he ran a very successful political and business operation, and had himself crowned "King" of this realm in 1846. At first he opposed polygamy; then, perhaps influenced by some comely devotees, he announced that his revelation now favored it. He eventually had five wives. This and other notorious behavior led President Millard Fillmore in 1851 to send a U.S. Navy gunboat to suppress such high jinks, but the colony survived. Strang's royal dream ended in 1856 when two former followers shot their King James; he died a few weeks later without appointing a successor. There are said to be a few Strangites still following his principles today.

more social experiments on the great road : Oneida

Polygamous Mormons were too much for most respectable folk to take, from New York to Ohio to Illinois and well beyond. Another sore test to the liberality of the Burned-Over District came with the establishment of the Oneida Community, founded east of Syracuse in 1848. Small but stable, it was more intelligently led, lasted longer, and had a larger impact on American life than most American communist sects. The founder, John Humphrey Noyes, had been influenced by a Charles Grandison Finney sermon on Perfectionism—the idea that we might become sinless and lead perfect lives here on earth. Of Finney, see more later in this chapter.

In its day, the Oneida Community was notorious as a promoter of the equality of the sexes. There's that pesky idea again! Members also practiced "complex marriage," i.e., every one was married to everyone else. "Free love" was an early term for this practice, a term that the community soon discarded as too inflammatory. Living the Perfect life, it seems it's easy to get one's *agape* confused with one's *eros*. And of course this doctrine meant that sex with anyone in the community—well, anyone of the opposite sex—was sanctioned and, if mutually desired, perfectly proper. That *does* sound "complex!" The rules for approaching one another erotically seem to have been as involved as a gavotte at a debutante cotillion. Lengthy, nonorgasmic sexual intercourse—in effect, fun sex with birth control—was another practice advocated by founder Noyes, to the horror of decent central New York folk. So was an early form of eugenics, as the community (really, its leaders) decided who should be permitted to breed. Not surprisingly, its leaders did a lot of the breeding. Children were taken from their mothers after weaning and communally reared.

One troubled soul who yearned for that community and sexual freedom, and lived briefly in the Oneida community, was a future presidential assassin; see chapter 3. Oneida disbanded as a community and a belief structure in 1881, its adherents tiring of the authoritarian strictures of its aging founder. Noyes withdrew to Niagara Falls, Ontario, perhaps to be out of reach of American lawsuits, and died soon after. Oneida is still organized as a business corporation, though its last related manufacturing operation in New York, Buffalo China, shut down in 2004. The Oneida Corporation filed for Chapter Eleven bankruptcy in 2006.

The Oneida Community Mansion House still exists. It is a large brick structure with a museum, a hall, apartments, and nine guest rooms, situated on thirty-three acres near Oneida, New York. Guided tours are offered and there is a golf course nearby. Thus do religious fervor and sexual and social experimentation dwindle into commerce, nostalgia, and putting greens. The corporate name Oneida survives only as a brand of tableware. The Oneida Indians are quite a different matter, and are surviving quite nicely, thank you. One of the six tribes of the Iroquois Confederacy, they are profiting handsomely from Turning Stone Casino, near the Great Road in central New York. They are using some of their casino big bucks in a Herculean attempt to revivify their nearly extinct Oneida language.

a message from East Aurora to Garcia

Elbert Hubbard, a writer and publicist, became rich and famous from his wildly successful, up-by-your-bootstraps, take-the-initiative moral pamphlet, "A Message to Garcia" (1899). Forty-two *million* copies were sold in his not overlong lifetime (1856–1915). I had the "Message" preached to me in a Presbyterian Sunday school on the Great Road in Illinois. Thanks, Mr. Humphrey. Hubbard had gained wealth early, selling soap for the Larkin company in Buffalo, New York. These wealthy industrialists, the Larkins and their associates, were among Frank Lloyd Wright's most important patrons. The grand house Wright built in Buffalo for soap magnate Darwin Martin still stands and is being expensively restored, though its outbuildings and the massive Wright-designed

Larkin soap company building have been demolished. The Martin house outbuildings are being rebuilt.

Disenchanted with the soap business that had made him wealthy, seeking a more meaningful life, Elbert Hubbard travelled and wrote and got even wealthier. In 1895, influenced by the work of Englishman William Morris, he founded his Roycroft Community on what is now US 20A in East Aurora, New York. It was an important part of the Arts and Crafts movement, dedicated to producing attractive consumer goods, putting style and simple beauty into everyday things. Roycroft became a large campus, with fourteen buildings built over the years to accommodate the craftsmen whose work Hubbard fancied and facilitated. He and they produced books, magazines, furniture, leather and metal goods, a whole array of attractive products. Important buildings here include a stone chapel, a large mock-Tudor printery, and a furniture shop. The former home of one of the craftsmen, appropriately built in what is called the "Craftsman style," has become a small Hubbard/Roycroft museum.

Actually, that architectural style was championed by another Great Road leader of the Arts and Crafts movement, Gustave Stickley (1858–1942). Also influenced by William Morris, he urged that houses should be in harmony with their landscapes, and he advocated an open floor plan. Both ideas influenced the career of the young Frank Lloyd Wright. Stickley lived and worked in several places, and he founded his furniture factory in 1904 in Syracuse, on the Great Road. In keeping with the spirit of the time and place, he started a Utopian community in New Jersey, which, like most, did not flourish. His furniture, like his houses, was simple, original, and handcrafted. His legacy today includes many handsome Craftsman bungalows along the route of US 20 in New York.

Roycroft died out as a business in the Great Depression of the 1930s. The Roycroft name lives on as a furniture style, and in the recently restored Roycroft Inn (1897, 1903–1905), a National Historic Landmark, built to accommodate the many visitors who came to the Roycroft world. The inn's exterior is undistinguished; not originally designed as an inn, it was adapted from other uses and expanded by Roycroft architect James Cadzow. The interior is nicer, rambling and woody and cozy, with some hints, especially in the furniture and lamps, of Louis Sullivan and Frank Lloyd Wright. It's a fine place for a meal on a visit to this interesting town. The Roycroft Campus Corporation that runs the inn has also acquired other parts of the Roycroft legacy: they hold a Book-Arts weekend in October, celebrating and perpetuating the lovely old crafts of letterpress printing (real lead type!!) and hand bookbinding.

Elbert Hubbard was a pioneer in media and the design of arts and crafts, not religion; his communitarian emphasis and his strenuous promotion of moral and artistic achievement link him and his community to other social and religious groups of the age. He was given to vague, noble pronouncements such as "Art is not a thing, it is a way." With his second wife, he perished at the height of his fame and wealth when the *Lusitania* was sunk by a German U-boat in 1915. True to the slightly weird Burned-Over tradition, his spirit is reported still to haunt his former office in the restored Inn (*Buffalo News*, October 28, 2001, E2). Headline: "Western New York is seething with the supernatural." The supernatural has certainly come to the right place.

East Aurora is also the site of the only surviving house in which President Millard Fillmore lived—except for the White House, of course. He helped to build it; see chapter 3 for more on Fillmore and this house. There's also a Gen-You-Wine Five & Dime store in East Aurora, Vidler's. It has expanded into half a block of stores on two floors, some with oiled wooden floors. Vidler's is loaded with fun and games, reeking of nostalgia. Whenever I have been there, it has been full of busloads of old folks remembering (and purchasing replicas of) the delightful knickknacks of their childhoods. Sometimes they bring along their grandchildren, who are acquiring their own toys and preparing for their own future nostalgia. There is also a toy museum in town. East Aurora is a very pleasant time warp, largely due to the Roycroft influence. Even the shoe repair shop's sign uses the attractive and distinctive Roycroft lettering.

Chautauqua : from sunday school to summer school to upscale resort

The best known place and idea (it's both) in the southwestern corner of New York is the Chautauqua Institution. Founded in 1874 by Methodists as an educational camp for Sunday School teachers, it has long outlived and far outgrown that. Theodore Roosevelt called it "the most American thing in America." It now has a long summer season of first rate concerts, plays, operas, and lectures. Its music students take private instruction, form ensembles, and play for the public. Significant events have occured there, such as FDR's famous 1936 "I hate war" speech at the Chautauqua Amphitheater. Bill Clinton spent a few days there as president. There was an important *glasnost* meeting there between Russians and Americans just before the end of the Cold War.

Many creative people have enjoyed Chautauqua, and some have flourished there. Thomas Alva Edison, born on the Great Road in Milan, Ohio, gave the world the electric light bulb, the phonograph, and the movies. Edison married Mina Miller, the daughter of one of Chautauqua's founders. Despite his distaste for organized religion, Edison often summered there with his wife. Jane Addams, from the Great Road in Illinois, published a book on peace with the Chautauqua Press in 1907. She personally took her messages of pacifism and social work to Chautauqua in 1915. George Gershwin wrote his *Piano Concerto in F* in a tiny studio there in 1925.

Chautauqua is mostly old, its well-preserved Victorian Gothic architecture coexisting with a few new buildings and many mature trees. It is conservative and traditional: no cars are allowed except for home owners, who can enter and park but not drive around. The speed limit is an oddly Babylonian twelve m.p.h. No alcohol can be sold on the grounds. (I hear this may change to permit wine with dinners.) Chautauqua might be senile and stodgy. It is not. Well, not very. It is an easy place to make fun of, and we who live near it and admire it, *do* often make friendly fun of it. I once heard it described as a place "where grandparents bring their grandparents," but that's a bit much. It can feel claustrophobic, with narrow streets and tidy, pricey wooden houses packed tightly together. Almost all have lovely front porches and/or second floor balconies, perfect summer spaces for self-improving, idling, or greeting the neighbors. Chautauqua is usually astoundingly quiet; many bicycles, few noisy cars. There are not a lot of young children here. Those who do attend play quietly, mostly, as though they were in church, which, in a sense, they are. You can hear the bell tower from anywhere on the grounds. This little time-warp town, home to about a thousand people in the silent winter, swells to accommodate many thousands in the summer without getting appreciably noisier. Motorboats on lovely Chautauqua Lake do not go VROOOOOOOOOOMM!!! They go put-put-put-put-put . . .

Chautauqua and cautious change

The vast, elegant Atheneum Hotel, built in 1881, has been carefully and lovingly renovated, but little altered. It was designated a National Historic Landmark in 1989. On a rural New York summer evening, there is no nicer place to sit than in a rocking chair on its huge front porch overlooking Chautauqua Lake. It's even better after table d'hote dinner at the Atheneum. The food is nothing special, but there is a choice among several desserts, and every diner gets to pick TWO. Sweet Methodist wickedness. Bliss. At least I hope that's still true; it's been a while since I dined there. Carl Carmer wrote that in the Chautauqua Instutution was "the last American tavern, so far as I know, to abandon the custom of serving cornmeal mush for supper every Sunday night" (*American Panorama*, Garden City, NY: Doubleday, 1960, 103). Well, why change a good thing? Isn't that the first rule of conservatism? "If the mush ain't broke, don't fix it?" Yet there is slow, cautious change at Chautauqua. Major events now include mellow rock concerts, nostalgic acts of aging rock groups for their aging baby boomer fans, along with the hymns and operas and plays. Three Dog Night, *All My Sons*, *The Music Man*, and *Madam Butterfly* cheerfully coexisted in the summer of 2005.

There is a large and very earnest "Relief Map of the Holy Land" laid out on the ground down by the lake, surely once a teaching aid for those Methodist Sunday school teachers. It has little sculpted hills and valleys of dirt, including, way low down, a moist "The Dead Sea." It has funny little toy buildings placed and labeled as "Jerusalem," "Beersheba," etc. The shore of Chautauqua Lake stands in for the Mediterranean coast. Since the Institution is on the west, or wrong, side of the lake, the sign must also read, for the literal minded: "Directions are Reversed." It is not only bewilderingly inaccurate; it is unintentionally hilarious.

Garrison Keillor and his Prairie Home Companion troupe did two summer *Prairie Home Companion* broadcasts from Chautauqua. He had only to expand his Lutheran jokes to include Methodists and Presbyterians, and do a bit more with white shoes and golf than with tractors and softball. Guilt is universal, and Chautauqua is as Middle American as Lake Wobegon, though a lot more prosperous. It is not quite all lily-white Protestant; African American visitors are few, but I occasionally see some. Though once excluded by restrictive WASP real estate covenants, some Jewish families, like their Protestant counterparts, have spent parts of summers at Chautauqua for years. Since 2006, the conservative Jewish group Chabad Lubavitch has held services at Chautauqua, and given concerts of Jewish music and classes in challah baking. They go back to Crown Heights, in Brooklyn, when the season ends in late August.

Chautauqua is the kind of place kids grow up and take their kids to, and their grandkids, too. Yet there's a price to be paid for the institution's success: many who went there regularly as children or young adults now can no longer afford rent there for a week or a month. Upscale rentals now go for up to four and five thousand dollars a week. Chautauqua is thus out of reach for many in the middle class, and that must limit the yeastiness of its mix of people and ideas.

Those who rent on the grounds, or pay a daily gate fee, are admitted free to most things inside, including some fine concerts at "The Amp," the grand old wooden outdoor amphitheater. You may be a fan, as I am, of "Music From Chautauqua," a nationally distributed series produced by the excellent Buffalo fine arts station, WNED-FM. Many of those concerts are recorded at The Amp, as were Keillor's shows, broadcast live, both of which I attended. Chautauqua has a slender claim to being the oldest continuous music festival in the world, antedating Bayreuth by two years. There is good theatre, opera, and symphonic music. Students come from all over the country to study dance, music, or literature. I have enjoyed teaching them. One summer my students included some earnest young Christian people attending on scholarships given by the International Order of the King's Daughters and Sons.

intellectual entertainment

True to its Christian roots, Chautauqua flings wide the gates and gives free admission, on Sundays, usually for a sermon in The Amp from a distinguished preacher, and good music from the pickup choir. Visitors can then stay free for a while for whatever the schedule affords, though it won't include a major evening concert. Chautauqua has a distinguished intellectual tradition. The Chautauqua Literary and Scientific Circle bills itself as the oldest continuous book club in America. It was founded in 1878, in the fifth year of the Institution. It annually puts on a series of fairly rigorous talks and readings by authors, few of whose books are light summer reading. I have enjoyed hearing friends and former Fredonia students do readings there. A very good book store supports these endeavors. Many of the Institution's invited star speakers come for a week, not just a one-nighter, and it is thus possible for visitors to engage a good mind over the course of several appearances and discussions in that week. Chautauqua is a serious place for serious people to come and have some serious fun. Seriously, folks.

Chautauqua earned its place in the American lexicon chiefly by exporting its unusual mixture of religion, entertainment, education, and uplift. Before radio and the other electronic media, "Chautauquas," distantly related traveling shows, toured the country, set up tents, and brought distinguished speakers and their ideas to places and people that could never have hoped to hear them otherwise. William Jennings Bryan made a lucrative late career out of reciting his "Cross of Gold" speech hundreds of times in hamlets like those of his native "Egypt," in southern Illinois. My father, unable to afford college, got some education and enjoyment from "The Chautauqua" in the summer in his little town of Genoa, Illinois, just off the Great Road. So did hundreds of thousands of others.

All of that ended, like vaudeville, with the advent of radio and movies. Chautauqua lives on, and thrives, largely because it is one of the most rational, least "Burned-Over" religious institutions in the Burned-Over District. It is a lovely and interesting place; it just no longer seems a particularly innovative one.[3]

the brotherhood of the new life—in my town!

There is yet another nineteenth-century Chautauqua County religious foundation to consider. I have saved it until near the end of this chapter not because it is especially unusual or interesting or influential, but because, remarkably, it happened HERE, not just in my home state or county, but in my little village, right across the street from my house. Land's sakes alive, if it can happen in Brocton, New York (current pop. 1,547, no more than half that then), it can happen ANYWHERE. If I'd lived here then, I'd be dead now, but I could have watched from my house right across what would become US 20 as the members of The Brotherhood of the New Life tended their fields. There are still vineyards there. The Brotherhood was a utopian community established in my little village in 1867 by Thomas Lake Harris.

Some time must elapse before a cult/becomes a sect/becomes a religion. The Brotherhood surely never got beyond a sect, if that far. It enrolled about seventy-five members at its height. It left here in 1883 and lives as the dimmest of memories in local history. "Vine Cliff," a handsome old house near the Lake Erie shore, with a fine classical pillared veranda looking south toward the sun, is the lone physical remnant of the Brotherhood's great days. The house still looks appropriately grand and patriarchal; it suggests graciousness and prosperity, Tara, not religious asceticism. As such dim memories do many social experiments survive— Brook Farm, Fruitlands, the Pantisocracy, and many less well known, like Brocton's.

Thomas Lake Harris (1823–1906) was born poor in Buckinghamshire, England, and moved with his parents at age five to the Great

Vine Cliff : the main house of the Brotherhood of the New Life

Vine Cliff

Road community of Utica, New York. Strongly influenced by Spiritualism (from the Great Road in central New York), he started his first religious community in West Virginia. When it failed, he returned to New
York and affiliated with the Swedenborgians. He established the first of
four locations of his Brotherhood in Dutchess County, New York, in 1861.
The community in Brocton was the third and largest, sited on two thousand acres stretching from what is now US 20 to the shore of Lake Erie,
two miles north. The agrarian Brotherhood grew hay, nursery crops, and
fruit, especially grapes—pretty much as the local farmers still do.

The Brotherhood was communistic and frugal, except, some grum-
bled, for the richer lifestyle of its leader. Harris smoked expensive cigars,
married three times, and kept company with attractive young women.
He preached spiritual cleansing for his followers through work, asceticism, and celibacy, though Harris's turgid hymn poetry drew criticism for
its perhaps figurative eroticism. He denied marriage (hence sexuality) to
those he deemed unworthy. There are lurid stories of the leader taking
sexual privileges he denied to his adherents, and unconfirmed tales of
naughty sexual behavior in his later years.

Harris's opaque theology need not detain us long. It resulted in what
we see over and over again in other cults: the expectation of the millen-
nium, abstinence from sex (for the followers, at least), the value of hard
labor, and the giving over of personal property and independence to the
control of a charismatic leader, who is sometimes thought of as a god,
and often becomes autocratic and claims special privileges. This then
leads to tensions, both external and internal, which result in the dissolu-
tion of the group. One flamboyant Brotherhood doctrine was "the bisex-
ual nature of the deity," which might have made a bit of a stir if anyone
outside the community had noticed it. Note again the tendency for these
religions to emphasize, or at least publicly assert the dignity of, the
female. Yet note also that the leader (like Joseph Smith and Brigham
Young, like John Humphrey Noyes, like David Koresh in our time) usually seems to get his pick of the nubile females. Fascination with and
unease about human sexuality is a standard motif in the creation of new
religions. Even Abraham and Sarah cut some capers. Perhaps anxious to
address the concerns of his more conventional neighbors, Harris wrote,
for publication in an 1873 volume of local history, a brief account of the
Brotherhood. He begins not with theology or organization, but with
physical and business operations:

> [W]e are laying out a village which we have named Salem-on-Erie
> designing to make it an industrial and business center. . . . Our product

of wines is from fifteen thousand to twenty-three thousand gallons annually. . . . [W]e also carry on a hotel and restaurant, and have just enlarged
our operations by erecting a steam grist mill. . . . [W]e are at present lay-
ing out and planting a public park and gardens . . ." (ed. Dr. H. C. Taylor, *Memorial Sketches of the Town of Portland*, Portland, NY, 1873)

Sounds just like the Chamber of Commerce, doesn't it? Nothing
too kooky there, although the huge wine production seems a bit surprising for a quasi-Protestant religious group at precisely the time and
place of the rise of the Temperance movement. The winery was quite
profitable, and Harris had no qualms about it. He built a tavern and
argued that his wine was filled with the divine breath, and hence had
no evil influences. He clearly could have written great modern wine
copy, perhaps something like

> We will sell no wine
> Before it's divine.

Harris continues: "In one sense the Brotherhood are spiritualists
[but not, as an uneasy editorial note assures us, in accepting] the general
mediumship and constant intercourse with the spirit world, [which they
reject as] profitless, dangerous, and even profane" (ibid.). "In another
sense the Brotherhood are Socialists"; yet Harris asserts that they revere
"Marriage, the Family, and Property, that triad of institutions most men-
aced by the revolutionary and distinctive spirit of the age." No lefty or
anarchist he. "In a word, the time-honoured virtues, Faith, Loyalty,
Honor, Purity and Obedience are believed . . . to be of infinite present
and real moment. It is the function of regenerate man to regenerate society; . . . these labors should be done from the inspiration of Divine Love
which have heretofore been performed from selfish greed or at the mere
spur of material necessity" (ibid.).

It is not surprising that this self-contradictory muddle of vague,
high-minded social tenets failed to keep a permanent hold on its over-
worked converts. Harris had considerable charisma, a piercing gaze, and
a fine patriarchal beard. He attracted many followers, including the poet
Edwin Markham. A wealthy English nobleman, Laurence Oliphant,
financed much of the Brocton scheme, and a later Santa Rosa, California,
project as well. Friends who work in real estate in Santa Rosa tell me that
building lots in the development of "Fountain Grove" (the former estate
of the Brotherhood there) now go as high as two million dollars. There is

a "Thomas Harris Drive" in Santa Rosa, too. I've visited it, and it's posh. Cultish erotic communism has become location, location, location.

> Birth, Copulation, and Death. / That's all the facts when you come to
> brass tacks.
> —T. S. Eliot, *Sweeney Agonistes*

Laurence Oliphant later broke with Harris, sued (successfully) for the return of some of his investment, and founded his own community in Palestine. Isn't that where religions should be founded?? Yes, in Israel or on US 20; nowhere else. According to my friend and fellow Broctonian Franklin Krohn, Oliphant became secretary to the author of the Israeli national anthem, "Hatikvah." Small world, ain't it? When Harris died, his followers, like those of Jemima Wilkinson, refused for three months to acknowledge that he was not just sleeping. He wasn't. Sex and death: these are the keystones, the wellsprings, often the shibboleths, of the religions of the Great Road.

Grass roots politics, Brocton, New York, c. 2000.
Assemblyman Bill Parment erects his sign in my yard on Route 20.
The grapes across the road were once part of the Brotherhood of the New Life land.

Brocton and yet another failed utopia : Pullman, Illinois

There is yet another remarkable link between my village and American Utopian experimentation. George M. Pullman was born in this little town in 1831, half a mile from where my house now stands, near what is now named "Pullman Street." I run past it almost daily. Pullman grew up poor in Brocton, one of ten children. After minimal schooling, he gained his first commercial experience working in a store here. Though he left Brocton at age sixteen, it was only to move east to Albion, New York, near US 20. He lived on or near the Great Road for almost his entire life, working first in cabinet making, then moving on to renovating and raising buildings above Chicago's swampy mud after the great fire of 1871. (That same mud later necessitated the ingenious use of structural steel frameworks for tall buildings and helped make Chicago the place where modern architecture began. It's still thriving there.) George Pullman's business life was long and interesting, culminating in the development and manufacture of the comfortable sleeping cars that bore his name: "Pullman Palace Cars." The Pullman car revolutionized long distance travel in America, and made him fabulously wealthy.

True to the spirit of the Great Road, George Pullman thought of himself as a social as well as commercial innovator. He cared about the lives of his workers, whom he sometimes called "my children." In 1880, he began to build a model town for them, just south of US 20, on Chicago's south side, where the sleeping cars were built: Pullman, Illinois. He wanted his namesake town to be an ideal, healthful place for them to live. No taverns were permitted, and no alcohol could be sold, except to guests at the upscale Florence Hotel, named for Pullman's daughter. (Pullman assumed that the hotel's high prices would discourage the workmen from partaking.) No private home ownership was permitted. The hundreds of attractive, well-designed brick rowhouses were rented to the workers at a profit to the company. They had gas heat and even indoor plumbing, remarkable for their time. Pullman's one church, a handsome greenstone Romanesque building, was rented, also at a profit, to all denominations. George Pullman even built a farm a few miles downslope from the town to receive the effluent of the town's sewers. The sewage (actually pumped there by a large industrial engine) was used to fructify the vegetable crops on the "sewage farm," which, like everything else in the town, homes and shops, sewage and church, turned a nice profit for the corporation and for George Pullman. Shit flows downhill, and the profits flowed to George Pullman, who lived about ten miles away on the then fashionable near-South Side, though he did maintain a suite at the Florence. Pullman was briefly a healthy, rational, profitable, patriarchal paradise for its twelve thousand residents—at least for those who didn't mind being aristocratically ruled.

Perhaps it was like Eden, when times were good. Skilled workmen took the jobs and rented the row houses and turned out Pullman cars and other types of railroad cars in great numbers, to meet the needs of the nation's great and growing railroad system. Then, in the terrible depression of 1893–1894, business slowed and faltered, and George Pullman made a simple business decision. He slashed wages without cutting rents or prices in the company stores. His "children" could no longer afford to buy food for *their* children in those stores, and the workers began organizing, oh, horror, a labor union. (I'm a faculty union leader. A dean once wanted to fire me for union uppittiness. He failed. He left. I stayed. Solidarity Forever, say I.) Three union leaders went to Pullman to ask for relief, and were summarily fired. A self-made independent plutocrat and visionary, George Pullman didn't like to be challenged, even questioned.

The new Pullman union was affiliated with Eugene Debs's American Railway Union, so its strike threatened to shut down the entire nation's transportation system. The previous years had seen increasing labor unrest and violent responses from capital and government: see the so-called Haymarket Massacre (Chicago, 1886) and the Homestead Strike (Pennsylvania, 1892). Businessmen and Chicago citizens were very worried, but Governor John Peter Altgeld of Illinois was sympathetic to the workers and refused to intervene. President Grover Cleveland, a progressive who had cut his political teeth on US 20 in Buffalo and Albany, would have none of this. There would be no labor anarchy in his country. He sent twelve thousand federal troops to smash the strike and enforce "peace." Ironically, six days later President Cleveland signed the bill that authorized Labor Day as a national holiday (NPR, September 3, 2006). The collapse of the Pullman strike was a massive defeat for organized labor.

Pullman's Utopian dream ended, as they all do. The workers, Pullman's "children," lost their homes and jobs. They hated George Pullman so much that, when he died three years later in 1897, his family feared the body would be stolen or desecrated. (He may have made these plans himself.) His casket was covered with a room-sized block of concrete, reinforced, appropriately, by railroad ties, when it was placed in its grand tomb in posh Graceland Cemetery. Or perhaps, as Ambrose Bierce wryly remarked: "It is clear the family in their bereavement was making sure

George Pullman monument and gravesite,
Graceland Cemetery, Chicago

that the sonofabitch wasn't going to get up and come back." George Pullman's paternalistic social engineering had ended in miserable failure.

Pullman cars are no more, though long distance travel on railroad
sleeping cars is still elegant and pleasant, if anachronistically slow. The
town of Pullman has survived and been reborn as a landmark district
after decades of neglect and deterioration. It looks (in 2001 and 2006) like
a very nice place to live, and it seems to be genuinely interracial. There's
a handsome mural depicting heroic-looking laborers. The state of Illinois
has taken over the Florence Hotel, which docents tell me was fortunate
in being ignored for years: it was never significantly changed or modern-
ized. It is gloomy and nearly derelict, but its four stories will soon be
restored to some of their former elegance. The old shops, just north
across 111th street from the hotel, have almost been destroyed by fire and
time, but enough remains to show how impressive they were. A docent
told me there were four thousand workers here at the peak of Pullman's

Florence Hotel, Pullman, Illinois

prosperity. The community Greenstone Church and the Florence Hotel are sometimes open to visitors, and the many row houses and the old stables are attractively kept. Some of the good impulses of the Burned-Over District and Brocton's most famous son survive in the town of Pullman.

Pullman and social justice, music and baseball

There is yet another link, and a wonderfully ironic one, between my Great Road home towns of Brocton and Chicago, between George Pullman and social justice. In the century between Civil War and Civil Rights, one of the few good jobs open to African American men was that of Pullman porter. About forty thousand black men became porters. For many years, all Pullman porters were jocularly called "George," in ironic honor of Brocton's George Pullman. The Brotherhood of Sleeping Car Porters, their union, led by strong, smart men such as A. Philip Randolph, was an early focus for black pride and economic power. The Pullman Company grudgingly recognized the union in 1937, after many years of struggle. There is a private museum dedicated to Randolph and the BSCP eight blocks north of the Florence Hotel, at Cottage Grove and 103rd Street; I have not seen it. The porters' job paid decently, though largely in tips. Porters traveled widely, communicated and built networks, and learned what was out there for them and for their people.

Without the porters and their union, Chicago, the nation's rail hub, would not have been so welcoming to and energized by the epic migration of blacks from the Deep South. The South's loss was Chicago's and the nation's gain. Gwendolyn Brooks and her *Bronzeville*, Richard Wright and his Bigger Thomas, the careers of Louis Armstrong, Kid Ory, King Oliver, Jelly Roll Morton, Sidney Bechet, Sippie Wallace, Big Bill Broonzy, Mahalia Jackson, and Muddy Waters, the migrations of jazz, ragtime, spirituals, gospel, and the blues up the Mississippi, on the Illinois Central Railroad, up US 61 to South State Street, would not have happened when and where they did. Benny Goodman, who made jazz swing and did so much to integrate American music, was born in Chicago in 1909. He was profoundly influenced by southern black musicians such as Johnny Dodds. In the words of legendary bluesman Robert Johnson: "Sweet home, Chicago!"

An aged Satchel Paige (at least forty-two, probably older) might not have had the chance to make his second major league start and pitch his first complete game in August of 1948. I was there, in Comiskey Park, with my dad, who had seen Paige pitch for the Kansas City Monarchs. Red Nelson, a good athlete himself, loved baseball and equity, and he knew what a historic moment this was. So did about seventy thousand other folks, way over Comiskey's capacity, most of them black South Siders. They had cheered Satchel Paige in Negro League games there for years. Comiskey Park had become the venue for most of that league's East-West All-Star games, and the South Side of Chicago had succeeded Harlem as the unofficial black capital of America. There were no vacant seats; we sat on concrete steps. It was goosebump thrilling, both the baseball and the occasion. Satchel won, of course; he and the Indians shut out the White Sox and their star lefty, Billy Pierce. I recall the score as 2–0, though authorities differ on this. Cleveland owner Bill Veeck had been criticized for hiring the old man strictly as a publicity stunt, and Bill Veeck was certainly a publicity genius. But he and his manager, Great Road Chicagoan Lou Boudreau, also knew baseball. Satchel Paige won six games in less than half a season, and

Satchel Paige's plaque, Baseball Hall of Fame, Cooperstown, New York;
Centenarian Ted "Double-duty" Radcliffe,
star of the Negro Leagues, gets his day at Wrigley Field.

helped pitch the Indians to the American League pennant and victory
in the 1948 World Series.

Without the rich cultural mix Chicago became, freedom and social
justice, so long delayed, would have had to wait still longer. How strange
and how fine that the most improbable unintended consequence of Broctonian George Pullman's patrician Gilded Age life was to promote racial
equality, creativity, and opportunity.

old wine in new wineskins

As I write, I often hear the noisy sounds of commerce on US 20
outside. Damn all Jake Brakes. The road, and the house, are not as
sweetly quiet and rural as they once were. Once in a while I do hear a

very old, rural sound: clopclopclopclop, an Amish horse and buggy going briskly by as though it were 1850. My Amish neighbors are fairly recent immigrants to the county. They live up and over the ridge behind me, on poorer, colder agricultural land, not the relatively warm and well-drained gravel bench/glacial moraine I live on. In the last fifty years, pressed by their large families and populations in Pennsylvania and Ohio, they have bought farms and created a community of several dozen families here in northern Chautauqua County. I often see their buggies parked en masse at one of their houses for a Sunday service. I see their kids at their little schoolhouses playing games barefoot in their earnest, dark clothes. Capture the Flag? PomPom Pullaway? Tag, in a German dialect? I don't know. I saw them sledding just last winter—not barefoot.

They are excellent neighbors, contributing their lumber and carpentry skills to many local barns and porches, and selling their baked goods and their beautiful hand-sewn quilts to all of us, thought not on Sundays. They certainly did not begin here on the Great Road—they are Old Order Mennonites, descended from stubborn sixteenth-century German Swiss anabaptists, still speaking a dialect of Old German among themselves and in their simple religious services. They happily tolerate us— "the English"—so long as we do not crash into their buggies on the roads. I'm glad that they have found sanctuary for their old ways here along the Great Road. They antedate and disagree with most of the innovations of our world and our Great Awakenings, but they live contentedly with this disconnect. They lead spare lives: limited education, dark plain clothing, no electricity in their houses, no internal combustion engines in their fields. Kerosene lamps, horses, and buggies are enough. Yet they are quite practical and will happily accept a ride in a motorcar or an order by telephone—so long as the phones are not in their houses. No radios or TVs either, thanks. I hear they are now using solar panels to light incandescent bulbs in their dark houses—good for them. They handle modern America much the way the Hopi of Arizona do—by ignoring it. They teach us simplicity and love and forgiveness. May they thrive; and they are.

Trappists on the great road

Another religious foundation fits comfortably into the lovely hills and valleys west of the Finger Lakes. Three miles north of US 20A, near Piffard, New York, is a Trappist monastery, the Abbey of Our Lady of the Genesee. The farmer monks there made such good bread that they turned it into their cash crop, widely available in Western New York supermarkets as "Monks' Bread." They now make five kinds, and some wickedly good cakes, too. Their abbey is surrounded by vast fields of sunflowers cultivated for use in my favorite bread variety.

Trappists have always been required to make their own living, usually as farmers. Not too different from a lot of the new nineteenth-century agrarian religions along the road, is it? Except, of course, that it's very old indeed and utterly different. Organized monasticism can be traced back to the rule of St. Benedict, in the sixth century AD. Trappists are Cistercians; their way of life began in La Trappe in seventeenth-century France, rather recent for a major Catholic order, though there have been Cistercians since the eleventh century. They are "O.C.S.O.," the "Order of Cistercians of the Strict Observance," and, boy, did they mean "strict" literally. Until the reforms of Vatican Two—i.e., until the late 1960s—a man who took a vow and became a Trappist took not only the usual monastic vows of poverty, chastity, and obedience. He also vowed *never to speak again* except in certain very prescribed circumstances, too complicated to go into here.

One example of an exception: if a Trappist monk were to be appointed Novicemaster, the teacher of novice monks, he must speak because he must teach. That happened to Brother Mary Louis, or Frater Louis (born Thomas Merton, in southern France, in 1915) in Gethsemani, his monastery in Kentucky. It didn't altogether please him, who had longed for the solitude and bliss of silence, but he obeyed. He once famously said of his monastic vows: Poverty is no problem. Chastity, well, that's not too hard. "Obedience, that's the bugger." Made a celebrity by his autobiographical book *The Seven Story Mountain* and many later theological and devotional works, he was eventually given permission to become a hermit on the grounds of Gethesemani. That he soon after died (in 1968) in a ghastly, very modern accident while attending a conference in a bustling city half a world away (Bangkok) is another of the sad ironies of his rich life.

Trappists' silence made sense. If a man wishes to dedicate himself totally to God, why should he chatter? If he's a priest, he can sing prayers seven times a day, and say Mass once a day. Shouldn't that be enough? The Brothers could and did arrange a system of hand signals to say things such as, "I'm going to begin to harvest the oats today, and I need you to help." Why babble?? Well, there are good, interesting answers to that, and, in fact, there is no longer a ban on conversation and speech in the Order. Something gained? Surely. A Trappist monk in the gift shop at Gethesemani told me in the early '80s that he pre-ferred the new rule. "You could spend years next to a Brother and never know him." True. But is there something lost as well? I think so: silence, single-mindedness.

The monks at the Abbey of the Genesee are polite and will answer your questions if you encounter them. Trappists will welcome you into their monasteries for a few days at a very modest price if you wish to make a retreat or just listen to silence for a few days. I have done it, and it's magical. But, accommodating as they are to visitors, they often give the sense that they'd rather be elsewhere: growing wheat and sunflowers, or making bread or jelly, or meditating, or saying Mass, or singing prayers, seven times a day. And why not? That's what they joined up to do. And that's why they fit so well into the rich, varied religious life of the Great Road. See more on Trappists in chapter 4.

religion, education, and social justice

The Great Road of the nineteenth century never officially ended any-where, though a reasonable terminus would have been northern Ohio, in "The Western Reserve," as it was called, land given to Connecticut in return for the relinquishing of land claims farther east. There, in Ober-lin, Ohio, on what was US 20, is a college by the same name. Both college and town were founded in 1833 by Yankee arminians and antinomians, evangelical Christians who were abandoning the rigid determinism of Calvinism for a belief in free will and an optimistic sense of man's poten-tial for salvation and perfectibility.

It seems as though anyone founding a town in the West in the nine-teenth century had to found a college, too, if in name only. Most of these colleges either died young or, more likely, never opened. Oberlin is a magnificent exception. It is also a good place to conclude this discussion of Burned-Over religion, and to make a transition to the political ending of this long chapter.

Charles Grandison Finney (1792–1875) has been called America's greatest early evangelist. Born in Connecticut, he moved with his family to Oneida County, New York, near the Great Road. He became a minis-ter and preached to great acclaim all over the Burned-Over District, and later held a pastorate in New York City. His core message was that God's Grace was available to all, not to just a predetermined elect. This evolved into what came to be called "Perfectionism," and it was a key motivator to religious experimenters such as John Humphrey Noyes of Oneida. Finney challenged and softened the hard Calvinist doctrine that, since God is omnipotent and omniscient, he must know the ultimate fate of all; hence, no matter what we do in this life, we are fated from before our births to be saved or damned—most likely, damned.

Finney began work at Oberlin in 1835 as its first professor of theology. The funds that provided for his hiring were contingent upon Oberlin's opening its doors to students of color. After sixteen years as a professor, he spent fifteen years (1851–1866) as an influential early president of the college, helping to give it that very American mix of godly morality, freedom of thought, and social consciousness that would come to distinguish the best of American religious-affiliated colleges.

My mother was a proud graduate of Oberlin, class of 1927. She taught me many of its fine songs before I was of college age; it has a great musical tradition. A distinguished conservatory is associated with it, well known for new music, "experimental ideas, and a free environment" (*New York Times,* February 22, 2007, B3). I almost chose to attend Oberlin, and I know I would have loved it. It was and is a special place. The college has many admirable Firsts to its credit, chiefly in coeducation and racial equality. Almost from its inception, women and blacks were admitted to study on the same basis as white men. It granted the first degree to

Formal dining room in the Seward House, Auburn, New York

a woman in 1841, to a "colored" man in 1844, and to a "colored" woman in 1862. All this was well before the Emancipation Proclamation, and it was unprecedented, groundbreaking, in American higher education. Jackie Robinson was a courageous social pioneer, and the most exciting player I have ever watched on a baseball field. But former Oberlin student Moses Fleetwood Walker, not Jackie Robinson, was the first African American to play major league baseball—for Toledo in 1884, before baseball instituted its apartheid.[4]

By the time of the Civil War, under Finney's leadership, Oberlin had become a hotbed of abolitionism. Equality of the sexes, and its concomitant, equality of the races, of all human beings, was tied in very closely with the progressive religious movements of the time. More recently, Oberlin appointed the nation's first openly gay athletic director. From all the nuttiness and clatter and religious frenzy of the Burned-Over time and place, came education, equality, human dignity, and social progress. What a mighty legacy from the Great Road.

all men and women are created equal : William Seward and Harriet Tubman

And there is much more, though it's not explicitly religious. In the very middle of New York State, on US 20, are two towns where great progress in race and gender equality was made. Two blocks south of US 20 in Auburn, New York, is the elegant house at 33 South Street, originally built by Elijah Miller in 1816–1817, and eventually occupied and greatly enlarged (in 1847) by his son-in-law, William H. Seward. It is the house that the sixteen-year-old Brigham Young helped to build, before he became a Mormon leader. Seward graduated from Union College, on the Great Road in Schenectady. He also lived for a time on the Great Road in Westfield, New York, and attended a historic meeting in nearby Mayville, the Chautauqua County seat (unpublished manuscript by Douglas Houck). Some local historians make the grand claim that that meeting in the Chautauqua County Court House on February 2, 1855, was the beginning of the national Republican Party. Though there had been Republican Party meetings much earlier, in Wisconsin, Michigan, and Ohio, resolutions made in Mayville, New York became part of the first national Republican platform at a convention in Philadelphia in 1856.

William Seward is best known to history as secretary of state in Abraham Lincoln's cabinet, and as the force behind "Seward's Folly," the purchase of Alaska ("Seward's Icebox") from Russia in 1867. This superb American land deal was second in importance only to the Louisana Purchase. Earlier, he had been a commanding political figure and a leading Abolitionist. He had gone to Chicago in 1860 hoping, even expecting, that he would become the Republican Party's presidential candidate. He was certainly the front runner and the most distinguished and best known of the candidates. Back in Auburn, a cannon was prepared to fire a shot of victory announcing his nomination, and thousands of his neighbors gathered outside his house on South Street. He led all candidates on the first ballot, but was short of a majority.

Some devious machinations occurred. Some of Seward's supporters were outmaneuvered and shut out of the Wigwam, the wooden structure built for the convention. Chicago police arrested many of them, in an eerie anticipation of the disastrous Democratic national convention of 1968. Seward was *not pleased* when Abraham Lincoln, the lightly regarded Illinois lawyer, won the Republican nomination on a vote change after the third ballot. (Lincoln came from a swing state, and that made him a hot property. Basic politics hasn't changed much since 1860.)

William Seward was a good man, a patriotic American, and a loyal Republican. He accepted his defeat and served with great distinction in Lincoln's cabinet. He was soon caught up, as all were, in the tumult of the Civil War. Seward seems to have thought that he could control or at least powerfully influence this relatively unknown and inexperienced Westerner. Some called him "the Premier." He soon recognized that he had underrated Lincoln's skills and character, as people tended to do. He came to regard Lincoln with great respect, ultimately with something like awe: "The president is the best of us," he said. Seward was murderously attacked on the same night Lincoln was shot and killed. Seward barely survived a severe stabbing—his cheek was nearly cut off—and went on to serve in President Andrew Johnson's cabinet.

Just a few blocks south of the grand Seward house in Auburn, also on South Street, is a piece of land and a humbler structure associated both with him and with the tiny, indomitable woman he befriended—Harriet Tubman. Modern Americans are more likely to know of her than of Seward, for her dramatic and courageous work as a conductor of the Underground Railroad, nineteen trips into the South to free slaves as "The Moses of her People." A map in one of her biographies shows "Roads to Freedom," the longest being the Great Road from Albany to Buffalo. Less well known is the story of her early life. She was born Araminta Ross, a slave, in Maryland. She escaped from brutal servitude,

The house where Harriet Tubman ran a home, and where she died.
Auburn, New York

freed dozens of slaves, and did astonishing work for the Union as a Civil
War spy and scout, perhaps even a leader of troops. In 1857, Tubman settled in Auburn with her parents, whom she had led to freedom. She lived
in a house provided by Seward, then a U.S. senator. Shortly thereafter, he
sold her the property at a token price, an illegal transaction at the time. It
would have been impossible for a poor black woman to get credit or buy
property without such help.

Ultimately, in another building—the one still standing on South
Street—she ran a home for old colored people. Tubman lived in it until
her death, in her nineties, in 1913. It fell into disrepair and was scheduled
for demolition, but has been modestly restored as a shrine to her and her
work. Though underfunded and understaffed, it is a memorial to mutual
respect and cooperation between an indomitable black woman who had
been a slave and a ruling-class white man. Good people did great things
here, and we are in their debt. These unconventional friends are buried
in beautiful Fort Hill Cemetery in Auburn.

Women's Rights National Historical Park Visitor Center,
Seneca Falls, New York, houses the Women's Hall of Fame

freedom for half of mankind

Finally, a brief statement of momentous events that happened in another small US 20 town twelve miles from Auburn: Seneca Falls, New York. It is said to have been the original for "Bellows Falls," James Stewart and Donna Reed's home town in Frank Capra's sugary classic *It's A Wonderful Life*. It's pretty enough to have been.

Seneca Falls is hugely historic as the birthplace, in 1848, of the modern women's movement. In the middle of the downtown district, on the main street (Falls Street, US 20), is a skeletal framework, all that remains of the Wesleyan Chapel, where meetings of the first Women's Rights Convention were held. For a time, the old building housed a car dealership, later a laundromat. It is now called Declaration Park, and it is the centerpiece of Women's Rights Historical Park. The National Park Service acquired this historic ruin just in time, stabilized what was left of it, and put an important document in stone on the walls: the delegates' take on the Declaration of Independence, known as the

Elizabeth Cady Stanton's home, Seneca Falls, New York

"Declaration of Sentiments." It was drafted in Mary Ann McClintock's house on the Great Road in the town of Waterloo, three miles west on Twenty. It states, for the first time in human history, that "All men and women are created equal."

In the parlor of the Hunt House in Waterloo, this announcement was drafted: "A convention to discuss the social, civil and religious condition and rights of women will be held in the Wesleyan Chapel at Seneca Falls New York, on Wednesday and Thursday, the 19th and 20th of July [1848], current; commencing at 10 o'clock AM. During the first day the meeting will be exclusively for women, who are earnestly invited to attend. The public generally are invited to be present on the second day, when Lucretia Mott of Philadelphia, and other ladies and gentlemen, will address the convention." Both houses still exist; the McClintock house offers guided tours.

Unlike the original Declaration of Independence, this one was intended to include ALL men and women, blacks, too. The renowned former slave, Frederick Douglass, was one of the signatories. Douglass spent his most productive years in Rochester, New York, just north of the Great Road, and is buried there. Harriet Tubman did not escape from slavery in Maryland until the following year. She later worked for women's suffrage in Auburn, dying just before it was realized. Frederick Douglass's name is there on the old wall with those of Lucretia Mott, Elizabeth Cady Stanton (whose house in town is open for tours), Susan B. Anthony, all the founding mothers, sixty-two of them signing, and thirty-eight good men, too. The times they were a-changing, all along the Great Road.[5]

American women finally achieved the right to vote in 1920, long after the original Womens' Suffrage leaders had died. Charlotte Woodward had been seventeen in 1848, a village school teacher living in a boarding house in Waterloo, New York. She attended the historic convention. Seventy-two years later, when people discovered that she had been a participant, they asked if she planned to vote now that women finally could. She said, "I'm going to vote if they have to carry me there on a stretcher!" She did.

What made the Burned-Over District of the Great Road so progressive and creative was its freedom of thought and expression, its acceptance and nurturing of novelty and strangeness. That creative freedom led to many social and religious experiments that quickly perished, and usually deserved to, but it also led to equality and justice. It all began here.

The Great Road was the Road to Justice and Freedom.[6]

chapter three

power and empire on the great road

six presidents and a plutocrat

power moves northwest

◆   American power politics began as a tug-of-war between New England and Virginia, with New York and Pennsylvania in between. Virginia won. All the early presidents save John Adams, who disliked the job and was not very good at it, were agrarian slaveholding Virginians. Later, the center of power moved slowly but inexorably west and north. Between 1870 and 1952, most elected presidents—nine of fourteen—were born in or elected from New York or Ohio, on or near the Great Road. A century of political dominance followed a creative century of social and religious freedom, experiment, economic development, and achievement. The center of political power followed the westward movement of the young nation's population.

That tide has turned. The nation's center of population has moved steadily west for centuries, but now it is also moving sharply south. Willis Carrier was born in Angola, New York, on the Great Road in 1876, at the time of the nation's centennial and the Northeast's greatest power. Ironically, the huge success of Carrier's invention—air conditioning—has combined with early retirement, longer lives, and immigration to shift the American nation firmly southwestwards. Political power has gone south with it.[1] Now it seems necessary for a president to be, in some way, Southern: from childhood, like Jimmy Carter and Bill Clinton, or by mobility and declaration, like the George Bushes, 41 and 43, Texans who were born in New England. All but two presidents elected in the sixty years since FDR can make some claim of Southern heritage. Georgians were said to have been glad that, in 1976, we finally got a president without an accent. Will we ever again get a president *with* one? Perhaps a Chicago accent?

Two important exceptions to this major shift of power to the South, John F. Kennedy and Ronald Reagan, are both, to some degree, children of the Great Road—from Brookline, Massachusetts, and Dixon, Illinois. George Herbert Walker Bush illustrates both sides of this power issue. Though elected president from Texas, he was born in Milton, Massachusetts, in 1924, just south of JFK's Brookline and US 20. A Massachusetts heritage now seems to have become death to national electoral hopes.

1850–1912 : power to New York and Ohio

It would be silly to claim that all northeastern presidents are significantly connected to the Great Road. Three Ohioans—Benjamin Harrison, William Howard Taft, and Warren G. Harding—had little contact with it. They are not part of the US 20 story. The two Roosevelts have a stronger connection to the Great Road. They were of Dutch patroon stock, thus more closely connected to the Hudson Valley and New York City than to upstate US 20. Both of them made their early mark on Twenty in Albany, TR as an assemblyman, FDR as governor. TR was inaugurated as president in Buffalo, New York. Yet their rich political careers are only tangentially part of the story of the Great Road, and I will not deal with them here.

Seven nineteenth-century presidents (and one near miss, Samuel Tilden) have deeper, longer, and more important ties to US 20: Martin Van Buren, Millard Fillmore, Ulysses S. Grant, James A. Garfield, Rutherford B. Hayes, Grover Cleveland, and William McKinley. They are truly of the Great Road.

Presidents from the great road : Martin van Buren

"Little Van," "The Little Magician" (1782–1862), doesn't get much attention from modern historians. He is the first of a long string of eight presidents who served one term or less, a skein that ended with Abraham Lincoln. Van Buren succeeded an earlier populist giant, two-term Andrew Jackson, who wanted Van Buren to be his successor. Unfortunately, Jackson bequeathed him, with the White House, a financial mess that pretty well assured he would not be reelected. It allowed his Whig opponents to label him "Martin Van Ruin." Martin Van Buren was an interesting and important figure who helped to shape the Democratic party and helped to build "Clinton's Ditch," the Erie Canal—the liquid equivalent of US 20 in New York State, a hugely significant commercial success. He took much of the credit from Governor DeWitt Clinton for his financing of the scheme. A very knowledgable anonymous reader of this book in manuscript states: "The Erie Canal is arguably the most important transportation project in American history, equal in importance to the Eisenhower Interstate System or to the transcontinental railroad system." Large claims, especially the latter, but a fair statement of the canal's commercial importance to the young country.

Martin Van Buren was the first American president to have been born after the Declaration of Independence and the start of the American Revolution—hence, the first not to have been a British subject. He was a member of the old Dutch society of the Hudson Valley, though of humble, not patroon birth—his father was an innkeeper. He was born in Kinderhook, New York, twenty miles south of Albany and the Great Road. Dutch was his first language. He is thus the only American president whose baby babble was not in English. His long and productive political life began in Albany, where he lived from 1816 until he moved to Washington in 1829 as a member of Andrew Jackson's cabinet. He served in the New York State Senate (1812–1820), the U.S. Senate (1821–1829), and as Governor of New York (1829), though he soon resigned that post to serve as Jackson's Secretary of State.

His political legacy is considerable. True to the spirit of the Great Road, he usually (though not always) opposed the expansion of slavery, that "firebell in the night," the smouldering issue that would explode in the Civil War in the year before his long life closed. As president, he opposed the annexation of Texas because it would expand slavery in the Union. He skillfully maneuvered John C. Calhoun out of the vice-presidency, and helped end Calhoun's bitter struggle with Andrew Jackson. He sided with the Spanish slave ship owners in the notorious *Amistad* incident. In 1838, he enforced Jackson's plan to push the Cherokees west to Indian Territory on the tragic "Trail of Tears."

Van Buren is also associated with the Jacksonian triumph of the "spoils system"—the idea that to the victor of the election belong the spoils of office, right down to the jobs of the local postmaster and customs clerk. That's certainly a great American tradition, or at least seems so to this Chicago boy. Interestingly, this thesis spawned its antithesis in the careers of three later Great Road presidents, and the creation of the modern civil service system.[2] Van Buren later ran, unsuccessfully, for president on two different splinter party tickets. With the Civil War looming, he supported Abraham Lincoln. On balance, his is a legacy the Great Road can be proud of. His Italianate Gothic mansion, Lindenwald, where he lived for more than twenty years, is now a National Historic Site. It is one mile south of his birthplace and his burial site in Kinderhook, New York.

presidents from the great road : Millard Fillmore

Millard Fillmore's life is intimately tied to US 20. He was born in 1800 in a log cabin in Cayuga County, New York, which is bisected by the Great Road. Fillmore Glen State Park in Cayuga County has a replica of the cabin. Fillmore's early years were spent in severe poverty. Like so many of his time and place, he moved west for better opportunity, and he prospered. He read law and was admitted to the state bar in 1823 in East Aurora, New York. The modest house he helped to build there in 1826 and lived in until 1830 is now about thirty yards north of US 20A, its original site on the Great Road. A National Historic Landmark, it is open for tours from June to mid-October.

The Fillmore house has an interesting history beyond its connection to Fillmore. It was moved back off US 20A, its original site, to make room for the Aurora Theatre; then saved from demolition and moved to its current site in 1930 by Mrs. Irving Price, of the family that founded Fisher-Price Toys. An artist, she used it as her studio. The house is much more refined than a log cabin; it is constructed of beams and hand split lath and plaster, much like my house, which was built eight years later. But it was still small and pretty primitive; its current large kitchen and elegant library are later additions. That was also the case when my house was moved along US 20; the original kitchen did not make the trip. The Fillmore house had had no running water. One of the Fillmore children was born in the upstairs bedroom, which at that time was probably reached by a ladder. The house now contains some original Fillmore furnishings, including an elegant bed from his later years, the bed that the Fillmores used in the White House.

Millard Fillmore soon moved farther west to Buffalo and began a very successful political career, including three terms in the New York State Assembly, a seat in Congress, and the politically potent post of Comptroller of the State of New York. Elected vice-president in 1848, he succeeded to the presidency in 1850 on the death of Zachary Taylor, at a dynamic and perilous time in American history. After his short two years in the White House, he returned to Buffalo, occupied a magnificent house downtown (sadly, long gone), and became the first Chancellor of the University of Buffalo. He died in 1874 and is buried in Buffalo's grand Forest Lawn Cemetery.

Millard Fillmore was never elected president—he ran a distant third in his only attempt. He was historically unfortunate in his party affiliations. "Whigs" and "Know Nothings" are not only far off the modern American radar screen; they sound ridiculous to a twenty-first-century ear, though Abraham Lincoln began his political life as a Whig. Fillmore generally runs not far behind Harding, Buchanan, Grant, Pierce, Hoover, Coolidge, and Nixon in historians' polls to identify "The Worst President." (He was number thirty-two and number thirty-six of forty-two in two recent polls.) Yet his brief time in office was important, and by no means all negative. He was the second president from New York, after Martin Van Buren, and his administration was the harbinger of a major power shift. It was the first northern administration in a skein that would run for more than sixty years, into the twentieth century and the presidency of William Howard Taft.

During this period, led by politicians from the Great Road, the nation survived the Civil War and, for good or ill, gained an empire. This age of outreach and industrialization greatly expanded the power and wealth of the United States. This power and wealth were facilitated by the opening of Japan to American trade, which was accomplished just as Fillmore's administration was ending. He signed the treaty that authorized this new relationship.

Domestically, Fillmore tried to be a conciliator, patching over rather then healing the deepening rifts in the young nation. With Henry Clay and Stephen A. Douglas, he was responsible for the passage of the Compromise of 1850, hailed at the time as the settlement to the explosive issue of whether slavery should extend to the western territories. Under the Compromise, California was admitted to the union, expansionism was affirmed, slavery accepted in the South, and boundaries settled. But this great Compromise came with a poisoned pill. The price of the South's assent was the enforcement of the fugitive slave law, the assertion of the grotesque legal right to own, retain, and regain human property. Without it, no Southern agreement; with it, no Abolitionist assent and no real peace. John Brown was hatching plans; Harper's Ferry and Bleeding Kansas lay just ahead.

Could another leader have done better? It took a Lincoln and a terrible war to settle these momentous issues permanently, and a century and a half later we are still grappling with the sociohistorical legacy of slavery. Unfortunately, Fillmore was no Lincoln, nor even a William Seward, another Great Road Whig who became Fillmore's political enemy. Unlike Seward, Fillmore had not much human sympathy for blacks. Unlike Charles Grandison Finney of Oberlin, he did not promote their education. Seward and Finney were, like Fillmore, men of the Burned-Over District of Upstate New York; from its free thought, they acquired respect for human freedom and equality for all. Fillmore did not.

Sadly, Fillmore grew more negative and nativist as he aged. In 1856, he ran for president as the candidate of the Know Nothing, or American party. His performance in that campaign did not enhance his historic status; he and they were trounced. He grudgingly supported Lincoln, but disapproved of the Civil War. During Reconstruction, he supported Andrew Johnson's postwar yielding of sovereignty to the Southern states, which meant economic and social slavery for freed slaves and a century of delay for their human rights. The Great Road did not permanently enlighten and humanize all who traveled it.

Ulysses S. Grant lived for a time along US 20. Born in southern Ohio in 1822, he left his home in Galena, Illinois, in 1861 to meet his destiny as a Civil War general and later, as president. His relationship to the Great Road, as well as Abraham Lincoln's, is better told farther west, in chapter 4.

Rutherfraud and Lemonade Lucy : the Hayeses of Spiegel Grove

The judgments of history can seem unfair and unkind. Millard Fillmore probably does not deserve the amused contempt his name usually elicits. Similarly, Rutherford B. Hayes might be remembered as the man who confirmed the nineteenth-century Ohio presidential hegemony, or, commendably, as the first president to move away from the "spoils system" toward a federal civil service. In keeping with social currents along the Great Road, he might be remembered for humane concern for freed slaves or Indians. He is not. Though his rating in those historians' polls may be edging upward, he's still firmly lodged in the bottom half. Gore Vidal calls him "dim but blameless."

As the scandal-ridden Grant administration ground luridly toward its conclusion, Hayes scandalously won the presidency in 1876, the proud nation's centennial year. He had lost the popular vote by a quarter of a million votes. It seemed clear that he had also lost the electoral vote to the Democratic nominee, Samuel J. Tilden, the reformist governor of New York. The presidential contests of this age were between New York and Ohio—East versus West, in a way. Hayes's Republican supporters contested the election and threw the issue to a commission which, suitably bought off, and by a margin of one, threw the electoral votes of three Southern states to Hayes, giving him a narrow (one electoral vote) and thoroughly crooked victory. Florida was one of the states. Isn't it good to know that that sort of thing could never happen again?

If American elections were always fair and honest, Samuel J. Tilden might have written a distinguished chapter in the book of Great Road presidents. He was born and raised on the Great Road, in the Shakers' nineteenth-century spiritual and political center, New Lebanon, New York (see chapter 2). As a young lawyer, he had argued against the expansion of the Shakers' land base and power. Ironically, some of their expansion land had been bought from Tilden's father's estate. In 1876, Tilden

Rutherford B. Hayes's home, Spiegel Grove

quietly accepted his patently unfair defeat, retired from active politics, and grew wealthy. He left much of his estate to fund the establishment of the New York Public Library. His is a quiet but positive and progressive Great Road legacy.

In the manner of nineteenth-century presidential candidates, Rutherford B. Hayes had said and done little during the campaign. He also had little or nothing to do with the subsequent stealing of the White House. Though he was a decent, honest man, he became known as "Rutherfraud" and "His Fraudulency." His wife, Lucy, was an ardent member of that new and vibrant Great Road institution, the Woman's Christian Temperance Union (founded in 1873), and he agreed that alcohol should not be served in the White House during his presidency. Mrs. Hayes promptly became known as "Lemonade Lucy."

Hayes's early years

Rutherford B. Hayes was born in north central Ohio in 1822. He got a remarkably good education for a boy from the western frontier, finally receiving degrees from Kenyon College and Harvard Law School. He practiced law in Upper Sandusky (later Fremont) and Cincinnati, and entered Republican politics. He served with distinction in the Civil War and was elected to Congress in 1864. He was thrice elected governor of Ohio. The crooked deal that brought him to the White House involved a devil's bargain with the political leaders of the Southern states. They would tilt to Hayes if the federal government would remove its troops from the South, thus leaving control of the defeated Confederacy in the hands of the former rebels, leaving the newly freed blacks with no federal protection. The Hayes administration came in under a cloud, and its legacy in the South was deadly: almost a century of segregation, brutality, lynching, inequality.

Custer and Indian policy

1876 was a portentous year for more than just a centennial and a fraudulent presidential election. On June 25, nine days before that centennial, George Armstrong Custer led his Seventh Cavalry in a wild and foolish charge into what he thought was a typical nomadic encampment of Plains Indians. Custer was part of a major three-pronged military plan

*The route Custer's Seventh Cavalry took west, in June 1876,
from the Rosebud to the Little Big Horn.*

to surround the Lakota and Cheyenne, whip them, and drive them onto
their ever-shrinking reservations in the Dakotas. He had led a similar all-
out charge before, at the Washita in 1868 in what is now Oklahoma,
when he easily won a bloody victory over a village of friendly, peaceful
Cheyennes led by Black Kettle. Hey, Indians are Indians, right? Black
Kettle had survived another even more brutal unprovoked attack at Sand
Creek, Colorado, in 1864. He did not survive at the Washita. So it goes
for friendly Indians in nineteenth-century America.

Federal Indian policy under the Grant administration was uncompromising. Nearly all the buffalo were dead, as government policy and
economics dictated, and there was no prey, food, or room on the plains
for free, nomadic Indians any more. The government, the railroads,
the banks, and the new immigrants all agreed that the plains should be

settled by white farmers, not roamed by red savages. That settlement was an economic, ecological, and social mistake that this nation is still struggling to deal with.

Had Custer exercised any common sense or foresight, he would have reconnoitered more carefully before he attacked. His colleague, John Gibbon (or perhaps his commander, General Alfred Terry), had called to him as he and his troops rode off from Fort Abraham Lincoln, Dakota Territory: "Now Custer, don't be greedy; save some Indians for us," or perhaps, "Wait for us." "I will not," he famously and ambiguously replied. He had refused to take cannon or Gatling guns, which would have slowed his progress. His scouts (Crows and Rees, Arikaras, historic enemies of the Lakota) warned him not to attack what they knew was a huge gathering. They sang their death songs before the battle began.

It is said that Custer badly wanted a quick victory this June 25th because he hoped to be nominated for president at the 1876 Democratic convention in St. Louis, which was to open on June 27. Hayes, the Republican nominee, would have to carry the scandalous baggage of the outgoing Grant administration, and the Democrats had a real chance at the White House. (They did win the popular vote.) Custer seemed to fear only that these Indians might cheat him of glory by escaping. They didn't. What he bumbled into with two hundred sixty-five soldiers (about half of his original command) was the great summer council of the Lakota and Cheyenne, at least five thousand people, probably two or three times that many. At least two thousand of them, perhaps twice that many, were the best, smartest, and bravest horse soldiers in the world. Sitting Bull, Gall, and Crazy Horse were among them.

Bad idea.

Custer's headlong charge was a foolhardy disaster. He and the five companies of men under his immediate command were soon surrounded and were all dead within an hour. Three of the Seventh Cav's companies had earlier been split off on Custer's questionable tactical orders to begin an attack from the southwest, along the Greasy Grass, the Little Big Horn River. They ran into more than they could handle and retreated desperately to a strategic hill southwest of Custer's position. Another three companies, equally desperate, soon joined them. With no drinking water, in the summer solstice heat, those who were still alive endured an awful night of attacks from gunshots and from arrows lobbed into their position.

Late the next day, June 26, the survivors were astonished and relieved to find that the Indians were not going to finish them off after all. The whole huge village was moving out. Such a massive gathering would have had as many as twenty thousand horses, and so many horses could not graze long in one place. The Indians were probably also aware of the approach of more units of the U.S. Cavalry, presumably with more sensible leadership. This great Indian victory, a disaster to whites, thrilled and horrified the nation as "Custer's Last Stand." A heroic and utterly inaccurate painting of it was reproduced and hung in thousands of American barrooms. A dramatization of it became, for a few years, the grand finale of Buffalo Bill's Wild West show. In one remarkable year, 1885, Sitting Bull himself took part in that show. (He probably had not participated actively in the Little Big Horn fighting, being in his mid-forties at the time.)

The Indian victory had an awful, ironic impact on the victors. The United States could not ignore this terrible military defeat, and the Army would soon round up and pen up or kill almost all the free bands of Plains Indians. Sitting Bull and his Hunkpapa band escaped to Canada, but they were soon starving there, and they stayed only four years. All this turmoil and conflict had to be addressed by the incoming Hayes administration. Crazy Horse was killed while in U.S. custody fourteen months later in September 1877, in the Hayes administration's first year, though Rutherford B. Hayes had nothing to do with that.

Hayes's home and library : Indian policy

Hayes did as he had promised. He served one term as president and retired to private life at his home, Spiegel Grove, on the Great Road south of Fremont, Ohio. It is an almost imperial place, with great green lawns, huge old trees, and two large buildings: his home and his presidential library. The home is typical upper class Gilded Age Victorian domestic architecture. President Hayes and his Lucy are buried on a little knoll amid grand old evergreens. The house and estate are bisected by a historic trail that connected the Great Lakes to the Scioto and Ohio Rivers. It was first used by Huron Indians, and later by their allies, the French, in war against the British. Seneca leaders such as Red Jacket, from the Great Road in western New York, are said to have walked it. It was a supply trail in the War of 1812. At this, its northern end, the trail meets and becomes part of, the Great Road. The trail south has been named the "Harrison Military Trail."

The Hayes Presidential Library was the first of its kind; it is thus interesting and historically important. Presidential repositories feature both permanent and temporary exhibits. The permanent exhibits here are dioramas and displays of personal objects dramatizing events in the

family's history, such as Hayes being wounded in the Civil War. I was fortunate to see a lengthy display of the the Hayes administration and its
relationships with American Indians, particularly with the Poncas, one of
the smaller Plains tribes.

Carl Schurz, a German immigrant whom history has deemed a
decent, progressive, and humane man, was Secretary of the Interior
under Hayes. Schurz usually gets credit for good treatment of Indians.
Not here. The exhibit—in an official presidential library—showed
clearly that the Plains Indians' cultures were designated to be destroyed, and destroyed they were. The displays spoke of the falsehoods
and treacheries employed in obliterating the cultural integrity of the Poncas. Indians belonged on reservations, no matter what they had been
promised or what they had or had not done. So the Poncas endured their
own small "trail of tears," as the Cherokee had: they were forcibly moved
from their ancestral lands in Nebraska to arid northern Oklahoma.
There the Poncas and five other small plains tribes are to this day, on tiny
reservations or agencies in what was by treaty supposed to be forever
"Indian Territory"—now the state of Oklahoma. (Since 1990, a tiny
Ponca footprint, not a reservation, has been reestablished in eastern
Nebraska. Don't expect much, Poncas.) As an interested amateur student
of presidential libraries—I've been to all but three—I applaud this one
for its remarkable candor.

race and reconstruction; spoils and workers

Given the devil's bargain that put him in office, Hayes seems to have
done his best to govern a shattered, newly reunited country. Modern historians tend to agree that Reconstruction was already ending by 1876, and
that Hayes's withdrawal of federal troops was necessary, perhaps
inevitable. The South would never reenter a unified nation while it was
powerless and bitter about its defeat and harsh treatment; Southern states
had to be permitted to resume sovereignty. Perhaps. Hayes could have
done little more than he did to help freed slaves. Later in life he worked
to improve conditions for blacks, and he defused a dangerous situation
involving the mistreatment of Chinese laborers in California. These
immigrants had been instrumental in another great accomplishment of
this age—the completion of the transcontinental railroad in 1869.

Hayes's most significant contribution to modern America was to
begin to reform the spoils system, i.e., "to the victor [of the election]
belong the spoils." It had always been assumed that party workers should

get all the jobs when an administration changed. Hayes enraged many of his fellow Republicans with this upright stand, and probably would not have gained another nomination had he desired it. He also caught a whiff of what he thought was revolution, the early stirrings of railroad workers' unrest and labor union organizing, in 1877. It wasn't a revolution, but he crushed it. Progressiveness on the Great Road went only so far.

James A. Garfield : Hiram, Williams, and Mark Hopkins

Like Millard Fillmore, James A. Garfield was born in a log cabin. Garfield's was southeast of Cleveland, Ohio, in 1831, on the Great Road. He was the last president to be able to claim that ironic humble distinction, and he truly was born and raised in poverty. He drove canal boat teams as a young man. He spent ten hard years trying to get a college education: first at Ohio's Geauga Seminary, then at the school that became Hiram College, and finally, at Williams College, from which he graduated with honors, aged twenty-five, in 1856.

In his years there, Williams College was young and poor, not yet a wealthy and influential institution. Its professors and students had to make do with little. Garfield's attitude toward what truly mattered in education and in life shows the grateful pragmatism of a once poor boy. Just before his early death, he said: "The ideal college would be one in which [Mark] Hopkins [a fabled early Williams College philosophy teacher and, for thirty-six years, its president] sat on one end of a log and a student on the other." I graduated from Williams College ninety-nine years after Garfield did. Garfield is something of a proprietary saint at Williams, particularly for this famous quotation, which has become a mantra, a koan, and a touchstone to define excellent liberal education. "Mark Hopkins and the Log" is the unofficial defining motto of a Williams College which has become excellent and opulent in ways he could never have foreseen. I think my portrayal of Garfield is good history, but it might incline slightly toward hagiography.

early years and military glory

After graduating from Williams, Garfield returned to Hiram, Ohio, to become a professor of classical languages. Like Charles Grandison Finney at nearby Oberlin, he became a campus leader and an abolitionist. Academic life was too small for him. He rose quickly in Ohio politics and, when the Civil War began, in the military. He was a General, a participant in the battle of Shiloh, a hero at the Battle of Chickamauga, and soon, in 1863, a member of Congress.

His career in Congress was lengthy—seventeen years—but undistinguished. His reputation was clouded by his involvement in the Credit Mobilier financial scandal, and he was also one of the Republican commissioners who stole the presidency for Rutherford B. Hayes in 1876. Garfield was elected to the Senate in 1880—partly as a reward for this shady party loyalty. President Hayes had been deemed insufficiently partisan by his party, so the Republicans in their convention searched long and vainly for a successor. Ballot after ballot failed to break a deadlock among U. S. Grant, James G. Blaine, and John Sherman. Seeking closure and unity, the exhausted convention selected the "dark horse," Garfield, on the thirty-sixth ballot. When he narrowly won the ensuing election, he gave up the Senate seat he had never occupied.

the "dark horse" and his brief presidency

Though he gave promising early signs of a strong executive hand, he had little time to achieve anything in his tragically short presidency. He did win an important struggle with Senate leaders over patronage, and made this ringing statement: "This . . . will settle the question whether the president is registering clerk of the Senate or the Executive of the United States." His victory left no doubt that he intended to be the latter.

He was shot in Washington in early July, one hundred and twenty days after his inauguration, while on his way to a meeting of the Williams College Society of Alumni. His assassin, Charles J. Guiteau, was a sad, delusional former Oneida Society member from the Great Road in central New York. (Guiteau had been born along the Great Road in Freeport, Illinois.) Guiteau became known to those Oneidans who disliked his society (more or less all of them, it seems) as "Charles Gitout," i.e., go away and don't join in our company or our "complex marriage" sexuality. He is said to have been disappointed, absurdly, insanely, not to have been appointed ambassador or consul to France. His lawyers attempted an insanity defense, which in retrospect seems eminently sensible, but Guiteau was soon tried, convicted, and executed. (Stephen Sondheim, Williams class of 1951, has him sing a jaunty cakewalk on his way to the scaffold in *Assassins*. The words are in part Guiteau's, from his poem "I am Going to the Lordy.")

Garfield died seventy-nine painful days after being shot, at the age of forty-nine. Gore Vidal called him "that most civilized of all our presidents." Among presidents, only John F. Kennedy died younger; only William Henry Harrison's one-month presidency was shorter. The wound should not have killed Garfield. Modern investigators speculate that the gunshot was fatal in part because of the fumbling, futile efforts of Garfield's surgeons to locate the bullet and extract it. A National Public Radio program suggested that when Thomas Edison tried to locate the bullet with an electromagnetic device, he failed because Garfield was lying on a mattress with newfangled metal springs. James A.Garfield died after only six months in office, of internal hemorrhaging and infection. Public sorrow and sympathy after his untimely death helped his successor, Chester A. Arthur, to further the work of civil service reform begun by Garfield's predecessor, Hayes.

Garfield's legacy : a phrase, a house, a tomb

James A. Garfield's gift for a phrase will ensure his name's survival, at least in Williamstown, Massachusetts, and in the lore of the American liberal arts college. His progressive Great Road social inclinations put him on the side of the angels on the burning issue of Emancipation. He left behind two significant physical artifacts: a grand property and its exhibits in Mentor, Ohio, and an even grander memorial tomb in Cleveland. Both are on US 20. First, his house and property.

I wrote in the Introduction that the setting of my house on US 20 is not so quiet and rural as it once was. That is even truer of James A. Garfield's house on US 20. It is set on ample grounds, whose size gave it its unofficial name. Reporters covering the candidate, and then the president-elect, literally camped out on its seven acres of grass. They called it "Lawnfield." In typical nineteenth-century fashion, the house was sited only a few feet from the side of what was once a quiet dirt road. A skilled watermelon seed spitter seated on the front porch would today be a danger to the urban traffic, which is swift and intense.

That front porch is an important historical site. Garfield bought the house in 1876, added the porch in 1880, and did most of his campaigning from it, setting a standard for "front porch" campaigns to be followed by later Ohio presidential candidates McKinley and Harding. The house and grounds are lovely. The house is very large, twenty rooms, expanded from nine in 1880, and further expanded by Garfield's widow in 1904.

Lawnfield, James A. Garfield's house, Mentor, Ohio

The property included a carriage house, which has become an excellent visitor center celebrating Garfield's career. There is a seventy-five foot tall structure on the property, once a windmill and pumphouse. It was built after Garfield's death under the direction of his widow, Lucretia. It cost $2,196, then a sizeable sum, and it was high enough to serve water to the bathtubs and "cascade closets," the flush toilets of the house. It fell into disrepair in 1930 and was rebuilt in 1998. "Lawnfield" is a fine relic of a bygone era; it became a National Historic Site in 1980.

James A. Garfield and his Lucretia are buried in a towering, ornate mausoleum on a hill in splendid Lake View Cemetery, on US 20 in Cleveland, Ohio, fifteen miles west down the Great Road from his home in Mentor. Their coffins are visible in a crypt, and there is a heroic statue of Garfield. The pomp of this pharaonic tomb is somewhat off-putting to me, though it is perhaps appropriate for a former president. Two other politicians of power and distinction are buried in Lake View:

the mighty Ohio Republican boss, Mark Hanna, who masterminded the 1896 election of President William McKinley; and Abraham Lincoln's personal secretary, John Hay, later secretary of state under McKinley. Hay is famous for describing the Spanish-American conflict as "a splendid little war." Garfield was succeeded as president by his vice-president, Chester A. Arthur. Arthur, born in northern Vermont, went to Union College in Schenectady, and is buried in Menands, New York. Both sites are on the Great Road.

Five sections away from Garfield's vast tomb in the same cemetery is a huge obelisk, and a modest headstone that reads simply

John Davison Rockefeller
July 8, 1839
May 23, 1937

The archetypal monopolist capitalist lies very near Garfield's grand tomb. Opulent Lake View Cemetery remembers and celebrates power.

*Lawnfield water tower
Mentor, Ohio*

a Democratic president from the great road

Before he was president, Stephen Grover Cleveland was mayor of Buffalo and, in Albany, governor of New York. He successfully worked both ends of the Great Road in New York, made his reputation, and prepared for his presidential runs. He was born in 1837 in New Jersey, and raised in a minister's family in the heart of the New York Burned-Over District, near Syracuse. He was schooled in Clinton, New York, on New York Route 5, a branch of the Great Road. (The modern routes run together for more than sixty miles in central New York.) When his father died, young Stephen Grover Cleveland was unable to afford to attend Clinton's Hamilton College. On his way to Cleveland, looking for advancement, he stopped near Buffalo, New York, to visit an uncle, who farmed five hundred acres in what is now the Black Rock section of Buffalo.

Cleveland saw opportunity in that growing transportation and industrial center, and he stayed on. The railroad had superseded the Erie Canal, which had made Buffalo, its terminus, prosperous. Buffalo didn't miss a step in the transition to rail. It soon became the eighth largest city in the nation, and the second greatest railroad hub, behind only Chicago. The Great Road from Boston to Buffalo to Chicago had become, in part, an iron road: the Great Railroad.

Cleveland dropped the name Stephen, studied law, and was admitted to the Buffalo bar in 1860. He worked his way into the Buffalo Democratic political structure as assistant district attorney, and made his mark in Erie County and New York state politics. He became Erie County sheriff in 1871, mayor of Buffalo in 1882, and governor of the state of New York in 1883. His Albany office was in the magnificent Renaissance chateau–like state capitol, then under construction. I am told it was the most expensive structure built in nineteenth-century America. I have often lobbied there. I believe it. It cost $25 million in nineteenth century dollars (*New York Times*, November 24, 2006). Cleveland was president of the United States two years later. His meteoric rise in these three years was based in part on his reputation for probity, honesty, and plain talk.

scandal : "ma, ma, where's my pa?"

That excellent reputation is one of the most characteristic and interesting things about the man. In his first presidential campaign, his opponents smeared him with the charge that he, a bachelor, had fathered a child out of wedlock. He had never denied the possibility, though Cleveland's paternity was never proven. He had paid for the child's upkeep. That did not keep Republicans from exploiting the issue, jeering, "Ma, Ma, Where's my Pa?," and thinking they had him beaten. When his political staff asked him how to deal with the scandal, he said: "Tell the truth." This astonishing political pronouncement seemed to win him respect and votes, and he won the close election of 1884, with some help from an ill-judged Republican/Protestant slur against "Rum, Romanism, and Rebellion"—whiskey, Roman Catholicism, and anything else disruptive that moneyed Protestant Republicans didn't like.

Cleveland became the first president from the discredited and disheartened Democratic Party since James Buchanan. He was the only Democratic president in the fifty-two years between Buchanan and Woodrow Wilson. A recent Cleveland biography (2000) is titled simply *An Honest President*. There is no record of his ever saying, "That depends on what the meaning of is is." Times have changed, not all for the better.

an honest president and his limitations

Cleveland is also the only president to serve two nonconsecutive terms. He won the popular vote three consecutive times, and is regarded (rather oddly, it seems to me) as both the twenty-second and twenty-fourth president. Amusingly, that means that when the U.S. Mint issues the presidential dollar coins in 2012, he will get two: twice as many as Washington or Lincoln. Cleveland furthered the cause of the federal civil service against the political spoils system. He paid more attention to Latin America than any president since Polk. He resisted imperialist yearnings for Hawaii. His Secretary of State, Walter Q. Gresham, argued against the nation's (and the Republican Party's) "impulse to rush into difficulties that do not concern it" ("Our 'Messianic Impulse,'" *New York Times*, December 10, 2006). That's a lesson we pay a high price to relearn every generation. Cleveland established the first National Forest in 1891, bless him. It is Yellowstone National Park's eastern neighbor, the beautiful Shoshone, in Wyoming. He was quick with a veto for what he deemed ill-judged or too expensive, and he maintained his reputation for honesty and for opposing corruption in a corrupt age. Grover Cleveland was clearly a man of good sense and great integrity.

Yet the progressive tendencies of the the Great Road, where he spent most of his life, went only so far. He consistently refused to intervene in matters and areas where he thought the federal government did not belong. During the withering depression that began in 1893, in his second term, he was deaf to the entreaties of the poor as expressed in what looked to him like Rebellion—"Coxey's Army." He was unsympathetic to the idea of women's suffrage. Like another honest Great Road president, Rutherford B. Hayes, he had no sympathy for labor unions. He intervened in Illinois—with no apparent doubts about *this* intrusive use of federal power—and helped to crush the 1894 Pullman Strike, which had threatened to disrupt transport all across the nation (see chapter 2).

Cleveland's first administration was in power when the Dawes Act became law. It purported to be a device to improve the lives of American Indians and give them private land and political power. Its effect was exactly the reverse. It was repealed in 1924 after it had done enormous damage to native communities and shrunk their reservations by about half. Nonetheless, Cleveland was a decent, honest man, and a good president, in an era when good presidents were scarce. He is perhaps best known today for a few sensational biographical facts: his secret cancer operation, his great girth, his beautiful young Great Road wife Frances (formerly, scandalously, his unofficial ward), and his daughter "Baby Ruth." Little Ruth became a national icon, and her celebrity probably helped Cleveland win his second term. She, not Babe Ruth, was the source of the name of the candy bar.

McKinley : president at the birth of the American empire

Democrat Grover Cleveland was succeeded in 1897 by Republican William McKinley. That was probably all right with Cleveland. He had always been a supporter of the gold standard. He did not approve of his party's being captured by the fervid oratory of the "free silver" candidate, westerner William Jennings Bryan.

William McKinley was born in Niles, Ohio, in 1843, into essentially the same rural northeast Ohio community that had ignored the arrival of James Garfield twelve years earlier. He attended Allegheny College in northwestern Pennsylvania, and Albany Law School in Albany, New York, both Great Road institutions. He began law practice and Republican Party politics in Canton, Ohio, and worked for the 1876 presidential election of his former Civil War commanding officer, Rutherford B. Hayes. For twelve years, from 1877, he was the congressman for the district in northeastern Ohio through which US 20 now runs. He represented the area of the Great Road in the House of Representatives, and his story belongs to it.

That story has much in common with those of his Ohio predecessors. He took up Garfield's "front porch" tactic and made it famous on his front porch in Canton. He did this in part, it is said, because he felt his delicate wife could not stand the pressures of a dynamic campaign. He was elected to two terms as governor of Ohio, during which he, too, put down a major strike, this one by coal miners. With the help of Cleveland industrialist Mark Hanna, he won the Republican presidential nomina-

tion in 1896, and defeated Bryan in the presidential election. As a harbinger of sectional politics to come, McKinley won the North and East,
but lost most of the South and West. Red and blue states, anyone?

remember the Maine—and take the Philippines

From the beginning of the Republic, despite protestations to the contrary, most American leaders had looked to dominate this hemisphere (cf.
"Manifest Destinies," *New York Times*, December 17, 2006, and *Dangerous Nation*, by Robert Kagan). Jefferson illegally bought Louisiana. The
United States invaded Canada in the War of 1812, and Henry Clay later
argued that Canada should be part of the United States. John Quincy
Adams enunciated the Monroe Doctrine in 1823, warning European
powers to stay out of the United States' sphere of influence. Under expansionist president James Knox Polk, the nation annexed Texas and California from Mexico (1848) and threatened a war with England over control of the Oregon territory: "54–40 or fight" (1846). Polk even tried to
buy Cuba from Spain. But after Polk's presidency, occupied with half a
century of Civil War and Reconstruction, most American presidents had
placed little emphasis on foreign policy or foreign expansionism.

McKinley's four and a half years in office marked a major shift, and
were a remarkable period for the growth of American global power,
especially in the Pacific. The explosion that destroyed the battleship
Maine in Havana harbor was the spark, or the excuse, for war with Spain.
William Randolph Hearst of the sensationalist *New York Journal* sent the
great Western artist Frederick Remington to Cuba to cover the war. The
following story, about a possibly apocryphal telegram (*New York Times*,
September 20, 2006), is too good not to retell. Remington is said to have
telegraphed his boss: "There will be no war. I wish to return." Hearst is
said to have replied: "Please remain. You furnish the pictures, and I'll furnish the war." Telegram or not, he did, and so did Remington. His pictures included a beautifully drafted fanciful erotic drawing of a chilling
event that never occurred: a lovely white woman, stripped, seen from
behind, her pretty butt naked, being interrogated by the dark, evil enemy.
Title: "Refined Young Women Stripped and Searched by Brutal
Spaniards While Under Our Flag. . . ." Porn sells. It even sells wars.

The brief Spanish-American War made a hero and, soon, a president: Teddy Roosevelt, famous for the charge of his Rough Riders up
Cuba's San Juan Hill. The collapse of Spain's American empire presented

the United States with Cuba, and we're still trying to figure out how to deal with that prize. Hawaii, Puerto Rico, and the Philippines also came under American hegemony at this time (1898), soon followed by serious, bloody imperialist warfare to hold the latter. McKinley justified that imperialist expansion by telling the nation, apparently with a straight face, that we would raise the Philippino people up to Christian civilization. The soldiers who fought in this bloody conflict had few illusions about it, much like the grunts in Viet Nam. To the tune of "Tramp, tramp, tramp, the Boys are Marching," they sang "Damn, damn, damn the Philippinos," and added that they would like to "Civilize 'em with a Krag," an Army rifle, "and return us to our own beloved homes." Estimates of civilian Philippino deaths from war, hunger, and epidemic in those years (1899–1902) run from two hundred thousand to a million. Brown people whom we bless with our gift of militant democracy seem always to pay a heavy price for it.

Secretary of State John Hay participated in the forced opening of Chinese markets to American goods, and McKinley sent troops to China to help put down the nationalist Boxer Rebellion (1901). American isolationism was crumbling; opposition to entering into World Wars I and II were its last gasps. Many Americans, including Mark Twain, spoke out strongly against this new Imperialism. Yet, for good or ill, the modern American Empire began when McKinley extended the western expansionism of the Great Road across the Pacific Ocean.

Pan-American irony and "that damned cowboy"

Resoundingly reelected over William Jennings Bryan in 1900, McKinley attended the Pan-American Exposition in Buffalo in 1901 to speak on America's growing role in the world. Up-and-coming Buffalo was then the eighth-largest city in America, with homes, businesses, and a street light system powered by electricity generated at nearby Niagara Falls. Ironically, McKinley's promotion of imperialist expansion took him to his death. He died eight days after being shot by an anarchist,[3] and was succeeded by America's youngest president, Theodore Roosevelt. TR was inaugurated in Buffalo in the Wilcox Mansion, a National Historical Landmark that still stands. Buffalo has never quite recovered from that assassination, though many economic factors have contributed much more to its decline.

Young President Roosevelt was not universally admired, even by his fellow Republicans. At McKinley's death, Mark Hanna famously said, "Now that damned cowboy is president of the United States!" "That damned cowboy"—a reference to TR's ranching days in North Dakota—proved mostly a good president, one who continued to turn American eyes outward to the larger world. Domestically, he played a major role in limiting the enormous power of the trusts, the monopoly industries.

the northeast and the great road dwindle in power

As noted, there are five more presidents with significant ties to the Great Road: Theodore and Franklin Roosevelt, John Kennedy, George H. W. Bush, and Ronald Reagan. Their administrations spanned most of the twentieth century, and helped to mask a truth: that the Great Road from Boston to Albany, to Buffalo, Cleveland, and Chicago no longer connects the power centers of the nation. The Roosevelts were essentially men of downstate New York, and Kennedy and Bush the Elder were men of a different age.

Ronald Reagan is more tempting as a subject for this book. His northern Illinois roots are deep and important, and the Great Road certainly helped to mould him. His folksy, down-to-earth Everyman image is pure Great Road Illinois hokum—Abe Lincoln with writers and an agent. How appropriate, if weird, that his most recent biographer felt he had to create a fictional friendship between himself and his subject, "Dutch" Reagan. I have visited Dutch Reagan's boyhood home in Dixon, Illinois. It is a fine old Midwestern frame house on a hill, not at all what one would expect from the stories of a feckless alcoholic father and a disadvantaged childhood. It is rapidly becoming a shrine. Dixon is where John Deere manufactured the steel moldboard plow that "broke the plains." And Ronald Reagan broadcast Chicago Cubs baseball games. What could be more mainstream Midwestern?

Yet Ronald Reagan became so wholly a man of California make-believe, a creation of La-La-Land, that the purported historical anecdotes in his stump speeches came straight from movie scripts, and he appeared to believe them to be real. In his triumphant campaign of 1980, his press people cheerfully admitted this, smiled, and said, "The Governor [of California] is rather hard to program." Ronald Reagan was from the Great Road, yes; but by way of Hollywood. His most famous movie line, from his best movie, *King's Row*, was "Where's the rest of me?!" Not, I think, on US 20. Despite Ronald Reagan's two terms as president, the Northeast no longer controls the White House or America. As presidential power has grown, it has shifted firmly south and west from the Great Road—to California, to Arkansas, to Texas.

postscript : power beyond the presidential

Power resides not only in presidents. That was especially true of the high-flying, laissez-faire Gilded Age in America, Mark Twain's ironic label for the late nineteenth century. Arguably, the most powerful Americans of that time were John Pierpont Morgan and John Davison Rockefeller, not their contemporaries who were presidents of the United States. J. P. Morgan has little connection to US 20, though his immense power and wealth supported the gold standard and helped save the credit of the nation in Grover Cleveland's second term (in 1895), and President Cleveland was properly grateful for it.

Born in central New York State in 1839, John D. Rockefeller moved early with his family to the area of the Great Road. He was the child of an odd family: a pious mother and a charming "sporting man," a ne'er-do-well father. That shady legacy might well have been a spur to achievement. John D. was educated in Cayuga County and Owego, New York, south of the Great Road. Some of the family's moves were said to have been motivated by the need for John's father, William, to escape the law. Three of William's friends did spend a term in the state prison for horse stealing in 1850, but he was said to have been "too smart to be caught."

Though it may be somewhat unfair, most modern Americans take their version of John D.'s life largely from the work of Ida M. Tarbell, who made a great journalistic name as a "muckraker," raking principally the muck of Standard Oil and John D. Rockefeller. Her work pushed President Theodore Roosevelt and the Congress to rein in the trusts, much as Upton Sinclair's *The Jungle* promoted a healthier meatpacking industry. (Sinclair, a socialist, was disappointed that his book didn't do much to change the nation's political system.) Ida Tarbell was raised in Erie, Pennsylvania, on US 20, and educated south of the Great Road at Allegheny College, where she was the only female graduate in the class of 1880. More sensational charges followed the biographical details I quote. *McClure's Magazine* published Tarbell's work as a series of

Chicago skyline

nineteen articles from 1902–1904; it then became a best-selling book. Her work is still fascinating to read, and it was profoundly influential. She has been secularly beatified, honored by the U.S. Postal Service in 2002, with a first-class stamp. She was also elected (in 2000) to the National Women's Hall of Fame in—where else?—Seneca Falls, New York, on US 20.

piety and sharp practice : god, wealth, and charity on the great road

The Rockefeller family soon moved west from New York along the Great Road to Strongsville, Ohio, when John D. was fourteen; then to Parma, and finally, in 1857, to Cleveland. This was the West where Grover Cleveland, two years John D.'s senior, had thought to find opportunity. John D. certainly found it. He left school at the age of sixteen in 1855, and went to work as a clerk in a warehouse on Lake Erie.

By parsimony and crafty investment, good record keeping and intense hard work, he amassed enough capital to become an important part of the infant petroleum industry, born just south of US 20 in northwestern Pennsylvania. Rockefeller and a few associates eventually controlled petroleum, railroads, ships, and steelmaking: transportation, energy, and manufacturing all tied up in a monopolistic system. Competitors had two choices: sell to Rockefeller and his companies at a low price, or compete and be wiped out, forced into bankruptcy. The smarter ones saw the handwriting on the balance sheet, capitulated, took stock in Rockefeller's enterprises, and got rich.

The story of his rise to power and unimaginable wealth is much too long to detail here. The old newsreels of the gaunt nonagenarian, looking like Death, handing out dimes to awed and probably creeped-out children, are a caricature of what he had been and done.[4] What fascinates me, as a student and chronicler of the Burned-Over District and the Great Road, is how differently the genius of the time and place motivated different men. Charles Grandison Finney and William Seward worked for equality and emancipation. The Seneca Falls delegates worked for the rights of all men, black and white, and all women, too. Joseph Smith and a dozen others started religions. John D. Rockefeller got unimaginably rich and powerful.

There is no mistaking the religious imprint of the place and the age in the career of this plutocrat. His mother's piety marked him deeply. Poor or rich, he always tithed, giving one-tenth of his income to his church. There is no doubt that he felt, like many laissez-faire capitalists of his age and our own, that his wealth was a sign of God's approval of his sharp, even brutal, practices. John D. Rockefeller said, "The good Lord gave me my money." Andrew Carnegie spoke highly of "The Gospel of Wealth." Mark Hopkins was the Williams College eminence so admired by President Garfield. Hopkins was an ordained Congregationalist minister and a leader of the American Mission movement, which began at Williams College. Though no millionaire capitalist, he weighed in on the side of god-given wealth. In his book *The Law of Love and Love as a Law* (1869), Hopkins placed "the grasping of property as requisite to the welfare of society and, rightly understood, as a noble implement of the law of love." Well, all right, then.

The University of Chicago, Rockefeller University, the United Nations buildings, the Rockefeller Foundation, Grand Teton and Acadia National Parks, Colonial Williamsburg, New York City's Museum of Modern Art and The Cloisters, and hundreds of less spectacular charitable or educational institutions are some of the ultimate results of John D. Rockefeller's parsimony, intelligence, foresight, selfishness, godliness, and ruthlessness. John D.'s great-grandson, Michael C. Rockefeller, was the son of Nelson Rockefeller. Michael lost his life at age twenty-three on a Harvard-Peabody expedition to New Guinea in 1961. His name lives on in a stunning collection of primitive art in the Michael C. Rockefeller Wing of New York City's Metropolitan Museum of Art, and more humbly in the I. M. Pei–designed Michael C. Rockefeller Arts Center on my SUNY-Fredonia campus. I saw the Rockefeller Arts Center officially opened by New York governor Nelson Rockefeller, who came to the dedication in 1969 to honor his son. (It was built with state funds, not with Rockefeller Foundation or other family money.)

Rockefeller Chapel, on the University of Chicago campus, is a glorious pseudo-Gothic paean to the greatness of God, and to the rectitude of Baptist John D. Rockefeller and his divinely or dubiously gotten money. This yeasty combination of religiosity or piety, acquisitiveness, self-righteousness, and charity is a distinctively American phenomenon. It grew directly from the religious and social ferment and experimentation of nineteenth-century upstate New York and the Great Road.

westering

prairies and plains : the big empty and the sandhills

westward to Indiana and beyond

◆　In this chapter, the Great Road heads west through the prairies to the plains. The West has long been more a shifting, elusive, creative metaphor than a region, more an idea than a place. Americans have always looked westward, though often to very different "Wests." I begin with a largely forgotten battle in the year 1794 in what is now northwestern Ohio. I take it as the arbitrary chronological and geographic starting point for our Westering, our national yearning, or, in the words of Robert Frost, our "vaguely realizing westward." The Battle of Fallen Timbers is commemorated by a statue in a park near Maumee, Ohio, a mile north of Alternate Twenty. The statue isn't much. It's a rather forlorn portrayal of three soldiers, with General "Mad Anthony" Wayne in the middle. A commission report on it correctly states that it "could use restoration."

The Battle of Fallen Timbers is usually ignored in the catalog of important American Indian fights. It should not be. It was, among other things, a historic first: "the first victory of the U.S. Army in the field" (John Mohawk, *The Treaty of Canandaigua*, San Diego, 2000, xii). Here General Wayne, a hero of the Revolutionary War, defeated and destroyed a confederacy of local tribes led by the Maumees, under the leadership of Little Turtle. This victory split the British from their Indian allies and opened a new "West"—Indian lands in western and southern Ohio, soon also Indiana. Illinois, Michigan, and Wisconsin—to further white immigration. (A young Tecumseh was there, on the losing side. He survived to become a great leader of his Shawnee people.) After securing an important inland portage by building and lending his name to Fort Wayne,

99

Indiana, General Wayne returned to Erie, Pennsylvania, just founded (in 1795) on what is now US 20. Anthony Wayne died in Erie in 1796, as important an Indian fighter as Crook or Custer.[1]

Much farther west, a little community was beginning to grow around an obscure fortification named Fort Dearborn for an obscure politician, at the southwest corner of Lake Michigan. A bloody battle there in 1812, part of the war with England, is now called the Fort Dearborn Massacre. Between forty and fifty whites were killed. The rest, forty-six, were taken into temporary captivity, and the fort was burned. Rebuilt, the little community would later take its name from an Anishinabe (Chippewa) word meaning something like either "Place of the skunks" or "Place where the wild onions grow": my sweet home Chicago, smelly even then. Illinois had become "The West," the Frontier.

the frontier moves west

The concept of the Frontier has been reinvestigated and seriously debunked since 1890 and the seminal paper and argument of Frederick Jackson Turner. I agree with chief debunker Patty Nelson Limerick and her fellows, but the word still has metaphorical resonance, and I so employ it here. When Tom Lincoln hankered for the West, the Frontier, and more space and opportunity, he left Kentucky for southern Indiana, where his Kentucky-born son Abraham grew up. US 20 in Indiana isn't especially interesting, unless you're a Notre Dame or College Football Hall of Fame fan. Both are in South Bend. A huge mural of the risen Jesus, raising his arms in triumph, adorns a wall of the Notre Dame University library building and looms over one end zone of the football stadium. His pose is reminiscent of a referee signaling a score. Campus wits have dubbed him "Touchdown Jesus." Religion followed the Great Road west beyond New York.

Once upon a time, twenty-six brands of autos were manufactured in Indiana. The Studebaker Museum in South Bend, new since my last visit, is said to be an excellent history of that now-defunct company's development from making Conestoga wagons to making automobiles. There's a historical American evolution for you! There is also an Auburn-Cord-Duesenberg museum in Auburn, twenty miles south of US 20. Are you into band instruments or recreational vehicles? Elkhart makes both, and has an RV Hall of Fame. Who knew? But I haven't seen it. If you would like to ride in an Amish buggy, in Shipshewana there are buggies stretched into three rows of seats for tourists: Take a Thrill Ride in a One Horsepower Amish Stretch Limo! These conservative Mennonites are not averse to coining tourist dollars from expanding, exhibiting, and judiciously sharing their "plain" lifestyles. Of their Friday horse auctions, they write: "You're sure to get wrapped up in the excitement of it all!" I didn't.

In northwestern Indiana, the Great Road leads to the Indiana Dunes National Lakeshore, a huge sweeping ten-mile beach with a dramatic view of Chicago just around the bend of Lake Michigan. The late Senator Paul Douglas of Illinois got little public praise for helping to preserve this superb place. Praise him now. Gary, a gritty steel-making extension of Chicago, earned fame in 1968 as the first large U.S. city to have a black mayor—Richard Hatcher. I'm proud to say I contributed to his campaign.

Ell-a-noy

Carl Sandburg sang:

> So move your fam'ly westward,
> Good health you will enjoy,
> And rise to wealth and honor in
> The state of Ell-a-noy

When Abraham Lincoln hankered for more space and opportunity, it was to Illinois that he and his father looked. When young Abraham struck out on his own, he went first to Petersburg and New Salem (where there's a superb state park remembering him and reconstructing his little village), then to Springfield, where he practised law and raised a family. In Chicago, in 1860, the Republican Party made him their nominee for president. Lincoln left Springfield and the only home he had ever owned to go to Washington. He came back to Springfield on a funeral train to be entombed there. By which time, of course, Illinois wasn't really the West, the Frontier, any more.

Chicago's placement and subsequent prosperity are due in part to a vital portage to its south and west. It was and is the connection, via the Chicago and Illinois Rivers, between the Great Lakes and the Mississippi and the Gulf of Mexico. When the Erie Canal was finished in 1825, the northeast was connected as well. A canal was hand dug southwest of Chicago in 1848; the Indian portage had existed for centuries. US 20 crosses the modern canal southwest of the city.

manifest destiny, empire, and resistance thereto

Well before Lincoln's presidency, the nation had begun to take on an expansionist American version of what Kipling would later call the White Man's Burden. This doctrine was usually expressed in the resounding phrase "Manifest Destiny." The precise date and origin of the phrase is disputed. John L. O'Sullivan signed his name to a piece in his *Democratic Ideas* magazine in 1839 that claimed it was our nation's manifest destiny, our clear fate and duty, to spread from ocean to ocean and create one great nation to rule the hemisphere, the world, and bring to a savage land and savage races the benefits of democracy and Christian civilization. This idea conveniently justified such imperialist adventures as the Mexican War (1846–1848), which greatly expanded the nation's territory southwestward. (Lincoln had opposed it during his term as a congressman from Illinois.) The expansionists' timing was good. One year later, gold was discovered at Sutter's Fort in the new California territory, which promptly became a taxpaying state in the union. Not all unnecessary wars are political and economic disasters.[2]

Back east, in Concord, Massachusetts, this westward expansionism put Henry David Thoreau in jail in 1846. He had refused to pay a one dollar tax levied to support the Mexican War. Friends (or his aunt) immediately stepped forward to pay it for him, but not before he had resisted to the extent of spending one night in Concord's jail. A legend about his brief imprisonment is too good to omit. His friend, Ralph Waldo Emerson, reportedly asked him: "Henry, what are you doing in there?" Thoreau allegedly replied "Waldo, what are you doing out there?" In this comeback is the germ of the most important social movements of the twentieth century. From Thoreau's experience came his *Resistance to Civil Government* (Thoreau's title: we call it *Civil Disobedience*), and his immense subsequent influence on epoch-making nonviolent revolutions led by Mahatma Gandhi and Martin Luther King Jr. Through them, Thoreau was a major influence on Nelson Mandela, and probably on Lech Walesa, *Solidarnosc*, and Pope John Paul II as well. Inspiring the empowering of the oppressed on three continents and helping to bring down the Iron Curtain and the Berlin Wall: no mean accomplishment for an obscure pencil maker and failed teacher. Thoreau's basic arguments are that there is a higher law than the civil, and that those who break the civil law must be willing to accept the penalty. Martin Luther King's *Letter from Birmingham Jail* is one classic result.

"American Progress," painting by John Gast, 1872

manifest destiny as art

The idea of manifest destiny is superbly represented in a large painting in the Smithsonian Museum of American Art: John Gast's *American Progress*, painted in 1872. It became widely known through an engraving by George Crofutt. The painting is not great art, though it is as sumptuous as the diaphanously clad, buxom blond lady—Progress? America? Columbia? Pamela Anderson?—flying or floating across it. She carries a school book (labeled "School Book") and a coil of wire in one arm. With the other she strings the telegraph wires that will unite the nation. Beneath her, in the foreground, are pioneers and homesteaders, heading westward with her. Behind her are a Conestoga wagon, a stagecoach, and a railroad in the distance, all westering. Just ahead of her, fleeing at her approach, are the indigenous Indians and a herd of bison. Snow-capped mountains, surely the Rockies, make up the left background. Behind her is the light she has brought; ahead of her, where the Indians and bison are, is the darkness she will dispel. Nope, not great art, but great propaganda, with a nice dash of soft-core barroom porn. Faith and faith alone would seem to be responsible for keeping her white dress up over her ample left breast. Or perhaps we should credit the uplifting power of Manifest Destiny, of American Progress.[3]

The new nation, exercising its alleged Manifest Destiny, almost exterminated the native bison—fewer than a hundred were left in the United States in the 1880s. It nearly exterminated the original human inhabitants, too. Estimates of the American Indians killed by disease, starvation, and war from the time of Columbus to 1900 range from two million to twenty million. Six million is not a bad guess, and it carries a scary echo of the Holocaust. Too bad if you're in the way—Here Comes America, though it may be disguised as a goddess or a lovely woman.

toward the Mississippi : west of Chicago

By the 1840s, Indiana and Illinois had already been occupied by whites. Now it was time to get beyond the lusty young city of Chicago, time to take this imperial impulse across the Mississippi to the former Louisiana Territory, current occupants be damned. The road west to Empire now approaches the Mississippi. US 20 passes near the town of Riverside as it leaves Chicago. Riverside, with its leafy, curving streets, is more than just a very nice old town; it is America's first planned suburb, designed by the great landscape architect, Frederick Law Olmsted. He planned the fine "green necklace" of parks in Boston, and less renowned strings of parks in Brooklyn, Buffalo, and other cities. Central Park in New York City and Yosemite Valley are not on US 20, but it is worth mentioning that these two utterly different places, three thousand miles apart, look strangely alike. Well they might. Olmsted designed the first and profoundly influenced the second, from his house and workshop just south of the Great Road in Brookline, Mass (see chapter 1). His influence on the national parks is aptly described in a well titled book, *Wilderness by Design* (Ethan Carr, University of Nebraska Press, 1999). Olmsted's fabricated wild-places-in-the-city have worn well. Riverside is still a pretty place to live, and Central Park is indispensable, a glorious refuge from Manhattan's hubbub.

US 20 ambles west from Chicago through anonymous strip malls, which have encroached on rich black farmland. Much of the Great

Road here is not so Great. It has become what I call Interstatificated: four-lane divided, featureless, exurban, dull. The city of Elgin was famous in my youth for watches and the state mental hospital. The watch factory is gone and the hospital is renamed and greatly changed. A century earlier, Gail Borden established in Elgin a large plant for the manufacture of his invention: condensed milk. Milk that could be stored indefinitely was a great boon to soldiers in the Civil War, and to campers and travelers ever since. Mari Sandoz quotes a Nebraska cowboy ode to the delights of canned milk:

> No tits to pull, no hay to pitch,
> Just punch a hole in the son-of-a-bitch.

The little farm town of Genoa is in DeKalb County, just south of the Great Road. DeKalb County is where Joseph Glidden invented, patented, and manufactured barbed wire, and DeKalb pioneered in the development and production of hybrid seed corn. Genoa is the home of my Nelson ancestors. My Chicago-born mother, Ruth Hutton Schlenker, met my future father while she was teaching Latin and French at Genoa High School. When the principal told her where she might live and with whom she might keep company (*really!!* this was 1928), he said that his favorite was "that red-headed boy at the bank." Harold ("Red") Nelson became my father. Genoa is now a growing exurb of Chicago. Impervious to change, Red's sister, my Aunt Kay, 94 and counting, still lives in Genoa in the house where she was born in 1914, before World War I began.

Aunt Kay and Mac, circa 2000

To see something of old Twenty, leave the US 20 expressway for the Business alternative, as I did, into Rockford, Illinois, to enjoy its old River District and impressive churches. Until the 2000 census, Rockford was the largest city on Twenty west of Chicago. Boise, Idaho, has now surpassed Rockford by more than twelve thousand people, as the nation moves westward. Even Northern Illinoisans would probably not have thought of Rockford as the last big city on this route between Chicago and the Pacific, but so it was. Twenty passes through or near some serious cities on its way to Chicago—Boston, Worcester, Albany,

Syracuse, Rochester, Buffalo, Cleveland, Toledo, South Bend, Gary. But once west of Chicago, the Great Road quickly becomes very rural.

land of Lincoln and Jane Addams

Abraham Lincoln is everywhere in Illinois. He appears on US 20 as a statue on "Debate Square" in Freeport, commemorating his historic second debate with Stephen A. Douglas in 1858.[4] The statue shows him seated, listening to a standing, speaking Douglas. Lincoln's key contention in an earlier speech in Springfield had been that no nation could

Aunt Kay and Mac, circa 1941, traveling in Lincoln land

exist "half slave and half free." Douglas responded to this issue and enunciated what became known as the Freeport Doctrine: that the people of a
territory had the right to decide whether it should become a free or a
slave state. This compromise satisfied the Illinois legislators, who were
the electors, and Douglas was reelected over Lincoln; but he lost his presidential prospects in the process. Douglas could no longer hope for support from Southern Democrats.

   Douglas's Freeport statue is a smaller one; "The Little Giant" was
barely five feet tall. Though born in Vermont, Stephen Douglas was a
product of the Great Road. He was raised and schooled in Canandaigua,
New York, the heart of the Burned-Over District. He left that laboratory
of free thought and experimentation, took the Great Road west to flourish in Illinois, and supported Lincoln and the Union when Civil War
came. He is buried in a towering tomb near the Great Road in Chicago.

   Eight miles west of my house on US 20 in New York is another
statue of Abraham Lincoln, erected in 1999. It commemorates a legendary moment when president-elect Lincoln came east along the Great
Road through Westfield, New York, on his way to Washington and
glory, sorrow, and death. The story goes that an eleven-year old girl
from Westfield, Grace Bedell, had written him to tell him that she
thought he should grow a beard: "You would look a great deal better, for
your face is so thin. All the ladies like whiskers and they would tease
their husbands to vote for you and then you would be president" (*New
York Times*, October 26, 2006, E8). Lincoln answered her letter, and he
did indeed begin to grow his famous beard at that time. On his way to
his inauguration in Washington, he asked that his train stop in Westfield
so that he could meet Grace. He is said to have said, with his usual
warmth and wit, that she might have got him elected. There are charming statues of both of them at this legendary event in a little park on US
20 in Westfield, New York.

   Five miles north of Freeport is Cedarville, Illinois, the birthplace
and burial place of Jane Addams (1860–1935), who almost singlehand-
edly began the settlement house/social work movement in America. She
was raised in Cedarville, and in 1882 earned a degree on the Great Road
at what would become the Rockford Female Seminary, then Rockford
College. Her father, John, had been a friend of Abraham Lincoln. Her
work was centered in and around Hull House, on the near South Side of
Chicago. Ultimately, she went far beyond feeding the hungry in the
depression of 1893 to political advocacy for workers' rights and women's
suffrage. She took fierce criticism for opposing U.S. entry into World

War I and was a founder of the American Civil Liberties Union. Her
lifetime's mighty achievements were honored in 1935 by the Nobel Peace
Prize. Her great work grew on and from the Great Road. She ennobled
the culture of the entire world.

Fifteen miles west of Freeport, Stockton advertises itself as "The
Highest Village in Illinois," and it does have a grand view over the valley
that leads down to the Mississippi River. The highest point in Illinois is

Statues of Abe Lincoln and Grace Bedell on Route 20, Westfield, New York

here, Charles Mound, 1,235 feet above sea level. Elevation is only a curiosity here, and Charles Mound is higher than only five other states' high points. But altitude will soon become a significant feature of the land, the climate, and the lives of the people. Once across the big river, the Great Road will rise slowly, inexorably, upslope to the Rockies. Twenty crosses Targhee Pass in Montana at its highest point: 7,072 feet above sea level.

Lincoln turns up again in Elizabeth, Illinois. This pretty little town has reconstructed Apple River Fort, an impressive log structure whose original figured in the Black Hawk war of 1832. Abe Lincoln's only military experience came when he was elected lieutenant of a company of volunteers in this brief Indian war. Local legend says that he and his men helped to save the fort from a siege, but Lincoln never claimed to have seen combat. Lincoln's tall shadow falls farther west on Galena, on the Mississippi River. This gorgeous old river town is full of fine Victorian houses built of local stone; a road sign on Twenty describes the area as "The Sandstone Corners"of Illinois, Iowa, and Wisconsin. Galena's old, narrow, gently curving Main Street has become almost a boutique mall. Galena has lots going for it, but nothing more important or historic than its connection with a sometime resident, born in southern Ohio: Ulysses S. Grant.

Grant and Galena

Young Hiram Ulysses Grant (1822–1885) left southern Ohio for the U.S. Military Academy without enthusiasm, graduated without distinction in 1843, and acquired the inaccurate but prophetic initials "U.S." along the way. (He had let himself be called Ulysses Simpson Grant after a muddled registration at West Point.) He served admirably but unspectacularly in the Mexican war (1846–1848), and soon, disillusioned by his limited opportunity for advancement in the stultified peacetime U.S. Army, resigned his commission. He failed in business ventures in California and in Missouri. He finally found employment in his tanner father's leather shop in Galena in 1860. He had little gift for retail, and hated his work. He seemed doomed to a life of genteel failure and obscurity.

Grant's big chance came in 1861 with the Civil War. He shaped up a group of Illinois volunteers and was given the rank of brigadier general. His Civil War record was brilliant and his spirit indomitable, from his victory at the pivotal siege of Vicksburg, Mississippi, in the west, to the final bloody, dogged, triumphant battles in the east. Urged to dismiss him for his alleged drinking, Lincoln said, "I cannot spare this man—he fights." Lincoln also allegedly inquired as to the brand of whiskey Grant drank, so that he might send a barrel to his other generals. Fighting would seem to be the main job of any general, but a surprising number of them, from Union Army commander General George McClellan on down, didn't, much. They preferred tactical maneuvering, cautiously avoiding large battles that might prove disastrous. Their delay and inaction tended to help the Confederacy: the longer any war drags on, the harder it is to justify to a democratic electorate. Lincoln's reelection in 1864 after four bitter years was no sure thing, even though victory in the war seemed near, and was. His Democratic opponent was none other than George McClellan, no longer the Union commander. McClellan supported the war, splitting his party, and Lincoln's electoral victory was massive. President Lincoln is said to have once quietly asked General McClellan: "If you're not using the Army of the Potomac, may I borrow it?" Always good for a laugh, that Abe Lincoln.

After the Civil War, Grant became far and away the most admired American of his time. His rise to the presidency was almost inevitable, though it brought him little happiness, some shame, and much sorrow. His decisive military behavior did not carry over into his political life, and his choice of subordinates was dreadful. Perhaps the best thing he achieved as president, though it was not much remarked on at the time, was the establishment of Yellowstone National Park, in March 1872. Few were sorry to see him leave the White House in 1877.

Grant and his family did not live in Galena for long, preferring to live among wealthy friends in the nation's centers of power, Washington and New York City, where he and his wife are buried. Grant is said to have wanted another term as president in 1880, Lord knows why. But the "dark horse" Garfield was the Republicans' choice (see chapter 3). Grant died in Saratoga County, upstate New York, in 1885, a few days after completing his excellent *Personal Memoirs*, which would become a bestseller. Thus, posthumously, he paid off the enormous debts his false friends and poor business decisions had led him to incur. In 1865, Galena had bought and presented him with a beautiful Victorian brick house on a hill on Bouthillier Street. Galena was the town he had left to become great and famous. Now it has claimed him as its heroic son. Good for Galena. Good tours of the house are available.

Retired Riverboat, Dubuque Museum Aquarium, Iowa

"you're in I-o-way, I-o-way!"

As the Great Road crosses the Great River Road and the Mississippi River, leaving The Land of Lincoln behind, it enters Old Iowa, a good description of Dubuque. River towns were usually founded early and were often more prosperous than nearby settlements. So it was with Dubuque, the oldest white settlement in the state. Its bluffs are adorned with handsome old houses and "The Fenelon Elevator," a pre–Civil War cable car system that lifts passengers up those bluffs. Add a 150–foot tall "shot tower" (1856)—an early low-tech gravitational method of making lead shot from the ore of the nearby mines—and you have a very interesting old place. "Galena," the name of the Illinois town across the river, is the Latin word for that lead ore. Down on the river bank by the shot tower, the great river smells fresh and alive as it heads toward New Orleans.

A young cub pilot named Samuel Langhorne Clemens learned how to handle a steamboat on this big river in the late 1850s. Of a river trip past Dubuque twenty years later, he wrote: "The majestic bluffs that

Mark Twain and tourist, Joyce Haines

overlook the river, along through this region, charm one with the grace and variety of their forms, and the soft beauty of their adornment. The steep verdant slope, whose base is at the water's edge, is topped by a lofty rampart of broken, turreted rocks, which are exquisitely rich and mellow in color.... And then you have the shining river, winding here and there and yonder, its sweep interrupted at intervals by clusters of wooded islands threaded by silver channels. . . . And it is all as tranquil and reposeful as dreamland, and has nothing this-wordly about it—nothing to hang a fret or a worry upon." It's busier today, but it's still lovely. The land and the river haven't changed much since Mark Twain described them thus in *Life on the Mississippi*.

There is a very interesting institution in Dubuque, new in 2003, featuring local river fauna: the National Mississippi River Museum and Aquarium. Huge channel catfish, sturgeon, and wondrously weird paddlefish swim lazily in their large tanks. There are excellent exhibits on the life of the river and its boatmen, then and now, from Indians and voyageurs and Mark Twain to modern towboat captains such as my cousin, Mike Slaby. There's a statue of Mark Twain sitting on a bench; you can have your picture taken sitting with him. Inside, you can steer your own virtual towboat. Outside is an impressive old boat-yard, which was still building mighty steel ships as late as 1973. It was kept very busy building military ships during World War I because it was inland and safe from enemy attack. You can tour a retired old towboat. This museum is well worth a stop.

"that's where the tall corn grows"

The Great Road here leaves the Mississippi, that great natural boundary, behind. There are two other interesting places to see to near here: a Field of Dreams and a Trappist monastery. Who ever said that Iowa was all corn? Well, actually, the Field of Dreams, near Dyersville, was all corn, until Hollywood plowed up some of it so that Shoeless Joe Jackson (played by Ray Liotta, batting, infuriatingly, from the wrong side of the plate) could play baseball with Moonlight Graham (Burt Lancaster) and farmer Kevin Costner in the sweet fantasy film *Field of Dreams* (1989). ("Is this heaven?" "No, it's Iowa.") The set soon reverted to tall corn until good old American initiative decided that it would make a tourist attraction, plowed up the corn, and rebuilt the field.

Actually, it made *two* tourist attractions: Battling Ballparks. (There's not an awful lot to do near Dyersville.) The infield and right field are run by a farm family, which asserts (as of 2001) that the other half (left and center field) are run by a moneygrubbing foreclosing bank and that theirs is the only *real* Field of Dreams. Theirs is free; the other charges a small fee. The entry roads are maybe thirty feet apart. So it goes in baseball fantasyland. Run the bases, buy a T-shirt, and head for Peosta.

Lord, have mercy on us

I have a serious soft spot for Trappists, as I noted in chapter 2. New Melleray, near Dubuque, is the second oldest Trappist foundation in America, dating from 1849, when Irish monks settled here. They wanted to spread their faith and their monasticism, of course. But they may also have left Mount Melleray, a beautiful abbey in County Waterford, Ireland, for the same reason many Americans' ancestors did, mine included—they were starving. Not all the Potato Famine Irish were "workin' on the railway."

When I first visited New Melleray Abbey forty years ago, there were many delightful Irish accents on the unofficial welcoming committee. I was told in 2001 that there was only one Irish monk left. Trappists are often quietly, wickedly, funny, and this abbey has long produced a witty newsletter. Now it has a lively web site. When a sister convent was established near Dubuque, the Trappistine nuns arriving from Massachusetts were greeted by the brothers with a big sign: "Welcome to the Wild West!" The brothers are farmers, of course; how could they not be, in this rich land where even the weeds in the highway cracks grow lush? But their leading cash crop is now caskets, beautifully made wooden boxes for eternity.⁵ Like the monks who bake Monks' Bread at the Abbey of the Genesee in New York, these Trappists must earn their living.

Leaving the ancient monk in the gift shop, I went into the impressive local limestone and oak chapel, completed in 1976, new since my first visit, and waited for the monks to file in to sing morning prayers. I sat behind a substantial wooden railing which separated me from the cloistered monks. At Gethsemani, in Kentucky, a sign at the entrance to the abbey church stated, as recently as 1985: "PAPAL ENCLOSURE: Women Forbidden to Enter on Pain of Excommunication." Does it still? Perhaps not, though the rule is surely still in force. Here the bar, the ban, is subtler, but still very real. These men have separated from the world.

I was alone in the still chapel until they came, except for one lone nun, in fairly modern dress. Why was she there? A crisis of the soul? A buswoman's holiday? To study modern monastic architecture? Monasteries don't encourage small talk, bless them, so I'll never know. It was very quiet, a beautiful sunny late spring morning. It was "terce," the "third hour" mid-morning prayer, the third of seven in the liturgical day.

Because of decisions made at the Second Vatican Council in the early 1960s, the Roman Catholic Church has flunked Latin; that is, its worldwide services are now, with few exceptions, in the vernacular, the local language. Roman Catholic priests now face forward toward their congregations to celebrate the mass. That's an advance in openness and lucidity, though a loss in tradition and mystery, and perhaps in beauty. Instead of "miserere nobis," the monks sang again and again "Lord, have mercy on us." The monks sing, sometimes with the organ, sometimes without. They sing plainly, functionally, not trying hard to make a beautiful sound. This is prayer, after all, not a choral concert. "Lord, have mercy on us." They are monks, not performers. This is their work. At Gethsemani in the 1960s, only priests sang; lay brothers did other work during these prayers. Here, I think, the whole community sings. "Laborare est orare": to work is to pray. And for the choir monks, to pray is to work.

Terce is a short service, one of the so-called "little hours." It was over in fifteen minutes, from 9:15 to 9:30. Back to other work for all of them until Sext, at midday, when prayer again becomes their work. They have, by the way, been up and at this holy work since 3:15 in the morning: their first service, Vigils, is at 3:30 a.m. "Lord, have mercy on us." They filed out; I left.

I walked slowly out into the warm Iowa sunshine and started the car. A news bulletin on the car radio stated that Timothy McVeigh had just been executed by lethal injection. I had forgotten the occasion: it was Monday, June 11, 2001. He had been alive when I arrived at the Abbey. "Lord, have mercy on us." On Timothy McVeigh, on his victims, on the monks, on all of us.

A supremely lovely place is New Melleray, built to address eternity. Yet I fear for its survival. A return trip (in 2006) and another terce showed a smaller group of monks, about thirty, nearly all old and gray, several with canes or a walker. (There had been 150 monks shortly after World War II.) Two-thirds of these men made their solemn professions before the 1960s. There were two younger men in a habit that I took to be that of the postulant or novice. Okay, there are some new recruits. But not many. There were young faces among the half-dozen retreatants, too. Though I am agnostic to my bones, I think northeastern Iowa and the Great Road would be much poorer without this abbey and its monks and retreatants and coffins and prayers. The monks will welcome you as a formal retreatant, involved in prayers and conferences, or just as someone who wants to share their silence: "We believe one of the special gifts we offer you is an atmosphere of silence and peace. This is integral to our way of life and spirituality. Silence and quiet help us hear the word of God speaking in our own hearts. We ask you to help us maintain an atmosphere of silence. . . . The fee for retreats at New Melleray is a free-will offering." Monastic silence, harder than ever to find in our noisy century, is exquisite. Try it while it's still there.

small towns, a western fort, and the Cardiff Giant—again

Twenty miles west, Earlville, Iowa (pop. 822) tells the world it has "two churches two schools a swimming pool." I stopped for gas in Parkersburg (pop. 1,804), next to a big smelly pig-hauling truck, across from the "HWY 20 Cafe." Hey, that's my research subject. It was irresistible. The burgers were good, the banter better. Ostrichburgers were on the menu. Ostrich joke:

Me to waitress: Have you ever eaten ostrich?

Waitress (of a great-grandmotherly age, wearing New Balance running shoes): Got one by mistake once. [wince]

Me: You didn't die, though.

She: No, and I didn't fly the coop or put my head in the sand either!

Sign in HWY 20 Cafe rest room: "We've had problems with needles in the garbage. Please dispense properly." Oh, my. If drug abuse is that common in Parkersburg, Iowa, it's everywhere.

Lest lovers of the building trades be dangerously overstimulated, I wish to make it clear that the Grout Museum (on Twenty in Waterloo, Iowa) does not have exhibits with names like "The Romance of Spackle," or "Plumbing Through the Ages." The legacy of Mr. Henry Whittemore Grout, it covers history and science, and has a planetarium.

Iowa Falls is "The scenic city." Jones Park. Aquatic Park. Nice parks. I couldn't find the falls. I think they may have been subsumed in a small dam. But there's a really big Wal-Mart. Webster City, a mile north of Interstatificated Twenty, grew two distinguished writer sons: novelist and screen writer MacKinlay Kantor, and journalist Clark Mollenhoff. Each won a Pulitzer: Kantor for *Andersonville*, Mollenhoff for his Watergate reporting.

Fort Dodge is the easternmost place on US 20 where I saw "Great Plains" as part of an address. Fort Dodge is still in the prairies, but the Great Road is getting closer to the West. This small city has collected several early buildings and put them together a la Sturbridge Village as though they were some real early Fort Dodge, a not very important fortification that was on the frontier briefly around 1850. There is an impressive rebuilt stockaded fort with exhibits, a school, a drugstore, a chapel, a gift shop, all the usual stuff. There is one unusual exhibit—the Cardiff Giant.

I beg pardon?? In chapter 2, I said the Cardiff Giant was in Cooperstown, New York. It's a fake, of course, a piece of rock, a bogus petrified Indian. But that one is the real Cardiff Giant bogus petrified Indian. Then what's this one, which, I must admit, looks a helluva lot like the other one? Okay: Fort Dodge sits on a huge layer of gypsum. Near Fort Dodge is the quarry where the block from which the original real bogus Cardiff Giant was carved.

Follow me carefully here.

Another block was quarried and carved to compete with the original bogus petrified Indian, and here it is, home at last: the Genuine Real Imitation Bogus Cardiff Giant Petrified Indian. Step Right Up!! Battling Blocks of Gypsum!! Battling Cardiff Giants!! Battling Ballparks, too!! Only in America. And only on US 20.

the population dwindles

Twenty miles farther west is Rockwell City (pop. 1,801), "The Golden Buckle on the Corn Belt."

Lytton (pop. 377) is the "Hottest Little Town for Business."

Early (pop. 670) is the "Crossroads of the Nation."

Is this where all the English majors go? Shelley called poets "the unacknowledged legislators of the world." They may also be the authors of the ridiculously overhyped town signs on US 20. The perceived need to promote the local economy, to save these dwindling towns and their businesses and real estate equity, produces this boosterism.

Twenty here is in prosperous farm country, if there is such a thing. Does anyone know a farmer who made money last year, or, at any rate, admitted it? Before the ethanol boom? This is certainly great farm land. Farms throughout most of Iowa look pin-straight, prosperous, neat, and tidy. Even some of the seemingly abandoned farmhouses and barns and silos look well kept up. Yet these little towns are slowly dying, more so as we go farther west. There are only two million full-time farmers left in the United States, down from ten million a century ago. We are said to have fewer farmers than we have people in prison (2.2 million). Lordy, isn't that one sad statistic? (NPR, *Talk of the Nation*, November 24, 2006).

first contact : Lewis and Clark and the Louisiana Purchase

At the western boundary of Iowa are Sioux City, the Missouri River, and the Sergeant Floyd Monument, a mighty sandstone obelisk marking the fourth and (one hopes) final resting place of the only member of the Lewis and Clark Corps of Discovery to die on the epic expedition. Poor Sergeant Charles Floyd died in August 1804, in his early twenties. Frontier diagnosis: a "Biliose Chorlick," i.e., bilious cholic. He probably suffered from an inflamed, then a ruptured, appendix, and died of septicemia, before penicillin could easily cure such infections. It's what killed my father's father, also young, in 1917. What was Sergeant Charles Floyd, a native Kentuckian, doing in this wild place?

In 1803, the young American nation was offered a deal it couldn't refuse, though it was patently illegal to accept it. Napoleon and his ministers were well aware of the difficulties of fashioning an American empire out of their recent acquisition, Louisiana, which had been Spanish-claimed territory. Louisiana was a long way from France, and the

French had other, more pressing problems, such as slave uprisings and yellow fever in the Caribbean, and the British Navy. They were planning to invade Britain and control Europe. So they gave President Jefferson's representatives—in Paris to try to purchase the mouth of the Mississippi, the strategic city of New Orleans—a chance to double the land area of their fledgling nation at a bargain price, fifteen million dollars, three cents an acre. We now know that that was more than eight hundred thousand square miles. *Done!*, and we'll worry later about legality, Congress, and finding the money. Louisiana was essentially all the land drained by the Missouri River, not just the modern state, and the potential was enormous, mind-boggling.

Thus, the young nation was forced, not against its will, to think northwestward as far as . . .

But of course, no one in Washington, D.C., no one anywhere, really knew what had been bought or how far it stretched. Hence the Corps of Discovery, the 1804–1806 expedition that Jefferson put under the command of Captains Meriwether Lewis and William Clark. The Great Road crosses their westward path twice: here at the Missouri, which they would attempt to navigate northwestward, and again in Oregon.

The Corps of Discovery buried their dead comrade Sergeant Floyd on a hill, now called "Sergeant Bluff" after him. They replaced him in their military hierarchy with one of their own, Sergeant Patrick Gass. Remarkably, they did this by voting. This was probably the first U.S. election west of the Mississippi. (The party's only woman, Sacagawea, and its only black, William Clark's slave York, surely did not vote.) The Corps climbed a nearby hill, Spirit Mound, in what is now South Dakota. It was said to be populated by short little devils who shot arrows at and frightened the local Indians. Then they were off up the Missouri to encounter the warlike Sioux (Lakota) and winter with the hospitable Mandans, who would soon be almost destroyed by the diseases (chiefly smallpox) that the whites brought. I will have occasion later to discuss this party and its remarkable achievements, not the least of which was losing only this one of its members on such a long and dangerous trek.

"are we west yet?"

Iowa is now behind us. Its legendary fertility fades a bit in its westernmost seventy-five miles. The land grows redder and hillier. Even before the Nebraska border, the term *ranch* begins to appear. As US 20 enters Nebraska, it passes two Indian reservations on the Missouri River, in the low hills to the south: the Omaha and the Winnebago. There are two more reservations on the Missouri farther north, those of the Santee Sioux and the Yankton Sioux, in South Dakota. These are the first Indian reservations near the Great Road for almost a thousand miles, the first since my local rez, the Cattaraugus Senecas' on US 20, twenty miles from my house in New York. The land is changing and the culture is changing. We are West. Sort of.

A roadside marker states that on August 21, 1804, Lewis and Clark passed the Sioux River and camped "along the Missouri River Northeast of here." There is a sign for a "feedyard," an odd locution: "feedlot" is the common term. There are many trees—we are still east of the Ninety-eighth Meridian—but the houses are fewer and fewer, and the farms (or ranches) are larger. Sometimes the 360 degree view shows no farmhouses at all. We are West. To an extent.

industrial beef, industrial pollution

At Randolph, Nebraska: a feedlot. Feedlots are fenced areas where beef cattle are "finished," taken off the farm or range and fattened for slaughter with subsidized corn and antibiotics. The medicine is necessary because cattle evolved to eat grass, not corn. Corn is a cheap and quick finisher, so that's what they get. Without the antibiotics, their feed would make them sick. This is not a big feedlot. Big ones smell like sewers, like death, like concentration camps, which is what they are. That stink is part of the price of cheap, industrialized McBeef. So, apparently, are dangerous strains of Escherichia coli in our spinach, probably caused by livestock manure runoff near huge factory farms in California. It's not just in spinach, either. Something else—possibly California lettuce or onions—transmitted virulent E.coli 0157:H7 to more than seventy Taco Bell customers in six eastern states in 2006. The precise cause was in dispute: cf. *New York Times*, December 8, 12, and 13, 2006. Given our mass production agricultural system, this problem can only get worse. California growers, usually resistant to any and all regulation, have asked for federal help to save their markets. I am not optimistic about our solving this problem any time soon.

As Michael Pollan and Wendell Berry remind us, cattle manure used to be boon, not bane. As cows graze a field, they manure it. Plop. But when you separate cows from fields by fencing them in feedlots, you have suddenly created two big new problems: how to fertilize those now manureless fields (with expensive petrochemical nitrogen, itself a pollutant), and how to contain the feedlots' pollution, bacteria-rich cowshit that was once a fertilizing blessing. So long as we feed not grass but subsidized corn and antibiotics to our beef cattle, we will be in danger from ever more virulent strains of adaptable bacteria, created in their stomachs by this feeding regime (*New York Times*, "The Vegetable-Industrial Complex," October 15, 2006).

A report on NPR's *Tech Nation* (October 23, 2006) stated that one and a half million tons of animal manure are plopped in the United States annually. Presumably that's just from domestic animals, not badgers, bats, or racoons. Manure happens, but who counts this stuff!? How!? Can you get grants to do it?! Who knew!? It's a mind-boggling statistic in any case, and it just underscores the problems caused by modern industrial McBeef production.

beyond the ninety-eighth meridian

It's time to start noting and codifying the signs of Westness. How do you know you're West? *W* will henceforth be the code for these signs.

Ashfall Fossil Beds State Park is an interesting side trip, an ongoing excavation of extinct animals trapped in volcanic ash thousands of years ago. It is also where I see *W*: my first yucca—a succulent dryland plant loosely related to cactus.

At O'Neill, Nebraska ("The Irish Capital of Nebraska", pop. 3,855), a really big town out here, the Great Road climbs to two thousand feet above sea level for the first time. O'Neill looks like much of the rest of America—convenience stores, fast food. It is clearly the shopping Mecca for hundreds of square miles around. It was founded by and named for an Irish revolutionary, John J. O'Neill. He led an invasion of Canada in 1866, his troops moving along the Great Road from Cleveland to Buffalo and briefly capturing Fort Erie, Ontario, just up the road from me. Who knew there was such an invasion, after 1812 at least?? After serving a prison term for these Fenian high jinks, O'Neill founded three Irish-American colonies; this one survived.

Ainsworth, Nebraska (pop. 1,862), is sixty-five miles west of O'Neill. It is trying hard to establish its identity, with slogans such as "Welcome to the Middle of Nowhere." Indeed, it holds a "Middle of Nowhere Festival" every June. I missed it, but I take their point. There are some row crops outside of town, but it looks more like ranch country. The reason is not far to seek:

W: We have crossed the Ninety-eighth Meridian of longitude, and the isohyet (I love that word!) where the average annual rainfall drops under twenty inches. The Great Road is now halfway between Boston, Massachusetts, and Newport, Oregon, midway between the oceans. At this midpoint, it's getting higher, dryer, and lonelier. Seventy-four of Nebraska's ninety-three counties have fewer people living in them now than in the 1920s ("Nebraska Settles for Nostalgia," *New York Times*, February 25, 2006).

Time to list some *W*s on US 20 in central Nebraska:

- Feedlots, of course,
- Grain elevators, "Prairie Cathedrals," get smaller and fewer as row crops diminish,
- Roads get red (iron and other metallic traces in the soil, washed down from the Rockies over the eons),
- Russian Olive trees, silvery green and lower than the cottonwoods,
- A store: "Sack n Save" (grocery bags become "sacks" in the West),
- A working windmill, the first, near Emmett, pop. 70,
- "Sandhills" in a sign near Atkinson (the Sandhills are the grassy steppes that cover most of northwestern Nebraska).

more Ws

Here are more *W*s, mostly from further west: watch for them:

- Old tires or old cowboy boots on top of fence posts. Trees are getting scarcer; fence posts are precious. Keep posts from splitting and decaying by covering them with something otherwise useless. There's a whole hunk of north central Kansas—"Post Rock Country"—that makes tourist copy of its limestone fenceposts, used there for the same reasons.
- Signs that include elevation above sea level as well as population.
- Signs where that elevation exceeds the population; usually by a lot.
- Signs where elevation is listed and population isn't—as in rural Kansas.
- Rocks with names, characters, even personalities: Needles, Jailhouse Rock, Courthouse Rock, Chimney Rock, even Molly's Nipple and Old Maid's Bloomers. (Molly got around some; there are said to be five Utah features by that name. Old Maid's Bloomers is a cowboy name for the bow-legged Delicate Arch in Arches National Park, Utah.)

- Oil rigs and endless full coal trains headed eastward to generate electricity.
- Erosion by many names: cutbanks, badlands, dry gulches, coulees, arroyos, mesas, washes, buttes.
- Signs that say "Open Range": watch for unfenced cattle wandering free.
- Speed limit: 75 (Nebraska). Distances are large. Western towns are sometimes described as "a six-pack apart." (Alcohol abuse among the bored young is acknowledged as a major problem. *New York Times*, September 2, 2006.)
- Antelope, mule deer, prairie dogs; even, behind fences, bison.
- Cowboys, sooner than you'd think—surely by central Nebraska. Jack Kerouac was just as surprised at this as you might be—he spotted one in Omaha.
- Big sky: endless horizon.
- Best sign of all: Cattle guards.

open range

Cows, it seems, are incapable of walking across horizontal convex-curved metal strips separated by a few inches. I take their point—it's not easy. Pickups handle 'em just fine. So if you don't want to open and close fences constantly, or even put up a gate, you can put a cattle guard at the head of a drive or road, and cows can't or won't cross it. They're called "Texas gates," too. In a world of fences, this might not be necessary; but out here you're frequently in "open range," places where cows may be on the road, and they must be kept out of (or in) some places. Hence: cattle guards. When you cross a cattle guard to enter an Interstate, and you will, you are *seriously* WEST.

Howdy.

At the Fort Niobrara National Wildlife Refuge, the fine scenic drive goes out onto the grasslands and gives good views of a lot of interesting things, chiefly mule deer and bison. You might see, as I did, a pair of golden eagles over a roadkill.

"semi-ghost" towns : Cody, Nebraska

Eleven miles farther west is Crookston, where a sign states its population as 99. Crookston is actually listed as a "ghost town" on a lively web site: "It still has a very few residents—semi-ghost." Boosterish Crookstonians, if there are any left, must hate this designation. In fact, Crookston does look somewhat "ghostly," with many boarded-up buildings. Clearly it was once bigger and more prosperous, but it lost the state highway route to Valentine and slumped. Federal figures from 1930 to 1980 show the population trend: 323, 262, 168, 139, 86, 86. Hang in there, baby! Still, it has a live post office, so I don't think "ghost town" qualifies. Not yet. Maybe soon. The next two towns confirm this trend: Kilgore, pop. 80. Nenzel, pop. 8.

The elevation climbs over 3,200 feet as the Great Road approaches Cody, Nebraska, "the town too tough to die." That frontier bluster was probably borrowed from Tombstone, Arizona, which has more historic right to it, though Tombstone has become tourist-kitschy. In his well-named book *Miles from Nowhere*, Dayton Duncan relates a long conversation with the indefatigably optimistic mayor of Cody. The mayor cites all the great strides the town has made, the superb new facilities, including an RV park and "one of the best softball fields in the state." Cody is a wonderful place to live and do business. Cody has lost no population between the last two censuses—it's still at 177. (It was more than four hundred in 1930.)

Duncan, like me, sympathetic to the land and the people here, is skeptical. He's not sure that's much to crow about, or that towns like Cody have much future. He's right. The 2000 census population of Cody: 149. That's a loss of almost one in six, down 16.4 percent in just a decade. The census says four of them are "Asians." Will Asian immigrants—East Indians, Vietnamese, Koreans, Chinese, Hmong—save, and change, the culture of the Great Plains, as immigrants from Asia so notably did fifteen thousand years ago?

Promotions don't seem to help much. US 20 in western Nebraska has been semi-glamorized as "The Cowboy Trail," and that's true enough. So many places along Twenty in northern Nebraska are rich with minerals and semiprecious stones that it has been called "Nebraska's Jewel Road." Okay, granted, but none of this fills motels and diners, or sells cars and tractors. The Great Road is well into the plains now, not the wetter, lush prairies, and its people are leaving, especially the young. North Dakota is the only state that actually lost population between 2000 and 2006 (New York Times, October 18, 2006), but there are losses everywhere in the Great Plains, especially outside the cities. Many counties here are back down to fewer than two persons per square mile, a marker that used to mean "unsettled," "frontier." Can anything stop the outmigration? Should we even try it stop it?

the Buffalo Commons

Two Rutgers University professors have argued that the dryer portions of the Great Plains will probably continue to depopulate whether the locals like it or not. Frank and Deborah Popper became darlings to the media and devils to the ranchers when they focused what many others have said in different ways, and said what seems to me more obvious and inevitable than outrageous. Here are some hard truths, not all from the Poppers:

• That this area of the West should probably never have been allotted, plowed, and farmed in the first place. It's great for native grazers, such as bison, but it's just too dry for intensive agriculture, and much of its soil was soon ruined and blowing away. Franklin D. Roosevelt, reacting to the tragedy of the Dust Bowl, said this quite plainly in his famous "I hate war" speech, delivered at Chautauqua, New York, in 1936. Too bad nobody listened to this truth earlier. Many Westerners still haven't, because they don't want to hear it.

There's a failed development story from the Hutton branch of my own family, four generations ago. Charlie Chown, an uncle by marriage, blew $100,000 (serious money in those days) on an irrigation/land development plan near Valier, Montana. As Ivan Doig's books show, all such schemes flopped. For years my parents owned worthless mineral rights to some dry Pondera and Teton County Montana range land. Oil shale was the hope, but it hasn't happened yet. Hapless Uncle Charlie is buried among my relatives in Chicago's Graceland Cemetery, quite near the mighty tomb of George Pullman. Mari Sandoz's *Old Jules* tells of another such futile irrigation scheme in Nebraska. There were many more.

• That the boosterism of politicians and the railroads sold a bogus bill of goods to immigrants.
• That rain does not "follow the plow," i.e., suddenly appear whenever and wherever needed for agriculture. Incredibly, people believed this magical thinking, probably because they wanted so badly for it to be true.
• That free trade and worldwide agricultural competition will continue to make this situation worse. Most crop prices have been dropping for decades. Corn prices are way up because of the ethanol boom, and so, therefore, are the prices of other row crops, but that's an anomaly, and it probably won't last forever. Nothing does.

- That there's already a glut of what grows best here, beef cattle. Colorado reported a drop from four to three million beef cattle in January, 2007.
- That cattle production is a major contributor (perhaps 18 percent) to global warming, at both ends of the cows: methane from their belches, nitrogen from their turds ("Meat and the Planet," *New York Times*, December 27, 2006).
- That the irrigation that permits bumper crops of wheat or corn here is getting more difficult and expensive every year, as the huge Ogallala acquifer and others are depleted much faster than they are recharged. Studies show that the Ogallala is dropping by an average of almost two feet a year. Farmers now have to pump the fossil water up more than eight hundred feet. The natural gas burned to pump it up can cost more than $100 per acre per year (*New York Times*, September 16, 2006). Estimates of how soon this life-giving aquifer will be empty vary from ten to one hundred years.
- That state and national governments would *save* money by buying out most of the family ranchers and farmers. They survive only with massive farm subsidies now.

Add that these messages were crystallized and brought by Jewish professors from New Jersey, the most suburban state in the United States, and that these professors proposed a "Buffalo Commons," a reversion to a nearly wild state for the land. These proud Westerners were enraged, and ready to kill any messenger they could find.

Angry questions: Hadn't their families ranched this land for generations? Weren't they justifiably proud of all the hard work and blood and sweat they and their ancestors had put into the Great Plains to help feed the world? Doesn't it matter that they love this life and know no other? What were their kids supposed to do, quit the 4–H and put on loincloths and be Pretend Indians in the Big New Theme Park, "Six Flags Over Buffalo Turds"?

Answers: Yes, yes, probably not, and no.

some possible futures for the Great Plains

Nobody is forcing anyone to leave or Go Native, certainly not the Poppers, who seem, by turns, surprised, irritated, exhausted, or amused by the fracas they innocently caused. No matter how much these good Western people have invested in the Great Plains, the brute facts of economics will continue to make painful changes inevitable here. Some of these proud, strong folks, or their descendants, will still be ranchers in fifty years. Perhaps some will go more organic, to meet a growing market ("There's more to like about grass-fed beef," *New York Times*, August 30, 2006). The senator Montana elected in 2006, Jon Tester, is a Great Plains organic farmer, missing several fingers from one hand in an agricultural accident. Many ranchers will sell out to big agribusiness factory farms, but even those don't always prosper here.

A partial solution to the eternal problem of "What's to be done?" might well be just benign neglect. Perhaps we should let this land go back to doing what it always did best: growing people and grass and native animals, making clean water and air, giving quiet and space and imaginative room to people who like it or need it or both. The American Prairie Foundation is now buying up thousands of acres of land in the northern Great Plains, looking to create a preserve (using federal grazing lands as well) of three and a half million acres. Buffalo and antelope in; beef cattle and fences out (*Buffalo News*, August 20, 2006). Local ranchers, whose cattle now graze some of these federal lands at bargain basement prices, are opposed. The Nature Conservancy is promoting different plans for the same vast area, more consistent with ranchers' continuing use of the land.

Space for nurturing people's hearts and minds and souls is another excellent use of such dry and open lands, from at least as far back as John the Baptist and Jesus, to our own time. Space is essential to people such as Edward Abbey, author of *Desert Solitaire*; Kathleen Norris, author of *Dakota: A Spiritual Geography*; Gretel Ehrlich, author of *The Solace of Open Spaces*; and Paul Gruchow, author of *The Necessity of Empty Places*. (An alternative view of emptiness in Wyoming appears in the funny title of a good book of poems by William Notter, Texas Review Press: *More Space Than Anyone Can Stand*.) One commentator says: "Over time, ranch families will find it in their interest to sell" (*Buffalo News*, ibid.). Okay. Maybe. But we have an obligation to manage change so that the people who choose to leave, or who adopt changed livelihoods and remain, can do so with dignity and without great financial loss.

beer and Indians

Whiteclay, Nebraska (pop. 30) is twenty miles north of US 20, on the South Dakota border. I didn't go there, nor does the Great Road. I mention it because of its cultural importance to the region. Four million cans or bottles of beer were sold there in a recent year. The roads out of town are notorious deathtraps, particularly the one going north into the vast Pine Ridge Sioux Reservation, four hundred yards distant. The rez's biggest town is two miles away. Alcohol cannot be sold on the rez, so Whiteclay fills a need and then some.

South Dakota's Indian reservations are places of massive unemployment, grinding poverty, and despair. Gasoline-, glue-, and solvent-sniffing kills unhappy adolescents. Fetal alcohol syndrome permanently damages many babies. Beer helps, short term. Activists both red and white have protested and marched into Whiteclay to try to stop this commerce in alcohol, mutilation, genocide, and death. Nothing has worked. Jobs, education, and a better economy might help. The little tribal casinos don't draw many tourists. I know. I went to one—in a double-wide.

Ten miles northeast of Whiteclay is Wounded Knee, the place of the slaughter (in 1890) that ended the Plains Indian wars, and gave the

Open road; Route 20 in Nebraska

Seventh Cavalry a chance to avenge its former commander, George Armstrong Custer, by shelling and killing two hundred ninety Lakota men, women, and children. The melancholy sign that marks the place once called it a "Battle." Now, more accurately, it has a patch covering "Battle" and reading "Massacre." In 1973 and 1975, Wounded Knee again figured significantly in American Indian history, but that is a story for another time and another book. See Peter Matthiessen's *In the Spirit of Crazy Horse.*

cowboys and settlers

Arthur Bowring Sandhills Ranch State Historical Park, just north of the Great Road, is a working cattle ranch morphing into a state park. It's got it all: barns, horses, cattle, cowboys, a bunkhouse, a nice ranch house, a good museum, and a name that's much too long and pompous. The Bowrings were well up in the state's social and political hierarchy, as big ranchers usually were and are. This institution demonstrates another good use for this land, retaining agriculture while emphasizing history and recreation. It is well worth a side trip and a stop. Among the mementos in the museum at the Bowring Ranch is a photo of a prosperous Nebraska ranch woman wearing a Nixon political button from 1956: "I Work for Dick." Hey, I'm just a reporter.

Just across from the Bowring Ranch is a mailbox with the name: "A. Sandoz. Bear Creek." The name "Sandoz" shows that we are now in the heart of the Sandhills, in vast Cherry County (larger than Connecticut), on our way from Valentine to Hay Springs, Gordon, Rushville, Chadron. This is and, I hope, always will be Sandoz Country.

Sandoz country : toil, heartbreak, loss, and triumph on the Great Road

There are no typical American immigrants or pioneers. From the aboriginal Indians and the Pilgrims to my European forebears and today's Asians, Latin Americans, Caribbeans, and Africans, very different peoples have come to North America for very different reasons. Poverty, hunger, and opportunity were usually involved. The Sandoz family of northwestern Nebraska is hardly typical, but it is representative, illustrative, and fairly well known, for one reason. Mari Sandoz

(1896–1966) was a hardworking and gifted writer, and many of her best stories are about her region, her own family and their experiences. She, even more than her pioneer father Jules, made this northwestern corner of Nebraska, its panhandle, into Sandoz Country.

Mari Sandoz's first book, published in 1935, was *Old Jules*, a biography not just of her father, Jules Sandoz, and his family, but of their entire immigrant community: farmers, ranchers, outlaws, Indians, women, children. It is tough, honest, painful, triumphant. It is the best book I know about the harsh lives of pioneers, especially of pioneer women. Laura Ingalls Wilder's books are sweet, but her publisher made her change one of her titles from "The Hard Winter" to "The Long Winter." Nothing "hard," please. Keep it light, upbeat, pleasant.

Old Jules : brutal patriarch

Nothing is easy in *Old Jules*, beginning with the character of the Swiss-German immigrant himself. In 1880, about to enter medical school, he left his well-to-do Swiss family in a rage after a quarrel. (The family would soon found a pharmaceuticals empire, starting with a dyestuffs factory in Basel in 1886.) Jules came to America and "proved up," successfully homesteaded, on a good parcel of Nebraska land, now known as "The River Place," on the Niobrara River. He was crippled and almost killed in a well accident, a practical joke gone wrong, in 1885. Ever after, he walked with a severe limp.

After the accident, his frightened, guilty friends left him for dead. He was found and taken to Fort Robinson, Nebraska, along what would become US 20, where an Army doctor from Virginia wanted to amputate his hideously injured leg. Old Jules told him that if he did, "I shoot you so dead you stink before you hit the ground" (Mari Sandoz, *Old Jules*, 43). His leg slowly healed, and the doctor lived, and a good thing, too. The doctor went on to fame by leading the team that conquered yellow fever, and has a nifty hospital in Washington, D.C., named after him—Walter Reed Army Medical Center. Without Dr. Walter Reed's work on yellow fever, it would have been almost impossible to build the Panama Canal.

Old Jules's disability later permitted him to leave the heavy work to his wife and children, and concentrate on hunting, quarreling, story-telling, and plant breeding. That suited him fine. He quickly went through three wives, some more legal than others, before landing the fourth, who stayed, bore him six children, and outlived him: Mary Fehr, also a Swiss immigrant. Old Jules didn't bathe or change clothes often. He was quick with blows for his wife and children. When he discovered his little daughter Marie was writing and thinking of publishing, becoming one of what he called the useless, lazy "maggots of society," he whipped her and locked her in the scary cellar. He was a crack shot, profane, hot tempered, always at war with some of his neighbors, especially the big money men who ran the Spade Ranch.

A display at the Bowring Ranch shows Old Jules's great enemy, Bartlett Richards, the unprincipled boss of the Spade Ranch. Like Theodore Roosevelt, he was an eastern dude who went west to try to improve his fragile health; like TR, he liked it, stayed, and became a cattle baron. Unlike TR, he stayed west and dominated a region. He had been preparing to enter Williams College, but he opted for western Nebraska. Before his twentieth birthday, he was running a half-million-acre cattle company. He ran afoul of the law and was jailed in 1905 for, among other things, illegally fencing open range land. He died in jail, aged forty-nine (display at Bowring Ranch). The owners of another big ranch had had Jules's brother, Emile, murdered by a hired killer while Emile sat at his own kitchen table. Adversity did not improve Old Jules's disposition, which had never been exactly sunny. He was, by the way, known as "Old Jules" even as a fairly young man.

"build up, build up"

Jules Sandoz was not a nice man, but he was smart and tough and talented, and he was a survivor. There were kinder sides to him. There was always a meal for a traveler at his house, and for the traveler's hungry family, too. Sometimes that meant that his own family went hungry. Mari coolly assessed herself as a child: "fifty-six [pounds], not much for thirteen" (ibid., 350). Old Jules was always ready to serve as a "locator," to help a new arrival stake out a claim and "find his corners," locate the precise boundaries of his land. For this, he charged little or nothing, as he wanted so badly to "build up, build up" the community.

His house was briefly the local post office, until he feuded with the officials and they took it away. Repeatedly. His place was the unofficial storytelling center of the community. His skinny daughter, Marie (later Mari), would hang back in the darkness to stay up and listen to the immigrants and Indians and, less frequently, the cowboys tell their tales.

Old Jules maintained a well-stocked medical kit and was the unofficial frontier doctor to one and all. He befriended the local Indians, some of the last Lakotas to live free in lodges, tipis, near his home. They called him "Straight Eye," honoring his shooting skill. He spent windfall money he could ill afford on a Victrola and phonograph records, because he liked good music and thought he and his family should have it. They loved it. Restless, he sold the attractive, well-watered River Place and developed a new claim on Mirror Flats in the drier Sandhills, planted fruit orchards, and opened a store.

the daughters of Mary and Old Jules Sandoz

He and Mary had six children. The oldest was Mari, named and called Marie in her youth. The sixth and last was Caroline, born in 1910, who is my source for everything I say here that doesn't come from Mari's work or her archives. I twice interviewed her for this book in her remote and beautiful Sandhills home.

Old Jules became a nationally known fruit breeder and grower, a correspondent of Luther Burbank. He was sure that his land was ideal for raising cherries and plums and apples. He was wrong. It wasn't. As his daughter Caroline tells it: sure, they had good years, bushels of fruit. But when they did, so did the neighbors, and the prices sank, just as crop prices do today. And they had bad years, too, as what farmer doesn't? If this land was made for any sort of economically productive agriculture, it was for what dominates it today—cattle ranching. It is covered with well-watered grass. Old Jules would have hated that truth, would never have admitted it, because he wanted more and more farmers to "build up" the community, but truth it is.

Caroline says that almost all the old families—though not all of the Sandozes—are gone now. So is much of the population, which was never large. Two of *Old Jules's* terse chapter titles are "The Kinkaider Comes" and "The Kinkaider Goes." That is, a second generation of new people came to prove up on six hundred and forty acres of land under the 1904 Kinkaid act. Most didn't make it, and they soon left, often selling out to the cattle barons.

The Poppers' Buffalo Commons argument doesn't specify the Sand-hills, but it certainly applies to them. Only along US 20, in the extreme north of the state, are there towns of any size, and many of them are slowly dying. It's more than a hundred miles from Gordon, on US 20, south to the North Platte River and the next big town. Western Nebraska is part of The Big Empty, The Empty Quarter. The Sandhills' second leading export (after beef) must be young people.

a hard life, a writer's life

Mari left home, too, in her day. Divorced and alone, she went to Lincoln in 1919 to try to get an education and become a writer. She was grindingly poor. She had sight in only one eye, having lost the other as a child rescuing cattle from a literally blinding snowstorm. She filled pill bottles in Lincoln to scrape together a living, and she often did not have enough to eat.

Though she had been a frontier schoolteacher, she had had almost no formal schooling, and she was only just permitted to attend classes at the University of Nebraska. She thrived in the writing classes, but she couldn't afford to stay and finish college. She went home, malnourished and defeated, after burning most of her early writings in the back yard of her lodgings in Lincoln. (There's a large apartment building there now.)

The Depression only made things worse. Mari built a lean-to room on a family barn and worked hard on her writing, a novel and a biography of her late father. The novel is *Slogum House*, a powerful naturalistic tale of an evil matriarch and her family, straight from her Sandhills experience. Its lurid ending depicts a nasty Slogum being accidentally strangled and borne in circles through the air by the windmill he had been repairing. A display at the Bowring Ranch states that one Spade Ranch worker "strangled when his coat got caught in the bevel wheel of a windmill tower." Writers find their material in unexpected places.

Had the biography *Old Jules* not been accepted for publication when it was, after sixteen rejections, Mari Sandoz might not have been able to continue her career as a writer. She had almost given up, and had returned to Lincoln to take an editorial position at the Nebraska State Historical Society. Then *Old Jules* became a Book-of-the-Month Club selection. Mari persevered, and became a distinguished Western historian as well as a writer of fiction, for both adults and children. Her subsequent career was successful, though her kind of writing, her frequently harsh and earthy language, her populist subjects, were too near some dangerous edges to bring her wealth and great popularity. Her prose is not always apt and idiomatic. Her first language was not English, but the Schweizerdeutsch of her parents.

Mari's was the first retelling of the Battle of the Little Big Horn to make major use of Indian sources. She traveled the local reservations extensively, and interviewed some of Crazy Horse's fellow warriors, such as the blind old He Dog, almost sixty years after Crazy Horse's death. She wrote excellent fictions about young Plains Indians for young adults. She

Mac with Caroline Sandoz Pifer, at her home in the Sandhills, Nebraska
Photo by Elizabeth Hoffman Nelson

was a flinty and contentious sort, quick to quarrel with her publishers: something of her father in that. Like many young Sandhillers then and now, when she could leave, she left. She left the Sandhills and Lincoln, and Nebraska, too.

She lived in Denver for a time, then moved permanently to Greenwich Village, New York City, the center of American letters in the thirties and forties. She loved being there; it was her home until just before her death from cancer. Yet she did at last return to the Sandhills. Her grave now stands alone on a beautiful, sunny, east-facing slope on family land. It was her expressed wish to be buried there, where she had no desire to live.

The Sandhills today are rich well-watered grasslands, surprisingly dotted with many small lakes, still producing fine beef cattle. On the nearly ten miles of dirt road to the house where Caroline Sandoz Pifer lives alone, visitors must compete with cattle for the right of way. Grassland birds are everywhere, and Caroline is a birder. She owns ten thousand acres. "Oh, that's nothing out here!" she says. Her land has become a wildlife sanctuary.

Poppers or no, the Sandhills seem to be reverting, at least in part, to what they were before Old Jules Sandoz and Mary Fehr and their contemporaries arrived. Is it sad that their lives and their backbreaking work had so little permanent impact? Perhaps not, so long as this beautiful land endures. I do find the Great Plains beautiful, though many do not. I really enjoy driving across this "flyover" land. It does not seem flat and boring to me. I remember reading some grumpy environmentalist who

Mari Sandoz's grave, Sandhills, Nebraska

Sandhills, Nebraska

accused those who undervalue grasslands of being "treeist" and "moun-
tainist," of overvaluing lush and/or spectacular landscapes. Those terms
are roaringly silly, but they make a point—there is great if subtle beauty
in these rolling steppes. "Why would I want to live anywhere else?" asks
Caroline, a "born Sandhiller," as she sometimes signs herself.

a tribute to a High Plains storyteller

Gordon, Nebraska (pop. 2,167), on US 20, is Caroline's shopping
town. Indians are conspicuous on the main street. Gordon gained notoriety in 1972 with the beating death of an Indian named Raymond Yellow
Thunder, and the angry, organized American Indian Movement's
response to it. I once stayed the night on US 20 in nearby Chadron, getting into the motel room just in time to (a) avoid getting caught on the
road in a tornado, and (b) enjoy the wild storm from the motel window.
This is Tornado Alley, and it was quite a show.

Alliance, Nebraska, is fifty-six miles south of Chadron and US 20,
yet I must mention two sites there. The first is the pretty cemetery north

Carhenge

of town where Old Jules and Mary Fehr Sandoz are buried. The second
is also north of town, within sight of the cemetery. On a long weekend
in 1987, a local family got together dozens of old cars, some large construction equipment, and probably a few cases of beer, and produced
Carhenge. It is just what it sounds like—a classic, unique, absurd American parody/imitation of Stonehenge, with junked cars substituting for
the neolithic dolmens and lintels. There is even a heel-stone (a half-
buried sedan) in the middle distance. The other people who were there
when I visited didn't seem to know quite how to take it. I think I did. I
laughed and laughed, and, cued and permitted, so did the others. It is
supremely silly, and great fun.

The next morning, after the tornado, on a day clear and sunny, I visited a good museum and a campus, and got an unexpected bonus. The
Museum of the Fur Trade, a small institution east of Chadron, has a vast
collection of historic guns, other good displays, and a roofed dugout that
recreates the feel of the famous old trading post there, maintained on the
Great Road from 1837 to 1872 by James Bordeaux. It is on the National
Register of Historic Places.

The campus is Caroline Sandoz Pifer's alma mater, Chadron State
College, "fifty years of Liberal Education, 1949–1999." I did my morning run across the pretty campus just after dawn, past the small football
stadium where the Eagles soar. There was a room devoted to Mari Sandoz memorabilia, though I didn't see it. The room in Caroline's basement was much more important, a research trove exceeded only by the

Save a fencepost with an old boot : Route 20 in western Nebraska

vast Sandoz collection I gratefully mined at the University of Nebraska's Love Library in Lincoln.

One prominent Chadron State campus building I ran by had a sign announcing the "CSC Tiospaye." Tiyospaye is a Lakota word meaning, roughly, "clan, extended family." How cool, a club, a meeting place, an extended family for Lakota students, who can surely use some social support in college. And then a wonderful surprise: a very nice older building, clearly one of the almost seventeen hundred Andrew Carnegie Libraries in the United States, had become "the proposed Mari Sandoz High Plains Research Center." It was in the process of renovation in 2001; it is now a going concern, with a striking bronze statue of Mari. It is now called the Mari Sandoz High Plains Heritage Center, a name warmer and fuzzier than "Research Center."

I talked to a nice construction guy working at the site early that morning. He didn't know anything about Mari Sandoz. He thought maybe she was some rich donor, a very reasonable guess. He was really pleased to hear that she'd been a dirt-poor Sandhills kid who'd made good. His daughter was going to Chadron that fall—he'd be sure to tell her. How delightful that this indomitable woman is getting her due in her own neck of the woods.

And how nice for Chadron State College that it's doing what Galena did with U. S. Grant: gaining glory by associating itself with a distinguished figure who had little to do with it in life. Mari did finally get a college degree, though not from Chadron State. It came in 1950—an honorary Doctorate of Literature degree from the University of Nebraska,

MARI SANDOZ
1896 - 1966
NOVELIST-HISTORIAN
FRIEND OF THE INDIAN

Bust of Mari Sandoz in the Nebraska Hall of Fame in Lincoln
Photo by Elizabeth Hoffman Nelson

which her poverty had forced her to leave. Though she had taught in a one-room school, her highest previous academic achievement had been an eighth grade diploma. Caroline told me that Mari cherished that degree.

There's a handsome bust of Mari Sandoz in the Nebraska Hall of Fame on the ground floor of the towering Nebraska State Capitol in Lincoln. She had written a scathing leftist novel, *Capital City*, about the greedy and fatuous society of the capital of the fictitious state of "Kanewa" (i.e., Kansas, Nebraska, Iowa). No one was fooled; nor, probably, did she want them to be. People snarled at her in the streets of Lincoln. It's very nice to know that her state has accepted her and now values her for what she was—a chronicler of Nebraska's greatness as well as its hardness and meanness. We need our Story Catchers (the title of one of her best young adult books), our Truth Tellers, and she was a fine and fearless one. She brought further distinction to the literary tradition of the Great Road.

chapter five

soldiers and Indians

the struggle for a continent

hostile encounters

♦   This chapter begins where the last left off, west of the Sandhills near Chadron, Nebraska. It may seem odd not to have finished discussing Nebraska there and then, but there is a reason. This chapter emphasizes conflict, not agriculture; racial and cultural struggle, not immigration. Northwestern Nebraska is rich soil for a piece of one of the most discreditable stories in American history: the Indian Wars.

The Indian Wars began a long way from Nebraska, though not far from the Great Road.[1] I know and love one stretch of the beach of Cape Cod Bay—"First Encounter Beach." I run there some May mornings. The name is a euphemism for the first skirmish between Anglo whites and Indians in New England. The Pilgrims first set foot on American land in Eastham, Massachusetts, on Cape Cod, not across the bay in Plymouth. They dug up some graves and took some sequestered Indian corn. There they "encountered" a group of Indians and exchanged shots and arrows with them. Some "encounter." The first encounter was a hostile one, as were so many to follow.

Another *"first* encounter," if first means "primary," really big, was George Armstrong Custer's disastrous attack, defeat, and death at the Little Big Horn, the Greasy Grass, in June of 1876. Talk about bad timing! Just before the nation's Centennial, just when this illustrious Civil War hero and Indian fighter may have been hoping to be nominated for president, he went and got killed, together with more than 260 of his men—all of his immediate command. That was some encounter, too. For more on Custer, see chapter 3.

Three weeks later, an American Army scout, William F. Cody, is said to have killed a Cheyenne chief, Yellow Hand, in a bloody little "encounter" that has become known as The Battle of Warbonnet (or Hat) Creek, July 17, 1876. A hyper-dramatized version of this feat appeared frequently in Buffalo Bill Cody's Wild West. The legend states that Cody shot and killed the Cheyenne chief, ran to his body, scalped him, and waved the scalp in the air, shouting, "This is the first scalp for Custer!" Always a great showman, that Bill Cody. Modern historians state that the victim was actually a young warrior named Yellow Hair, not the more important Yellow Hand. Buffalo Bill made sure that it was Yellow Hand in the show. That's show biz.

This tiny skirmish—one death—was of some importance. The Fifth Cavalry stopped a large group of Cheyenne warriors who had left their agencies, intending to join the victorious Cheyenne and Sioux leaving the Little Big Horn. They were driven back to their agencies, in keeping with government policy. There is a marker denoting the place of this battle, in the Nebraska National Forest, about twenty miles north of US 20, just south of the South Dakota border.[2] I begin with this story of this small encounter because of when it happened, so soon after the Custer fight. That greatest of American Indian military triumphs soon turned, ironically, into Indian disaster.

the real payback for Custer

The U.S. Government and the U.S. Army could not let such a great Indian victory go unpunished, so most of the "hostiles" were quickly pursued and almost as quickly killed, or rounded up and forced onto reservations. Never mind that Custer and the Seventh Cavalry had attacked an unsuspecting and peaceful Indian gathering. Never mind that the Lakota and Cheyenne had been defrauded and cheated in all their dealings with the whites, most notably by Custer himself. He had led soldiers and miners into the Black Hills in 1874 after the federal government had signed a treaty in 1868 giving the Black Hills to the Lakota forever. Justice had nothing to do with this 1876 campaign against the Indians—it was economics and conquest, pure and simple.

Meanwhile, there was great tension and unease at the important military outpost of Camp Robinson, near Crawford, Nebraska, on the Great Road. Two Lakota leaders, Red Cloud and Spotted Tail, had been granted agencies, embryonic reservations, for their people nearby, under the watchful eye of the U.S. Army. These were the agencies that the band of several hundred Cheyenne warriors left in July 1876, to be intercepted and turned around at Warbonnet Creek.

Red Cloud's is a particularly interesting life story. He had gained respect early for his courage and sagacity. Indeed, that was the only way to become a leader among his people. He fiercely opposed the white man's advance into Lakota territory. He refused to "touch the pen," sign a treaty, that gave up Indian territory. He opposed the whites' building and defending the Bozeman Trail into Montana, a trail the Lakota called "The Thieves' Road." Red Cloud led the successful concerted Indian war effort to expel the whites from this trail and the forts they had built along it. He helped to win the Fetterman Fight (or Massacre) near Fort Phil Kearny in December 1867, the worst U.S. Army defeat in the West before the Custer debacle. A treaty very favorable to the Lakota soon followed. For more on Fetterman, see below.

The Army grudgingly withdrew in 1868, leaving Fort Phil Kearny and the other forts to be burned by the victorious Indians, giving them total, if brief, control of the Bozeman Trail. Red Cloud and his people had temporarily halted the white advance—a remarkable achievement of warfare and diplomacy. But as Red Cloud saw more and more whites come near or into his territory, and as he four times traveled to Washington, D.C., he came to know that further resistance was useless. His people were simply overwhelmed. He was courageous, but not foolish. He gave in, made permanent peace, signed a treaty, and retired to a quiet life in a square frame house at his agency near Camp Robinson, where he would die in 1909.

a great man's life and death

Not all Plains Indian leaders or Indian bands felt or did the same. Two major leaders held out: Sitting Bull and Crazy Horse. Sitting Bull's story has little to do with the Great Road. He led his Hunkpapa Lakota people to freedom in Canada in 1877, came back when they were starving there in 1881, and joined Buffalo Bill's Wild West show for a year (1885), giving away most of his wages to the urban poor of North America and Europe. Like the sixteenth-century Indian savages Montaigne quotes, Sitting Bull could not understand why so many poor people should go hungry in the midst of such plenty. Montaigne and I both ask, ironically: Who were the real savages? Sitting Bull eventually retired to a cabin on his Standing Rock Reservation in northern South Dakota. Thought to be a threat during the Ghost Dance days, he was killed by reservation police in the fateful month of December 1890, two weeks before the massacre of Wounded Knee. He was close to the bitter truth when, late in his life, he said, "There are no Indians left but me."

Crazy Horse's story is more closely related to the Great Road. He is as important a figure as Sitting Bull, and more elusive. Mari Sandoz's magnificent fictionalized biography of him is entitled *Crazy Horse: The Strange Man of the Oglalas*. He was "strange" not only to whites, but often puzzling to his own people as well. He was light-skinned, and of average height or less. He almost never spoke in council. He was fearless in battle, often choosing the dangerous work of the decoy, getting perilously close to the enemy, drawing their fire, and enticing them into ambush. If the enemy was foolish—as was Captain Fetterman—this tactic was deadly.

Crazy Horse seemed impervious to bullets, and he may have believed that he was. His vision quest dream had told him that he would not be killed by enemies, but would die only when betrayed by his own people. He often dismounted from his horse to make his shooting more accurate, something no one remembered anyone doing before him. He was so respected as a leader that he was able for brief periods to shape the warriors who followed him into an effective tactical military force, not simply a collection of foolishly brave risk takers to whom counting coup[3] and gaining glory was more important than defeating the enemy. The Fetterman Massacre, the Battle of the Rosebud,[4] and the Battle of the Little Big Horn were three such tactical triumphs—all major Indian victories. Crazy Horse was a leader at all of them. But the buffalo were almost gone by 1877, tens of millions of them slaughtered by whites, partly to force the Indians into submission, and his people had little to eat. Even this proud and fiercely independent leader knew that his people could take no more, and in May 1877 he came in, surrendered, at Camp Robinson. Those who watched said that the parade of his people seemed more like a triumph than a surrender. He asked for and was promised his own agency for his people.

a hero's death at Camp Robinson

Red Cloud is said to have objected to this, fearing Crazy Horse's power. Other men misinterpreted his behavior and his words, making him seem more aggressive and threatening than he was. He "went out" again to hunt for buffalo, and was brought back and taken to the camp's jail. The plan was to send him to prison, probably to Florida to the Dry Tortugas Islands.[5] Crazy Horse realized what was happening when he saw bars in the windows of the jail. This freest of men drew a knife to fight his way out. His former comrade, Little Big Man, pinned his arms, receiving a severe cut in the process. Someone shouted something like, "Stab him! Kill the son of a bitch!" A soldier on guard duty bayonetted him twice and he sank to the ground, mortally wounded, betrayed by his own people, as his vision had foretold. (The parallel to Jesus betrayed by Judas is moving and inevitable, but it would have made no sense to Crazy Horse.) They took him into the adjutant's office next door, where he refused to lie on a bed, preferring the earth. He died around midnight, on September 5, 1877, after telling his father, Worm, and his tall friend Touch-the-Clouds, to tell the people they could not depend on him any more. He was in his middle thirties (Mari Sandoz, *Crazy Horse: The Strange Man of the Oglalas*, New York: Knopf, 1942, passim).

His parents took his body, exposed it to decay in Lakota fashion, and buried his bones somewhere on what is now the Pine Ridge Reservation. No one living knows where; at least, no one is telling. "It does not matter where his body lies, for it is grass; but where his spirit is, it will be good to be," said his younger contemporary, the Lakota shaman, Black Elk (John G. Neihardt, *Black Elk Speaks*, New York: Pocket Books, 1972, 122). He Dog was Crazy Horse's old comrade-in-arms. Blind, in his eighties in the 1930s, he said of his own life, "Maybe it would have been better to die fighting" (Mari Sandoz, *Interview with He Dog*).

Today, travelers can take the Great Road to Fort Robinson, whose long and interesting military history stretched past World War II. Its life as an active post included periods as a cavalry barracks, a prisoner of war camp in the 1940s, and a training base for Army dogs. Reportedly, some of the aging cavalry horses became military Alpo. The fort has long been militarily decommissioned, and has become a Nebraska state park. It was also the site of the epic "Cheyenne Outbreak" in 1879, as a local sign calls it. Mari Sandoz wrote another excellent book about this epic event: *Cheyenne Autumn*. There is no reason to retell this painful story here; her account is definitive.

For me there is only one great story here, Crazy Horse's. Thomas Babington Macaulay called Tower Green, London's venue for centuries of royal beheadings, "the saddest spot in Christendom." A great American died—was murdered? assassinated?—here at Camp Robinson, and a people's freedom ended. The reconstructed jail at Fort Robinson is, for me, the saddest spot in the West.

sacred mountains : the Black Hills

The Black Hills are not on US 20, but they play an important part in the history of the Great Road, which is the historic southern access to them. The Black Hills of South Dakota are a huge uplift dome of volcanic rock, thrust up into the middle of a vast flat land. Higher than their surroundings, higher than any land form between the Atlantic Ocean and the Rocky Mountains, they are often green and wet when the plains around them are hot and dry. In the East, they would be called mountains. They appear dark, "black," from a great distance because of the dark green conifers that cover their moist slopes. They were sacred territory to the Indian tribes who lived nearby.

The Lakota, latecomers in this region, venerated the "Paha Sapa," the Black Hills, though they did not live there permanently. The Black Hills were their main source of trees for their tipi poles, and were one of the sacred places where their youths would go for vision quests to seek their destinies. The Lakota regularly held important gatherings there, and a few miles north and east, at Bear Butte. When the white man came west in great numbers, the Lakota grudgingly retreated from much of this vast and beautiful country. In 1868 they were given, by the treaty of Fort Laramie, exclusive rights to the Black Hills "so long as the rivers shall run and the grass shall grow." The builders of the transcontinental railroad wished to push the Oglala Lakota toward the Black Hills so that they would not interferfere with the construction of the railroad farther south. The hills were thought to be unsuitable for farming and white settlement in any case. Six years later, in 1874, gold was discovered in the Black Hills, and the U.S. Army, pledged by treaty to keep whites out, led them in. So much for treaties with savages. The Custer fight in 1876 was one consequence of this treaty breaking.

The terrible ironies of this history are manifest in the Black Hills today. Few corners of the United States are more lovely; and few are more degraded. The northern Black Hills are full of cheesy tourist attractions and billboards that blot the landscape. Casinos have overwhelmed and destroyed the once appealing authentic Old West town of Deadwood, where Wild Bill Hickock was murdered and is buried. Lead (pronounced "Leed"), Deadwood's mining neighbor, is boom or bust, mostly bust, depending on the world price of gold. Sturgis is great if you're a Harley-Davidson; it is the Mecca of the bawdy annual pilgrimage of thousands of hogs and their riders. Nearby Bear Butte may soon lose its sacred character to noisy development to accommodate these bikers.

Many of the northern Black Hills towns are as bad or worse, mostly wall-to-wall T-shirt shops. Keystone, in the shadow of Mount Rushmore, is Four Blocks of Hideous, so awful it's almost fun. There are a few good stores in Keystone, notably one called The Indians.

Those small areas of the Black Hills that have been preserved as parks retain much of their original magic. Custer State Park and Wind Cave National Park, contiguous in the southern Black Hills, contain between them about a thousand bison, discreetly fenced in, but seeming to roam free. Some say that the emergence myth of the Lakota issues from Wind Cave, though I have not been able to confirm this and I am skeptical of it. These parks' roads and vistas are magnificent and unspoiled. The Old West is only a rumor to anyone who has not seen a hillside black with bison, or the cavorting red calves of a large summer herd. The degredation of the northern Black Hills should be a warning: this is what the entire West might become if we let it happen.

Crazy Horse would have hated it

About sixty miles north of Fort Robinson, in the heart of the beautiful Black Hills, a Polish-American sculptor's family is slowly progressing on an apparently endless task: creating the Crazy Horse Memorial by blasting an image out of the limestone of a mountain, as Gutzon Borglum did at Mount Rushmore. So far they've got a head, a model, and a plan: a REALLY BIG head and a REALLY BIG plan, much bigger even than Mount Rushmore.

The original sculptor, Korczak Ziolkowski, worked with Gutzon Borglum on Mount Rushmore. His rather ugly statue of Sitting Bull near Mobridge, South Dakota, is a famous target for sharpshooters and other vandals. Korczak Ziolkowski has been dead since 1982; work on the mountain has stopped and started again several times. The family charges a stiff admission to the site—ten bucks in 2006, or"$24 a carload"—to keep the work going. Their rap says that a Lakota chief approved of the memorial, even "requested" it. Maybe. Whites could always find some Indian to agree with them and "touch the pen," agree to a treaty that ceded Indian rights. Caroline Sandoz Pifer told me that her sister, Mari, admired the sculptor and liked his plan. Ian Frazier, in *Great Plains*, says it's the only place in the Black Hills where he saw "lots of Indians smiling." That's the good news.

Here comes the bad news.

I don't know if this thing is being done out of genuine respect for Indians and for Art, or as a gimmick to guarantee perpetual Ziolkowski family employment, and I don't care. Either way, it's a terrible idea. So far, the head that has emerged is nine stories tall ("eighty-seven and a half feet high") and butt-ugly, a caricature Indian. The plan is for the statue to be more than five hundred feet tall—"the largest statue in the world." And the most hideous.

It is deeply offensive to call this a "Crazy Horse Memorial." There are multiple photographic images of all the other nineteenth-century Indian leaders—Sitting Bull with his family at his lodge, or with his boss and sometime pal, Buffalo Bill; Geronimo at a campsite, with a rifle, or in a touring car. Some images, such as those of Edward Curtis, are gorgeous, noble, romantic. Some are bogus and cheesy.

But no one has ever produced an authentic image of Crazy Horse, because there aren't any. He saw to that. He refused to let anyone take his picture, just as he rejected most contact with whites. In short, we don't know what he looked like because he didn't want us to. How horrible, then, that his name is being used as the identity for this emerging monstrosity. It's right up there with a recent commercial product, "Crazy Horse Malt Liquor," and a lot harder to ignore. I cannot speak for this "strange man," but I think he would have hated it, too.

A side note: While I was working with the Mari Sandoz collection at the University of Nebraska Library, I asked about a painting on the wall. It was a painting that Mari had commissioned—a painting of Crazy Horse. It was, like her description of him, of a young, light-skinned Indian warrior. The subject was also a very handsome young man. Do all biographers fall in love with their subjects? Probably not, but Mari must have yearned to make her biographical portrait come to pictorial life, even though she admired his refusal to sit for a photograph. This might also explain why she favored the Crazy Horse Memorial, if she did.

Let's let it all hang out here: Mount Rushmore National Memorial, that most sacred of American icons, is almost as bad as the Crazy Horse Memorial. The four presidents' portraits are striking, and they are not ugly. They were all great leaders, though TR just got his spot on the mountain at the last minute. The Memorial's Park Service Superintendent, Gerard Baker, is a Native American, though he's Mandan-Hidatsa, not Lakota. That's the good news.

The rest of the news is all bad. On a mountain ceded to and sacred to the Lakota, their conquerors have dynamited the faces of four leaders who, to different degrees, all helped kill Indians and destroy Indian cultures. A Native American group, Defenders of the Black Hills, would like it blown up. "We all hate Mount Rushmore . . . it's as if a statue of Adolf Hitler was put up in the middle of Jerusalem" (*Smithsonian*, May 2006, 83). Exactly. I respect the remarkable work that Mount Rushmore is, and I love this country, but I hate this place. End of rant, and end of the Great Road in Nebraska.

mile high, emptiness, ghosts

The elevation is nearing five thousand feet above sea level as US 20 enters Wyoming. Van Tassel, (pop. 8), is at 4,736. Antelope and tumble-weed, uprooted Russian thistle, begin to appear. So do huge freight trains with gondola cars full of coal, heading east toward electricity-gen-erating plants such as the one in Dunkirk, New York, that I can see on my commute.

US 20 passes "Node Post Office." No town, just a house.

We are *W*est.

Lusk is a sizeable town: pop.: 1,501. elev.: 5,015.

A historical marker sign fourteen miles farther west anounces a "ghost town," Jireh. According to the marker, there's a ghost college, too. As in the Middle West, town founders here liked to claim and trumpet higher education. The sign is the only thing left of Jireh, at least above ground. Frankly, this isn't much of a ghost town. A ghost town should be a place that once had a population that is now gone, or almost gone, with decaying buildings left to attest to it. There are hundred of such sites all over the West, most associated with boom-and-bust mining. They testify eloquently to the fleeting nature of human endeavor, especially in the dry, enormous West, beyond the hundredth meridian, west of the twenty-inch rainfall line.

Some are called "semi-ghost," like Crookston, Nebraska—see chapter 4. Some have dwindled and nearly died, then been revived, by retirees or hippies, like Jerome and Bisbee, Arizona. Some true ghost towns have been lightly commercialized and stabilized, like Shake-speare, New Mexico. One is a disguised amusement park—Cisco, Cal-ifornia, owned and operated by Knott's Berry Farm. Bodie, California, has become a fascinating state park. So has South Pass City, Wyoming—see my Introduction. In different ways, they're all inter-esting. But Jireh? No. There's nothing there, nothing above ground, at least. That it's on a major highway seems the only reason for the historical marker. Seeing most true ghost towns requires excellent directions, dirt roads and paths, and a hike.

interstates and cities and jackalopes

Sixty-three miles into Wyoming, US 20 briefly loses its independence and joins I-25. Ten miles farther on is the attractive little city of Douglas, which boasts the Wyoming Pioneer Memorial Museum. Its collection is diverse and rich, if a bit cluttered. There is a good little museum shop, and there was as well a fat, friendly dog named Maggie.

Douglas is renowned, or infamous, for its creation of a tourist attraction known as the Jackalope, a giant jackrabbit with antelope antlers. It is the Bigfoot of Bunnies. Postcards of this improbable exotic beast are for sale everywhere in Douglas, and there is a very large white statue of it in the center of town in a place of honor, "Jackalope Square." Except for the statue and the postcards, I've never seen one. Some spoilsport biologists want us to believe that the myth began with rabbits afflicted with papilloma virus; they may grow large warts that look something like horns (*New York Times*, August 29, 2006). I'm not buying it. I prefer imaginative Great Pumpkin-type explanations. I recall a Douglas guy's obit that claimed he had invented the jackalope just for fun, and maybe for a little PR for tourism. Maybe he got the idea from science. Good for him either way.

Indian fights and forts

Seven miles north of Douglas is Fort Fetterman State Historic Site, some restored buildings of an important fort named for one of the stupidest and most arrogant of American military leaders. Captain William J. Fetterman, posted fresh from West Point to Fort Phil Kearny on the Bozeman trail, boasted that he could ride through the entire Sioux Nation with eighty men. Eerily, that was the exact number in his command on December 21, 1866, when he disobeyed his commanding officer's explicit orders and led his men over a rise out of sight of the fort. They were decoyed, ambushed, and killed to a man— eighty-one—by the combined forces of Crazy Horse and Red Cloud. Their corpses were then mutilated. The site today clearly demonstrates exactly the route they took, and there is a memorial, just over the ridge,

Mac at Fetterman Massacre Memorial, Wyoming
Photo by Elizabeth Hoffman Nelson

near the point of the disaster. It's scary. No other battlefield I have ever seen gives such a graphic sense of what happened there, how, and why, though the Little Big Horn battlefield comes close.

Want to contact Wyoming's largest Harley-Davidson dealership? Just dial 1-800-Fat Hawg.

Near Glenrock, Dave Johnston's name is immortalized in a huge power plant belching carbon, sulphur, and fly ash into the Big Sky. Did anyone ask his permission, clear this with Dave?

W alert: These Interstate exits and entrances are protected by cattle guards. We are *West* for sure.

The road south to Ayres Natural Bridge Park at milepost 151 is very pretty and the little park is sweet. The natural bridge isn't much. A little strip mining and a lot of sagebrush are visible from US 20 here.

Casper, Wyoming, is named for Lt. Caspar [*sic*] Collins, a young soldier who admired and befriended Indians but died in an Indian skirmish anyway. So it goes in the American West. Some McMansions burned near there in the dry, fiery year of 2006; that's a growing theme in the globally warming West. Casper is the second-largest city in Wyoming, and, happily, the end of Interstate travel on US 20 until Oregon. Business 20 is "Yellowstone Street," a nice foreshadowing of what lies ahead, though Casper is almost three hundred miles from the park.

The reconstruction of 1860s Fort Caspar is detailed and interesting. There's a facsimile of a Mormon handcart in the excellent small museum. There's a good life-size model of part of an old toll bridge over the Platte, which was built and tended by Mormons as a moneymaker on their trek west. The price of the toll went up with the river; i.e., if it was shallow and easy to ford, they didn't charge as much. Sharp folks, those Mormons. There's a good little bookshop at the fort, specializing in things Western.

"this land is your land" : the BLM

As soon as the Great Road leaves the well-irrigated city, the land gets very dry and empty and open. It is desert, or nearly so. This part of the road is almost all on land managed by the Bureau of Land Management. The process of giving out free land to pioneers began in 1812 with the establishment of the General Land Office. Homesteading on free land swelled, then slowed and finally stopped in the 1930s, killed by the Depression and the Dust Bowl. When I was one month old, the General Land Office stopped giving out free land. In June 1934, hundreds of millions of acres, "the land that nobody wanted," remained unclaimed all over the West.

Unless you're a Westerner, you may never have heard of the BLM. Yet it administers almost as much land as the national parks and national forests combined—270 million acres—about one-eighth of the land surface of the United States. It is also responsible for regulating the use of the mineral rights to another three hundred million acres. Its stewardship of these lands is clearly of enormous ecological importance and economic consequence. That stewardship is very precarious, even more than that of the National Park Service or the National Forests, as it is consistently underfunded and under intense local political pressure.

The Taylor Grazing Service was given control of most of these lands in 1934. In 1946 it was joined with the Land Office to form the Bureau of Land Management. Today, more than eighteen million acres of Wyoming are managed by the BLM; the federal government manages almost half of the state. That federal control rankles many Westerners, and prompts such movements as "Wise Use" and "The Sagebrush Rebellion," local attempts to take control of federal lands.

Most of the public land is allotted to ranchers for cattle grazing, at very low rates. As of 2006, ranchers are charged a miniscule fee of $1.36 for each AUM, "Animal Unit per Month," one cow and her calf. Pennies: 2.3 cents per cow per day. In Wyoming, liberal mining provisions permit local companies to exploit mineral resources, chiefly coal and natural gas. Some regions of the BLM have long been closely connected to, even beholden to and controlled by, local business interests. Its critics sometimes disparagingly refer to the BLM as the "Bureau of Livestock and Mining."

That culture is slowly, sometimes painfully, changing. Under a 1967 charge (FLPMA, Federal Land Policy and Management Act), recreation and land and water conservation attained a higher priority in the BLM's activities, to the distaste of many Westerners. On Christmas Eve, 2002, the Bush administration announced a rollback of many of the Clinton rules to adminster these lands; so the tug-of-war between development and convervation continues. That rollback has since been rolled back; see chapter 8. The West has been reinvented many times. The New West that is now coming to birth will surely continue this social and political process.

back country byways and energy

This process and its conflicts are graphically visible on US 20 west of Casper, in the relatively empty middle of Wyoming. There are two BLM

"Back Country Byways" leading north off US 20. They demonstrate the BLM's admirable attempt to reach out to the public by citing the scenic values of some of their land. The South Big Horn/Redwall Backway is fifteen miles west of Casper, leading toward the Big Horn mountains in the far distance. This is open range. If you have an eye for spare beauty, you can find it here. Herds of antelope, from a few to dozens in a group, are common. Horned larks fly along the dirt road.

There are many signs of methane exploration. There is an enormous reserve of oil and natural gas here in the Powder River Basin, and gas is a relatively clean fossil fuel. Extracting it, however, has high environmental costs, especially the heavy use of scarce and precious water. Interestingly, many Powder River basin ranchers are just as strongly opposed to gas drilling as are Eastern environmentalists like me. Most ranchers are good stewards of their land, environmentalists of a different, more practical stripe. Some are now beginning to make common cause with those who oppose unbridled energy exploitation. Ranchers often do not own the mineral rights to the land they own and tend. They get nothing from the drilling's disruption, and they properly fear the pollution and degradation of their land and water. This is complicated by the fact that ranchers often do not own the land on which their cattle graze—much of it is leased from the BLM. This is an important, even historic struggle, still playing out. See, for example, Hannah Nordhaus's excellent "Confessions of a Methane Floozy," *High Country News*, December 25, 2006.

The Byway loops back to US 20 just west of another attraction— Hell's Half Acre. US 20, indeed the entire West, is rich in real estate owned or operated by Lucifer. There are two Hell's Half Acres on US 20 alone; the other is in central Idaho. This one is a three hundred acre eroded badlands area with pretty pastel colored cliffs and a small curio shop. Long ago, it was used by Indians as a buffalo jump: that is, a cliff to stampede buffalo over so they could more easily be killed, skinned, butchered, and consumed.[6]

The Byway rejoins US 20 at Waltman. The Bighorns are closer here, but the paved road is less attractive. There are oil and gas rigs and construction equipment everywhere, lots of heavy truck traffic, high tension electric lines. The scenic designation has been thoroughly trumped by the energy crunch. Chevron has a heavy footprint here. Thirty miles north of the Great Road is Teapot Dome, the locus of the great energy scandal of the corrupt Harding administration. The scandal, and a conviction for bribery, sent Warren G. Harding's Secretary of the Interior Albert B. Fall to prison for nine months. Contemporaries joked that he was so crooked that when they buried him, they had to screw him into the ground.

Bush administration Interior operatives such as Steven Griles are starting to serve prison sentences, too. Energy scandals in Interior are not just ancient history. Flaws in 1990s oil leases, hugely favorable to Big Oil, were covered up by department personnel until 2006. The Interior Department inspector general, Earl Devaney, said that "short of a crime, anything goes at the highest levels of the Department of the Interior." Tens of millions of dollars are involved (*New York Times*, September 15 and 16, 2006). Auditors have complained that Interior suppressed their efforts to recover millions of dollars from companies they say were cheating the government (*New York Times*, September 20, 2006). And Indian tribes have been shorted, cheated out of millions of dollars of revenues for oil pumped on Western Indian lands. The matter has been in litigation for a decade.

At Moneta, trying to get onto another Scenic Backway, I was held up by construction vehicles and a flagman, who quite correctly said, "There's a lotta work goin' on up there." The road north toward Lysite and Lost Cabin turned out to be a not-so-scenic Byway. In front of the colorful, low distant hills are signs like "Poison Gas Production—Hazardous." Thank you, Louisiana Land and Cattle Co. I'll try not to breathe. Cattle guards here, too. Cows and poison gas? Mmmmm. Yum.

Lysite is a tiny town built on a green patch, among cottonwoods along a small creek. The cafe is the "Eat & Run." Before the poison gas arrives? Lost Cabin is three miles farther, just a very big, very sumptuous old house built and left empty by a cattle baron who died in 1930. On the way back to US 20, I encountered a truck carrying a cargo of molten sulphur. Don't ask. I don't know either.

a great love story

Twenty-seven miles south of Moneta, off US 20 on a dirt road, is an archaeological area called Castle Gardens, which I did not visit. I have seen pictures of the pictographs there, and they are impressive. Even more impressive is the remarkable story of the Love family that homesteaded sheep ranches in this region for half a century. Their story has been beautifully told in two different media: in John McPhee's superb book *Rising from the Plains*, through Mrs. Love's journal and their son David's recollections; and in Ken Burns's lavish PBS Documentary *The*

West. I urge you to seek out this heart-tugging story in more detail. Here is a brief summary.

John Love, born on the southern Wisconsin farm of his legendary Scots uncle John Muir, went west in the 1880s, worked as a cowboy, and became a sheep rancher. His friends included Robert LeRoy Parker and Harry Longabaugh—Butch Cassidy and the Sundance Kid. He was on familiar terms with the legendary Shoshone Chief Washakie. In 1910, John Love won a recent Wellesley graduate for his wife; she had come west to be a teacher. They spent half a century in the lonely center of Wyoming, gaining and losing potential fortunes in sheep. Mrs. Love once described her future husband as a "muttonaire" (*Rising from the Plains*, 304). The Loves eventually grew old and frail, retired to town, and left the ranch forever. Its buildings are now empty and derelict. The Loves had nothing to show for their years of hard labor but love, Love, memories, and three high-achieving children. David Love, who survived growing up amidst highwaymen and rattlesnakes and droughts and floods and wild killer dogs, became the preeminent geologist of the Rocky Mountains.

Thermal Feature, Hot Springs State Park, Thermopolis, Wyoming

Washakie and the Wind River reservation

US 20 turns north at Shoshoni and runs through a beautiful canyon in the Wind River Indian Reservation to the town of Thermopolis, named for its historic hot springs. Wind River Canyon is shorter, eleven miles long, but almost as spectacular as the better known Glenwood Canyon in western Colorado, and a lot like it. It is probably less well known because of its obscure location. Near the northern end of the canyon, as the road rises through eons of geologic time, signs tell travelers they are moving swiftly from the Cambrian age, half a billion years ago, to the more modern Triassic. Down at the sparkling Wind River, the canyon is green and gorgeous. Farther north, beyond the canyon, this river is called the Bighorn.

Thermopolis, once part of the territory of the Shoshone, is just north of the canyon and off the rez now, as are its famous hot springs. Thereby hangs a tale, both of a region and a great man. In 1896, Washakie, the powerful old chief of the Eastern Shoshone, grudgingly gave up control of these hot springs. He insisted that they be kept freely available to all as a place of communal healing. They were known as a place where even enemies could come together peacefully and ease tensions. Earlier, in 1874, the federal government had extorted South Pass and its gold fields from Washakie and his people—for four cents an acre.

The hot springs area is still open to all; indeed, it's a state park, to which entry is free. The big outdoor hot spring ("World's Largest") is as impressive as all but the biggest thermal pools in Yellowstone. But the area is quite commercial now, tarted up with restaurants and water slides, and the outdoor pool and the premiere indoor pool cost fairly big bucks. There's a fine rich sulphur smell (not molten, I hasten to add), and happily screaming kids.

There is one small state bathhouse, sans bells and whistles, one pool where hot soaks are free. Technically, the promise to Washakie has been kept. During the four times that I have been there, the park has been busy, but no one was in the gloomy little state bathhouse. It's not surprising. A sign and a lonely attendant state the rules. You can soak for twenty minutes free. Then you must "leave the facility for two hours before you can return." So much for meditative relaxation and slowly bringing disputes to a peaceful resolution. HURRY UP AND SOAK!!!! RELAX RIGHT NOW!!!! Sorry, time's up. Get out. It's sad. I haven't tried it yet, in all my visits to Thermopolis. I should point out that the rap on this restriction is that more than twenty minutes could be bad for your health. Okay. Maybe.

Thermopolis also boasts the fairly new Wyoming Dinosaur Center, on a hill south and east of the center of town. It contains huge fossils excavated from the nearby Morrison formation. Kids love it, for the reasons Steven Jay Gould cited: because dinosaurs are "big, scary, and dead." There's a current flap (2006) among paleontologists over the center's acquisition of an archaeopteryx fossil, one of only ten of this lizard-to-bird life form known to exist. Some scientists sniff that it should not be housed in such an out of the way place, but instead be where scientists can examine it. Still, when it is goes on exhibit, it'll be another good reason to stop in.

The story of Shoshone Chief Washakie is about much more than hot springs. Early on, this courageous, intelligent man realized he could never resist the swarm of whites heading west, and he tried to accommodate without crumpling. He lived an enormously long life, essentially the entire nineteenth century. His gravestone in Fort Washakie gives his dates as 1804–1900.

He had been a great warrior. Crowheart Butte, which dominates the horizon for forty miles on his reservation, commemorates his response to criticism that he was getting too careful and passive to lead his people. It is said to have been so named because Washakie killed an enemy Crow there and ate his heart. No wimp, this. According to John McPhee in *Rising from the Plains*, John Love once asked his friend if he had "really eaten his enemy's heart?" Washakie said, "Well, Johnny, when you're young and full of life you do strange things." He was buried, with full military honors, in the only place in this country where a U.S. fort is named for an Indian—Fort Washakie, Wyoming. In 1868, he accepted this huge (it is larger than Yellowstone National Park), dry hunk of central Wyoming as his people's last retreating place. Along the western boundary of the rez is the gorgeous Wind River Range: thirteen of the fourteen tallest peaks in Wyoming are in the "Winds." Washakie thought that he and his people were home, and were done compromising.

Then his tribe's enemies, the Northern Arapaho, whipped by the U.S. Army and the Shoshone in 1874, needed a place to survive a hard winter. Washakie's place, of course. He hated the idea, but he knew they could go no farther, and he said they could stay for a while. The Arapaho have been there ever since. Their headquarters is about five miles east in Ethete. Indeed, the Arapaho now outnumber the Shoshone on Washakie's Wind River Reservation. That may be what you get for being hospitable and accommodating on the Great Road, or anywhere else in America.

Shoshone days

Every June the Eastern Shoshone put on Shoshone Days: a rodeo, a powwow, and sometimes a giveaway. Around one o'clock, the rodeo began with Indian singers and drummers, and a horrid taped country and western rendition of "The Star Spangled Banner." The Indian MC, from New Mexico, was a real pro—chatty, funny, informative, booster-ish. Cowboys and cowgirls lined up formally in the center of the ring, and the rodeo began with bull riding.

The rodeo was minor league. Only one of the young Indian contestants was able to ride his bull for the required eight seconds. On the other hand, the crowded bleachers were right next to the chutes, and giving superb views—and whiffs—of the livestock. It also gave a good view of the handsome Indian cowboys, such as Lamar Wandering Medicine: tight jeans, ribboned chaps, short hair, boots, Stetsons.

The Shoshone people had been a little vague on when the powwow started. I asked four different people. I was told it began at 4, 5, 5:30, and 6. It started around 7. Maybe a little later. "Indian Time" is a running in-joke that seems to be shared by American Indians all across the country. Things start whenever it's time to start them, not necessarily when they are scheduled to begin. They end when they're finished. This makes perfect sense, but it can drive planners, employers, and tourists nuts.

The first event was a giveaway, a special memorial dance. Giveaways are an important part of Plains Indian culture. In this case, the grandfather of a girl who had recently died honored her memory by saying a long prayer in his language. ("Never give an Indian man a microphone"—Sherman Alexie.) Family members carried large framed photographs of the girl as they slowly danced around the powwow ground. They were followed by anyone who wished to join to honor her. They shook hands with the family, went to the back of the line, and danced around the circle once. I have danced with my New York neighbors, the Senecas; I felt too much an outsider to join in here.

Next came the women's traditional dance contest, three different dances sponsored by the girl's family, who judged the competition. The family made another circle around the grounds, this time throwing coins as they danced for kids to run in and pick up. The powwow's announcer called out names and people went up to receive beautiful quilts and blankets and other gifts. The family placed small plastic baskets around the circle and invited anyone who wished to to take them. These gifts were items like pieces of cloth and apples. After nearly an hour, the girl's uncles led the final, "going home" dance. In some cultures, famously the Kwakiutl of the Northwest Coast, the lavish giving of most or all of one's wealth, the potlatch, was the primary route to prestige and power. In groups such as the Shoshone, it serves to honor the dead, to help the needier members of the society, and increase tribal solidarity. The dance was deliberate, stately, and moving.

My friend John Haddox tells a wonderful story about such Indian giving. He is an adopted member of the Pawnee nation. As a young man, he worked on the railroad one hot Great Plains summer—long, hard labor. His main aim was to save enough money to buy a beautiful shawl to give to a lovely young Pawnee woman he fancied. At a giveaway dance for the young woman's family, he danced around the circle with the other Pawnees, and gave her the precious shawl he had worked so long and hard for. She smiled, shyly acknowledging his gift. Later, as the dance continued, he saw "his girl" give "his shawl" to someone else! Astonished and angry, he saw still another person, then another, and another, giving and receiving *his* beautiful shawl. Ultimately, he understood. He had made the girl happy with his gift. She knew that giving it away would make other people happy and bond her people together. The gift was not the point. It was the act of giving that mattered.

The remainder of the Shoshone powwow was dance competitions for men and women: men's traditional, grass-dancing, and fancy dancing; women's fancy shawl and jingle dancing. It went on until twilight ended. There was also a "tiny tots" competition, which was predictably adorable; the winners of this received two dollars. Winners in the grownup categories make a lot more. Indeed, some Indians make a good living on "the powwow circuit."

sacred relics

There is another grave on the Wind River reservation even more celebrated than that of Chief Washakie. To the north, outside of town, in what one writer has called "the most beautiful cemetery in Wyoming," reputedly lies the body of Sacagawea, Bird Woman, the remarkable young Shoshone woman who traveled with the Corps of Discovery, carrying and nursing her infant son, Baptiste. She's a Madonna figure, complete with child. A Catholic priest on the reservation said in the 1920s that the woman buried here was Sacagawea.

Sacagawea's presence with Lewis and Clark was enormously valuable, but not because she was their guide; she wasn't. She helped them with trails and landmarks when they arrived in her home country, but that was all. She was invaluable in two other ways. The Indians they encountered immediately dropped suspicious, hostile attitudes when they saw the Americans traveling with a woman and a child: this could not be a war party. And her astonishingly fortunate meeting with her long lost brother, Cameahwhait, when the Corps desperately needed horses and help, is the most absurdly improbable coincidence in American history. Ridiculous, romantic, and true.

Does she lie here, next to her son, as the headstones state? All myths are true, aren't they? Every cemetery is entitled to its sacred relics, isn't it? Sacagawea's bones are important bones, and I'd surely like to claim them for *my* road. What a legend, what celebrity! There are more statues of Sacagawea in America than of any other woman. She has been elected to the Cowgirl Hall of Fame, in Fort Worth, Texas (Ken Burns and Dayton Duncan, *Lewis and Clark: The Journey of the Corps of Discovery*, New York: Knopf, 1997, 92). Could I make this stuff up?? She now shares celebrity with Lewis and Clark on the new, politically correct, trail signs. She is even on our golden dollar coin, and you don't get any bigger than that in the USofA! Larry McMurtry offers a hilarious insight about one famous incident involving her: "In the saga of the Charbonneaus—Toussaint the bumbling husband, Sacagawea the competent wife calmly picking up the articles that have floated out of the boat—you have the axle of American television comedies from *The Honeymooners* to *Malcolm in the Middle* . . ." (*Sacagawea's Nickname*, 2001, 148–49). "Sacagawea: the Sitcom!" "Sacagawea Simpson!" I love it.

Sad to say, she's almost certainly not buried here on the Great Road. There is a plausible account of Birdwoman's early death in December 1812, in her twenties. She died and was buried in her husband's home territory at or near Fort Manuel in what is now the Dakotas. The woman buried in Fort Washakie with her sons may well have been named Sacagawea. There were several Sitting Bulls and several Crazy Horses, too. The gravestone—the biggest in this colorful cemetery—says she died in 1884. Two stones flank hers; one for her adopted son "Bazil," and one supposedly for "Baptiste . . . Papoose [*sic*] of the LEWIS and CLARK expedition. . . ." It is a memorial stone for someone who died and was buried in 1885 "in the Wind River Mountains." But it's not the Baptiste that Sacagawea nursed and William Clark loved.

Baptiste Charbonneau was born to Sacagawea just before the Corps set out from their winter with the Mandans in the spring of 1805. He led a fascinating, cosmopolitan life. He was classically educated at the

Sacagawea's grave (sorta), Fort Washakie, Wyoming

expense of Captain William Clark, who loved the little boy and nick-named him Pompey. ("Pompey's Pillar" is still a minor landmark on the Missouri in Montana.) Baptiste toured Europe, learned music and several languages, met and served as a guide to the wealthy and famous, and caught gold fever. He died in southeastern Oregon in 1866 at the age of sixty-one, on his way to a gold strike, and is buried there, near the Great Road. Like his mother's, his was a remarkable, characteristic, questing American life.

There has been a big recent rush (2006) for natural gas just outside Washakie's Wind River rez, near Pinedale, Wyoming. As usual, it's boom and bust in the energy biz in Wyoming. Pinedale is a pleasant little town, its Museum of the Mountain Man a minimal tourist attraction. I hear that Pinedale has been outed by some magazine, and the locals are now either cashing in or lamenting the end of their quiet lives or both. I did my morning run in nearby Dubois once, when that town was still pretty sleepy. Even then, it had a lot of trailer housing, as do most towns in Wyoming. Now it's going BOOM too, and nobody in this area can hire enough motel and food service food workers. Is it too much to hope that the Eastern Shoshone might share in this bonanza? Probably.

Route 20 in central Wyoming

winter in June : Cody

The Bighorn River waters its lush valley as US 20 heads north through Worland. Twenty West actually runs almost straight east for a few miles.

Hand-scrawled business sign on Twenty in Basin, Wyoming:

> Mountain Man
> Crap and Salvage

The land here is relatively green and flat and populated; there are even some row crops in the irrigated fields, not just cattle grazing. Horses are everywhere. In these high plains, winter leaves grudgingly. On one thirteenth of June, I felt my way west on Twenty from Greybull to Cody through a dark afternoon snowstorm, the road slippery, snow blowing around the sagebrush and covering the ground. The radio said that my goal, Yellowstone National Park, was temporarily out of reach. East Entrance: Closed. Beartooth Pass: Closed. Dunraven Pass, in Yellowstone: Closed. Call this number at nine A.M. tomorrow. Stuck. Time to be philosophical, enjoy the town, and hope for a thaw. Yellowstone Ranger Aphorism: "There are two seasons in Yellowstone—Winter and July." July was still eighteen days away. The Great Road here crosses the Bridger Trail, blazed in 1864 by the famous scout and explorer Jim Bridger. He used it to lead immigrant trains to the Montana gold fields without ruffling the feathers or attracting the rifle shots of the Lakota, who dominated much of this territory in the 1860s. The trail is more than five hundred miles long, essentially from Casper, Wyoming, to the northern Bozeman Trail and Virginia City, Montana.

Although Cody is more than fifty miles from Yellowstone's East Entrance, it is a "gateway town," i.e., a town at or near a major entrance to a major national park. That can be both an economic blessing and a social curse. Gateway towns tend to become tacky tourist traps—cf. Gatlinburg, Tennessee—and Cody does have more than its share of shopping strips and blowsy attractions. Furthermore, it's not exactly an old Wyoming town. It was founded in 1896 by real estate speculators and front man Buffalo Bill Cody much as his Wild West show was—as showbiz and as an investment. Improbably, Jackson Pollock, the great abstract expressionist painter, came into the world there in 1912. Cody is where it is because its winter climate is usually milder than is most of northern

Yup, we're west, all right. Laundromat in Cody, Wyoming mall

Wyoming, because of chinooks, warm winds that come south from Canada down the mountain front. Buffalo Bill was always a commercial creation. His fame as scout, hunter, and mythic hero owed as much to dime novelist Ned Buntline, who gave him his catchy nickname, as to Western derring-do. The town of Cody is just such a creature of marketing and publicity.

Yet both Cody and its eponymous founder are hard not to like. Is Old Trail Town just an odd assemblage of old buildings of modest importance? Yes. Are the nightly summer rodeos and staged gunfights in the streets (check out the purported prostitutes in bright red bloomers) sheer tourist claptrap? Sure. It makes little difference. Who am I, raised on *The Lone Ranger*, *Shane*, and *High Noon*, to separate the bogus from the authentic? Or even from the authentically bogus? Buffalo Bill was a crack shot and a promotional genius. A great showman, he brought The Wild West to the world, which loved every minute of it. He seems to have been a sweet man with a taste for pretty women and the bottle, a soft touch for the down and out, and a good, though not always provident, businessman. He was a friendly and respectful employer of Indians. In addition to hiring Sitting Bull in 1885, he employed a young Black Elk to work in his show from 1886–1889. Forty years later, Black Elk, who as a boy observed some of the 1876 Custer fight, would create the important book *Black Elk Speaks*.

Bill Cody made a *lot* of money and lost almost all of it. "Buffalo Bill hauled in the equivalent of about $30 millions in today's dollars overseeing his Wild West show at Chicago's Columbian Exposition in 1893. . . . A financial panic in 1907 ruined him and his show; when he died there wasn't enough money in his till to pay for his burial" (*New York Times*, "Why the Rich Go Broke," September 17, 2006). The town of Cody is mostly showbiz, and pretty good showbiz at that. Dinner at the historic old Irma Hotel, named for Buffalo Bill's daughter, is fun, even if the country music is too loud.

Cody's Buffalo Bill Historical Center is superb, especially the Whitney Gallery of Western Art. Only the Heard Museum in Phoenix may outdo it, and the emphases of the two collections are very different. Cowboys and Indians dominate here, pueblos and kachinas there. (I should note that I have not yet seen the Amon Carter Museum in Fort Worth, Texas, or the Gene Autry museums in Los Angeles. I hear The Old Cowboy, whom I saw riding Champion at a rodeo in Kansas City in 1941, had quite a collection.) There's an overly grand equestrian statue of Bill Cody. His boyhood home, a house moved here from south of the Great Road in

Iowa, is on the grounds. He should surely be buried here, too, but an entrepreneur spirited his bones to Golden, Colorado, where they are still a successful tourist attraction. A sizeable sum was paid for the use of these famous relics. Remember, Bill Cody died almost broke.

LDS kids re-enacting Mormon history, Cody, Wyoming

The Buffalo Bill Historical Center firearms collection is commercialized, huge, and mind-boggling, but instructive. It connects back to the Springfield Armory on the Great Road in Massachusetts, where many of the repeating rifles that "won the West" (or stole it, if you're an Indian) were designed and made.[7] The Plains Indian section is very good, as is the newer Draper Natural History Museum. Cody would be a must-see stop if it offered nothing more than this excellent museum complex. Also in Cody is a huge mural on the dome of the local LDS Temple, depicting the early history of the Latter Day Saints. When I was there, some Mormon kids were dressed up as Mormon pioneers, posing for pictures on the front steps. Mormons love to reenact their story, and a wondrous story it is.

a strange ghost town, with a heart

North of Cody, Heart Mountain, named for its odd cleft shape, dominates the landscape. It shelters an unusual Western ghost town that recalls a sad moment in American history. It was the site of one of ten internment camps built to jail Japanese Americans in 1942. Here and elsewhere, 120,000 American citizens who had committed no crime were held in prison for three years without legal recourse. George W. Bush's first Secretary of Transportation, Norman Mineta, was, at the age of eleven, one of the internees at Heart Mountain.

A huge smokestack and three decrepit dormitory barracks buildings remain on the bare plateau under Heart Mountain. There is a moving memorial to the people who shivered there and tried to lead normal American lives after being torn from their homes, mostly in warm California. Four hundred sixty-eight barracks buildings without running water housed the internees. They ate in mess halls, and handled their washing and toilet needs in separate utility buildings. A faculty union friend of mine was jailed as a child in such a camp near Parker, Arizona. When his family was finally permitted to return to the Imperial Valley in California, they had lost their farm. His mother soon committed suicide. Ike (Akira) survived, and he attends reunions in Parker. The human

Japanese internment camp barracks, Heart Mountain, Wyoming

spirit is indomitable. At Heart Mountain there is a typical veterans' honor board with the names of some very atypical veterans: men who were freed from this prison to fight for their country (in Europe, not in Asia) in World War II in "The Fighting 442," an infantry division. There is soon to be an "interpretive walk" built there to commemorate this needless suffering. Good.

It must have been dreary and awful in these uninsulated barracks in the long, cold winters. A striking *Life Magazine* photographic record of the grim lives of the people jailed here is on permanent display in the Bannock County Historical Museum in Pocatello, Idaho, just south of the Great Road. The *Life* photographers were Hansel Mieth and Otto Hagel. Gretel Ehrlich's moving novel *Heart Mountain* chronicles the interaction of a local ranch family with the internees, and the internees' struggles with despair, idleness, and racism. A trove of eight hundred Dorothea Lange photographs of internees at the camp in Manzanar, California, has been rediscovered and published by W. W. Norton. "They tell us that conditions in the camps were much worse than most people think" (Linda Gordon, *New York Times*, November 6, 2006). The Park Service has recently been enjoined to preserve these melancholy places. Good again, so long as it doesn't further dilute the slender NPS budget or divert them from their other responsibilities.

Cody folks know the Heart Mountain story, the older ones fondly, if inaccurately, remembering the camp. "It was the biggest town in Wyoming." Well, no, but at more than 10,700 souls in 1944 it would seem to have nosed out Rock Springs for fifth place, and that's impressive enough. "Some of the families liked it here and stayed after the war." True, though not in the camp, to be sure. "Some farmers and ranchers made a good thing out of provisioning the camp." Sure. This was ranching country and there were profits to be made. This was and is America.

But people don't come here to see hotels, dioramas, murals, or internment camps, nor to relive the Indian wars, where this chapter began.

Yellowstone is waiting.

chapter six

the best idea:

Yellowstone, the peaceable kingdom

getting there

◆   The most dramatic approach in all of American westering is one
that the Great Road just misses—the Tetons rising suddenly, stunningly
high, eight thousand feet above the high plains of central Wyoming. In
this book, we'll see them from US 20 in Idaho, on the west, the other side.
Wyoming's US 20 takes us west from a touristy cowboy capital, Cody,
along one of the many roads claimed to be "the most scenic in America."
If you favor this route, you have on your side the author of that quote,
former cowpuncher and president Teddy Roosevelt, a man given to
sweeping enthusiasms.

He was right; it is gorgeous. It is now officially "The North Fork
Scenic Highway," that is, a pretty road along the North Fork of the
Shoshone River. The Shoshone National Forest was America's first,
established by President Grover Cleveland in 1891. Now nearly two hundred million acres are so designated, and the last, best hope for retaining
large wild areas in the lower forty-eight lives in them. The Absaroka and
Washakie Wilderness Areas are on the north and south sides of the road
respectively, and trailheads invite you to enter them from US 20.

In my opinion, there are no bad ways into Yellowstone, only bad
ways out. All ways out are, by my definition, bad. There are two other
ways to come into Yellowstone from the east, and they're even more
breathtaking: Chief Joseph Highway, Wyoming 296 via 120 and the
Sunlight Basin from Cody—more on this route later; and US 212 from
Red Lodge, Montana, the justly celebrated and highly vertiginous
Beartooth Highway.

Chief Joseph Highway, Sunlight Basin

Just west of Cody on US 20 are some things worth seeing, and one that has vanished from the tourist radar screen. "Trail Town" is an assemblage of more or less historic Western log buildings placed together on both sides of a dirt street as though they had been built together, like Old Sturbridge Village on US 20 in Massachusetts, and Old Fort Dodge on Twenty in Iowa. What appealed most to me were the small museum; the livery stable; and the cabin that once belonged to Curley, the Crow scout who was the only human survivor of George Armstrong Custer's immediate command at the Little Big Horn. (A young man at the time, he was told to make his escape before the battle began, and did.) There are modern gravestones memorializing Western figures, who were disinterred and reburied here to attract the tourist trade. Every Western tourist attraction, just like every medieval cathedral, needs its relics, such as Sacagawea's alleged grave (see chapter 5). "Liver Eating" Johnson, said to be the original of Robert Redford's "Jeremiah Johnson," lies here. Another stone commemorates a murdered local shady lady, named "Belle." (What else?) Relics needn't always be holy.

Near the rodeo ground, busy every night in the summer, or on a float trip on the North Fork of the Shoshone River (great fun), you can sometimes smell a hint of the sulphurous fumes of the Yellowstone "hot spot," the volcanic magma chamber lurking just half a mile under the surface. Locals refer to this area as "Colter's Hell." For the same reason, this river was first known to whites as the "Stinkingwater." See below for a fuller account of John Colter and his explorations.

Just four miles west of town, near the top of Cedar Mountain, which dominates the western Cody viewscape, was Shoshone Cavern National Monument, established in 1909. Horace Albright, in his amiable book *Oh, Ranger!* (1922), describes it as "a regular story-book robbers' cave, its secret entrance located high up a mountain cliff among the trees. . . . Inside the cavern are interesting and beautiful formations." But this limestone cave failed to attract many tourists, or meet the quality requirements of the national park system, and was summarily decommissioned in 1954. Directions to reach it (published in 1930) suggest why: a thousand foot climb and two ladders to reach the entrance, five more ladders once inside. Even in Albright's early

Float trip down the "Stinkingwater," the North Fork of the Shoshone River, near Colter's Hell, west of Cody, Wyoming

account, the cave is described as "at present . . . not open to visitors," and statements from the '40s and '50s say much the same. It seems never to have been much of a draw. I recall a faded sign vainly advertising it in 1955. The cave is still there, of course; it's now called Spirit Mountain Cave, or Cavern. There's a good book in this political process—how national monuments become national parks, how parks and monuments are created and sometimes un-created, how minor national parks (such as the former Platt National Park, in Oklahoma) get downgraded to recreational areas or worse. But it's not this book.

West from Cody along US 20 toward the park lies the glistening blue of Buffalo Bill Reservoir. The dam that creates it was completed in 1910 and heightened and enlarged in 1993. It is well worth a stop, if you're not acrophobic. It's a longer walk to the good visitor center than it used to be. Since 9/11, fear of terrorist car bombs and burst dams and floods has forced tourists to park several hundred feet away. Peregrine falcons and other raptors swoop along the steep canyon walls east of the dam, and there are lots of pigeons for them to prey on. West of the dam is Buffalo Bill State Park, created for camping and water sports in the reservoir.

Past the dam and park, trophy McMansions dominate distant hilltops, with grand views to the horizon. Greenness, wetness, and trees increase with the altitude in the Shoshone National Forest, and Yellowstone's East Entrance is 1,935 feet higher than Cody. There are many dude ranches and campgrounds along the way. The most famous of these is Pahaska Tepee, founded by Buffalo Bill himself, just east of the park. ("Pahaska," meaning "Longhair,"was Bill Cody's Indian name. Hence the melodious phrase means simply "Bill Cody's Lodge.")

Yellowstone's famous wildlife doesn't pay much mind to artificial boundaries, so it's wise to start watching for bear and deer and moose as soon as you reach Wapiti, twenty miles west of Cody. Near here is the site of the first National Forest Ranger station. Note a sign five miles farther west: "Grizzly Bear Area—Special Rules Apply." They do indeed. Disclaimer/Warning/ Admission: US 20 does not officially traverse Yellowstone National Park. But since it ends at the East Entrance and begins again at the West, it is fair to assume that the road to Old Faithful, and indeed to everything else in the park, is US 20. Since there is no official U.S. highway designation here, I take the entire park, the whole figure eight Grand Loop Road, for my province. What highway could more deserve the right to be called the Great Road than the road that leads to all these treasures?

early visitors

Yellowstone has been receiving visitors for centuries, starting well before even legendary history. A branch of the Eastern Shoshone inhabited the park long before the white man came, and other migratory tribes hunted there in the warmer seasons. White men called these Shoshone the "Sheepeaters," once thought to be a dismissive, contemptuous name for a "degenerate race." But killing bighorns with atlatls, spear-throwing sticks (until about AD 500), then bows and arrows, surely took great skill and hunting knowledge. The name was probably originally intended to distinguish them (*duku-deka*, meat-eaters) from their relatives farther west (*agai-deka*), whose main protein source was salmon, not mammals (Gregory E. Smoak, *Ghost Dances and Identity*, Berkeley: University of California Press, 2006, 19). There are said to be vestigial wikiup rings in the park to this day—remnant circles of stones once used to weigh down the animal hides used to cover a brush structure. I've not seen one. I have been told of a place in the park where I might see authentic Crow Indian tipi poles two centuries old. I won't say where. The Shoshone probably hunted and gathered there in the summer and left for warmer areas in the winter—such places as Thermopolis or the Snake Valley or the Wind River country, where they left prehistoric petroglyphs.

The Lewis and Clark expedition (1804–1806) didn't come within a hundred miles of the present park. One of its number, however, may have. Private John Colter asked permission of his military commanders on the Corps of Discovery to leave the expedition when the work was essentially finished, as the expedition was on the way back to Missouri and civilization. He wanted to return to trap beaver, and to trade with the Indians for more. (European demand for beaver pelts to make fashionable felt hats was a prime motivation for opening the Northwest. When felt hats went out of fashion, the trade collapsed, and the hard-pressed beavers recovered.) Colter, a Virginian, became one of the earliest whites to fall under the spell of the high plains and forests of Wyoming. Clark wrote that Colter's behavior "shows how easily men may be weaned from the habits of civilized life to the ruder but scarely less fascinating manners of the woods . . ." (Albert and Jane Salisbury, *Two Captains West*, Discovery Press, 1960, 209). Clark's words are an early statement of the romantic American attitude toward wild nature, which culminates in Thoreau's "In wildness is the preservation of the world."

Captains Lewis and Clark gave Colter their permission, provided that no one else should seek to leave. Colter separated from the Corps of

Discovery near Fort Mandan, in what is now North Dakota. His subsequent adventures were wild and woolly, including being captured and stripped naked by a Piegan (Blackfeet) war party in 1809 and forced to run for his life—literally. He said that he survived by killing the only Piegan quick enough to stay with him, and then by hiding under the water of a small river. Almost naked, almost starving, he walked two hundred miles to safety at Fort Raymond, on the Missouri River in Dakota Territory. On his traplines, Colter had encountered some of the thermal features of the area and, telling of them, was not believed. "Colter's Hell" became one more in the long list of tall tales of the early American West.

Was it Yellowstone? There is no way to know. Majority opinion long inclined to the view that the thermal features Colter saw were east of the present park, along the route of US 20. They were the reason for that area along the North Fork of the Shoshone river to be named "Colter's Hell Hot Springs." These features have dwindled in the two centuries since Colter's time, as thermal features will. A recent Yellowstone Park publication speculates otherwise: that Colter "probably skirted the northwest shore of Yellowstone Lake and crossed the Yellowstone River near Tower Fall, where he noted the presence of 'Hot Spring Brimstone'" (*Yellowstone Today*, History of the Park, 19). I'd like to think that that was true; nobody should get that close to Yellowstone and miss it. John Colter soon went back East and died young in 1813, a farmer in Missouri. He had become a near neighbor of that quintessential frontiersman-adventurer, Daniel Boone, settled down in old age at last.

tall tales and expeditions

Whether or not John Colter saw what is now Yellowstone National Park, other early mountain men did, as dozens of small parties explored this marvelous region. The most famous of the guides was Jim Bridger. This remarkable man was long dismissed as an amusing liar, but his contributions to geographical knowledge were immense. In 1842, in southwestern Wyoming, he founded a trading post that became Fort Bridger. It soon became a major way station on the Oregon Trail just west of South Pass, and was strategic enough to have been bought by the federal government. It's now a Wyoming state park, an interesting stop for Western history buffs. In 1991, I happened on a Civil War reenactors' encampment there. Jim Bridger went everywhere in the Old West. His third Indian wife was a Shoshone, and he became a good friend of Washakie,

Old Faithful Geyser, Yellowstone

whose fascinating life is discussed in chapter 5. General Grenville Dodge, no mean explorer himself, said of Bridger that "[a]s a guide, he was without equal. . . . He was a born topographer; the whole west was mapped out in his mind."

Ferdinand V. Hayden was a member of the first official exploratory party that Bridger led into the Yellowstone region in 1859 (Michael

Beehive Geyser, Upper Geyser Basin, Yellowstone

Frome, *National Park Guide*, Prentice-Hall, 1989, 151). Hayden's descriptions and recommendations were essential to the designation of Yellowstone as the first national park.[1] No other explorers except Lewis and Clark and Jedediah Smith deserve as much credit as Jim Bridger for our early knowledge of the West. But of course almost no one believed his stories, and, it must be admitted, he did tell some "stretchers," as Huck Finn called tall tales. There are many petrified trees in the park. Jim Bridger added that there were also, sitting on them, "pee-trified birds singin' pee-trified songs." There are a few places in the park where steam vents, thermal features, issue right out of cold lakes and rivers, as at West Thumb Geyser Basin. Jim said you could catch your fish in the lake and just throw it back over your shoulder into a hot pot to cook it. A tall tale, to be sure, but just possible.

Jim Bridger, old and blind, died in a log cabin in 1881 on a farm in what is now the south side of Kansas City, Missouri, around 103rd St. (*Kansas City Star*, March 2, 1941). That's where I first yearned for the West, sixty years later. He was buried near his home; then his bones were moved to Mount Washington Cemetery in Independence, Missouri, under a massive gravestone provided by General Dodge. A few miles away in the same county, in Forest Hill Cemetery, lies the body of Leroy M. ("Satchel") Paige. Satchel's imposing gravestone immortalizes his aphorisms on "How to stay young," which include "Don't ever look back. Something might be gaining on you." It would be hard to imagine two more different trailblazers; yet with their skills, courage and wit, they showed us great things.

The Washburn-Langford-Doane party (1870) and the second Hayden expedition (1871) were soon formed and funded to investigate the Yellowstone region. Many of the grand old names, such as Old Faithful, were given to thermal features by the Washburn party. This party scored another First. One member of the group, an unpleasant fellow named Truman C. Everts, got lost. He also lost his glasses, his horse, his equipment, and nearly his life. His companions searched for him but gave up after a week, thinking him dead. He would later complain bitterly about his abandonment. His loss "cast a deep gloom over the little party and seriously interfered with the progress of the expedition" (Hiram Chittenden, *The Yellowstone National Park*, University of Oklahoma, 1973, 72). Well, yeah! Everts wandered in the wilderness for "thirty-seven days of peril" before miraculously staggering back and surviving. His weight on his return was estimated at between fifty and seventy pounds. His Historic First: First Tourist Getting Seriously Damaged Doing

Really Dumb Things In Yellowstone. He has had many imitators. His feckless exploits got a park mountain near Mammoth Hot Springs named after him. I'm jealous.

Mt. Everts, view from my tent, Mammoth Campground

the first national park anywhere—sort of

The Hayden party left us a rich creation myth to deal with. It is unlikely that the pretty story of the campfire under the shadow of what was later named National Park Mountain, and the decision to preserve the area as a public park, happened exactly as some of the participants later claimed. Supposedly, all spontaneously agreed that this place was too magnificent to exploit for personal gain; it should instead be preserved as a "pleasuring ground" for all the people. This has the suspicious sound of religious conversion, of Roman Emperor Constantine seeing a vision of The Cross in the sky: the Hayden party seeing National Park Mountain, or The Light, and being converted to twenty-first-century environmentalism. No. See Paul Schullery, *Searching for Yellowstone*, for a gentle but thorough debunking of this myth.

It doesn't matter much. As these explorers' stories began to circulate, painters, photographers, and writers helped to make the Yellowstone region better known to the centers of American population and power in the Northeast. Painter Thomas Moran and photographer William H. Jackson were members of the Hayden party, and their work there made them justly famous. Moran's "Grand Canyon of the Yellowstone" once hung in the U.S. Capitol, and now hangs in the Smithsonian Museum of American Art in Washington, and, boy, does it deserve to! It is epic, romantic, gorgeous. It makes a great case for Official Art. N. P. Lang-ford's articles in *Scribner's Magazine* in May and June of 1871 spread the word. They're still very good reading, well illustrated with woodcuts. Within a year, "the best idea America ever had"—the national park idea—had taken root. (That apt phrase is often, but not definitively, attributed to Viscount James Bryce, Lord Acton, distinguished historian of America, and British Ambassador to the United States from 1907 to 1913.) President U. S. Grant signed the legislation, and the first national park in the world was born on March 1, 1872.

But it isn't quite that simple. Those who argue that Yosemite was the first national park have a case. It was the first federal land set aside as a park, if we don't count downtown Hot Springs, Arkansas, in 1832. (See? This is complicated.) President Abraham Lincoln set aside part of what would become Yosemite National Park in 1864. But Yosemite began as a state park, and did not become a national park until 1890. And Hot Springs, just a pleasant nineteenth-century spa town with a mildly lurid Arky past, doesn't have the majesty or razzle-dazzle to serve as the Eden of the national park creation myth. So Yellowstone it is, and why not?

So, by consensus, Yellowstone is the place where the national park idea began. It is indeed remarkable that, in 1872, a raw, shaken, splin-tered, and painfully reuniting young democracy decided it could afford to set aside two and a quarter million acres of land for people, for scenery, for animals, for fun, for the future, for the environment. Never mind that they wouldn't have understood that term then. What a gift!

Some American Indians were said to consider all important decisions keeping in mind the previous seven generations—their ancestors—and the next seven generations—their offspring. We do not inherit the world from our ancestors—we borrow it from our children. No one in the grasping history of Western America got closer to that ideal than these very ordinary nineteenth-century politicians, bless them. Alfred Runte, a distinguished historian of the national parks, argues that Yellowstone (and most of the national parks) were saved, set aside, only because they were considered economically worthless: had the land had more imme-diate economic potential, it would have been exploited like the prairies and the plains. Maybe. I prefer to think that there was at least some genuine vision and selflessness at work. And what glory came from it.

an Indian epic in the new park

It didn't take long for tourists to get the idea that there was something very special here. Only five years after the park's official establishment, other less benevolent political actions had stirred up the usually peaceful Nez Perce Indians in their ancestral home in eastern Washington. Harassed and pursued by the U.S. Army, they began a strategic retreat of more than a thousand miles under, among others, Chief Joseph, Hin-Mah-Too-Yah-Lat-Kekth in his language. Six hundred Nez Perce and their two thousand horses entered the area from the west across Targhee Pass. They traveled into the valley of the Madison River, past the site of the modern town of West Yellowstone. Their route led them straight through the center of Yellowstone National Park from west to east, along Nez Perce Creek, later so named for this event.

North of Yellowstone Lake, along the Yellowstone River, the Nez Perce encountered a surprising and bewildering novelty on the Great Road: tourists. They briefly took the tourist party prisoner, and nearly killed one of them. Their behavior was summed up by Emma Cowan, the wife of the man who was shot and almost killed: "Knowing something of the circumstances that led us to the final outbreak of these Indians, I wonder that any of us were spared. Truly a quality of mercy was shown us during our captivity that a Christian might emulate, and at a time when they must have hated the very name of the white race" (Erin H. Turner, *It Happened in Yellowstone*, 2001, 23).

The Nez Perce left the park and took a beautiful but difficult trail— the Chief Joseph Highway, we call it now, Wyoming 296—east and north toward their eventual capitulation to General Nelson Miles in Montana, about thirty miles south of the Canadian border and freedom. It was the occasion for one of the most eloquent speeches in American history, translated and recorded on the spot by an interpreter, on October 5, 1877:

> Tell General Howard I know his heart. What he told me before, I have in my heart. I am tired of fighting. Our chiefs are killed. Looking Glass is dead. Toohoolhoolzote is dead. The old men are all dead. It is the young men who say yes or no. He who led the young men is dead [Ollokot]. It is cold and we have no blankets. The little children are freezing to death. My people, some of them, have run away to the hills,

Yellowstone River upstream from Tower Fall

and have no blankets, no food. No one knows where they are—perhaps freezing to death. I want to have time to look for my children and see how many I can find. Maybe I shall find them among the dead. Hear me, my chiefs! I am tired. My heart is sick and sad. From where the sun now stands, I will fight no more forever. (Robert M. Utley and Wilcomb E. Washburn, *Indian Wars*, 260–61)

Chief Joseph kept his word. His reward for his honesty, nobility, and military genius was to spend the rest of his life in exile from his beloved homeland in what we call eastern Washington. Of the leaders of the government who lied to him and never let him return to his home, he said, "Such a government has something wrong." Yes. In August 2004, some Nez Perce, in traditional regalia, met near Nez Perce Creek at the end of Fountain Flat Drive in Yellowstone. They conducted a ceremony commemorating their people's trek through the park to northern Montana. If you would relive a smidgen of this epic journey, take the spectacular switchbacks of the Chief Joseph Highway into and out of the Sunlight Basin, on Wyoming 296. Think of doing it in chilly autumn weather, carrying children and household goods and supporting old and sick people, not driving in a modern car. Homeric.

Friction with Indians in Yellowstone country didn't quite end with Joseph's heroic retreat and noble surrender. In 1878, "The Bannock War" erupted over resentments over Indian mobility, and access to land and hunting grounds. Buffalo Horn led his warriors effectively, but at his death the war fizzled out. This small conflict was nonetheless significant: its conclusion "effectively marked the end of militant resistance to the reservation system" (Smoak, 150). That was the last time that this area was the site of serious Indian-white conflicts.

the Army and the Park Service

By 1877 the park was occasionally patrolled by the U.S. Army, but mostly left to survive on its own. In 1886, Lieutenant Daniel Kingman,

Black bears near Roosevelt, Yellowstone

under the command of Civil War hero General Phil Sheridan, laid out the earliest of the park's dirt roads for military horses and wagons, and for the early tourists. These tracks would develop into the modern figure-eight Grand Loop (Tim Cahill, *Lost in My Own Backyard*, 36). The new park had a superintendent, Nathaniel P. Langford—inevitably, N. P. Langford acquired the nickname "National Park"—but no budget and no staff. The first unofficial ranger, Harry Yount, was hired as a "game-keeper" in 1880, and lived alone in the Lamar Valley. Harry quit after a year of hopeless frustration. It was absurd to expect one man to patrol and protect more than two million acres, and he said so in a very articulate letter. He recommended what has since happened: that a small and reliable police force be assembled to protect the park and the animals. Today the supreme prize for outstanding National Park Rangers is called the "Harry Yount Award." Before there was a Park Service, hunters freely entered to poach the large animals.[2] Locals and some of the tourists knocked chunks off the geyser cones or pieces of travertine from the hot springs to sell, or to take home to Aunt Myrtle.

Black bears, a mating pair, foraging for flowers, Yellowstone, 2005. The male is larger and cinnamon colored.

Into this destructive vacuum stepped the U.S. Army, whose thirty-two-year stewardship of the park (1886–1918) is a noble chapter in its great history. At its peak in 1910, the Army contingent here numbered 324 soldiers, not counting military families and nonmilitary workers. Despite the harsh and lonely winters, soldiers regarded service in Yel-

Mule deer, Yellowstone

Yellowstone has hard winters : A spring scene, an elk carcass

lowstone as good duty, and it's easy to see why. They enjoyed catching poachers, riding, hunting, fishing, hiking, lots of fresh air and natural wonders. Still standing today is the architectural legacy of this early period—the handsome old military buildings at park headquarters at Mammoth Hot Springs. A walking tour of this area is instructive. I love the big former gym in an admin building that's been divided into modern Dilbert cubicles, still under a basketball hoop and backboard. Do they shoot hoops with crumpled-up memos? I hope so. There's a very funny signboard discussing the five mile walk (downhill) to nineteenth-century Gardiner, Montana, with its fleshpots, its bars and brothels, and the five mile walk back (uphill), during which the soldiers were said to have contemplated "the wages of sin." I only recently discovered that the old dirt road, now one-way north, still exists, starting from the Mammoth cabin area. Sharing it with a hiker, cyclists, and bighorn sheep, I travelled it in 2007. Downhill. In a car. Not to the fleshpots, if there are any left in Gardiner. The sandstone chapel, the last structure built by the Army there (1913), is gorgeous. Built by Scots masons, it is low and muscularly buttressed, giving it the look of an old Saxon or Norman parish church. Its interior is light, warm, and inviting. A National Parks Christian ministry holds Sunday services there in season.

Pressure was building to create a genuinely professional park service and a national park system. Both came into being in 1916 under the lead-

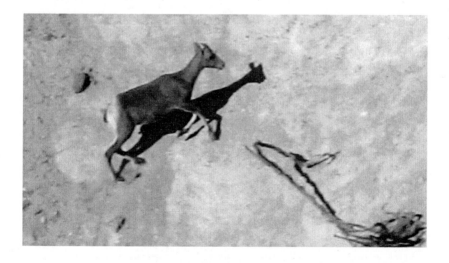

Bighorn ewe on cliff near Tower Fall, Yellowstone

ership of Stephen Tyng Mather and Horace F. Albright. The Park Service took over the administration of Yellowstone and bade farewell to the Army. (Those wonderful, silly "Smokey Bear" hats the Rangers sometimes wear are a vestigial reminder of the Army's precedence.) The birth of the Park Service came at something of a cost, not least in the founding charter of the National Park Service. The Service was enjoined by the National Park Service Act of 1916 to do a difficult, almost self-contradictory job: "to conserve the scenery and the natural and historic objects and the wild life therein and to provide for the enjoyment of the same in such manner and by such means as will leave them unimpaired for the enjoyment of future generations" (Richard West Sellars, *Preserving Nature in the National Parks*, 38. Sellars credits Frederick Law Olmsted Jr. with writing it). Ever since, there has been inevitable tension between "providing for the enjoyment," such as stocking rivers with nonnative fish for tourists to catch, and "conserv[ing]" the resources "unimpaired."

In 2006, Interior Secretary Dirk Kempthorne resolved (for now) a long-simmering argument between the recreationists and the preservationists by stating that conservation must come first. Good for him. It must indeed. Once a resource is lost, there's no getting it back. Early Park Service leaders also knew that for the national parks to grow and prosper, they had to develop a nationwide politicial constituency of people who enjoyed them, even loved them. Equally important, many people would come to have a stake in them because they made big money off them, and still do. Recently, Park Service retirees have put together a small ad hoc group of geezers, the Coalition of National Park Service Retirees (*High Country News*, December 11, 2006). They function as watchdogs over an Interior Department that has been known to propose and do stupid things that would damage the parks forever. You go, fellow geezers!

building a constituency—bears as performers

Shocking things were proposed, and some were done, to attract tourists and build political support for the parks. No tramway was ever built to the bottom of the Grand Canyon, though Horace Albright is said to have favored it. Shudder. In Yellowstone, bears both cute and scary were permitted, even encouraged, to interact with visitors. Albright, both as Yellowstone superintendent and as director of the National Park Service, promoted this. There's a photo of Albright introducing a bear to President Coolidge, while the president's security guards look on disapprovingly. In his twenty-third summer in 1936, Yale law student Gerald Ford was a seasonal ranger in Yellowstone. It was an idyllic experience which our thirty-eighth president loved to recall. But the work he did was a far cry from what modern park rangers do: his main job was as an armed guard on a "bear-feeding truck." Ye gods. Young Jerry also welcomed dignitaries at Canyon Lodge and kept records of the license plates of cars in parking lots—useful information for building park political constituencies in far-off states (John Heilprin, Associated Press, December 27, 2006).

In the old days, until the 1970s, tourists could pretty well rely on encountering several "bear jams" in the course of a summer day's drive around the Grand Loop. A bear, preferably a black bear mama with two adorable cubs, would wander onto the road and approach a car. Cars would back up for hundreds of yards to watch and participate. I remember a black bear in 1968 standing up at the (closed) right front window of our Olds Vistacruiser, and my family's reaction of terror and delight. People in cars would throw food out for the bears to eat, or, worse, get out and feed them by hand. When the food ran out before the hand did, a bear might become a bit testy, and a tourist might be injured. Dads would hold their children up so the kids could hand the bears a goody, while Moms got a snapshot of it. Really!

In a remarkable link between the Great Road in Massachusetts (chapter 1) and the Great Road here, Ted Hughes wrote two poems about his visit to Yellowstone in 1959 with his American wife, Sylvia Plath. In "Fishing Bridge" (still a famous Yellowstone landmark), Hughes speaks of her delight in walking toward the wilderness near Yellowstone Lake in her bikini. In "The 59th Bear," Hughes gives a fervid description of encounters with dozens of bears. Bears, bears, bears everywhere, fifty-nine of them, raiding the campgrounds for garbage. A bear attacked the poets' car (borrowed for the trip from Plath's mother) and wrecked a food chest to get at three trout (and some pancake mix) stored there (*Birthday Letters*, 87, 90–95). I never saw Yellowstone's bears quite *this* thick on the ground, but I believe that it happened. The park has since instituted excellent bear-proof garbage cans, and bears are rarely seen in campgrounds today.

Garbage feeding like this was terrible for the bears, though it did help them stock up on crucial calories for their winter hibernation. The calories were all the wrong kind—Twinkies and Hersheys and wieners, not berries and carrion, nuts and grubs. Tourists and "bear-feeding trucks" trained the bears to associate roads and cars and people with

Bear jams! Yellowstone

yumyums. As a result, a lot of bears were killed on park roads. It trained the bears—cubs are smart—to be beggars, not to lead the life of wild bears. It was awful, but by god, it was fun to watch.

There was worse. Before Ted Hughes's and Sylvia Plath's and my visits in the 1950s, grizzlies would congregate at large garbage dumps to eat the leftovers of the old hotels. People came every night to watch them scavenge, and sometimes fight for, the garbage. At Canyon, there were bleachers built and lights strung so that tourists could come and enjoy The Big Show, which must have been stunning. I never saw it. Garbage-watching began in the 1880s. The spectacle was ended in the early 1950s, but garbage was still a major food source for Yellowstone's grizzlies until 1974.

a sudden end to garbage bears

When garbage dumping and feeding was suddenly ended in 1974, and all garbage was trucked out of the park, the grizzlies lost a major food source. This policy change led to a sad and bitter battle between the Park Service and two pioneer bear researchers, Frank and John Craighead. The Craigheads agreed that ending this corrupt free lunch was a good idea, but that it should be phased out slowly, so as not to starve the bears. The Park Service said no, Now, and ended the Craigheads' research access.

No one doubts that grizzlies died as a result of this decision. Today, though the size of the grizz population in Yellowstone is disputed, most agree that it is still dangerously small—perhaps seven hundred bears. The genetic pool is narrow, the population isolated, and the loss of any bear, particularly a breeding female, is serious. Even outspoken critics of the Park Service agree that the current management plan for Yellowstone's bears is better than the devil-may-care approach of fifty years ago. A series of recollections from my personal Yellowstone experience will illustrate both the changes and the problems.

how bear watching has changed : Ranger Ted

1955: Half a day in the park—my first—produced twelve bear sightings. It was wonderful. They were everywhere, especially on and near the main roads.

1968: Took a five-year-old daughter out of a plumbingless cabin at night for a pee. "Daddy, there's a bear there!!" and indeed there was. We figured out a way to handle the matter inside the cabin. Bears were everywhere in the '60s, too.

1974: Park policy changes: no more garbage for the bears.

1981: Went to a ranger talk given by Ranger Ted. (I never got his last name.) Ranger Ted was a tall, gaunt, retired biology professor from the

University of Utah, one of the hundreds of great people, seasonal rangers, whose dedication and knowledge, and love of the national parks, make those parks work every summer. Ranger Ted explained to a large and attentive audience why changes in the park's bear policy had been necessary. He was mouthing official park policy, but he also clearly bought into it.

His talk was focused on one of his career's major scientific research emphases—bear poop. The main reason we needed to keep bears away from people food, from places like the old garbage dumps where they would congregate and forage, was bear poop. When they ate, especially in groups (grizzlies are not usually real groupy, social beasts), they would get excited and defecate; and when they defecated, in a group, they would surely also "STEP IN IT!" That was Ranger Ted's repeated horrific vision—that the bears would "STEP IN IT!" If they did, they would eat with the same paws and spread disease among themselves, and Yellowstone's bears would sicken and die.

What the fascinated audience learned from Ranger Ted was "DON'T LET THEM STEP IN IT!" or at least keep them from grouping around food sources that might encourage them to mis-STEP! Bears became

Grizzly in burned lodgepole forest, Dunraven Pass

harder to find; no dumps, no roadside feeding, and it was okay with me. I found Ranger Ted's ursine scatology convincing, if a mite obsessive. And so it rested until

1984: Went to a ranger talk given by Ranger Ted. Really! I asked at a visitor center what evening programs were scheduled. I was told that Ranger Ted was there for his last summer at Yellowstone, his last ranger talk, which I saw as a diva's Farewell Tour. His topic was Bears. (Bear poop, I was sure.) I could drive twenty miles to Canyon to hear him if I wanted to.

Did I want to!? Is the Pope a Catholic!? Do bears poop and step in it?!? It was the same loony, wonderful, compelling, obsessive talk, down to the last "WE CAN'T HAVE THEM STEPPING IN IT!" Thank you so much, Ranger Ted.

But I saw no bears that year.

2001 and 2002: Saw no bears the first few days of my visits. Darn. Poop, even. Might get shut out again. I wouldn't even mind if they would STEP IN IT! if I could just see a few bears. And then there they were, black bears, grizz, in the dawn and the dusk and at noon, near and far, where you'd expect them to be and where you wouldn't. Bears

Black bear munching on flowers

are harder to find now, but they're there. They've always been there. They always will be.

2003: June: Coming around a bend in Dunraven Pass, wow, there's a young grizz feeding just upslope. We stop and watch him for an hour, well within the hundred yards we're supposed to be from all bears. (He decided the distance, not us.)

2004: Slow year, slow month, July: Still, a grizzly sow with three cubs far away across the Yellowstone River in Hayden Valley.

2005: June: Bears everywhere again, including one memorable morning when my partner Joyce and I saw six black bears, two of them large cinnamon males, feeding on flowers just outside the entrance to our cabin area, Tower/Roosevelt. Later that same morning, up Chittenden Road toward Mt. Washburn, we saw six grizzlies, including a sow with two cubs, and one boar (male) only forty yards away in heavy timber. It doesn't get much better than that.

2007: Friends report seeing *seven grizzlies in the same spotting scope field* in the Antelope Creek drainage, on the north slope of Mount Washburn True, it was two sows with two and three cubs respectively, but it's still seven grizz. I repeatedly saw the same family groups, though never at the same time. Awesome. There are many more grizzlies in the park now than there were thirty years ago, probably reaching up to or near the grizz-carrying capacity of the ecosystem. Grizzlies have been removed from the Endangered Species list, and I doubt the wisdom of that. Bear jams now don't involve bears feeding on the roads, and bears are harder to find. Yellowstone has become wilder and less predictable, and that's good.

If people love them to death and develop their parks too much, the very reason for their being can be undermined and destroyed. Would Yellowstone be better or worse if it contained places where bisons and bears were penned up and people could come watch them as if in a zoo? Would the Grand Canyon be better or worse with a tramway from rim to river? I have no problem answering that—MUCH WORSE—but not everyone would agree. This is the delicate balance that we as a people are continually striving to achieve.

tourism : the stagecoach and the automobile

Just one year before the Army left and the Park Service took over, another fateful political decision was made that would have an enormous impact on Yellowstone and all the other parks. On August 1, 1915, the first automobile was admitted into the park. Since the advent of the automobile, the national parks, not to mention the nation, have never been the same. Traffic jams and parking hassles can severely damage a national park experience. Buses or trolleys now replace private vehicles at some times in some parts of some great parks: Grand Canyon, Yosemite, Zion, Mesa Verde, Dinosaur National Monument. These programs have been very successful, but they are limited. No one wants to "Pave Paradise," or Yosemite Valley, "and put up a parking lot," but we all love our cars. Hey, so do I!

The railroads exploited and opened Yellowstone, as they did Glacier and the Grand Canyon. A signboard at Yellowstone's North Entrance in Gardiner, Montana, shows how this vista looked in the nineteenth century. What was a busy railroad yard downslope from the entrance road has become Gardiner's school athletic field (Go Bruins!), where football games are sometimes delayed by grazing elk. Most tourists arrived by train, then traveled into the park in horse-drawn wagons. A nostalgic reminder of this period survives today in the northern part of Yellowstone, in the Roosevelt area trail rides and stagecoach and chuckwagon

Stagecoach at Roosevelt

outings. A signboard near the Roosevelt corral states that travel companies charged as much as $50 for a five and a half day trip around the park (upscale), or as little as $35 for six days. This was for stagecoach travel and sleeping in hotels or rather nice tents. A large dinner was included; I don't know about other meals, but I suspect they were included, too. Sounds cheap enough for those with significant disposable income. But it cost big bucks, about $175, to travel by railroad coach from the eastern seaboard to Cody, Wyoming, so tourism was limited. Average stagecoach speed: six miles an hour. (Or less: there must have been lots of wheel and team problems or road washouts.) The record year is said to have been 1915, when 21,151 came. It is estimated that 310,000 tourists visited the park during the thirty-two years of the stagecoach era. That's a very sizeable number, though nothing like what was to come. Once the public was permitted freely in and around by private car, tourism grew exponentially, until today nearly three million tourists a year visit the park, almost all in cars or buses. There are a lot more visitors on motorcycles these days, too, and that looks exciting, though I would much prefer to be inside a vehicle when bison are ambling past.

In 1912, H. W. Child, president of the Yellowstone Park Transportation Company, argued that we should maintain the stagecoach monopoly.

Retro tourist bus, Yellowstone

He Viewed With Alarm the dangers to tourists that would come from the mixing of horses and automobiles. He also warned, in deliciously oro- tund prose, of the dangers that would occur when "some of our most law- abiding citizens . . . uniformly disregard speed limits and rely alone for justification on a kind of intoxication superinduced by the ecstasy of auto- mobile travel." Zowie!! I love and concur with his "ecstatic" phrasing, and his prediction was pretty accurate, too[3] (*Yellowstone National Park Chat Page*, February 19, 2007, and C. E. Knight, "New Roads in Yellow- stone National Park, " 62nd Congress, 2nd Session, Doc. 871, Washing- ton: USGPO, 1912, 18, with thanks to Roadie).

Mr. Child's prescient warnings notwithstanding, autos entered the park on August 1, 1915, and everything changed. Coach tours ended suddenly in 1916. The Fountain Hotel, near Lower Geyser Basin, was once (1891–1916) the newest and loveliest of the park's establishments. 14,814 visitors stayed there in 1905. "The summer of 1916 was a disor- derly one, with both motor and horse-drawn vehicles plying park roads. The simultaneous operation of both types of vehicles caused chaos: car engines frightened horses and park roads were not engineered properly for cars. But cars could get further in a day than could stagecoaches. . . . The Fountain Hotel closed abruptly following the summer of 1916 . . . motorization was the reason" (Whittlesey, "Music, Song and Laughter," *Montana* 53, 4, Winter 2003).

Only during the wartime travel restrictions of the 1940s did the growth of automobile tourism slow and stop. The first million-visitor year was 1947, when gas rationing had ended and new tires and new cars were available. There were predictions that three-dollar-a-gallon gas would significantly cut visitation in 2006. Didn't happen. A 9 percent boost in travel in the usually quiet month of September pushed the 2006 total to more than 2.7 million, just over the total for 2005 (*Billings Gazette*, October 25, 2006). "The ecstasy of automobile travel" has trumped the higher costs.

here come the sagebrushers

Early car campers were colloquially known as "sagebrushers," for the roadsides where they pitched their tents or parked their prehistoric RVs. Although camping hurt the hotel business, large hotels built for the growing tourist trade rose and fell and rose again, culminating in the wonderful Old Faithful Inn, which opened in 1904 and has been lovingly restored. Gateway towns—West Yellowstone, Jackson, Cody, Gardiner, and Cooke City—geared up to service and profit from the swelling human flood. In his cranky, delightful *Desert Solitaire*, Edward Abbey decried "Industrial Tourism" for the way it was turning his once obscure Utah desert paradise into "Arches National Money-mint." (Try to get a campsite at Arches National Park in the spring and you might agree with him.) Some lament the crush of traffic at Artist Point or Old Faithful, which has, I think, the only cloverleaf highway junction in the national parks. So far. Traffic and people can be oppressive, wearying; but the park is so big and diverse that, like Walt Whitman, it can contain multitudes. On a busy summer day, Yosemite Valley, about the same size as Manhattan Island, can feel like Times Square. But three million tourists a year don't overwhelm Yellowstone. If July is too busy for you, try May. Or September. Or December. (I haven't tried winter yet. I will.)

A sadder fact is that those who stay cooped up in their cars—canned tourists, I call 'em, adopting the point of view of a bear at an old-fashioned bear jam—don't really see much of the park. True enough. It is also true that most of the hundreds who come to watch a summer eruption of Old Faithful turn around and leave before the great show is quite over, in a hurry to get to gift shops or cafeterias or toilets. Rangers call this "the

It's MY road!

geyser flush," which makes me giggle. It's easy to deprecate this behavior. But I'd rather have at least part of their attention here than at Disney World or Six Flags Over Secaucus.

Does it really do people any good to commune, however sketchily, with nature? I dunno. That questionable dogma is behind many worthwhile projects, like sending poor city kids to summer camp. Do people behave better in the parks than, say, at NFL games, or at Coney Island? Crime stats and many conversations with law enforcement Rangers suggest that a good, cautious answer might be "Yes, some." The Park Service's Morning Report can make harrowing reading, but most of its catastrophes are traffic or hiking accidents, not violent crimes. High-tech marijuana growing is common in the national parks and forests, but that's commerce, supply and demand, utilizing wild green places that don't get much surveillance. Drug- and people-trafficking make some beautiful Southwestern border parklands—Big Bend, Organ Pipe Cactus, Cabeza Prieta—dangerous; but so is the whole Mexican border. People do smile a lot at Yellowstone, and they don't seem to need to whine much or play music too loud. The park seems to calm them. It might be good for you, too.

Nursing bison calf

finding the peaceable kingdom

At its sweetest, Yellowstone can seem something like Edward Hicks's vision of *The Peaceable Kingdom*. Hicks (1780–1849) was a Quaker and a self-taught early American painter. He made many versions of a scene based on Isaiah 11:6: "The wolf also shall dwell with the lamb, and the leopard shall lie down with the kid; and the calf and young lion and the fatling together; and a little child shall lead them."

This iconography—placid animals and child or children—often appears in the right foreground. In some versions, William Penn is in the background, peaceably negotiating with Indians in an idealized landscape, his ship at anchor in the harbor. It is a naive vision of the Earthly Paradise, a glorious moment in the providential future, though Hicks conflates past, present, and future into a time that somehow seems *before* the Fall, before war, before sex and death, when all animals must have been vegetarians. The Elizabethan poet, Michael Drayton, called the unspoiled New World "Virginia, / Earth's only paradise." Hicks's paintings are a lovely vision of "America, Earth's only paradise." A late Hicks

Pronghorn antelope, Yellowstone

is projected to sell in 2007 for about $4 million. So much for folk simplicity. Hicks's paintings sort well with other early American religious visions such as those of the agrarian, egalitarian Shakers, and many of the other Great Road Utopian experimenters.

This Edenic vision is in some degree what many people seek when they go to Yellowstone. From watching real bison, elk, and moose quietly grazing and ruminating, to cartoon visions of Yogi Bear raiding Jellystone picnic baskets, the Yellowstone experience is partly about a sweeter, calmer time when man and nature were not at odds, when we could "talk to the animals," before we heeded the stern Biblical injunction to "subdue" and "have dominion" over the earth. Did such a time ever exist? Of course not, but it doesn't matter. The question is immaterial. It is what many of us yearn for, and what some of us can think we have found in Yellowstone.

predator and prey

Whoa, Charley! What's this about the wolf dwelling with the lamb? Tell that to the latest newborn wapiti (elk) calf ripped apart by a wolf pack to feed its pups. The last original gray wolves in the park, a pair of cubs, were shot in 1924 as part of a misguided predator control program. Since their reintroduction in 1995, wolves have been a significant, grow-

Elk, near Firehole River, Yellowstone

ing, and violent part of the natural landscape of the park. Tennyson's "Nature red in tooth and claw" is closer to the literal Yellowstone truth than is Hicks's *The Peaceable Kingdom*.

The presence of gray wolves restores much of the natural balance to a landscape previously tipped heavily against predators who compete with us for prey species such as elk, deer, and sheep. For a moving statement on this issue, see Aldo Leopold's seminal essay "Thinking Like a Mountain." Leopold recalls shooting a mother wolf. "I was young then, and full of trigger-itch; I thought that because fewer wolves meant more deer, that no wolves would mean hunters' paradise. But having seen the green fire die [in the eyes of the dying wolf], I sensed that neither the wolf nor the mountain agreed with such a view" (*Sand County Almanac*, "Thinking Like a Mountain," "Arizona and New Mexico," 130). Predator and prey are part of a natural dance, and they are good for each other. They test, sharpen, and improve one another, though the truth of this grim dance is hell on sloppy sentimentality.

Killing these predators wasn't real good for the park, either, despite people's desire to see large "charismatic megafauna," i.e., bear, elk, deer, antelope, bison, moose. Too many elk for the land, starving to death in hard winters even though they were and are still fed near Jackson; too few aspen and willows, browsed to death by hungry elk; fewer trees, fewer beavers, and so on and on. Wolf researcher Doug Smith says that wolves have made elk more cautious, avoiding areas where they might be surprised by a hungry wolfpack. As the elk avoid river bottoms, more willows and cottonwoods grow and mature. The resulting shade cools the rivers and improves conditions for the native trout. There are nearly twice as many beavers in the park now as there were before wolf reintroduction: more willows, more beaver. And because beavers make ponds, and willows like to "get their feet wet," still more willows. That should be good for moose, too.

There is a competing explanation. Some scientists think the park's warmer climate is the main reason for the change. The park's growing season has apparently expanded by a startling three to four weeks since wolf reintroduction (*Billings Gazette*, September 19, 2006). The wolf-induced "ecology of fear" brings back not only beavers, but also songbirds such as the yellow warbler. Former Park Ranger Paul Schullery quotes a ranger colleague: "In the summer, [the elk] eat the cereal. In the winter, they eat the box." It's not a jungle out there, but it's tough and competitive. Forage is limited, and the winter is long and hard. It's life and death. What isn't?

the illusion of paradise regained

Still, the feel of Yellowstone, in summertime, "when the livin' is easy," is often quiet, uncompetitive, peaceful. Grizzlies are omnivores; vegetation makes up as much as 90 percent of the steady eating they must do to sustain themselves and prepare for hibernation. In Yellowstone, the presence of so many large prey animals means that the local grizzlies eat a lot more meat than that, perhaps 40 to 50 percent of their diet. In the spring, they scavenge carcasses of the many ungulates, chiefly elk and bison, that didn't make it through the winter. In the late spring, spawning cutthroat trout were a valuable staple, but that source is severely declining, and seems largely to be used by boars, the more aggressive males (*Yellowstone Discovery* 22, 1, 1–7, Spring 2007). In summer, when there are abundant berries or roots or forbs or insects, they rarely need to kill anything, though they'll surely kill and eat a ground squirrel or pocket gopher if they raise one while searching for roots, nuts, or ants, or a newborn elk if it's easy prey. In the fall, bears turn hyperphagic, consuming (a ranger told me) as much as *thirty thousand*

Mac at Loop A Norris Campground, Yellowstone, 2005. Gibbon River in background
Photo by Bernie George

calories a day. It's simply easier and more efficient to eat berries and insects than to chase and kill large things. Much of the big bears' chasing is protective, chasing persistent scavengers such as ravens, wolves, and coyotes away from their kills.

Remarkably, a very substantial part of the huge bears' diet is small, protein-rich moths, at one calorie each, taken from under rocks in the park's high country in late summer. Yellowstone grizz also fatten up in late summer, prepare for hibernation, on the nutrient-rich nuts of the whitebark pine, often by unearthing caches made by squirrels. The trees that provide this crucial food source are severely threatened by attacks from mountain pine beetles, and a fungus called white pine blister rust. Whole mountainsides have gone from green to russet—i.e., dead—as global warming lets the beetles move higher up the mountains. What will the grizz eat when these trees are gone? No one knows, but it won't be good for them ("In the Rockies, Pines Die and Bears Feel It," *New York Times*, January 30, 2007).

In July 2002, I got out of a car on a narrow dirt park road to ask the people in the car ahead why they were stopped and blocking the road— did they see something interesting? They did: a young grizz just off the road, sitting in the bushes, totally engrossed in foraging, for berries, I think. I suppose I should have been afraid, and indeed, I was breaking the park rule of staying twenty-five yards from most animals and a hundred yards from bears—it was more like ten. My car was between us, and I could easily have made it into the car if he'd made a rush—but of course, that was the last thing on his mind, and therefore on mine. He didn't give a damn that a few people were watching him, though he surely knew it. Nothing short of a high powered rifle could have induced him to stop eating. In most bear encounters—especially grizz encounters—the bears are like this: quiet, aloof. I've never bumped into one around a bend in a trail, or been near a sow with cubs. That might be different.

There is metaphorical truth in our yearning for this quiet, amiable relationship with the rest of nature, and at least metaphorical gratification of this yearning in Yellowstone. "The Peaceable Kingdom" may exist only in our imagination, as it did in Isaiah's, and Edward Hicks's, but it is none the less real or wonderful for that.

danger in paradise : common sense

Another reality is danger. Hiking in Yellowstone is pretty safe, probably safer than walking in an American city. Only six human

Zzzzzzzzz . . . bison just off the boardwalk at Mud Volcano

deaths have been definitely attributed to bears in Yellowstone since the park's inception in 1872. Most victims were people who did the wrong things, like a photographer in 1989 who got too close and provoked a charge. Another did the same thing in 2007 and was lucky to live, after hiking three miles and getting a ride to the hospital. Yet some people apparently do all the right things and are still attacked, especially if they are traveling alone.

A worker at Canyon in 2002 was approached near her dorm by a young grizz, who actually tested her thigh with his mouth. She had stayed very still, unthreatening, trying to look unafraid—the recommended way to react to a grizz. But this was too much, and she threw a cup of water in his face. Startled, he released her, and shambled off. Another visitor, same summer, was gored by a bison standing next to a boardwalk. The visitor walked right up to the bison, thinking (if that's the right word) that boardwalks belong to tourists, and are sanctuaries. They don't, and they're not. Common sense will keep you out of danger—most of the time. A story a ranger once told me contains excellent advice. Her friend was playing Frisbee in a meadow near a bull bison. The Frisbee flew pretty close to the bull, and the bison's tail went up. As she said, "That means one of two things—charge or discharge—and in either case you don't want to be around." Her friend dodged behind a tree and lived to play Frisbee again.

You are more likely to be hit by lightning, or hurt in traffic, than to be attacked by an animal in Yellowstone. Like Dr. Johnson's dictum on the knowledge of one's imminent hanging, "It concentrates the mind wonderfully" to know you are walking where there are creatures that could, if they wished, kill you and turn you into breakfast. Yet in the words of Aldo Leopold (who was writing of riding a high ridge amidst lightning bolts), "It must be poor life that achieves freedom from fear" (essays with *A Sand County Almanac*, 126). I enjoy the feeling of not always being at the top of the food chain. It's intense. I like to feel vulnerable, but you don't have to. You can enjoy the wildness of Yellowstone without it.

planning for Yellowstone

I'd like to suggest what you should see in Yellowstone, always remembering that this is not a detailed guidebook, and that dozens of

What's for lunch?
My campsite, Bridge Bay, Yellowstone

good ones are available with many different emphases—general, mammals, birds, geology, thermal features, hikes, plants, deaths, rangers, waterfalls, and so on and on. Prepare for your trip, and have a lot of fun, reading about the things you might want to see and do. If you have questions, go to the Web's Total Yellowstone Page, find the chat page, and ask. You'll find scores of helpful people, smart amateurs who are nuts about the place. We call ourselves Loons and I am proud to be one of them. We will rush to inform you and give you good information and opinions about anything you can think of to ask about. These chat pages are undergoing major changes as this book goes to press. "Yellowstone Chat" still lives. See also "The Home of the Yellowstone Loon" for excellent Yellowstone info and advice. Many of these folks also contribute to "The Great Outdoors Chat Page" and the "Loon Zone Chat Page."

Try to allocate at least four days for the park, more if you can. You can drive to and stop at the major highlights in two days, but almost everyone leaves lamenting not having had enough time. Some people will need time to acclimate to the altitude. Serious altitude sickness is not a problem, but you may feel lightheaded or out of breath, or have difficulty sleeping. I'm in good shape, fit for my advanced age, run every morning, etc., but I sometimes have sleeping problems in Yellowstone. The problem usually disappears in two or three days, and you might plan, as I do, to begin your trip at the lower altitudes, below seven thousand feet, in the northern half of the park. Drinking lots of fluids and going light on caffeine and alcohol helps.

Get a good map and familiarize yourself with the lay of the land, the main points of interest and the major areas of tourist facilities. Make reservations as early as you can, even a year or more ahead, if you're staying in the hotel or cabin facilities, which come in all levels and prices except luxe. Yellowstone will be full except for cancellations if you wait. Some campgrounds, the larger ones, can be reserved, though the small, out-of-the-way ones I like best can't.

Here are some personal, highly opinionated tips.

Mac's top ten, part one : thermal highlights

Yellowstone was famed first for its thermal features, and indeed there are about ten thousand in the park. The molten magma of the earth's core here is only half a mile below the surface. There are more geysers here—about three hundred—than in all the rest of the world combined. (Dan Sholly, *Guardians of Yellowstone*, 63). The word *geyser* is Icelandic; only in Iceland, New Zealand, and Yellowstone do geysers exist. Five thermal highlights that I would hope no one would miss are:

One: Old Faithful, and the entire adjacent Upper Geyser Basin. Old Faithful has slowed a bit, it isn't as regular as clockwork, and you may have to wait an hour and a half to see it blow, but do it, and then do it again. See all of it. And remember that Old Faithful is only one great geyser at the south end of the Upper Geyser Basin. It always astounds me to see people stand or sit waiting for the old girl to blow while they ignore wonderful geyser spouts just a few yards away to the north—Giant or Lion or Beehive. Go enjoy the rest of the basin when Old Faithful quiets down.

Two: Norris Geyser Basin, the hottest in the park. This is really two areas, Porcelain (cooler, with lovely pastels) to the north and Back Basin to the south. Don't miss either one. My favorite geyser in the park was Echinus, in Back Basin—once almost as predictable as Old Faithful and more intimate. It has a large pool that slowly fills with hot water and then blows, formerly every two hours or so. There are bleacher seats built all

Mammoth hot springs terraces, Yellowstone

around one side of Echinus, as if to watch a baseball game. But in 2003, changes just under the crust here closed a section of the Back Basin trail and changed Echinus, perhaps, I feared, forever. For several years it blew less than once in four hours, then went dormant for nearly a year. The bleachers were barren and empty and sad. Remember the wonderful old Frank Sinatra song?

"Yes, there used to be a ball park, right here. . . ."

But there is good news: Echinus is partly back. I encountered a ranger near it in July 2006, and sadly asked him about Echinus, and he told me excitedly it was back to pretty much its old pattern—frequent and spectacular eruptions. "It's my favorite gesyer in the park!" he said. "Mine too!" I replied. I didn't have time to stop and watch that day, but I will. See it before it quiets down again, as it will. (And, sadly, it has. It erupted four times in the first half of 2007, but it's mostly quiet now.)

Mac at Mud Volcano, Yellowstone, c, 1982
Photo by Diana Hume George

This constant change is typical of the thermal areas of the park, particularly of Norris. The Yellowstone caldera will surely one day blow its top again. The floor of the northern part of Yellowstone Lake is slowly rising in reponse to the intense magma (molten lava) chamber below. When it all blows, perhaps in a quarter million years, perhaps

Mac and Bernie, Gardiner, Montana
Electric Peak is in the background.

much sooner, it could destroy much of North America and most of its life forms. That might well include us. Be sure to see Yellowstone before that happens.

Next to Echinus is the tallest geyser in the world, Steamboat, so named for the puffing sounds it makes when it erupts. The three hundred foot eruptions happen very rarely, so if you see one, you are REALLY fortunate. I never have. It has gone dormant for as long as half a century. Still, it's a fine show even when quiescent, constantly bubbling and fizzling, and sending up jets a few feet in height. It's been unusually active in recent years.

Many Yellowstone visitors get hooked and become "geyser gazers." They spend quiet, happy hours waiting for eruptions. Predictions for many geysers are listed at the Old Faithful Visitor Center, and *real* geyser gazers communicate with each other by phone or scanners, so they can get the word around quickly when an eruption begins. But note: not all thermal features are geysers. For example:

Three: Grand Prismatic Spring, in the Midway Geyser Basin. Words almost fail in trying to describe this astonishing hot pool, nearly four hundred feet across, brightly colored in blues and russets and yellows and oranges by the heat-loving algae who live in it. It is the chief, but not the only, attraction of this basin; the adjacent Excelsior Gesyer Crater is a dormant feature, but its pool is deep and blue and gorgeous. The use of enzymes from bacteria in hot pools near here has led to enormous advances in our study of DNA (*New York Times*, November 28, 2006). See chapter 7 for more on this.

Four: Mammoth Hot Springs is the name of the enormous travertine terraces built up over the centuries by slow seepage from underground vents. Yellowstone is the world's greatest hot spot, and the seepage continues, the process is active and ongoing. It is located near the administrative center of the park, Mammoth, inside the north entrance. The currently active areas are most easily seen by driving and parking just above the terraces, then walking down toward them. The colors here are subtle—largely off-whites and pale oranges. Elk often lounge around at Mammoth. Don't get too close to them, especially during the fall rut, when the males can be very aggressive.

Five: Finally, one of my personal favorites: Mud Volcano, north of Hayden Valley in the eastern part of the park. Since there are no great geysers here, some people bypass this area. Don't. The features here are as diverse as those anywhere else, including great names and sights such as Dragon's Mouth Spring and a grand, big roiling pool called Black Dragon's Cauldron, which abruptly burst out of the ground here in 1948. It has calmed down in recent years, but who knows when it might kick up again? Or when a totally new feature might appear? Just across the road are, to my nose, the best stinks in the park, at Sulphur Cauldron. Bison often wander the trails, the boardwalks, even the parking lots at Mud Volcano—don't dispute priority with them.[4]

Mac's top ten, part two : non-thermal features

Six: Grand Canyon of the Yellowstone, Lower Falls. The distant view of Lower Falls (more than three hundred feet) and the canyon from Artist Point is the most famous sight in the park not involving a geyser, and it is magnificent. The stone is volcanic rhyolite, and it is indeed yellow; hence the name French explorers gave the area and then the river—Roche Jaune, yellow rock. Artist Point is, like Old Faithful, very crowded in the summer. The parking and viewing areas are being rebuilt as I write this. Enjoy the view even more by hiking to the Point along a fairly easy trail (South Rim) from the parking lot at Uncle Tom's Trail, a mile to the west. Wonderful views of the canyon show themselves here, without the crowds. In the summer, you can almost count on seeing an active osprey nest on a rock pinnacle. Artist Point is the viewpoint of Thomas Moran's great painting. I once traveled Yellowstone with Terry and Dori, two painter friends, and I learned from watching them work how to take in and process such extravagant natural beauty.

Seven: Upper Falls of the Yellowstone River: This is the companion to the Lower Fall and Canyon view. You can easily get right to the brink of the falls and watch, indeed, almost *feel* and *taste* the river tumble more than a hundred feet.

Eight: The Lamar. This is the name for the Lamar River Valley in the northeastern corner of the park, east of Roosevelt, where, in 1995, wolves were reintroduced into a park that had lacked them for seventy years. It has become the wolf-watching capital of the park, and, south of Alaska at least, it is America's Serengeti: the best place to watch antelope and great herds of elk and bison, and the attendant coyotes, wolves, and bears. The Absaroka Mountains form a gorgeous eastern backdrop. The road up the slope from Tower toward Dunraven Pass and Mount Washburn, along the Antelope Creek drainage, is becoming another animal-watching hot spot. More on this later.

Nine: Hayden Valley. Named for a son of the Great Road, geologist and surveyor Ferdinand V. Hayden, it is the lushest, grassiest, loveliest part of the park, usually full of animals, especially bison, elk, and Canada geese. The Yellowstone River meanders through it, and there are many viewponts to pull off the road and just enjoy the view. As of 2006, there's a new wolfpack, the Haydens, sometimes very visible, hanging out east of the river. If a grizz wanders through the valley (and one surely will eventually), all the better.

Ten: The lakes. Majestic Yellowstone Lake is a huge underused part of the park, and its southern reaches give an opportunity to explore real wilderness away from the cars and crowds. Shoshone Lake is even more remote: the largest backcountry lake in the lower forty-eight. You can't get to Shoshone and its geyser basin except by walking or paddling: no motorboats allowed. More on how to see these wonderful places later.

additional suggestions for finding the Peaceable Kingdom

One: Cliches got that way by once being new, fresh, and true. Don't avoid things just because they may sound trite, like Old Faithful. Yellowstone cliches include ranger programs. Most of them are insightful and substantive and fun, for both kids and grownups. Hey, grownups turn into kids in Yellowstone; at least I do. I'm about fourteen when I'm there. Twelve when a bear shows up. You haven't been to Yellowstone National Park until you've been to a ranger campfire program there, even if Ranger Ted is no more.

Two: Go where you hear the big animals are. They move (duh!), so ask at visitor centers for recent sightings. Big animals are usually visible

The Peaceable Campground, Loop A, Norris, Yellowstone

in the Lamar Valley, probably the most reliable place to see bison and wolves, and Hayden Valley, where bison are pretty predictable. Tower Junction is famous for black bears. Along the Madison River, between the west entrance and Madison Junction, and the headquarters at Mammoth, are the best places for elk. Government elk, I call 'em, right there next to the post office and the visitor center.

Three: Watch for traffic jams, most often bison jams these days, cars stopped along the roads, or groups of people with spotting scopes. That almost always means something worth watching. Stop and park carefully off the road. Most folks are delighted to help you spot what they see. I have never known a more welcoming, eager-to-help group than these regular professional and dedicated amateur animal watchers. Thank you so much, Brian and Kathie and Bill and Kathy and Rick. You'll see more animals from the road than you will on a hiking trail, but not if you whiz by at fifty m.p.h. Slow down and enjoy.

Four: Watch early and late and long. "Bears are where they find you," but not if you're not out looking, especially in the early morning and early evening. (Large animals often bed down in the heat of midday.) You have to work harder for your sightings now, but that just makes them sweeter.

Five: Do some of the grand, silly, civilized things. Stay a night or two at the newly renovated Old Faithful Inn, or, at the very least, wander in its lobby for a while. It's a time warp: welcome to 1905. Architect Robert Reamer's creation is six glorious stories of logs, some, admittedly, with steel supports hidden in them. It is a breathtaking space with a huge fireplace and a big clock, a silly, wondrous vision of the Enchanted Forest morphing into the Waldorf. It is the ur-example of the faux woodsy style that has come to be called "Parkitecture." Have a meal at Lake Hotel, where the breakfast trout is grand, and listen to pop tunes from the string trio or quartet before dinner. Does this stuff belong in national parks??? Of course not, but enjoy it anyway.

Some of the more absurd tourist shows are gone from the national parks forever. I am glad I got to see the Firefall off Glacier Point in Yosemite. Every summer night, a big bonfire was built, then shoved off the sheer cliff so tourists in the Valley could go "Oooooh!" and "Wow!" My family went "Oooooh!" and "Wow!" I am also glad it doesn't happen any more. Reservations are required for dinner at both Old Faithful Inn and Lake Hotel.

Six: If you can manage it, camp. That can be in a small tent, like me, or in a posh RV. The big payoff is that elk and bison don't come into the Old Faithful Inn, as they do to Loop A of Norris Campground, in the floodplain of the Gibbon River. A river site at Slough Creek can put you

The Peaceable Kingdom, mule dear bedding down
near our Slough Creek campsite

in touch with water ousels, weasels, mink, foxes, mule deer, moose, bears, coyotes. If you're already a camper, no prob. If you're not, consider renting an RV and staying in the park, not just near it. It's also more convenient—distances are long and speed limits low.

Seven: "Yellowstone" in these pages has been shorthand for Yellowstone National Park. There is a larger truth roughly eight times the size of the big park, a huge area now often called the Greater Yellowstone Ecosystem, comprising the park and large portions of the five national forests that surround it. These forests are lovely, dark and deep. The GYE area would be a great place to camp and hike and watch animals even if you never went into the park. Taste and enjoy these forests, perhaps stay a night in them before you enter the park. It's not a bad idea to do this if you're camping in Yellowstone, because you need to get to the best campgrounds by midmorning if you're to get a site. What great threshholds the Absaroka, Shoshone, Gallatin, and Bridger-Teton National Forests make! Consider joining the Greater Yellowstone Coalition, a lobbying group that promotes the health of the entire Yellowstone ecosystem. Get into "Y-2-Y," Yellowstone to Yukon, the grand plan to keep a corridor of wildness all the way from Yellowstone (the first "Y") to Canada's Yukon (the second "Y"). Animals don't understand political boundaries; Y-2-Y would let animals transcend them to some extent.

Eight: If you can, boat, canoe, or kayak. The easiest way to get deep into real Yellowstone wilderness is to get to the bottom of one of the eastern "arms" of Yellowstone Lake, where (whoopee!) motorized craft are not allowed. Almost one in five of the seventeen thousand backcountry campers in 2005 got into the wilderness by boat, me included. If you can't paddle long distances, a park concessioner from Bridge Bay Marina will ferry you to the entrances to these arms for a modest fee. Reserve a campsite by mail or at a back country office in the park, and the wilderness is yours. If you're not into wilderness, rent a motorboat and take a self-guided tour, fishing if you like.

But be careful. Yellowstone Lake is dangerous, much more dangerous than the famous bears. Even Shoshone Lake, much smaller, regularly claims lives—two in 2002, two in 2007, and one in adjacent Lewis Lake in 2005. The water is often so cold that, if you tip over, hypothermia can kill you in less than an hour. Wear flotation devices and stay close to shore on windy, wavy days, if you go out at all. Paddle early, before wind and waves get high. Boats with outboard motors are for rent at Bridge Bay Marina, and there are tour boats on which you can take a cruise. I finally took my first cruise in 2007, and it was delightful. If that's the only way you can get on the big lake, *do it*. I have read that people sometimes hear heavenly music coming from nowhere on these big quiet lakes (*Outside*, November, 2006). I've never heard it. Just being there is the music of the spheres, heavenly music, to me.

Nine: Yellowstone is a fishing paradise, though only in the lakes can you keep some of your catch and eat it. Every river is catch and release, unhook it and let it go. Barbless hooks have been required everywhere since 2006, a good idea. Yellowstone's cutthroat trout are big and beautiful and not hard to catch. Paul Schullery, a devoted fly fisherman, thinks they may have a "stupid gene." He also wonders about the propriety of catch-and-release fishing in the streams. Snag wildlife with a hook and drag 'em out of their habitats?? We don't do that to things that live *above* water. Why not catch-and-release elk? He's joking, I think, but he makes a good, funny point. "Rope 'em, Elkboy!"

Ten: At all costs, hike a little. Get just a few yards off the crowded main roads, and off the boardwalks around major thermal attractions, and you are in a quieter, sweeter Yellowstone. Long hikes are better, such as the fairly difficult walk to the top of Mt.Washburn, altitude 10,243 feet. The park contains more trails (1,200 miles worth) than almost anyone could walk in a lifetime. (Ranger Orville "Butch" Bach Jr. just might have done them all, and a lot of backcountry canoeing, too. See his good books in my Bibliography.) A few hundred yards, at any pace, will serve. If you're disabled, there are places for you, too— the hike to Lone Star Geyser, for example. It starts as a good, flat, former road, easy for wheelchairs. It follows the Firehole River for the first mile, and it's gorgeous.

Eleven: Or just stop at one of the many trailheads or picnic areas and go a few yards into the forest. Sit, be quiet, and listen. Get to know one of the rivers this way, by fishing or splashing in it. Swimming is not encouraged because most park waters are very cold. There are two exceptions: "Hot-potting," swimming at "Boiling River," where the Gardner River is warmed by thermal features just north of park headquarters at Mammoth; and, to the west, a swimming hole on Firehole Canyon Drive, one-way south from Madison. This drive is gorgeous even if you don't go to swim. Under no circumstances should you hot-pot in any other thermal features. It's destructive to them, and boiling is a nasty way to die.

Twelve: Don't spend all your time in a car, but do try to get a feel for the very different areas of the park: The geyser basins (chiefly southwest); the Lake (southeast); the lush valley and high peaks and passes (east); and the whole northern third, which is low, sagebrushy, warmer, and forested only at its higher altitudes. I used to prefer the southern loop of the Grand Loop road system. Now I spend most of my time in the north, where tourists are fewer, and large animals, especially bears and wolves, are usually easier to find.

Thirteen: Again, don't spend all your time in a car, but take whatever dirt or gravel roads are available. (They're not always open). Blacktail Deer Plateau Drive is a one-way seven mile loop off the road from Mammoth to Tower. Don't worry about the road surface. They wouldn't let you on it if it required high clearance or four wheel drive. If the Park Service has a fault in its treatment of the public, it is that it's often a fussy nanny, always warning and scolding. Yeah, I know, there's a lot of meat-heads out there and they need to be protected from themselves. True. Point taken. But it should make you realize that if a road is open, it's probably quite safe. Drive slowly, stop among the wildflowers (parking off-road), take a little hike, and soak up the views and the animals, the silence, and the absence of traffic.

Fourteen: At least once, stop at a signed feature on impulse, one you've never heard of. Some of the best features in the park are relatively little known: Monument Geyser Basin (a short but very steep hike) comes to mind. If possible, take a short hike to a minor thermal area such as Artist Paint Pots or Clear Lake/Mud Lake. The former is signed on the main road; the latter takes some seeking, walking, and planning. The rangers and the other staff at the visitor centers are mostly great people, patient, knowledgeable, and helpful. They'll gladly direct you to a hike within your competence.

There. Mac's Fourteen Points. No more suggestions. You can't do it all the first time. I haven't done it all in twenty-seven visits, so I keep going back. One of the joys of Yellowstone is that no one can ever know it all, so there are always wonderful new things to see and do, and reasons to return.

fire : naturally reseeding yellowstone

One of the things you will doubtless notice on your trip is the impact of the famous fires of 1988. Some of the media (and many local politicians, who should have known better, and shut up) fulminated against the Park Service's patient fire policy, and wailed that the park was ruined forever. Well-meaning New Jersey schoolkids sent tree seeds, sure that the park would need replanting.

Summer 1988 was indeed a harrowing time. See Dan Sholly's *Guardians of Yellowstone* for a good blow-by-blow account of it all, the firefighting and the political pressure and the hysteria and worrying and, finally, the late arrival of the rain and snow that put the fires out, as they always do. In fact, most of the park did not burn at all, despite the presence of explosive fuel levels from a century of fire suppression. Those areas that did burn—about one-third of the park—did not lose every tree. In about half of that third, undergrowth burned without starting crown fires, so most mature trees survived. Approximately four hundred elk died of asphyxiation. Very few other large animals were killed: five bison, one bear, a few deer and moose (*Guardians of Yellowstone*, 278). No significant structures were destroyed, though the glorious Old Faithful Inn came perilously close to fiery destruction. Yet there are large areas—west from Mt. Washburn or just north of the South Entrance—that are still seriously scarred.

A small fire at Mary Mountain fills the sky, Yellowstone, 2006

The situation is best summed up by the inconspicuous signs the Park Service has put in burn areas all over the park: "Naturally Reseeded by Wildfire in 1988." True. The lodgepole pine is the dominant, climax tree species in most of the park. It takes its name from being tall and strong and slender, perfect, when young, for tipi poles. Lodgepole pine cones (and the seeds in them) fall to the ground every year, where the seeds are eaten by birds or ground squirrels or other small rodents, or buried, or left to rot back into the earth. Lodgepole pines in some areas produce cones that are serotinous: they remain tightly closed even after they mature, protecting and preserving their seeds. These seeds can remain viable for decades. Only very high temperatures can melt the cones' resins and permit the seeds to fall out. Thus, there are always huge quantities of viable seeds ready to sprout after fires such as those of 1988 (Romme and Tinker, *Yellowstone Science* 14, 1, Winter 2006, 16). Seeds from these serotinous cones are incapable of generating *until* what humans regard as a catastrophic event—a major forest fire—occurs. When the cones are burst open by the heat of the fire, the seeds take root in the rich ashy soil left behind, and are fertilized by minerals from the dead trees. The loss of mature trees opens areas so that sunlight can foster new growth. From death, life. No fires, few new trees.

Now, when you drive the roads or hike the backcountry, you see whole roadsides and hillsides covered with young trees, some three or four feet tall, some ten or twelve, growing vigorously among the deadfalls. It's gorgeous, it's natural, and it's a triumph, not a disaster. The road from Norris to Mammoth is especially rich in this regard. I have heard tourists say, "It's nice, but they oughta clear out those old dead trees." No. Not if we want the new trees to have the minerals of the old trees to grow on. Not if animals who love dead trees, woodpeckers, for example, are to survive. Not unless "park" has to mean something like Versailles. Yuck. Here it comes, the heretical truth: despite the temporary loss of some tourist income in the gateway towns, *the fires of 1988 were the best thing that's happened to the park in many years.* There, I said it and it felt good. 2006 was a record fire season in the West, and there were many small fires in Yellowstone, one ominously covering a quarter of the sky with smoke when I was there in July 2006. But it went out naturally. 2007 looks even worse, major fires in Utah and California, even east in Georgia and Florida. But I would bet there won't be major damage in Yellowstone any time soon, because a century's worth of fuel burned up in 1988.

change and the new west

This irony—that change can look disastrous but be beneficial—can be extrapolated to a historical truth about the national parks. Their establishment often faces serious opposition from local people who fear that their livelihoods will be locked away behind elitist walls. Grand Teton National Park, that glorious land of spectacular mountains and lakes just south of Yellowstone, was established only after a long and nasty struggle. The Rockefeller family quietly, secretly, patiently, bought up the necessary land, but the park's establishment was bitterly opposed and long delayed. People in Jackson still grumble about the intrusive Fedral Gummint. Yet consider Jackson. It's not to everyone's taste, including mine. It's tres fou-fou, hugely upscale, not the raw cowtown I first saw in 1955. But no one can deny that it has profited richly from its park, as northwestern Wyoming has from Yellowstone, indeed, as almost every park area has.

It's hard to get people, particularly independent Westerners, to change their ways. But the gold and the silver are mostly gone, or at least so hard to extract that they're not economically productive any more, at least not without poisoning the land and water. Bernard DeVoto, who loved his native West, once called it a "plundered province." There are more cows in feedlots than even McDonald's needs. Farm prices are chronically low and getting lower, except for feed grains, not grown much here, whose prices are currently sky high because of ethanol. Timber and cattle prices are low, and agricultural competition is stiff and increasingly international. Coal and natural gas are abundant and their prices are rising, but the environmental cost of burning or retrieving them is high.

The truth that many Westerners are coming to know is that their dirty, exciting, romantic, extractive, dig-it-up-and-leave-a-mess-and-run, boom-and-bust past is mostly just that: past. And the best economic things they've got going for them are open space, clean water and air, forests, wild animals, hunting and fishing, and Yellowstone and all its younger siblings among the national parks. In August 2002, the prestigious journal *Science* published a landmark study demonstrating that conservation is as much as one hundred times more valuable—in dollars and cents, not even figuring in scenery or fun—than the economic gain from using and damaging the environment. True, and we are slowly beginning to adjust to that truth.

regaining paradise

There is little left in the East of the dense forest the first Europeans encountered. Pilgrims and Puritans thought of nature as "a hideous and desolate wilderness, full of wild beasts and wild men," in the words of William Bradford in 1620, and they cut down the forests as quickly as they could. It took Thoreau and the Romantic Transcendentalists to teach us that we had lost a paradise in gaining control over and diminishing nature. When Thoreau walked Cape Cod in 1849 and 1855, much of the Cape had become nearly treeless. In two centuries of settlement, almost all of the trees had been cut down for fuel and building, and the land cleared for subsistence farming. Here's how he described it:

> In short, we were traversing a desert, with the view of an autumnal landscape of extraordinary brilliancy, a sort of Promised Land, on the one hand, and the ocean on the other. Yet, though the prospect was so extensive and the country for the most part destitute of trees . . . the solitude was that of the ocean and the desert combined. (*Cape Cod*, Parnassus, 72–73)

Cape Cod has many trees again, and it's green and lovely, one of my favorite American places. But except for the lovely expanses of the Cape Cod National Seashore, the Cape is now mostly building lots. Cape Cod has turned into a nice, quiet, safe, temperate, pretty place for well-off people to retire to, where they can build cottages in the woods or McMansions next to the National Seashore. Where will our descendants find space, openness, freedom, wildness? Where will they find what Aldo Leopold loved and insisted that we needed? "Man always kills the things he loves, and so we the pioneers have killed our wilderness. Some say we had to. Be that as it may, I am glad I shall never be young without wild country to be young in. Of what avail are forty freedoms without a blank spot on the map?"

Yellowstone is showing the way again, as it did at its founding. The New West will one day be valued more for its beauty and its wildlife, its sweet spaces and silences, than for its mineral wealth. Perhaps Paradise can be Regained, as Milton's fallen Adam and Eve can hope to rediscover it at the end of *Paradise Lost*: "A paradise within thee, happier far." Will the Peaceable Kingdom ever come? If it does, US 20, the Great Road, will run to it and right through it.

chapter seven

the great road to wilderness

◆ Roads are a sure sign and necessary feature of civilization. They grow from tracks and paths because of our need to connect villages and hunting grounds, or cities and farms, to move people and products. Some roads also go to wilderness. The Great Road goes to America's greatest wilderness treasure, Yellowstone National Park.

Yellowstone National Park is so big and diverse that it presents different faces to different people, gives different answers to their different questions. The previous chapter has discussed its most famous attributes: charismatic mammals, gorgeous vistas, and thermal features, largely visible either from the main tourist roads or from boardwalks conveniently close to those roads. The main park road, the figure-eight Grand Loop, was built to go to those thermal features. The animals are everywhere, especially in spring, and are easier to spot near the openness of a roadway than in the adjacent forest. Thus, the road is a great way to see much of the park. Buses full of senior citizens, vans and RVs full of families, nearly three million people a year, show up to get in touch with their natural heritage. They hit some other, more civilized places, too, such as the magnificent Old Faithful Inn, a century old in 2004, and its restaurants and shops.

It is thus quite possible to have a Yellowstone experience of several days' duration and never leave the society of crowds of people. You may log two bears and six geysers, sleep and eat in very nice hotels, listen to pop tunes from a string quartet, buy yourself a cap and Aunt Myrtle a trinket, and go back to Cleveland refreshed, enriched, and ennobled, thinking you have done the park. Most of Yellowstone's visitors would agree that you have. And there's nothing wrong with this; it's a glorious way to spend a summer vacation, and the kids will remember it forever.

There are other Yellowstones that I think are more thrilling and more important. This chapter is about them. In what follows I will raise the troubling political issues of how the national parks should be used; of how much wilderness should be set aside within or separate from the parks; of what wilderness is and what it is for; and of how and how much it can be exploited and used without ceasing to be wilderness.

wild Yellowstone and the American wilderness

"In wildness is the preservation of the world," wrote Henry David Thoreau in 1862, a century ahead of his time, and most of us agree with this radical idea to some extent. Even the most output-determined of strip mine bosses probably wants his operations to rest lightly enough on the land so that there will be antelope as well as tailing piles and leaky containment pools for his grandchildren to recognize as his legacy. His main aim is and should be profit, but he likes a good viewscape too, and it's good PR. Maybe he enjoys hunting, and he knows that conserving habitat and wild animals, even nurturing Bambi just so we can blow him away, is good for the corporate image. We all know that without Thoreau's Wildness, without some concern for animal species that do not yield an immediate profit, we would lose key parts of our historic national heritage. Thus, places such as Grand Teton and Yellowstone National Parks have evolved into a sanctuary and breeding ground for animals such as elk and bison.

Two hundred years ago, there were an estimated thirty to sixty million bison living in the area that would become the United States, many more bison than people. Seventy-five years after that, in the 1880s, there were fewer than one hundred bison left south of Canada. Their last refuge was—where else?—in the recently created Yellowstone National Park. Park literature says there were fewer than two dozen bison remaining in the park in 1901. Their ancestors had been slaughtered for hides, for meat, for fertilizer, for sport, and as government policy, to end the independent life of the Plains Indians. When Indians could no longer live off the buffalo herds—their Wal-Mart, Rite-Aid, Safeway, Cineplex, ESPN, and Home Depot rolled into one—they had little choice but to "come in," to accept a dreary, fenced-in reservation life. Though interbreeding with Canadian animals and even with domestic cattle has changed the species somewhat, we can still see in them something of what our natural world looked like before "the white man's buffalo," beef cattle, replaced the bison. The purest of the *bison bison* breed, not surprisingly, survive in Yellowstone and Wind Cave National Parks (*New York Times*, January 9, 2007).

Flo Gardipee is a University of Montana grad student who describes herself as a "professional pooper scooper." She follows bison in Yellowstone and Grand Teton National Parks, whisks bits of their fresh turds away, and studies the mitochondrial DNA from those samples. Gardipee studies poo. I'm not making this up, you know! This noninvasive

Pronghorn Antelope, Blacktail Deer Plateau

technique has yielded important information: that there are at least two quite distinct breeding groups of bison in the park. That's the straight poop. The two thousand in Hayden Valley are genetically distinct from the nine hundred to the north in the Lamar, who are more diverse genetically. Are these Lamar bison more likely to leave the park and die? If so, we are in danger of losing much of their precious genetic diversity (YubaNet.com, University of Montana, January 29, 2007).

By and large, even very conservative, profit-oriented Westerners agree that some bison and other wild animals should be preserved. But the devil is in the details and the numbers. Bison don't know about boundaries, so in the winter, in search of forage and warmth, they often leave Yellowstone National Park at its north entrance, thereby losing their protection, and walk to their deaths at the hands and the guns of Montana Department of Livestock employees, or of licensed hunters. Montana ranchers are concerned that their cattle might catch brucellosis, a cattle disease some of the bison have, and abort their calves. There has never been a documented case of cross-species infection from the bison herd, but ranchers say they are working on a narrow profit margin—that's certainly true, truer all the time—and they can't take the chance. Thus, most winters, we see the grisly spectacle of bison being slaughtered while Indians and environmentalists struggle desperately, on the ground and in the courts, to stop the killing. The winters of 1990–1991 and 1996–1997 were bad, but it got worse. As many as nine hundred were shot and killed in the winter of 2005–2006. Licenses

Bison, Lamar Valley

awarded to Montana hunters for the 2006–2007 season grew from 50 to 140, with an increased focus on bison cows, to decrease the size of the herd. Yellowstone now plans to reduce its herd from approximately 3,500 to 3,000; in plainer words, to kill hundreds more bison (*New York Times*, November 13, 2006).

How to end this awful impasse? It seems simple enough: let the federal government aquire the rather small area the bison move into, and

Pronghorn Antelope, Lamar Valley; note the radio collar

add it to the park or make it an adjacent sanctuary. In fact, the neighboring Church Universal and Triumphant did agree to a land sale and swap with the federal government for just this purpose—for a hefty $13 million. But there still isn't a functioning winter sanctuary outside the park for Yellowstone bison, because the church has retained grazing rights to the land, and we're back to the brucellosis issue again: cattle and bison mixing. Another $3 million might fix it, paying a whopping price to retire the grazing rights. In addition to financial constraints, there is usually local opposition to the creation or expansion of park lands, though it often fades quickly when a good deal is offered to the local people. We as a nation will not do the right and sensible thing if we do not have a fundamental respect for wildness and its values, which transcend (but often include) the purely economic. And we certainly cannot do it when federal leaders are savagely cutting back on expenditures for land acquisition and park maintenance. That's one example of the value of wildness and the struggle that competing views of it can generate.

wildness and wilderness

"Wilderness" is not quite the same thing as wildness. As I was writing the first draft of this section, I saw a tiny gray streak scuttle behind a filing cabinet. Mouse. Damn. Doesn't belong here. A wild thing in a computer room. As Mary Douglas taught us, dirt is matter out of place. Set the trap. I did. SNAP! Wildness is lovely if it doesn't screw up our civilized behavior patterns. We may know we need it, but not in our houses, thanks. This old house, in the falling-down state it was in when I bought it, has harbored mice, rats, squirrels, bats, a racoon, a skunk, a groundhog, a robin, a chickadee, and insect species galore. Who knows what else? Pretty wild, huh? "Wild Kingdom," right here in my house.

But wilderness is something very different. The definition adopted by the Wilderness Society, then used in the Wilderness Act of 1964, a century after Thoreau, is both geographic and cultural. Wilderness is "an area where the earth and its community of life are untrammeled by man, where man himself is a visitor who does not remain." That's a very good start. But it automatically follows that it must also be a place of significant size, or it would be under constant barrage from its civilized boundaries, and it must be a place that is not privately owned and used.

One example:

There is a tiny National Forest, 16,032 acres, in the Finger Lakes region of New York, in the town of Hector, just south of the Great Road. It's an odd, unique remnant of a Depression-era soil conservation program. It became Finger Lakes National Forest only in 1985. It's a pretty place, and you can hike, ski, and snowmobile there. Its contains twenty-five square miles. That makes it seven-tenths of one percent the size of Yellowstone. It is publicly, federally owned, and probably will not soon become a subdivision; but it is surely too small and too close to farms and towns ever to be considered wilderness. Designated wildernesses can officially be as small as five thousand acres, but they would need to be surrounded by something other than farms and busy roads: something like a real, sizeable national forest.

Another example:

There are large forested areas in the North, West, and especially the South, owned and planted by lumber and paper companies, where trees are planted and left to grow until they are big enough to harvest. Monoculture: one crop, clear cut every X years. Fairly big, kinda pretty, surely harboring many wild animals, but not old or diverse or wild enough. Not wilderness.

And another example, quite different:

On December 1, 2006, President Bush signed into law the New England Wilderness Act, designating 76,000 acres of forest as wilderness in Vermont and New Hampshire. This land was carved out of the Green Mountain and White Mountain National Forests. It's small, it's precious little, but it's precious nonetheless, especially in the highly populated northeast. It will be a sanctuary for black bears and many other animals. Well done, Mr. Bush, and thanks to the states' congressional delegations as well.[1]

We can't afford to be too exclusive, or the only wilderness we could claim would be at or near the lonely, frozen poles—and even they, especially the heavily studied and continually occupied and littered South Pole, would be questionable. If only old growth forest qualifies, there wouldn't be much in the national forests, and precious little in the national park system. Biodiversity, size, wild animals, limited or no hunting, no economic exploitation—we're getting closer.

What about regulation and mapping and control? True wilderness, it might be argued, should be unregulated, unknown, and uncontrolled, even dangerous. That's certainly what wilderness meant to civilized Europe and America before the Romantic movement made it Byronic, fashionable, madly and dangerously beautiful. If that's a necessary criterion, then Yellowstone—even the wildest patches of it—might not qualify. William Blake's "London" was full of "chartered streets," i.e., land marked and squared and owned and known and controlled, like its people. Yellowstone is marked and managed and controlled, too, not just left to run wild.

Indeed, Yellowstone has never been officially declared to contain any wilderness at all. In 1972, nine-tenths of the park—more than two million acres—was recommended for federal wilderness designation. For a third of a century, dilatory Congresses have failed to finalize this recommendation, but wilderness lovers know better. In 2005, 16,970 backcountry visitors spent an average of 2.3 nights in the wilderness (*Yellowstone Today*, 165). That's a lot of happy campers. I'm happy to say that my son Bernie and I were two of them. For six nights. And it was wilderness we were in, whatever its official designation.

Those of us who love the national parks sometimes grumble about the tendency of their keepers to be fussy, bureaucratic, and intrusive. But really, what choice do they have? If they are to keep them "unimpaired" for the future, and keep the dimmer visitors from committing ecological atrocities or unintended suicide, they *have* to be fussy. It does jar one a bit to be in the Yellowstone wilderness, many miles from a road, looking for a place to pitch a tent, and find a sign that says "6A2," meaning, essentially, "You can camp here if you've got the right permit and it's in season, but not otherwise." Yet the main criterion—where man himself is a visitor who does not remain—is still met.

Another issue beyond size, wildness, and control, is use. Why lock up millions of acres of wilderness that no one can put to good sound economic use? Alfred Runte has argued that the great American parklands would never have been created if their land had been thought to have significant economic value. They are what and where they are because settler-developers thought them too mountainous or arid or wild to exploit successfully. Even if we agree that economic potential is not the sole criterion for land use, what good is a gorgeous forest or desert or marsh for those who can't go into it, and will never see it? Isn't it undemocratic, even elitist, to reserve large swatches of the national heritage to gratify a few, young and fit and venturesome enough to enjoy them?

The answer is NO, in thunder. And I am a real good example of why it's no.

In my seventieth year, I asked several friends if they wanted to have a wilderness experience with me. Though relatively fit, I thought I was too old to go very far into the Yellowstone backcountry wilderness on my feet. I thought about it. I run (slowly) at least two miles every day. I could have made the attempt. But could I carry food, tent, kitchen equipment, sleeping gear, extra clothing, and water or a water filtration system? Probably not, not very far, at least. The legs go first, athletes say. I hadn't been smart enough to do it when I was younger. But I could paddle a canoe, sit and pull for hours, and thus I could get far from any road, far from any crowd, and find out what, if anything, wilderness means and does. I did, and it was magical.

planning a wilderness canoe trip

Two of my friends, in their fifties, leaped at the chance. A third, much younger, pouted the next day that I hadn't asked him, and I quickly did. Our story is one that any reasonably fit septuagenarian could, if he or she wished, imitate. Wilderness is available for any and all who wish it, and what a delight it is to know that. Four paddlers, two canoes, perfect. If one canoe tips in cold water, a second can give aid. We found a time when we could all devote a bare two weeks: early June, hardly an ideal time for paddling a cold high mountain lake, but it would have to do. We live 1,900 miles from the park, so we needed to rent canoes on site. This was harder than I'd expected, because the park concessioner had recently decided that the danger of lawsuits was too great for the profit involved. No canoes for you! But we found a

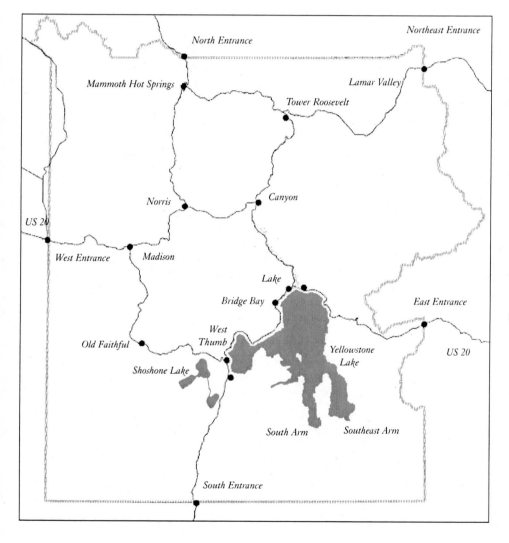

Map of Yellowstone

good guy in Livingston, Montana, who agreed to rental, shuttle, and pickup for a reasonable price. Thanks, Jason, and thanks to Mardie, too, another year.

Yellowstone Lake has earned its reputation for being cold and dangerous. Many more people die in its waters than are killed by bears or bison. I decided that a one-way paddle, keeping the prevailing southwesterly winds behind us, was relatively safe and achievable. We would never have to be more than two miles from shore; in a lake this big and stormy and cold, that seemed scary enough, and, believe me, it was. In just a few days we could go from the big lake's southwest corner—the Grant boat launch at West Thumb—to the extreme southeast corner, my true goal, the very bottom of Southeast Arm. (Do follow this on a map, won't you?) We would traverse the entire south shore of the huge lake, and pass by or enter the openings of its three great bays, the "arms." In addition, we would get to the bottom of at least one of the arms, where no boats with motors are allowed. Want silence? Space? Earn it: paddle or walk.

rules and regs in the wilderness : selecting campsites

Next step: Get the backcountry rules, regulations, and maps. Our timing was not ideal; many good lakeshore campsites are closed in June. Bears are largely vegetarian, but, like us, omnivorous. Cutthroat trout are relatively easy to catch as they spawn in the shallow streams, so bears gorge on the piscine protein. Yellowstone's backcountry managers properly insist that this buffet should be reserved for the bears until mid July, so some lovely sites are out. Okay, we can deal with that.

With help from Yellowstone Ranger Roy de Walt's fine photos and descriptions of all the campsites on the lake, available on line, I chose three that looked fine. We would do 7L7, at the entrance to South Mountain Arm, for the first night; cross that arm and South Arm to 5L5 for night two; and spend three whole nights at 6A4, the last campsite on the lake, near the marshy delta where the Yellowstone River enters the lake, as far as we could get on the lake from anything civilized. 6A4 was also appealing because it had a bear box for food storage—heavy metal, man, no bear could get at your trail mix there! That implied lots of bear activity—a mixed blessing—but it also meant less work hanging food over a pole to keep it from the bears. And the mice, which are equally voracious.

Send in your choices by April 1, please, with a check for twenty bucks and some personal info, and hold your breath.

Comes a call from the Backcountry Office checking out our abilities and my sanity.

"You weren't planning to paddle back across the lake, were you?"

"No, ma'am, we're doing a shuttle for the return trip."

"Looks good to me," she says. And in a week I got a confirming letter, no changes required, and we really *were* good to go. *YES!*

the trip : problems, solutions, and animals

This isn't the place for lengthy discussions of tents or clothing or canoeing techniques. Moderate skills, equipment, and knowledge, mated to cautious judgment and good sense, are quite enough for this sort of

Cow moose and calf
Floating Island Lake, Yellowstone

trip. I delegated the kitchen and food planning to two other paddlers. We expected to be working hard and eating voraciously, so we packed lots of food, especially trail mix and jerky. Surprisingly, we brought much of it home. One of my favorite photos from the trip is of a large bottle of waffle syrup, sitting lonely and unused. On the long travel days, we were often too tired to eat much; the exercise had suppressed our appetites. We ate very well, including fresh-caught lake trout (Thanks, Tom) but we ate lightly. That's usually a good idea, perhaps especially in wilderness.

I have sometimes experienced at Yellowstone the beginning symptoms of altitude sickness, my chief symptom being insomnia, inability to breathe and sleep well and comfortably in oxygen-thin air. I decided we needed to acclimate before the trip. We had three days on the road, starting near sea level; two days at Slough Creek campground in the park (c. 6,100 ft.); and one night at a motel unit at Lake (c. 7,750 ft.). Those three days did the job. We worked and slept well. For once, good planning.

Our two days at Slough Creek were magnificent. We entered the park at the northeast entrance in the morning, still without a campsite, anxious to set up. (You can't reserve the campsites I like best.) We stopped to look at the Pebble Creek campground. I had read online that there had been some recent grizz trouble there—a young bear had actually jumped on and rolled around on a tent—and I'd thought the campground might be closed. (I later learned from a ranger that this bear had earned a nickname: "Pounce.") When we arrived, we found a partial closing—no soft sided units (tents, like ours) allowed—and a partially flooded campground. Wet ground is not nice for campers, but it was lovely for the two moose browsing on water plants in the creek there—our first large park mammals, and the only moose we would see on this trip. (Moose have declined here since the great fire year of 1988, as they need old growth forest, and about one-third of that burned. There are probably fewer than five hundred moose in the park today, perhaps no more than three hundred. Yet I saw more in June 2007 than I ever had before.)

Back on the main road, heading west toward a campsite. Bison and elk across the Lamar River. Then, "Dogs!" says Ted.

Wolves.

Thirty minutes into the park and we are seeing a life and death chase. Three members of the Druid wolfpack are trying to run down a pronghorn antelope, chasing it, testing its speed and condition, turning it, following it. (Wolves would have difficulty catching a healthy pronghorn.) What Barry Lopez (in *Of Wolves and Men*) calls "the conversation of death" goes on for ten long, riveting minutes. "I think we'll see a kill."

Wrong. Potential tragedy for the antelope turns into farce; the antelope is now attacking, or at least charging, the wolves. They scatter and melt back into the trees. Antelope male in his territory, irritated by all this fuss? Female with young hidden nearby? We'll never know. When the encounter breaks off, we can breathe again. And we *still* don't have a campsite. (Slough Creek and Pebble Creek campgrounds, small and well located for animal watching, tend to fill up early. Mammoth campground is a good nearby last resort, and larger, often not filling even in high summer.)

I went back to the same wonderful places the following year, with different friends. It was later in the season, July, so the watching crowds were bigger and the animals a little scarcer. Our first morning in the Lamar was cold and relatively unproductive. Just after dawn on the second day, we watched bison and wolves for two hours, culminating in the thrill of seeing the Druid wolves run across the road in front of us to their home area on the flanks of the mountain they're named for.

Lamar River
Photo by Jack Berkley

Slough Creek campground

Of all the developed campgrounds in Yellowstone, my favorite is Slough Creek. It is in the heart of the Lamar River region, once lightly visited, now the prime place to see predators and prey in their mortal dance. Slough Creek is northern, low, relatively warm. It has a stunning backdrop, the Absaroka Mountains, on the eastern boundary of the park. It has a gorgeous river (forget "creek") running through it, so strong in the spring that it is dangerous to ford or swim in. Minks and water ousels ("dippers," small diving birds) work its banks. Across the river is a large meadow, sometimes occupied by grazing moose. The campground is two and a half miles of bumpy, twisty gravel from the main park road, so nobody just drives by. There are twenty-nine campsites, three pumps, three clean outhouses, no crowds. We take the last, farthest site, still with a lovely view of the river, set up, talk to the campground host, and find that a young grizz has been here, too—probably the same one, "Pounce"—last night.

Moon at dawn over Sough Creek

Grizzlies have strong family values, if we count just sows (females) and their cubs. Boars (males) sometimes kill cubs, as it brings the bereft sows into heat sooner. Cubs usually stay with their mothers for two years. Then, ready to be impregnated again in a brief encounter with a boar, the sow chases off her cub or cubs, who must make it on their own. Much of the odd bear behavior we observe, such as the grizz at Pebble and Slough, is from these two-year-olds, grizzly adolescents, trying to find and establish their place in the world.

We talk to campers who describe the young bear's path along the creek the night before. They clearly loved it, though it gave them the shivers. We're jealous. We'd like to see him tonight, though we certainly don't want the campground closed to tenters. After a day of hiking, writing, resting, and wildlife watching in the Lamar, we settle for coyotes yipping in the distance, and eight mule deer who bed down quietly within fifty feet of our three tents. It's the Peaceable Kingdom, sort of, and we are flattered by their trusting proximity. Not bad for less than a day in Parkadise.

first full day in the park : the top dogs Are back

Up early to catch the best wolf watching time, back to what we call "Spotting Hill" in the Lamar Valley. (It's called "Dave's Hill" by veteran wolf watchers. We have no clue who Dave is or was.) When wildlife are around, it's full of people with impressive optical equipment. Be sure to take binoculars when you go, but the animal-watching community is always happy to let you take a look at what they've come to see. And they have really good scopes. We arrive in time to see two dark wolves testing a bull elk; the elk did most of the chasing. The crowd was large and appreciative, but no business resulted, and we wondered about the hungry wolf cubs.

These Druid wolves are among the oldest of the many packs of gray wolves here. They're named for Druid Peak, a mountain north of the road that dominates this area. In 1995, members of an interagency wolf reintroduction team brought captured Canadian wolves into a holding pen south of the road to acclimate them to their new surroundings. The wolves were from the area of Hilton, Alberta, east of Jasper National Park; they were proficient at preying on elk. Later, the team introduced wolves from British Columbia who had preyed on both elk and bison. The Alberta wolves were fed with elk roadkill brought by wildlife managers. When the pen's gate was opened, the wolves at first didn't leave.

They were suspicious of the open gate, afraid of this brave new world. When the fences were cut and they left the pen, they soon formed into several different packs. They found themselves in Wolf Heaven—among abundant prey species, chiefly elk that had never seen a wolf, though they harbored a proper fear in their genes.

Ranger Doug Smith supervised the complex operation. Interior Secretary Bruce Babbitt was there helping carry the cages, as was the late Mollie Beattie, then head of the U.S. Fish and Wildlife Service. (Mollie now has a Yellowstone wolf pack named after her.) It was a great and historic moment, long dreaded by local ranchers, long overdue to environmentalists. Ranger Rick McIntyre, who has studied these wolves since they've been here, spoke of that pen—I saw it, with him—as "Plymouth Rock," where the new wolves first put a paw in an ecosystem they'd been gone from for seventy years. When the wolves left the pen, the most important missing piece of the park's original natural ecology was back. Eight separate reintroductions were carried out from three different pens in 1995 and 1996; the Druid pack was one of those established in 1996. Of the large mammals who once lived in Yellowstone, only the black-footed ferret is still missing. (There are no prairie dogs here to feed ferrets, though ground squirrels might do.)

the ebb and flow of life in Yellowstone's wolf packs

Nature is pitiless. The Druid Pack, once solidly established, has experienced hard times. The year 2005 was very hard on wolves, especially pups; parvovirus, probably caught from local dogs or infected park coyotes, is the suspected cause. The Druids lost all that year's pups, but the pack is still around, though it became much weaker in numbers (four adults) and was forced out of its original territory. The Druids moved farther east, near Cache Creek, then farther, beyond the park's eastern boundary. As of August 2006, the Druid adults had raised eleven apparently healthy pups. All were alive as of October 2006.

Of the Sloughs' 2005 pups, only three survived. (Source: interview with Brian Connolly.) Now the Sloughs seem to be making a comeback, too. They appear to have reclaimed their territory in the central Lamar Valley (Ralph Maughan's Wolf Report, August 30, 2006). They had a "howling bout" with the Unknown Pack in October (Ralph Maughan's Wildlife News). As of January 2007, they seem to have accepted a new alpha male; they were down to seven adult females, as all their original males had died. An Agate Creek pack yearling seized this great opportunity and became their new alpha male. I was thrilled in June of 2007 to see them (from a great distance) make a chase and a kill, running down a pronghorn across the Lamar Valley.

I was delighted to be with Rick McIntyre in July 2006 when, with the help of radio telemetry, he spotted the Sloughs for the first time in three months. In June 2007, I watched the Sloughs feed on a dawn bison kill, near the top of a distant hill in clear telescopic view. The bison's stiff forelegs wobbled as they worked the carcass. They left their prize to a cinnamon black bear, who kept them away for a time; then they retook it when the bear left. Coyotes waited their turn. As of December 2005, Yellowstone's wolf population was at 118, down 30 percent from the 171 of 2004 (*Yellowstone Today*, 174). That's hard, but that's how nature works. The wolf population was up 16 percent to 136 at the end of 2006, though 45 percent of those were pups. There were ten breeding pairs in thirteen packs (Ralph Maughan, January 23, 2007). Mollie's Pack lost all its 2005 pups, too; they had six in 2006. Mange, a serious canine disease caused by

Ranger Rick McIntyre leads hike to historic wolf site

Ranger Bill Wengeler and wolf watchers, Antelope Creek, Yellowstone

a mite, has been diagnosed in the alpha male of Mollie's Pack. That's real bad news. Hitherto, because all wolf migration had been outward, the park's wolves had not been infected with mange.

But the good news is that, despite problems and cyclic ups and downs, the park is nearly whole again, for the first time in seventy years. That historic 1995 pen, by the way, has been disassembled. Rick tells me you can still tell where it was from the many elk bones still on the site.

There has been trouble when wolves leave the park and kill cattle or sheep. As there are now (in 2007) about 325 wolves in the entire Greater Yellowstone ecosystem, some cattle predation is inevitable. For a rancher who sees a wolf, the mantra is said to be "Shoot, shovel, and shut up." You'd think that Yellowstone's wolves would mostly stay in the park. Why would they leave such a banquet, such rich hunting grounds? (There are as many as twenty-five thousand elk, their main food source, in the park in the summer.) Wolf predation of nearby livestock has proven to be less than was predicted—an average of about thirty sheep and four cows a year, according to one source (*Yellowstone Today*, 174).[2]

But researchers note that the main reason for the loss of adult wolves in the park is that they migrate out. Wolves *do* leave the park. Pressure for territory in the park pushes them toward and beyond the park's boundaries, where there's less wolf competition, though a lot more cows, sheep, ranchers, and rifles. Western wolves have been recommended for removal from the Endangered Species list. In at least two states, Idaho and Montana, that would surely mean the early death of most of them, as the states, not the federal government, would be in control, and wolves would have less protection. Now, when there are demonstrable wolf predations outside the park, ranchers are compensated, as they surely should be. The compensatory money is currently provided by the private group Defenders of Wildlife.

There's also a huge local economic bonanza from wolf reintroduction, estimated by one economist at $35 million a year (*New York Times,* February 5, 2006). The gateway towns to the north and east—Cooke City, Silver Gate, and Gardiner, Montana—have seen their motel and

Mac and Ted wolf watching, Lamar Valley, 2003

restaurant businesses flourish. Housing in the northeast part of the park—at Mammoth and Roosevelt—is full to bulging every summer, so Xanterra, the concessioner, is happy. People *really* want to watch wolves. Unless you're a nervous elk (chief prey) or a grumpy coyote (no longer top dog), you have to agree that wolf reintroduction is a smashing success. In 2005, Ranger Bill Wengeler told me that the park's coyote population might be down by as much as 50 percent. A year later, he told me that down 30 percent is probably more accurate, but at any rate there are fewer than there were, and more ground squirrels—a main coyote food source—as a result. Even the surviving coyotes may have gained something. Wolves are better than coyotes at killing large prey, so there are now more elk carcasses for coyotes to scavenge (James C. Halfpenny, *Yellowstone Wolves in the Wild*, 63). Interestingly, the number of red foxes seems to be increasing, probably as coyote numbers decrease. Park publications say so, and I certainly see more foxes than I did in the past.

officialdom and a messenger from the wild

Even with a letter with backcountry campsites and dates settled, you still need a backcountry permit, available at three ranger stations in the park. We also needed permits for our rented boats. We went to Bridge Bay, where we would be picked up the next day by our canoe concessioner and taken to Grant, our put-in point. Getting the permit takes a while, including viewing a good video on backcountry ethics and bear country behavior.

Yellowstone's road system is old and creaky, barely up to the demands of today's heavy traffic. Every summer, some large section of the double loop road is closed or temporarily shut down for widening or repaving. This summer (2003), Dunraven Pass was to be closed. The widening had been scheduled for the previous summer, but environmentalists had sued to stop construction to save whitebark pines along the side of the old road; their nuts are a major source of food for bears, as I discussed in chapter 6. The closing would have required a long detour to get back to our Slough Creek campsite in the northeast section of the park. We got the good news that the roadwork had been postponed, which let us get northeast more easily. We stopped at Norris Geyser Basin, my favorite, the hottest in the park. We also stopped to see the beautiful Norris campground, and found a typical Norris tableau in Loop A: two huge bison flanking a tent, sitting not thirty feet from it, with the Gibbon River rolling through the meadow in the background. Bison own the park; they sit where they want to. Fine by us. Then a few miles farther on: GRIZZ, and our heart rates increase.

We had seen a bear in the Lamar the day before, but at a great distance. Coming around a high curve in Dunraven Pass, along a steep gray-black slope of grass and volcanic breccia, we saw three cars parked on the outer berm. Incipient bear jam? YES! We pulled over, too, and saw a grizz just up the slope from us, young, sub-adult, maybe two hundred pounds, sturdily digging under the volcanic rocks, perhaps looking for insects. Soon there was a huge bear jam—dozens of cars, like the old days—and a ranger with pepper spray, there to keep the traffic moving and, ostensibly, to protect us.

But there was no danger. The bear knew we were watching and didn't care. He was an eating machine, hyperphagic, providing for his survival in what was probably his first summer on his own. We watched

You lookin' at me? Young grizzly, Dunraven Pass, 2003

for an hour as people came and went, as he worked slowly up and across the slope, dislodging sizeable rocks that tumbled down to the road, crashed, and split. I really wanted to take home a doorstop fashioned by vulcanism, time, gravity, and *Ursus arctos horribilis*, grizz. By 2006, this slope was gone, or at least significantly altered, by the new, wider road, which is, by the way, very beautiful and much safer. Will the grizz be back?? We don't know. These are the sorts of questions that arise when we manage wilderness, as we must. We felt privileged to share this moment with this messenger from the wild.

At this bear jam, we asked the traffic control ranger about an emergency vehicle we had seen the day before near Tower. Serious accident? What happened? Well, a touron (tourist/moron) had stopped his car on a slope to see some animals, but he hadn't properly set his brake or transmission. Result: the car rolled into three people. All survived, though one had to be med-evaced. When I show friends a photo of the bear, they love it, but usually say they're glad they weren't eighty feet from a grizzly. I tell 'em we were pretty safe. Many more people get hurt by cars than by bears in Yellowstone. Six people have been killed by bears in the park since it opened in 1872; at least ten have died since 1900 by falling into thermal pools. That sounds worse to me than becoming a grizzly's lunch.[3]

no longer top dog : off to the lake

Canned beef stew for a quick dinner. A red fox trots nonchalantly past, still shedding his heavy winter coat. Long day, no plans for more travel today, until we hear a bear had been seen at the junction between the main road and our campground road. Why not? Sure. No bear, but dogs again. A group of four husky canids was trotting northwest through open country: wolves, I was pretty sure, though they seemed very tan. Then one of them did one of those frisky rodent-hunting jumps straight up into the air, and it was pretty clear—they were coyotes, not wolves. (Wolves make this move, too, but it's more often done by coyotes.) As it grew darker, the coyotes simply disappeared; we never saw them return to the woods. Some Indians called coyotes "ghosts." Good name.

Strike camp, get final permits, head for a scruffy '60s motel unit at Lake Lodge. On the way to the lake at Bridge Bay, we saw a fascinating event in Hayden Valley, a lovely open area usually full of wildlife. The Yellowstone River was high. As it ran through the valley, it had made a few large islands by extending an auxiliary channel. On one small island

Wilderness campsite: Terry and Ralph in South Arm, 2004

were sixteen elk—nine cows, seven calves—looking spooked, wondering whether to stay or go. A watcher who'd got there earlier said that "something large and dark" had chased them there. A bear, surely. Eventually, three cows came back across the channel, leaving the others on the island, still looking nervous. As often happens, we saw neither the beginning nor the end of this adventure, but the middle was great. We had dinner at the rustic Lake Lodge cafeteria. We sat on the front porch as the night descended and looked into the distance at the great headland looming over the south end of the lake, diminished by the distance, twelve miles away: the Promontory. Four years later I heard a ranger on a Yellowstone lake boat ride call it "the crocodile." Okay—it looks ominous enough. It's our goal; we'll be there in three days, I hope. It was a little scary to see where we would soon have to go, on a huge and darkening lake.

onto the lake : dangerous paddling on Friday the 13th

Up early to meet Jason, our outfitter. A perfect morning to put in at Grant: sunny, warm, no wind. Two big canoes full of gear and food and professors, tied up right to the gunwales (all but the professors, that is). We began paddling blithely on the glassy pond of West Thumb, a huge circular bay, a former volcanic caldera, protected from the wind and weather of the big main lake. This was easy. But by early afternoon—this was planned to be a long day's paddle—the wind and rain in the main lake were making progress difficult. We pulled onto a beach to rest and wait for better weather. It eased a little, then, after we started again, got worse. As Jack said later, "It got nasty, and we were wondering what Mac had gotten us into." Quite a lot, as it turned out. Long afterwards, they told me they were referring to me as "Captain Ahab." I'm taking that as a compliment.

Yellowstone Lake is so vast and mighty that it makes many a paddler's decisions for him. It laughs at plans. We'd done about eleven of our planned twelve miles, the last seven tough and choppy. We had still another mile, another bay, more wind and chop and rain to endure to get to 7L7, our first designated campsite. As we rounded a point into Eagle Bay, it seemed really dangerous to continue, and we were nearly exhausted. We knew we should go no farther. We beached and checked out the next available site—7L6. No one with any sense is on the lake this early in the season, and we hadn't seen another soul since launch, so we weren't poaching anybody else's site. Indeed, it was a huge area, a double site, with a dock and a privy—practically a summer resort. Yet I still felt guilty and worried that we weren't proceeding according to plan.

Q: Won't the rangers come and scold us? Or worse, make us pack up and go where our permit says we should be?

A: No, Silly. Nobody knows, nobody cares.

True, at least this time.

Delicious potato soup for supper, power bars and fruit for dessert. Thanks to Ted, chief cook and fire builder. The weather was cold and threatening—there was rime ice on the tent in the morning—but we managed to stay warm and dry.

We four are not just friends, colleagues, and canoeists; we also sing together in an a cappella group, the Fredonia Catch Club. A former member once called it "a drinking group with a singing problem," but we do sing well. I expected there'd be a a good bit of singing on this trip. Wrong again, Mac. Little so far, none later. (We had sung for my Aunt Kay in her house near Chicago, on our first night out, after a great Yankees-Cubs game at Wrigley Field. Thanks for the tickets, Stan.) We don't sing here—we paddle. We are concentrated on NOW, the moment,

Canoeists embark, Bridge Bay Marina, 2004

preoccupied with doing what's right in front of us, pull, lift, pull, lift, occupied with surviving, with staying balanced, afloat and alive in harsh conditions. It concentrates the mind wonderfully. My stern man, Ted, said, "You get this great awareness of all the things you don't need." Exactly. Henry David Thoreau, a great canoe tripper himself, would agree. He wrote in *Walden*: "A man is rich in proportion to the number of things he can afford to let alone." We have let many things alone to be here: problems, research, careers, loved ones. There is excellent talk when we're together on shore. Everyone is dazzled by the animals and the landscapes we've seen. That's enough, and more than enough.

Furthermore, we have an embarrassment of riches here in the wilderness at 7L6. Our own private loon swims back and forth, calling, in our bay. Our outhouse has a door, toilet paper, and a great view. What is this, Hilton Head? Hilton Privy? Good weather tomorrow would be very nice, of course, and I know I will be stiff and sore in the morning.

day two : open water

As usual, not much wind in the morning; that's why it's the best time to travel. We pack and start early. We have more open water to cross on this day than on any other. We need to cross the mouths of both Flat Mountain Arm and South Arm, the latter a two-mile reach. Our goal is the Promontory, that looming presence we saw after dinner two days ago. Once we land on it, we are almost home and dry. Well, at least then we will be done with major open water crossings. That significant danger will be behind us.

There's good news. The old guys, even the oldest, me, find we do not hurt as much as we had expected. We are all in decent shape, but none of us had had time to do a course of lifting or running to prepare for this. You don't approach your eighth decade on this planet without picking up physical and spiritual dings. Me: sore back, sore left shoulder, sore left wrist, chipped on a fall on ice years before and never quite healed, arthritis complicating all this. Can I paddle very long on the left side, my natural power side? Can I keep up? Will they have to drag me home? Or just bury me here???

That's a joke, but I worry. Jack has an iffy shoulder too. Yet today we both felt fine; I checked. We actually felt stronger and more pain free at the end of the trip than at the beginning. The canoeing turned out to be less difficult physically than we had feared, though it was perhaps more dangerous. Does God temper the wind to the shorn lamb, as Laurence Sterne wrote in *A Sentimental Journey*? Maybe. Actually, my wrist hurts more from the repetitive motion of typing this tale than it did from living it, paddling on the lake.

And so back to our work: long transits on open water, some wind and chop even on a quiet morning. It's a calm day. Good. I planned it to be a short day, though not an easy one. I had blithely assumed we would skip past all the bays, going across relatively quiet open water, saving time and energy. Tom, an experienced river canoeist, doesn't buy this. He wants to hug the bay shores. Who can blame him? Wind can come up quickly and put us in peril, as it did yesterday, though then we were very near shore. Tom reads the morning weather, finds it good. We leave, and arrive on the shore of the Promontory well before noon. Whew.

Yet even in this crossing there was some danger. We had a quartering wind most of the way, which encouraged us to come up into it, to

Stan solos, South Arm, 2004

point farther north than our intended direction. As we watched the Promontory shore rise to meet us, and wondered which green patch was our designated campsite (5L5), we found it prudent to head left, northeast-ish. When we arrived on shore at what was obviously a campsite, we found ourselves at 5L7, two campsites, two miles, north of our target.

Yup, this'll do fine, despite turbulent clouds of mosquitoes from nearby Alder Lake. So "Mosquito Beach" it was for us, and we were glad to be there. No more open water crossings. We could see busy Lake Hotel—about twelve miles away—from our beautiful volcanic black sand beach. The Promontory rose impressively just north of us; around that corner was Southeast Arm and the end of our quest. We'd made it. Tomorrow: 6A4 and the Yellowstone River Delta. Even a big midnight thunderstorm, lightning bolts crashing all around us, couldn't stop us, though its winds bent my tent poles some.

Yellowstone Lake laughs at plans—again

Hold it. Not so fast. Tom, our resident weather pessimist, squinted at what looked to me like perfectly normal morning clouds and announced that we'd spend another day here. Hey, cool by me; I've given up taking my silly planning seriously. "Man plans; God laughs." We could have pro-

Blustery day, South Arm. Yellowstone Lake, 2004

ceeded, as the day turned out to be lovely. Two of us (Mac, the Old Fart, and Ted, the Kid, sixty-nine and thirty-three) actually swam, sorta, in the very cold lake. Low forties Fahrenheit, I'd guess. The ice had been out of Yellowstone Lake for less than three weeks. Tom caught two lake trout for dinner. Four otters swam past us. It was a sweet Day Off in Paradise. Jack, our geology lecturer, walked north and discovered a creek with drifted sand choking its mouth, making a geologic feature we christened Berkley Slough in his honor. It had muskrats and LOTS more mosquitoes.

As a survivor of north woods canoe trips in the 1940s, I must say that these swarms of mosquitoes were more a nuisance than a plague. Insect repellents have improved enormously. The bugs may get in your face, but they won't sting you much if you're covered with DEET. The only significant exception to that truth is The Problem No One Mentions:

Q: What happens if you're female, or when you have to poop and expose untreated skin?

A: You do it very quickly.

Mac, Stan, Ralph, and Terry, Lower Falls, 2004

day four : 6A2

Well, by God, we got here. Not 6A4, of course. Would we ever go where we're supposed to? Nah, not us. We're Oh for Four. Still, we're near the bottom of the Southeast Arm in a glorious campsite with its own lake/lagoon/inlet, and a stunning view east to the Absarokas. It reminds me of the northern Italian lakes, Como, Lugano, south of the Alps. It's breathtakingly beautiful, even before a storm produces a double rainbow over the mountains.

It took serious sweat to get here. It was nine or ten miles, placid at first, then tough; major chop, heavy crosswind, tippy canoes. When we rounded a point into quieter water and saw a campsite sign, we headed straight in, you bet. We fought our way in and suddenly it was quiet and calm. This site (6A2) is excellent. Only when the trip was over did I realize that 6A2 was not officially open until July 15—another four weeks.

Ted, Mac, Tom (l to r), canoeing Yellowstone Lake, 2003.
Absarokas in the background. Photo by Jack Berkley

Oops. The tent area is mostly blowdowns and burnouts from the fires of 1988. It's hard to find a place to pitch a tent, but it's gorgeous, and only half a mile from the Trail Creek trail I will explore tomorrow. (When Jack and I did, we saw a marten—Yellowstone's largest weasel—cavorting on some blowdowns.)

On our way to this campsite, we stopped for a breather at a park (an open grassy meadow) full of elk. Diverse birdlife was everywhere, deep in this wilderness: lesser scaups and buffleheads and goldeneyes and Canada geese. One pair of cinnamon teal; two golden eagles; two bald eagles. Many western sandpipers are PEEPing at our campsite. Most majestic of all are our near neighbors, the hundreds of white pelicans who nest and breed in our front yard, the two small, rocky Molly Islands half a mile from us. Ungainly on land, they are exquisite in their coordinated flights above us. Tom especially enjoyed this.

We are bushed; we all took naps. When we beached, I just rolled out of the canoe onto the ground and lay there for ten minutes. Jack is happy as a geologist in rocks, which he preeminently is. Everywhere he goes we get a lecture, and I love it. We are camping, he tells us, on a volcanic moraine. Most of these rocks are malachite, a volcanic copper ore.

We are still not eating much. Fine by me, who's been on a diet for a while anyway. I have never been with such an abstemious crowd. NOBODY DRINKS. ("Where's the three cases of beer?" asked Jason, our canoe concessioner, as we embarked.) When we got to our last campsite, three of us (the non-Mormons) ceremonially split one bottle of Moose Drool brown ale—a whimsically named good Montana brew. Should you take less food when you go? I dunno, but I will. (And I did.) If you're like me and most Americans, how great is it to do two weeks in the wilderness and come back fifteen unneeded pounds lighter? I plan to write *Dr. Nelson's Gin, Jerky, and Canoe Trip Diet* and die very rich.

the end of the quest

Our last full day was the day to get deeper into the Southeast Arm, to see the marsh where the young Yellowstone River empties into the lake. We did, and we also got a good look at 6A4 and the Trail Creek Patrol Cabin. Wilderness purists might disdain any site such as Slough Creek or Trail Creek or Hawk's Rest, where the alleged wilderness includes a small cabin built for patrolling rangers. Not me. "Man himself is a visitor who does not remain." If he leaves a cabin and some firewood and a match, and nobody lives there permanently, it's fine, it's still wilderness. Indeed, the empty cabin underscores the astonishing unpeopledness of this area. We haven't seen another boat or another person for three days. It's wonderful.

We beached for a rest around the last point with this vista in view. Okay, says I, that's it, that's far enough, I can see it, I been here. If we went farther we'd be going over open water again, and I said there'd be no more of that. I've used up my open water leadership initiatives. Thanks for getting me here, guys—I love you all. If they wanted to go farther, it was up to them.

Bless them, they did, of course. Ted and Tom say, "We'll go explore the river." "Not without us, you won't," say Jack and I, and we're off across open water again, heading for the reeds and twisting channels of the Yellowstone River: a good five miles round trip. In the deep reeds and channels of the river's marshland, we felt like Bogey in *The African Queen*, without the bugs and leeches. Or the gin. Jack's GPS tells us that our southeasternmost point was W 110 degrees 12'31"; N 44 degrees 18'25". That's as far as you can get from cars and crowds in Yellowstone. Heaven.

returning on the Grizzly

It was ending, though none of us wanted it to. We struck camp and paddled four miles back to the tip of the Promontory, where we had arranged to be picked up by the "Grizzly," a concessioner boat, at 3 p.m. We arrived well before noon, and one of those pesky benefits of modern civilization got us earlier service. Tom's cell phone still had a charge. I called and left a message at the office. ("Your call is very important to us . . ." Oy. Voice Mail. Civilization. Oy.) Ted leaped into the lake to save Tom's fishing pole, and we all snoozed in the sun. Then we saw a small boat heading for our point.

"Doesn't look like what I expected, but it sure is coming toward us," and it was. Turns out it's a funny old wheezing power boat redeemed from a life of ferrying workers to and from Pacific Ocean oil drilling platforms. (It's since been retired and replaced, gone to its wheezing reward.) We perked up, loaded all our equipment, and headed back to noise, people, and problems. Ted said what we all felt: " I felt sorrow as I saw the mountains close off the bay where we'd been."

We set up at big, bustling Bridge Bay campground amidst a gazillion RVs to spend our last night in Yellowstone. Bison lounged very near our tents. We had time to go see Old Faithful before dinner. We were glad the thousands of people we saw were having fun, but their numbers seemed oppressive to us, spoiled as we were by the silence and beauty of the wilderness. Three days on the road and it was over, we were home, on June 21, the first day of summer.

Economic note: This was all amazingly inexpensive. We took my car, a great little horse of a Honda CR-V, with Ted's luggage rack on top. I didn't charge mileage, just gas. We spent six nights in motels, the rest in cheap or free campsites. Including motels, gas, food, campsite fees, canoe rentals and shuttles; not including souvenirs, film, film processing, or Yellowstone Jack's magnificent cowboy hat:

We did it all for forty bucks per day per person. Really!

Spiritually invigorating? Physically testing? Magnificent? Scary? Yup, all those. And CHEAP. And if I, seventy years old and forty pounds overweight (then—not now) can do it, so can most of you.

Dawn, South Arm, Yellowstone Lake
Photo by Jack Berkley

do it again

So delightful was it that I have since repeated the experience three times, with different friends and different itineraries, but twice including a canoe trip into the wilderness. Hey, I knew how now. I knew the rental sources, the winds and waves, the mosquitoes and the otters, the quiet of a wilderness lake as a June evening falls. For some, a week in the wilderness is quite enough for a lifetime; for some, it would be a week too long. For others, it would be grand to go back every year, but life presses, responsibilities clamor, other opportunities beckon. My three mates, all thrilled by their experience, reluctantly said they couldn't go again. I found three more to take their places, the ideal sized group again, but with a difference. On the next summer's trip (2004) I was no longer the

Mac at Shoshone Lake, 2005

oldest. Two—Ralph and Stan—were friends from high school, and we three were all seventy. Terry, this trip's Kid, was fifty-two. Our average age was a mellow sixty-six, which might be thought more suited for shuffleboard than for canoeing. Our physical and wilderness skills were not as high as those of the previous group, but that wasn't a major problem. We did a Promontory Point shuttle both ways, paddled a little less, hit our assigned sites, went back to Southeast Arm, thoroughly explored South Arm, and had a great time. Lots of good talk, cards, backgammon, and painting. (The Kid is a fine artist.)

We learned another thing: don't believe maps, even fancy pseudo-topos from National Geographic. We got to what we thought was our last campsite in South Arm and were unloading our canoes, when a bunch of kids in kayaks paddled up and correctly claimed the site as theirs. Oops. Lesson Learned: make sure you're where you think you are. Another mile and a half south down the lake, we found home for the next few

Happy camper: Bernie at Slough Creek, 2005

days in a site with spectacular sunsets over the lake, great fishing, a broad beach, and an island, a river, a bay, and a swamp to explore.

At Promontory Tip, where we went to await a shuttle pickup, we encountered our first lake ranger, a guy in a power boat who moored and asked to see our permit. They really do check sometimes! Seth was friendly and knowledgeable, like most of his associates. When I questioned him about his experiences, he said he'd spent the previous summer at the the patrol cabin near 6A4 with his wife and his infant son, Weston. That's as far away as you can get from traffic jams and drug deals and whiny tourists. Must have been something like Eden, after sex but before the serpent.

"Was it as magnificent as I think, Seth?"

"Oh, yes."

"May I assume you like your work, Seth?"

Quiet reassuring smile and nod. Rangers may get paid off in sunsets rather than dollars, as they wryly say, but mostly they like their work. Paradise Regained, that's what wilderness can be.

Bernie on a very still Shoshone Lake, 2005

Then, the following summer (2005), my son Bernie and I had a different backcountry experience, in Shoshone Lake. It's the largest backcountry (wilderness) lake in the lower forty-eight, though it's less than
one-tenth the surface area of Yellowstone Lake. This trip required him
(not me, you bet) to pull our canoe more than a mile against the swift
current of the cold, rushing Lewis River channel. It was tough. (Later,
Ranger Stein told us that it was the early season that made it so hard: "In
August, you can do it in Tevas." If I do it again, I will.) We passed ten
canoes leaving the lake the next morning. Awful busy, I thought, grumble, grumble. But after we got to our stunning campsite high over the
lake (8R4, Flat Top), we saw no one for four whole days. We did see bear
scat, and Bernie, the lucky bum, saw a lone wolf from the Bechler pack
lope through our campsite—but no other people. We had the whole
Shoshone Geyser Basin—the only major thermal area in the park not
reachable by road—to ourselves. Can you wonder why I go back every

Bernie and brown trout, Shoshone Lake, 2005

year? After Shoshone Lake, we spent three days watching bears and wolves, and showing them to other tourists through our little spotting scope. We did much the same the following year.

the Agate creek pack and coyote woman

In July 2006 I swapped Bernie at the Bozeman airport for my partner, Joyce. She and I spent the next four days mostly watching wolves, bighorn sheep, and a nest of three fledging osprey chicks and their parents. Joyce is a sophisticated non-camping woman who's very fond of Broadway musicals, nice motels, and ballroom dancing backward in high heels. She wasn't quite sure that Yellowstone wilderness, even from a comfortable distance, would be her thing. Why did she need wilderness? Then we saw twelve bears up close by 9:30 one morning in 2005—six blacks, six grizz— and her heart raced and she came around. One morning in 2006 we spent *three and a half hours* intently watching a wolfpack rendezvous site: the doings, the comings and goings, the playing with the pups, the sunning and the sleeping, the ecstatic greeting of returning pack members, of the

Joyce's coyote

Agate Creek wolf pack. Everything but a kill. Glorious. We left only when they bedded down for the hot midday hours.

We returned that evening to the same prime viewing area, a pull-out over the Antelope Creek drainage in sight of Mount Washburn. We asked our friend Brian Connolly what was up: "Whatcha got, Brian?" "Nothing yet." Okay. We settled down to join maybe forty people straining to find wolves or bears. Nothing happening. Boring evening, then, "What's that? That's a coyote!" Joyce shouts, and eighty eyeballs swing right to find our visitor, who lopes past very near us. We watched him hunt for ten minutes; it was the best sighting of the evening, and everyone was happy and grateful. I christened Joyce "Coyote [with three syllables] Woman," and people laughed and agreed. Next night, back we go. "Whatcha got, Brian?" "Nothing yet. We were kinda waiting for Ca-yo-te Woman to find something for us." Funny; but by god, she did—back came her coyote. Ballroom Joyce was now clearly Queen of the Wilderness.

We left Yellowstone the next morning, having seen no wolves that day—just a huge grizz working the Antelope Creek area and slowly crossing the road. When we got home from our trip, I learned we had

Joyce and Mac

missed, by two days, a dramatic elk kill by the Agates, right below that pullout. Another friendly veteran wolf watcher, Kathie Lynch, gave a memorable description of the mercifully quick kill, the stripping of and gorging on the carcass, and the comic look of the overstuffed Agate wolves. We had seen a cow elk dangerously near the pack before we left, and wondered if something big might happen soon. It did. Darn.

Moral: Never leave Yellowstone.

The Agate Creek pack has since left its summer rendezvous area, Antelope Creek, "where summer wolf watchers had so much to see." Sure did. As of October 2006, all thirteen are alive and thriving, following the elk who are coming down from the mountains. Their alpha male, 113M, at nine and a half years, is tied for the honor of being the oldest wolf in the park (Ralph Maughan's Wildlife Report, October 23, 2006), though he has recently been seriously injured.

Coyote Woman and I will go back, you bet.

what's wilderness for?

What about those who will never get close to Yellowstone's wilderness, or into any wilderness, who don't even want to think about the difficulties, the dangers, the privations? Those who may like the idea of wilderness, but know they don't want to shit in the woods, for esthetic as well as practical reasons? Good question.

As you read this, you may know you'll never get there, even if you now know that it's not so hard as you'd thought it was. Okay. Too bad. But aren't you glad somebody did? And that others will? Aren't you pleased that there are emissaries, outreachers, to tell you what it's like beyond the boundaries, to send you a message from the edge? In a recent biography, poet Edward Dorn is called a "noted survivor of our edges and boundaries and scout of far-off places and distances." A noble calling. I've read many messages from such scouts and survivors, and been grateful for them. Mine is one more such message from the edge, and it wouldn't, couldn't have happened, without wilderness to do it in.

There are also important economic and scientific reasons for preserving wilderness. Mushroom Pool is an unremarkable looking hot pool along the Firehole Lake Drive, a one-way road north of Old Faithful between Midway and Lower Geyser Basins. The drive goes by the spectacular Great Fountain Geyser, one of the best erupters in the park. I've never stopped to look at Mushroom Pool. I should have, and I will. In 1966, a heat-loving bacterium was discovered in this pool and christened

Thermus aquaticus ("Hot Water Critter"), now just Taq for short. In the 1980s, a heat-resisting enzyme, Taq polymerase, was developed from it. Taq polymerase has since been proven invaluable in DNA research and sequencing, and in many practical medical and forensic applications of that research. The man who used it to make such a useful tool won a Nobel Prize for his work, and we are all wiser and healthier for it. Companies that use Taq have made hundreds of millions of dollars from it; Yellowstone has earned not a penny, which vexes the folks at the National Park Service. Some scientists call this "the great Taq rip-off." It has created pressure to search for more such applications with big pay-offs, searches some environmentalists find utterly inconsistent with the basic purposes of a national park (*New York Times*, November 28, 2006). This controversy simmers on like a thermal pool, but one thing is crystal clear: preserving Mushroom Pool led unexpectedly to enormous benefits for mankind. In July of 2007, NSF announced the discovery of a new bacterium in the park's hot springs. It transforms light into chemical energy through photosynthesis. Historically, many great scientific break-throughs and medical advances, such as penicillin, have come unexpectedly from apparently noncommercial research.

If Yellowstone and other such biological preserves cease to exist, our descendants will lose their chance to make such great discoveries. Digitalis comes from the foxglove plant. Quinine comes from tree bark. Who knows what other useful compounds might be out there? Yet the world is losing hundreds of acres of rain forest every hour, from the pressure of population and subsistence farming, and large-scale coffee plantations. We must save as much of the wild as we can, not just so Mac can go canoeing, but because, quite literally, "In wildness is the preservation of the world," the preservation of the health not only of our planet but of each one of us.

All such practical benefits aside, just having wilderness out there is a lift to the spirit, a thrill, a sense that boundaries can be transcended, and that life can suddenly, unexpectedly, expand and grow more luminous. As Aldo Leopold wrote: "I would hate to be young again without wild country to be young in, for what avails 40 freedoms without a blank space on the map?" I love to sit in my old house in the bleak midwinter and know that there are people planning trips to the wildest places they can find, whether I am one of them or not. (I usually am.) That's part of what wilderness is for.

Our species is expanding dangerously quickly. There will soon be fifteen billion of us, but only a few thousand tigers, pandas, rhinos, gorillas, grizzlies. Wild animals need habitat, and so do we. Even under America's beautiful spacious skies, people now overwhelm our most popular play spaces. We need to preserve everything we can save, so that people can get off by themselves and find out who they are, and what, if anything, life is about. Mary Midgely said it superbly: "We need a vast world, and it must be a world that does not need us; a world constantly capable of surprising us, a world we did not program, since only such a world is the proper object of wonder" (*Beast and Man*, Ithaca: Cornell University Press, 1978).

Early Plains Indians didn't have much trouble getting off by themselves. When young men, and some young women, too, needed to find their destiny, their identity, they went on vision quests. They headed alone for a butte or a mountain and fasted, hoping for a meaningful vision or dream to interpret and learn from. It often came only after days of privation, even suffering. Sometimes it did not come at all. I've been to many of the places they went to—Bear Butte, peaks in the Black Hills, the Badlands, Devil's Tower, and the bluffs near Fort Laramie, where Crazy Horse had his momentous vision. They're all still there. They have beckoned to me. But they're now often full of people, touring, climbing, picknicking, partying, camping, drinking, fornicating, hiking, motorcycling, you name it. A very few of these sites are now reserved for quiet spiritual questing at certain times of the year, to the noisy griping of disappointed climbers and partiers. People certainly need and deserve places to be boisterous. But where will we go to find silence, to know ourselves, to search out our destinies? "To be young again?"

Does this sound absurd coming from someone in his eighth decade on this lovely planet? Probably, but it shouldn't. One of the most essential and appealing characteristics of our species is that we quest, we seek, we stay curious until we die. One of the best ways to seek is to test one's self against the wilderness, at any age. I know. I've done it. I do it every summer. I urge you to try it. As Wallace Stegner wrote in his "Wilderness Letter": "We simply need that wild country . . . even if we never do more than drive to its edge and look in." Wilderness is a necessary "part of the geography of hope." That's another reason for preserving wilderness. If it's not there, you can't do it. It still is, and you can. The Great Road leads to many busy and historic places. It also leads to wilderness: to solitude, silence, peace, joy, knowledge, wonder, and a healthy, happy spirit.

chapter eight

"ocian in view! o! the joy!"

◆ William Clark entered this jubilant cry in his notebook in 1805 when he thought that the Corps of Discovery had reached the Pacific. They hadn't—what they saw was only the Columbia Gorge, the very wide mouth of the Columbia River—but they were very close, within five miles of the ocean. Moving west out of Yellowstone, US 20 hasn't reached the ocean yet either, but it is on the downslope from the continental divide to the Pacific.

The road out of Yellowstone National Park is, for me, always a sad one. Any road out. In the words of a great American phrasemaker, the Crow chief Arapooish, about his favorite region, his homeland, "Anywhere you go away [from Crow Country] you fare [eat, live] worse." I hate to leave the 'Stone, but it's good to see "US 20" on the signs again, though I've never really been off it.

"West"

Drive west out of Yellowstone National Park and you are in that quintessential gateway community, West Yellowstone, Montana, known to locals simply as "West." There's not much here except motels and restaurants and tourist attractions, yet the town has some history, style, and grace. The Western railroads did a lot to develop the national parks, seeing them as destinations that would encourage long distance, high end travel. Earlier, for similar reasons, the railroads had promoted homesteading in the West, often in places where conventional farming was doomed to fail.

The first railroad to arrive in West Yellowstone, Montana, was the Oregon Short Line, in 1907; the Union Pacific came soon after. The town was founded rather late, in 1908, in response to the growing demand for tourist services. At its terminus just outside the park, the Union Pacific built a handsome stone and timber depot. It has become a museum, complete with a wondrously wacky looking propeller-driven early skimobile.

The UP also built a lofty dining hall, usually empty now. It has much of the "parkitecture" grandeur of the great dining room in Yosemite's Ahwanee Hotel, and it should. Both were designed by Gilbert Stanley Underwood, an architect employed by the Union Pacific. Most of these old buildings have been taken over by the town of West Yellowstone, for use as courtrooms, or for youth programs, or as the town library. The Greater Yellowstone Coalition (GYC) holds some of its meetings here.

The railroad did not dominate travel to Yellowstone quite so much as it did at some parks, but it was very important. A lovely railroad promotional publication of 1876 cites this table of distances for reaching the park:

Ogden, Utah, to Franklin, Idaho, by rail:	80 1/4 miles
Franklin to Virginia City, Montana (stage):	317 miles
Virginia City to Bozeman (stage):	66 miles

And so on and on. It sounds exhausting, bone-rattling. In our time the railroad no longer goes to West Yellowstone (as it still does really to Glacier, and nostalgically to the Grand Canyon), but it has left these graceful historic reminders of its former presence.

I didn't much want to like West Yellowstone. Some of its attractions seemed cruel and bogus, such as using captive grizzly bears and wolves to attract a crowd, and I don't patronize such places. Yet on a hike into the park just after sunrise in 2002, it was hair-raisingly beautiful to hear a morning chorus, a wolf pack howling. I was so close to the town that I thought, skeptic that I am, it might be a tape played and broadcast by the West Yellowstone Chamber of Commerce. It was live wolves, all right— captive wolves at the West Yellowstone Grizzly & Wolf Discovery Center. I'm counting that as real. The Grizzly & Wolf Discovery Center is right on the line for me. Wolves and bears, once wild, are kept in cages and behind fences and fed by keepers. They regularly play to a crowd who may not be lucky enough, or have the time or patience or legs, to see wild bears and wolves in the park.

"a robin redbreast in a cage / puts all heaven in a rage"

Wild animals in cages. Not William Blake's style, nor mine. Yet these bears and wolves are billed as animals that would have had to die if they were not here. Most of the bears—their biographies are posted—are orphans of mothers who were shot for raiding human food caches or garbage dumps, and were teaching this risky behavior to their intelligent offspring. Should civilization just pull back from grizzly territory? Maybe, but it never has and it won't. (Grizzlies have already retreated to the mountains. They were once the dominant predator on the plains.) So the simple truth seems to be: these bears would be dead if they were not here. Okay. Fair enough.

The big, beautiful bears are let out into a small grassy area several times a day in twos and threes, often in sibling groups, and they busily

Bison, big and little, on the road in the Lamar Valley

overturn rocks to get at treats left for them by the Discovery Center workers. This is designed to keep them alert and interested bears, not just torpid jailbirds. (Lions and tigers are said to be relatively content in zoos; after all, cats sleep most of the time anyway. Bears—mobile, curious, and questing—are less well suited to captivity.) These bears have to contend with ravens for the treats; the smart local birds soon learned that goodies would be available every ninety minutes or so. Some of the grizz are still wild or aggressive enough to chase the ravens "off the kill," as it were. It's a hell of a good show, and you're not likely ever to get so close to a big bear in the wild. I have, and I have loved it, but you might not be able to or even want to. The bears are

Lame scruffy coyote

also used to test new varieties of bearboxes, solid metal or plastic caches to protect campers' and hikers' food.

The center seems to me to be an apt metaphor for all of West Yellowstone: not quite authentic, but close enough to be appealing, even exciting. Many people think so; West is the busiest entrance to Yellowstone National Park. It is also the snowmobile capital of the Greater Yellowstone Ecosystem, worse luck. The Bush administration has repeatedly rejected its own study groups' repeated recommendations (studies that cost eight million dollars) to end snowmobile use in the park. Former Interior Secretary Gale Norton took a well-publicized spin on one in 2005. Up to 720 of these noisy fuming beasts are permitted into the park every winter day. (I must admit that it sounds wonderful to be empowered and riding one in that gorgeous winter wilderness. Unfortunately, it makes that wilderness a lot less wild and gorgeous.) In 2002, rangers at the entrance shacks wore respirators because the air was so polluted with exhaust fumes. Now the snowmobiles are required to be cleaner—four-stroke, not two-stroke. And they must travel in escorted groups, partly to keep them from chasing down, and thus weakening, animals such as bison and elk.

Interestingly, their popularity is declining in favor of the more ecologically friendly snowcoaches, larger vans on treads and skis. Two hundred fifty has been the average number of snowmobiles in the park on recent winter days. All to the good, say I—keep 'em out—though I wouldn't say it too loud in a bar in West Yellowstone, which makes mucho bucks off the $200 a day rentals.

more Yellowstone roads

I leave Yellowstone grudgingly, glad that there are two more anomalous bits of the great park to enjoy, on roads in and out that can't be accessed from the park's main road system. One is US 191, the road north from West Yellowstone. There is no political reason why 191 should take a bit of a bend east to spend sixteen miles within the western border of the park, but it does. Roads here tend to follow river valleys, and the valleys of the Grayling, then the Gallatin, lie just inside the northwest corner of the park here. It's an anomaly, but a pretty one, though not exactly woodsy. There are excellent views and many trailheads off it. Except for the trailhead signs and a few others, you'd never know you were in a great national park. To the north and west, in Montana, is the Gallatin National Forest. In it is Quake Lake, formed by a massive 7.5 earthquake that dammed the Madison River and killed twenty-eight campers in August, 1959. My Fredonia colleague Gordon Baird was there as a kid that month; he and his family narrowly avoided death by deciding not to camp there for two more days. That may be the only time in history when I would agree that leaving the Yellowstone area was a good idea.

Off to the west is Red Rock Lakes National Wildlife Refuge, a sanctuary for *Cygnus buccinator*, the trumpeter swans, gorgeous birds that almost went extinct fifty years ago. They now grace Yellowstone's skies and streams, especially the Madison. Forty years ago, a small

Trumpeter swans, Madison River, Yellowstone

flock of them flew over my head, trumpeting, as I entered the park from the south. It was soul-stirring. When they're gone, I hope I will be too. I've also seen them swimming in the Snake in upscale downtown Jackson, Wyoming.

In the second anomaly, you'd surely know you were in a great national park even before you got to the Bechler Ranger Station. Yellowstone National Park yields its finest secrets to those who get off the main roads. You haven't quite been West if you haven't done some serious miles on gravel or dirt. As US 20 heads southwest across Targhee Pass, out of Montana into Idaho, Idaho 47 turns southeast toward Mesa Falls. Idaho 47 is a scenic alternative running parallel to US 20. Nine miles south of Lower Mesa Falls is Targhee National Forest Road 582. It goes east into the national forest, then into the park. It is eighteen and a half miles from the beginning of 582 to the park boundary, much of it paved, the rest (in 2002) very good gravel.

Bechler : cascade corner

Five eighty-two takes you into the Bechler region, one of the many backcountry areas in the park, and the only one you can drive a car into. Bechler is the wettest part of the park, getting nearly eighty inches of precip annually. It's often difficult to hike here in June because the long winter's snow is still melting and the woods are just starting to dry out. Bechler is called Cascade Corner because there are so many waterfalls. Cave Falls, on the Falls River, is a fine sight, wide (c. 250 feet) and powerful, though not high. It drops about twenty feet in two stages. There is a pretty national forest campground very near Cave Falls in the Targhee, just outside Yellowstone. The Bechler River is a tributary of the Falls River; the falls is a tributary of the Henrys Fork of the Snake River. The water you see here will soon go over Mesa Falls. If you wish to find solitude in Yellowstone, Bechler is one very good place to do it. But be warned: it will be damp.

Backtrack to the Great Road, up and over Targhee Pass, which, at 7,072 feet, is the highest point on US 20 coast-to-coast. Probably named for a Bannock or Shoshone chief, it is the end of eight miles in Montana and the beginning of four hundred and eight in Idaho. The Targhee is dotted with recreational sites, but it's a major timber producer, too, hideously clear-cut in some places right up to the line where it stops and Yellowstone begins. Along US 20 there are stands of young pines, planting dates given, to replace clearcuts—logging that cuts down every tree. There are no "cosmetic strips" here, shallow ranks of big trees left along main roads to give the appearance of the forest primeval. This is *logging* country.

America's national forests

What are the national forests for anyway? The first National Forest Chief Forester, Gifford Pinchot, had no doubts: they were essentially tree farms. "Get Out The Cut" was and is the great cry of the National Forest Service. They're not in the Department of the Interior, as are the parks—they report to the Secretary of Agriculture. Agriculture is about crops, product. An early-twentieth-century attempt to move the national forests to Interior failed after a bitter turf fight. The national forests' budgets depend, in part, on how much timber they produce.

The nation certainly needs lumber, and a modest fraction of that lumber comes from the national forests, though a lot less than you might think. If I am reading the bar graphs correctly, in 2001 just over a billion cubic feet of timber was harvested from the national forests. That's a big

Firehole River

number, but it's not so big compared to the *sixteen* billion cubic feet total U.S. forest harvest. And it's only about one-third of what the national forest cut was twenty years ago (*National Report on Forest Resources*, Forest Inventory and Analysis, USDA Forest Service). In short, way more than nine-tenths of the nation's lumber comes from private forest lands, especially those in the Southeast, "which provides nearly 60% of all the Nation's forest products annually." (ibid.). Remembering a morning run past central Mississippi clearcuts in the '80s, I believe it.

The nation surely needs lumber. But Americans also need recreation and clean air and water, space and good watersheds, and rivers fish can live in. Build a road to get timber out, and you change the character of a forest forever, often severely damaging its rivers and wildlife. Many areas in the national forests are uneconomical to cut because of difficult access, or steep slopes. Surprisingly, many have few trees in them, at least few trees worth cutting for timber. The main purpose of these forests is to stabilize land and make clean water. As it went out the door in 2001, the Clinton administration's Interior Department issued rules requiring that forty-nine million roadless acres of the national forests remain roadless. The industry-oriented Bush administration soon attempted to overturn that restriction by issuing new regulations. That move was itself overturned by a federal judge (*New York Times*, September 21, 2006) on the ground that environmental concerns had not been properly considered. Similar recent repudiations have slowed resource development in Utah, Alaska, California, and New Mexico (*USA Today*, October 11, 2006). So it goes. Environmentalists have been successfully playing Dee-Fense! on this issue since 2001.

My bias is clear. Most of what's left of the national forests, certainly all the old growth, should be retained, cutting very modestly and not destroying anything environmentally sensitive, beautiful, or precious. Aldo Leopold's oft-quoted environmental folk wisdom applies here: "The first rule of intelligent tinkering is to save all the parts." As our population passes three hundred million (as it did in October 2006), we are plowing up and losing to sprawl three thousand acres of land a day. We better save some serious space to run to.

fire policy in the national forests

What about fires? As the globe's climate heats up, and no responsible person seriously doubts it is doing so, this problem will grow. "Thinning" forests to prevent fires is often used as a justification for major cuts in old forests. Yet thinning does not eliminate fires, and the trash left after logging is great fuel for fires. The total fire suppression policy of nearly a century has proved to be, in the long run, a bad idea. Smokey Bear has been mostly retired except as a friendly poster icon. In most forests, we should manage naturally caused wildfires by letting nature take its course and burn the accumulated tinder.

And yet: many people have built homes or cabins or motels in or near the national forests, and there are more every year. Can we "let it burn" if it means the destruction of million-dollar homes? Major fires in Boulder Canyon, Montana, just north of Yellowstone—in and near the Gallatin National Forest—are evacuating residents, burning homes, and promoting intense discussion in the fall of 2006. As of October 3, 2006, a record eight million Western wildland acres burned in this fire season. It finished as the worst on record: 9.5 million acres burned through early December (*Dunkirk Observer*, December 15, 2006). Two thousand seven looks as though it will break that record. The season gets longer and deadlier as the globe warms. Five Forest Service firefighters died in the terrible Esperanza wildfire near Palm Springs, California (*New York Times*, October 27, 2006). Firefighting costs precious lives, and it costs a lot of money, too: for 2006, through September, $1.2 billion dollars (*High Country News*, October 16, 2006, 3). Should we log and thin all our forests, or should we leave them essentially wild, cutting only if we replace mature trees with a new, diverse forest?

There are no simple answers to these questions—no simple political answers, at least. Many people who live near the national forests have lived on them, and from their abundance, for decades. They are understandably upset when mills close and logging slows or ceases, even if the causes of such closures are more often global and socioeconomic than environmental. This is essentially the same issue as that of the BLM lands in Wyoming. People of good will need to inform themselves, talk to one another, and make wise decisions about the future of our forests. Some are talking and trying. I hope they save a lot of the Targhee. It's gorgeous.

the sound of mountain water

Harriman State Park is a gift to Idaho of a private estate, once owned by the wealthy Eastern railroad family. Locals still refer to it as "the railroad ranch." There is a visitor center and good fishing access to the Henry's Fork of the Snake River, some of the finest fly fishing water in the West. In coming over the Continental Divide and Targhee Pass, the Great Road has entered the valley of the Snake, the penultimate great Western river. (The last big one is the river the Snake flows into—the Columbia.) To follow these two mighty river valleys is to retrace most of the historic American trails from the northern Rockies to the Pacific.

Leave the Great Road briefly for Idaho 47, noted earlier as the route to Bechler. Forty-seven is the designated Mesa Falls Scenic Byway. It leads to breathtaking and quite different views of Upper and Lower Mesa Falls. An easy walk with a few switchbacks goes near the brink of Upper Mesa Falls. This is very near where Wallace Stegner camped as a child when his feckless father moved his family from Saskatchewan through Montana to Salt Lake City. Stegner recalled the magic of this place, the spray and the sound and the taste: "By such a river it is impossible to believe that one will ever be tired or old" (*The Sound of Mountain Water*, New York: Dutton, 1980, 42).[1] You can still feel the same luscious spray. In June, baby marmots, bustling in and out of cover along the path to the falls, reinforce this sense of eternal youth. The observation point for Lower Mesa Falls is just south on 47, and its view of the falls is distant and picturesque rather than close and tactile. There is a small campsite here, new (in 2002) since my last visit.

the backs of the tits

Back onto US 20, and soon another stunning view, one I've postponed for hundreds of miles: The Grand Tetons. They rise higher from their plain than any other range in the lower forty-eight. The wondrous cliche view of the Tetons is not visible from US 20 in Wyoming, but the view of the back of them in Idaho, though more distant, is almost as grand. It's subtly different from the distant Wyoming approach. There the land is dry, used for grazing. Here the ranchers and farmers have irrigated massively, and the land is green and productive. The name "tetons," in French "breasts" or just "tits," is not very accurate; they are far too sharp and rugged for that. It makes you realize how long those French trappers had been out among the beaver. The Tetons are the spectacular roofline of another crown jewel national park, Grand Teton. They may be seen best close up from the other side from the plains, or from the shoreline of absurdly picturesque Jenny Lake; but they are gorgeous from anywhere. The museum of Indian art and artifacts at the park's Colter Bay Visitor Center is a must-see.

The Grand Tetons

rexburg, thomas ricks, and good clean fun

The best view of the Tetons from the Great Road is from near Ashton (pop. 1,114), "The Gateway to Adventure." US 20 soon becomes Interstatificated again, so that Rexburg (pop. 14,302) is about a mile from the highway that used to run through it. Rexburg is recognizably, unmistakeably, a Mormon town: wide streets, green trees, shiny, clean, with a logical grid plan. It was the home of Ricks College, a two-year college so wholesomely, patently Mormon that I irreverently thought of it as "BYU-Idaho"; that is, the Idaho branch of Brigham Young University, the archetypal Mormon University in Provo, Utah. Ho ho, big joker, that Mac Nelson. The next day, I learned that that is exactly what the name would be changed to in the fall of 2003, and it has since been done. Who knew?? Me, I guess.

The late, or former, Ricks College was a gold mine of Mormon ways. On my morning run, I found this list on a large board outside the Hyrum Mainwaring Student Center:

top 10 summer activities for all students

1. Fri 6/15   Jackson/Bar J Trip
2. Sat 6/16   Manti Temple Pageant
3. Fri 6/22   Playmill & W. Yellowstone Trip
4. Sat 6/23   Yellowstone
5. Fri 6/29   Moonlight Serenade Dance
6. Sat 6/30   Jackson/Jenny Lake Hike
7. Wed 7/4   Whoopee Days Parade & Fun Run
8. Sat 7/7   Big Springs Canoe Trip
9. Sat 7/14   Snake River White Water
10. Every Wed   Country / Swing Kids Dances

All this with a Viking ship logo, at the Central Plaza, off Viking Drive.

Golly gee, Wally, that's all keen stuff, especially Whoopee Days and the Manti Temple Pageant, and I know I'd enjoy a lot of it myself. But don't these Latter Day Saints ever want to raise a little Heck, excuse my French?

The college's agriculture building is named for Ezra Taft Benson, former secretary of agriculture under President Eisenhower. Another building is named for Spencer W. Kimball. Both Benson and Kimball were octogenarian presidents of the patriarchal Church of Jesus Christ of Latter Day Saints. There are some dorms on campus, but much of the housing is private, with la-de-da names such as "Royal Crest" or "Heritage Manor" or "The Carriage House." All these are billed as "college approved housing for young ladies." "Beehive Manor" (the beehive is the state symbol of Utah—don't ask) offers "Fine Young Ladies Housing." ("Ladies"—not "women.") There's also at least one that's "college approved for young men." I suspect the men can live in unapproved housing, the women not.

A sunny-voiced DJ on KRIC, the campus radio station, blared, I kid you not: "IT'S 6:30—TIME TO GET UP!" The station's drivetime chat and music (though almost everyone seems to walk, briskly and early) is cheery, full of uplift and injunctions to exercise.

Sign on baseball field on campus:

NO FREE PLAY
ATHLETIC USE ONLY
TRESPASSERS WILL
BE PROSECUTED
FREE PLAY ALLOWED ON FIELDS 2 BLOCKS SOUTH

Ricks's approved creation myth appears on a campus sign:

RICKS COLLEGE

RICKS COLLEGE COMMENCED AS A
CHURCH OF JESUS CHRIST OF LATTER-DAY
SAINTS STAKE ACADEMY IN 1888.

Ricks was first known as Bannock Stake Academy, the Fremont Stake Academy, Smith Academy, and Ricks Academy before becoming Ricks College in 1918. The name memorializes Thomas E. Ricks, founder of Rexburg in 1883. Today Ricks College, Idaho's largest private college, includes a modern campus surrounding the historic 1903 Jacob Spori building.

More of Mr. Ricks later. Meanwhile, sign on campus cop car:

REXBURG POLICE

COLLEGE DIVISION

No separation of church and state in *this* theocracy.

There are attractive gardens, billed as a "Horticultural demonstration." "PUBLIC WELCOME DURING DAYLIGHT HOURS." Translation: Don't come in here at night to suck face.

A Daughters of Utah Pioneers sign states more college history, and the objective of the college: It "has been to train young people to adjust to their social environment and meet their community responsibility with moral leadership." Ricks that was is so heavy earnest. Makes me wanna yell "DARN!" just as loud as I can. They do get some things right: separate, reserved faculty and staff parking. That's been gone from my campus for many years, after a fit of late '60s egalitarianism. Maybe there's something to be said for patriarchy.

the Teton dam collapse

Rexburg has a very specialized town museum, housed in the basement of the former LDS "Rexburg Tabernacle." The main section memorializes a terrible event, the leaking and collapse of the earthen Teton dam in 1976, six weeks after it was declared finished. It was finished, all right, as were a number of other similar projects after its disaster. Rexburg was overwhelmed when the dam burst and the Snake unleashed an estimated eighty billion gallons of water into and down the valley. Ten people were killed, many fewer than might have been; a warning had been issued in time for most people to evacuate. Photo of a sign from nearby Sugar City: WANTED / DAMN ENGINEER / DEAD OR ALIVE.

more on Mormon life

The museum's friendly and knowledgeable docent explained some cryptic LDS terms to me. A "Stake," as in the Ricks College sign, means a group of five Mormon wards. Every five wards had a school. This one grew into an academy, then a college. That's much the same route that my college, SUNY-Fredonia, took, though without the ward/stake organization. My docent has two sons: the prospective engineer is off to BYU; "the artistic one" will enroll here. Rexburg, she said, used to be "Ricksburg," after its founder, Thomas E. Ricks. But "they took the town away from him . . . the polygamy thing . . . and changed its name. . . ." Got it. The old polygamous order changeth, grudgingly, yielding place to new. When, in 1890, Utah and the U.S. government decided they needed and could just stomach each other, the Mormon leaders announced a new revelation: polygamy was no longer God's will. Anyone in the way had to go, or at least go underground. Pretty Rexburg and shiny Ricks, now BYU-Idaho, are clear, open windows into Mormon life and thought.[2]

Rexburg shooter bulls on the loose

Keeping the wild and the domestic separate is often a good idea and a difficult task. About a hundred elk, bred for their huge antlers, escaped from a fenced "game farm" near Rexburg in August 2006, at the beginning of the elk rut. These "shooter bulls" were raised to be killed by trophy hunters, but instead had to be targeted by Idaho game wardens. The reason? They might carry brucellosis, tuberculoisis, or chronic wasting disease; they were never tested and cleared of these diseases. If they carry disease, and interact with wild elk, the tainted domestic elk could threaten the existence of the wild herds. Idaho is intensely antiregulation, very lenient toward entrepreneurs and hunters; but this leniency could prove disastrous for Idaho's game animals (*High Country News*, October 30, 2006, 23). This danger of disease transmission is one cause of the ugly winter bison shoots north of Yellowstone National Park. See chapter 7.

Back to US 20, which here is the road to the heavily billboard-advertised "Yellowstone Bear World." Bears in cages, without the justification of the West Yellowstone Discovery Center. Yuck. No way. On to Rigby, Idaho, where signs claim it was the "Birthplace of Television." Actually, as Western boosterism goes, this is pretty accurate. Near Rigby is the farm where Philo T. Farnsworth, born in Utah, grew up. He was more responsible than anyone else for the development of the cathode ray tube and the technology of early television. He was also a pioneer in nuclear fusion research. Farnsworth may have envisioned electronic scanning from observing the neat perpendicularity of the row crops on his family's farm. He profited little from his invention, and he later struggled with clinical depression. He is said never to have owned a television, nor to have permitted his children to watch one (*Writers' Almanac*, September 6, 2006). There is a happier story that, shortly before his death, Farnsworth watched live television pictures of the first moon landing in July 1969, and said that this made his invention worthwhile. My family watched that magic moment live from our rental on the English Channel in Shoreham Beach, Sussex. I agree with you, Mr. Farnsworth, and thanks.

onto the lava flows : atomic city and goodale's cutoff

The Great Road enters Idaho Falls like an Interstate and exits as a two lane, heading west into forbidding country. It leaves the lush valley of the Snake and enters one of the largest surface lava flows anywhere,

black volcanic rock on both sides of the road. The landscape is flattish—
the mountains to the north recede as you head west. It is lonely and dry
here; the grasses are sparse and short. Twenty miles west of Idaho Falls is
the second "Hell's Half Acre" of this trip; there are actually more than a
hundred thousand acres of this rough lava. There's a good short hike
through a little of Hell's Half Acre right off US 20 to the south. Then a
sign for "Atomic City." That name is explained when, in another ten
miles, Twenty enters INEEL: "The Idaho National Engineering and
Environmental Laboratory."

INEEL covers a large chunk of Idaho, with all the serious buildings
secure and fenced and unattainable, way off to the north of Twenty. This
is a tightly guarded atomic research laboratory, and, with one exception,
it doesn't welcome tourists. Its original name lacked the second "E."
Then some governmental public relations genius thought (correctly) that
it would soften and sweeten the aspect of the place to add "Environmental." One of its ongoing environmental projects is to try to figure out how
to handle atomic waste—a big national issue that gets bigger every day.

The landscape here is not to everyone's taste, but it has strong features. US 20 passes "Three Buttes" here, three huge batholiths, low
mountains to the north composed of rhyolite and basalt. The road follows
a historic part of the Oregon Trail known as Goodale's Cutoff. It was
named after guide Tim Goodale. In the early 1850s, the local Shoshone
became understandably inhospitable to the immigrants who swarmed
across their country, especially into the well-watered, lush valleys of the
Camas and the Snake, which were crucial to their hunter-gatherer economy. So formidable was this Shoshone threat that settlers from the East
were willing to travel a hundred miles across this lava flow, with no grass,
water, or shade, just to avoid the Shoshone. It was also a quick route to
the brief Idaho gold rush. It's still a little scary to cross this grim land,
even in an air-conditioned Subaru.

duck and cover

The tourist attractions here are two: EBR-1 and Craters of the Moon
National Monument. EBR-1 is "the world's first nuclear power plant"; its
primitive reactor provided power for nearby towns. The tour of the small
dormant facility is interesting if a little spooky; it has the look and feel of
cheapo '50's sci-fi movies. EBR-1 is a reminder of the naive days when it
was thought that atomic power would be so cheap that its use wouldn't

even need to be metered. "Duck and Cover," everybody; here come Homer Simpson, Chernobyl, and Three Mile Island.

Way more than fifteen hundred miles back east, the Great Road passed the site of the world's first controlled nuclear reaction, in 1942, in a former squash court (since demolished) under the stands of Stagg Field at the University of Chicago. Here, the town of Arco is a historic site of "Atoms for Peace," as the first city to be powered entirely by electricity generated by atomic energy. Pickles' Place is the "Home of the Atomic Burger." Hey, if it glows and ya got it, flaunt it. Soon the land grows a little greener, irrigated hay fields and grazing cows. No lava is visible. True fact: passed a BLM truck on US 20 full of people in funny white jump suits. Hazmat? Martians? Fashion victims? Aliens from Area 51? Who knows? It all fits nicely into the eerie feel of this land and its atomic past and present.

craters of the moon, sort of

The centerpiece of this land and its strangeness is Craters of the Moon National Monument and Preserve. Created in 1924, it was greatly enlarged in 2002 to include a huge Bureau of Land Management area of lava fields to the south: the Preserve. Twenty clips the northwest corner of it, the older, more developed Monument section. "Craters of the Moon"is an uninspired metaphor. It looks more like parts of Hawaii than it does like the moon, though early astronauts did train here. There are drives and hikes and climbs and an "Indian Tunnel," a partly collapsed lava tube. Lucifer did his usual homesteading here: there is an "Inferno Cone" and a "Devil's Orchard." In the visitor center, "bombs" are on display: large blobs of molten lava that flew up, cooled in the air, and fell in an aerodynamic shape. (A similar principle was used to make lead shot in the shot tower back in Dubuque, Iowa.) Ice Cave, a neat site to walk through thirty years ago, is off limits now. Is the National Park Service being nannyish again?

One really neat thing about this weird landscape is the microworld at your feet. Nothing could be less hospitable to plant growth than a recent lava flow, either pahoehoe, the ropy stuff, or aa, the jagged stuff. (The luscious words are Hawaiian.) Yet the young rock is fairly rich in minerals. When it begins to break down, cracks catch windblown grains of soil, seeds find the cracks and begin to grow. Thus, a lava flow that, from a distance, looks like solid basalt may turn out to be full of tiny brilliant

blooms in the summer. The campground is even—a-a, watch out!—a little dangerous. It's not easy to drive tent stakes here, and the careless can
get cut on the jagged rock. Altogether a wild, strange, interesting place.

back to the valley of the snake

In the next thirty miles the lava flow gradually ends. Near Carey is
a sizeable herd of cattle, several hundred head, and good grass for them.
Carey (pop. 300) has a Latter Day Saints temple, and a "sport shop" with
"beer and wine to go." Sport is where you find it. Between Carey and
Picabo the road goes through a notch that reminds me of the landscape
of Mesa Verde, in southwestern Colorado. What are "Picabo Resi-
dences" like, I wonder? Picabo is the town that hell-for-leather Alpine
skier, Olympic downhill medalist Picabo Street, was named for. The
Sawtooth mountains are visible to the north, where Picabo was born.
Hailey (the birthplace of poet Ezra Pound, of all people), Sun Valley, and
the "Sawtooth Scenic Byway" are all up that way. I've driven the byway
and it's super.

At the Magic Reservoir, pines reappear on foothills to the north,
toward the "Princess Mine Road." It is much greener here, almost lush,
good range, some irrigated row crops, as US 20 heads west and south
toward the Snake. Actually, Twenty here follows a migration path much
older than Goodale's Cutoff, which adopted it. We are in Camas Prairie,
the vast green summering ground of the Shoshone and Bannock people,
and the Nez Perce and Blackfeet from much farther north. They came
here to dig the bulbs of the Camas plant, a vital food source, and to trade
and flirt and prepare for the annual bison hunt. "The Camas Prairie
War," also known as the "Bannock War," a minor struggle of 1878, was
fought over access to this area, after settlers and their hogs began to compete with the Indians for the nutritious Camas bulbs. The Indians at the
Fort Hall reservation thought they had reserved rights to the area. A mistake that substituted "Kansas" for "Camas" in the treaty may have been
one of the causes of the disagreement, then the brief war.

The Great Road spends eleven miles in a corner of the Boise
National Forest, comes out into open range, and there it is, the Snake
River plain below. The Snake is brown, flat, low; unbeautiful. Yet how
happy and relieved immigrants must have been to see the big river again
after the volcanic grimness of Goodale's Cutoff. US 20 is now back on the
main line of the Oregon Trail.

Boise and west

Twelve miles west of this view of the Snake, US 20 briefly joins Interstate 84 and its cross-country rival, US 30, for the ride into Boise. Just off Twenty east of Boise is the National Interagency Fire Center, which I visited. Its task is to organize and coordinate federal firefighting, a job that gets bigger and harder every year. Twenty separates from I-84 at Exit 54 and becomes Broadway in the city center. The classical state capitol is visible two blocks away to the north. Boise was named by trappers from the French word meaning "woodsy." It still is. The Boise River flows among old trees through a pretty park in the middle of the mellow downtown. Thanks to Kate and Michael, "The Spuds," for showing me this. Though Boise's population is now (2000 census) more than 150,000—the largest city on US 20 west of Chicago—it still has an appealing small town feel.

There are thirty-six more miles of US 20 in Idaho. East of Notus are fields of irrigated row crops, and a sign for "Redneck Trailer Supplies." This is strong Second Amendment country. Greenleaf (pop. 862) is considering "recommending" that homeowners maintain firearms to stop

Fort Hall replica, Idaho

crime that might encroach from Boise (*USA Today*, October 2, 2006). One gun owner there, Alan Weinacht, is pastor of the local Friends Church— the peaceful Quakers. He and some others think the law is "stupid." "This is not exactly crime central." The mayor, Brad Holton, says he keeps twenty-five guns, all but one in a safe. "But you don't want to run into that one at night" (*New York Times*, October 12, 2006).

In Parma is an unlovely stucco "replica" of Fort Boise, once an ungracious but important stop on the Oregon Trail. Why ungracious? There's a good BLM Oregon Trail visitor center near Baker, Oregon, seventy miles north of US 20. Its exhibits make clear that Fort Boise was built—by Francois Payette in 1834—to encourage the fur trade, not to provide succor for Oregon Trail immigrants. They were considered a nuisance by the trappers and traders. One immigrant, Charlotte Pongra, wrote in 1853: "Crossed Snake at Fort Boise, that world renowned spot of one miserable block house all gone to decay . . ." (caption, BLM Oregon Trail visitor center). The displays at this center are interesting, though the mannequins and recorded voices are absurdly over the top. I shared the visitor center with a large group of young Oregonians, kids whose T-shirts identified them as "Young Grangers Making Their Mark." My workplace, Fredonia, New York, more than two thousand miles east on US 20, claims to be the birthplace of this once important rural organization, the Grange, "The Patrons of Husbandry." Only connect. Two miles farther west is another historic survival: a real functioning drive-in theater, the "Motor Vu." Probably wasn't an important stop on the Oregon Trail.

Oregon desert

US 20 crosses the Snake into Oregon. Nyssa bills itself as the "Thunderegg Capital of the World," and, inevitably, holds a "Thundereggs Days" festival. Thundereggs are a weird and marketable variety of a geode or a similar nodule sequestered in compressed volcanic tuff. They sometimes contain semiprecious stones such as opals, and are beloved of rockhounds. There are many Hispanic people here, presumably originally migrant agricultural laborers. Of the few radio stations on the dial, two are Hispanic. Ontario is home to the Four Rivers Cultural Center, a pleasant, small museum that celebrates the ethnic diversity of the local people—Anglo, Hispanic, Asian, Basque. The valley of the Snake is huge and lush; the irrigated crops are chiefly onions and potatoes.

The altitude back in Boise was over five thousand feet; at the Malheur River, in eastern Oregon, it is under two thousand. The land quickly gets browner, dryer, hotter as US 20 enters BLM land. This is serious desert, with brown hills and sagebrush; yet the Malheur River valley is irrigated and green. Easterners tend to think of Oregon as wet, even soggy. That is probably true of Portland, hundreds of miles away over the Cascade Mountains, but not here. This is harsh, dry country.

water and the modern west

An unknown nineteenth century wit said, "Whiskey is for drinking, water is for fighting over." That's truer than ever today. Southeastern Oregon, like most of the West, has become a battleground over water use. Who should trump whom? Fish? Farmers? Subdivisions? Indians? Toilets? Golf courses? There never was enough water to satisfy everyone here. With rampant growth and ever hotter summers coming, it's getting worse.

Oregon Trail, near South Pass

The seven years from 1998 to 2004 were unusually dry in the west. 2005 was a little wetter, but most reservoirs remained less than half full. There is every sign that this scarcity will recur or get worse; 2006 has been very dry. The scary possibility exists that the recent "'Drought in South-west May Be Normal" (*New York Times*, February 22, 2007). Maybe it's been unusually wet in the West, and we're just going back to a more normal pattern. Can we keep using subsidized irrigation water to grow crops that must be price supported? Cotton grows well in California's Mojave Desert, with the aid of copious amounts of scarce water sold to farmers way below cost. This subsidized cotton can be produced at about seventy cents a pound. The price of cotton on the world's markets: less than half that (*High Country News*, October, 2002). Should this continue? If so, why? Free trade agreements and international competition are threatening to end it. Some farmers and ranchers in southern Oregon are seriously thinking about taking a government buyout, like the ones suggested for the Great Plains, and it's probably a good idea. It surely would be cost effective, unlike so many things ostensibly done in support of the family farm. Other societies, from the Babylonians to the Ancestral Puebloans in Four Corners, have been destroyed by misuse or lack of water and consequent agricultural failure.

brown and dry

The color palate here is narrow yet rich. There is every shade of brown imaginable. Extruded lava flows and long volcanic dikes appear. In Juntura, huge cottonwoods; beyond it, buckets o' rocks. They're used in the hard rock West as ballast, weight to hold fences in place where drilling postholes is tough, rocks are plentiful, and fenceposts are scarce.

As the elevation climbs again toward three thousand feet, pinyon pines and juniper trees—"P-J" landscape in Western lingo—dominate the landscape. Higher tends to mean wetter. The summit of Drinkwater Pass is 4,212 feet and the beginning of the Pacific Time Zone. The rocks here are both igneous and sedimentary, volcanic and limestone. At Stinkingwater Pass—ya gotta love the name, if not the smell—4,848 feet, US 20 offers a view of the enormous block fault of Steens Mountain, forty miles off to the south. The Steens area is being both preserved and used by an unusual coalition of environmentalists and local ranchers. Good for them. In late June, Steens is still snow-capped.

The 126 miles from Burns to Bend is low, a geologic fault, a basin in this down-and-up, basin-and-range topography. Indeed, this is the northermost tip of the Great Basin, which dominates so much of the interior West. Just east of Burns is a small Paiute Indian Reservation, looking moderately prosperous. The houses and yards are neat and clean. The community building is nice-looking and pleasingly round. The empty message board shows that nothing much is happening. Getting through Burns (pop. 2,913) is easy, and then BANG there it is, the glitzy Paiute casino. Is this the reason for the relative prosperity? Who gambles here? Aliens from Idaho? Bluehairs from busses? There's no local population to speak of. Sherman Alexie has called casino gambling "the new buffalo": that is, with the buffalo gone, no longer the main source of sustenance for many Indians, gambling revenue is taking its place, and that can be true. Gambling is certainly a bonanza for the few remaining Connecticut Mashintuquet Pequots and their white financiers. Gambling is making money for some on my local Seneca rez in Western New York, and causing major political battles in Buffalo, the Catskills, and elsewhere. Yet most of these lonely outpost casinos surely can't make big money.

Near Riley, a turnoff for Reno, Nevada, there is a historical marker about the Bannock War of 1878, a brief but important settlers-Indians

They often are

conflict that included skirmishes as far east as Yellowstone National Park. When the Bannocks' leader, Buffalo Horn, was killed in Idaho, the tribe fled west into more sparsely settled Oregon, where they joined forces with some Northern Paiutes. Several battles with the U.S. Cavalry were fought near here, ending in the inevitable defeat of the Bannocks and Paiutes, and their confinement on reservations. That was the end of the Indian Wars in the northwest. Descendants of those Paiutes are now dealing blackjack on the rez back in Burns. There are huge, even majestic plains on both sides of US 20—ideal pronghorn habitat, I'd think. It is at the western end of their range, but I've never seen one there. The low foreground to the south is an ancient volcanic caldera twenty miles across—the Harney Basin. Up over a ridge beyond Hampton are the distant Cascades, snow-capped and stunning, a cool blessing after a hundred miles of high desert.

world's frankest historical roadside marker

Near Brothers, still in the desert, is my all-time favorite historical marker, bar none. It reads, in toto:

HISTORICAL SITE
OBSERVATIONS FROM HOMESTEAD ERA

Homestead cabins were so numerous that at night as kerosene lamps blazed from the small windows, the lights viewed from nearby Pine Mountain looked like twinkling stars. It usually took about 5 years for a man to arrive, build a house, fence some land, plow it, put in a crop, wait in vain to harvest, lose his money, get tired of jackrabbit stew, and leave. About 1916 the land rush was slightly in reverse due to crop fizzles and a growing shortage of sage hens, deer, and antelope. The June frosts blighted the town of Imperial as well as neighboring settlements and they eventually faded into oblivion with heaps of tin cans, pickle jars, and catsup bottles left as a memorial of these citadels of high hopes. From society's standpoint a serious consequence of homesteading was that it was hard on the land in that most of the acreage should never have been plowed. (*High Country News*, Sept 25, 2000, 20)

Wow. As my father used to say, before his son became a poet and poetry teacher, there's more truth than poetry in that. But there's a lot of poetry, too. "Jackrabbit stew." "Pickle jars." "Crop fizzles." Great stuff.

There are "No ideas but in things" (William Carlos Williams). This marker should be required reading for everyone west of the twenty-inch rainfall isohyet—roughly the ninety-eighth meridian. Too bad the boosters and politicians and railroads couldn't see all this coming. But of course nobody wanted to see it, even if it was perfectly plain.

the posh new west—but you're already too late

North from US 20 on Oregon 27 is the Lower Crooked River Back Country Byway: sagebrush, good views of mountains, hawks in the sky. I didn't take it. Instead, I went to Bend, and apparently everyone else did, too. Bend is one of those formerly pleasant small cities that has been outed by Outside Magazine or some such media tattletale. It's clearly the next FILL IN THE BLANK: Aspen? Moab? Telluride? Spokane? Silver City? Durango? Bozeman? Whatever, it's clear that, in the wise words of Lawrence ("Yogi") Berra, nobody goes there any more—it's too crowded. It seems to be all strip malls and fast food and outlet stores and traffic congestion. It probably was a really nice place to live. My friend Brian Connolly, who gets his mail there and lives nearby, says it was. Stu Gilbert, whose excellent unpublished manuscript on the Oregon high desert country was most helpful to me, agrees. Brian says the Bend area has more than 150,000 people now, though the 2000 census claims only 52,000 for the city. It's in a pretty place, and it has a moderate climate. If you own property there, rejoice, sell, cash in, and move away. It's so o-ver. Too many people. The histories of Brothers and Bend, the dry, brown places and the wet, green places, are rapidly changing as the New West arrives. Cows and mining are Old West; new urbanism, tourism, and ranchettes are New.

Q: Is there an uglier word in the English language than "ranchette?" A "ranch" should be sweaty and rugged and dirty and vast. Put an "ette" on it and it becomes a bogus little toy poodle, perfumed, coiffed, dinky, adorable. Yuck. Blech. In the interest of full journalistic disclosure, I hereby admit that I once owned forty acres on the western slope in Colorado, and five acres on the Colorado Plateau in southeastern Utah. They were both dry and had spectacular views. I never built anything in either place, and the land is no longer "mine" (whatever that legal construct means), but I might have. I guess that makes me a former potential "ranchetter." Yuck encore. Yet my motives, my aims, were probably the same as many others'. I like the views, the sun, the skies, the air, the stars at night, the silence, the animals, many of the people, the low population density. Goodbye, Old West.

new west, latest version

Almost every American who moves west, whether to Fredonia, New York, two centuries ago or to Alaska now, wants some version of the same thing: space, opportunity, freedom. And they also want nobody else to come out after them, Please Close The Gates Now That I'm Here, Because The Damn Easterners, Maybe From Idaho, Maybe Even From California, Are Ruining Everything. Don't Californicate My Paradise! I have no answer to this problem, except more and better birth control. The West is always remaking itself. This is just the latest incarnation. Those that follow may well be worse.

South of Bend and US 20 on Oregon 97 is The High Desert Museum, a fine place. I especially liked the outside trails with otters and porcupines, and the good Indian displays. On the way to it is a sign whose wisdom is hard to dispute: "Extreme Fire Danger—When Dry." There be philosophy there if a man could but find it out.

more lava, less water

Ninety-seven heads south into the Deschutes ("many waterfalls," pronounced "duh-Shoots") National Forest to Oregon's largest Ice Age volcano, now the Newberry National Volcanic Monument. Its ash was the source of much of the soil in the area. Don't miss the neat corkscrew drive up Lava Butte, and the unspoiled views of the Cascades it provides. Farther south on 97 is Sunriver, an unattractive resort/subdivision with good mountain views. The road winds through the national forest, past tacky inholdings and huge ponderosa pines. There's been extensive logging here, though cosmetic strips hide most of it. The Deschutes is a major locus of conflict, legal and political, between environmentalists and the timber industry. (Elizabeth Arnold did a fine report on how the Deschutes should be managed for National Public Radio on Sept. 27, 2002. Some of this information comes from it.) The Deschutes River is also reeling under heavy agricultural and urban use, and its former great salmon and steelhead runs are as diminished as its flow. Thousands of fish have died there in times of low water, some of it diverted at

Dick Cheney's orders. As a fellow Yellowstone Loon once hilariously posted about dead salmon and water use in the Klamath River, "This Just In: Fish Need Water." A conservancy group is trying to restore the Deschutes and its tributary creeks, with the help of the Warm Springs, Wasco, and Paiute Indian tribes, who have treaty rights to half the river's fish (High Country News, October 16, 2006). Agricultural irrigation pipes are replacing open canals, which lose half their water to evaporation. Any time Westerners of good will and diverse interests are talking rather than suing or fighting, that's good news.

Close to the base of the lower Cascade Mountains, it becomes clear how volcanic this whole area is—lava flows are everywhere. In midday, few large animals are visible in this exploited forest—all I see are ground squirrels. US 20 goes west to Sisters, a town perhaps too beautiful and green for its own good. Nestled in the woods, it was warned to prepare for evacuation during the fires of 2002. In the end, only two houses in the area were destroyed. It is named for the Three Sisters, mountains to the south of the Great Road. Sisters, pop. 911 and growing fast, is said to have the largest concentration of llamas in North America. There are indeed a lot of them. Sisters is just One Big Adorable Boutique. Dinner at Bronco Billy's, an old hotel, is mandatory. Sisters is already on the slippery slope, just starting to go the booming, gated subdivision way Bend has already gone.

The McKenzie Pass-Santiam Pass Scenic Byway is a loop that leaves Sisters for McKenzie Pass, 5,325 feet. The road is surrounded by lava. There are ferns and rhododendrons, and snow still on the ground in June. Sahalie Falls is absolutely gorgeous, a lot like Upper Mesa Falls in Idaho. Animals? Not many in midday: one deer. Back toward Sisters, US 20 heads east through more pines and lava. There is smoke in the forest to the south; "Controlled Burn," says the sign at the roadside. That's one way modern forests are managed, but it's tricky. In Los Alamos, New Mexico, in May 2000, enormous damage—235 houses destroyed—was done by a backfire set to stop a controlled burn in the Bandelier National Monument. At Santiam Pass, there are fields of stumps, thoroughly logged slopes, and big logging trucks.

wetter and greener

US 20 heads west toward the ocean. Here there are mossy pines and more deciduous trees. The last vista before the Great Road leaves the Willamette National Forest is (or was in 2002) a really ugly clear-cut hillside. Farther west is an area almost as rich in covered bridges as Indiana or Vermont. Example: Short Bridge, just off US 20 east of Sweet Home, is a covered bridge built in 1945 over the South Fork of the Santiam.

Signs: "Highway 20 Church of Christ." For a beauty shop: "Hairway 20." Every few miles there are sawmills, every one with stacks of big beautiful dead ponderosas. Sign: "Central Bark—we deliver." Another "Motor Vu" theater. Much of US 20 here, what's called Santiam Wagon Road, is lined with orchards. It is fruit country, like my Twenty in western New York, nearly three thousand miles east. Albany is a big town with a lot of Mexican restaurants—probably established by and to serve agricultural workers. Albany, Oregon, is 3,081 miles of US 20 west of Albany, New York, for which it was named.

Corvallis' name means "Heart of the [Willamette River] Valley." It has a charming old downtown. Linus Pauling, twice a Nobel Laureate, was a graduate of what became Oregon State University. Pauling's Institute and his papers are here. Corvallis is also the home of the Oregon State University Beavers; US 20 passes almost under the south end zone bleachers of the gigantic OSU football stadium. When I was there in 2002, *Sports Illustrated* featured their football team on its cover (a famous jinx), picked them 1–2 in the nation, with their rivals, the Oregon Ducks. The Beavers flopped, as beavers will. They did better in 2006, when they defeated high-flying USC in a corker, 33–31. I enjoyed watching it on TV and figuring out that my Twenty was just off the screen to the right. Bernard Malamud taught English at OSU in Corvallis; his novel, *A New Life*, may be reasonably supposed to have been based on his experiences there. It's a very good book, and a funny one. Malamud's mythic *The Natural* also dates from his Corvallis years. It is based in part on the weird shooting of Philadelphia Phillies' first baseman Eddie Waitkus by a lovestruck fan in 1949, way back east on Twenty in Chicago. A maniacal fifteen-year-old Cub fan at the time, I knew nothing of Baseball Annies. I was shocked and puzzled by such homicidal obsession; Bernard Malamud was inspired. Waitkus survived. After a similar horror story thirty-one years later, John Lennon did not.

Some Oregon State forestry grad students did a study in which they concluded that "salvage logging," commercially clearing out logs after a big south Oregon fire (the "Biscuit" fire, half a million acres burned in 2002), was harmful to the future growth of the forest. When they published in *Nature* in 2006, you'da thought they'd shot Barney, the president's dog. Some of their professors (whose programs are largely funded by the timber industry) protested bitterly and tried to suppress or deny their findings, which did contradict timber industry dogma. A later study of the fire tends to confirm the students' conclusions: thinning without burning increases future forest fire damage (*New York Times*, November 14, 2006).[3]

Philomath (pronounced "fill OH muth") is the home of the "Philomath Frolic & Rodeo." Yee-hah! Like so many ambitious Western hamlets, it once had its own college. That college's main building, still handsome, is now the town hall. There was a nasty struggle here in 2003 over a school superintendent's decision to do away with "the Warrior," a statue of an Indian mascot. The result was the loss of some college scholarships, the departure of the superintendent, and a documentary film: *Clear Cut: The Story of Philomath, Oregon* (*High Country News*, October 2, 2006, 9). In Blodgett, the elevation is down to 770 feet above sea level. East of Eddyville, north of US 20, are more hideous clearcuts. Pioneer Summit is at elevation 337. The small Siletz Indian reservation is eight miles to the north. The Siletz footprint is much heavier in the glitzy, ugly casino they run twenty miles north along the great beach road, US 101.

Just north of US 20 is the unmarked site of an oceanfront blockhouse built by soldiers in 1854 under the command of Lieutenant Phil Sheridan, fresh out of West Point, not yet a Civil War hero. It does not survive, though a photo of it does. In the excavation process, his men encountered the bodies of Indians buried in ceremonial canoes. Later famous for his views on dead Indians ("The only good Indians I ever saw were dead"), Lieutenant Sheridan was not long deterred. He ordered that the canoes be put out to sea with their grim cargoes, and so they were. So much for NAGPRA! (that's the Native American Grave Property Repatriation Act, which came a century too late to save these corpses and their grave goods).

"Ocian in view! O! the joy!"

US 20 : ocean to ocean

Actually, US 20 stops within a mile of the Pacific, on a hill within sight of Yaquina Bay and the ocean.[4] I really like Newport, Oregon. It is raffish and real; it welcomes the world to its fine bay and beaches. The motel on the beach between my motel and the ocean view hosted two conventions while I was there: first the National Rifle Association, then the Veterans of Foreign Wars. Is this America or what?! In 2006, the people of Newport rejected a very tempting poisoned apple—a "ship-breaking" company wanted to set up shop there and pay good wages for dismantling military vessels, with possible serious consequent pollution of the bay. Despite its economic problems, Newport's citizens felt that the danger to their beautiful seacoast was too great. Good for them, and for the strong independent tradition of Oregonians (*High Country News,* February 20, 2006, 5).

On Cape Cod, looking east toward Portugal, Henry David Thoreau wrote: "Here a man can stand and put all of America behind him." Newport, Oregon, is similarly on the edge, but America comes along for the ride. Newport's bayfront is handsome but unglamorous, with good, cheap seafood restaurants. Here, Newport smells like what it is—a working fishing town.

Newport has a rather new world class attraction, the Oregon Coast Aquarium. Be prepared for an intense experience here. The big underwater exhibit areas do not actually go out into the bay, as I had been led to believe. They are only huge exhibit tanks full of marine life. Yet when you walk in the middle of all of it, with the aquatic life, fish of all kinds, eels, skates, sharks, all around, above as well as below, it can be dizzying. I loved it, found it enchanting. Some people need to get out fast.

the Pacific : in tanks and at the beach

There are also outdoor pools and exhibits with libidinous birds and gloriously loafing sea otters, who are bigger up close than you might expect them to be. The aquarium's most beautiful and surprising exhibits are the several rooms devoted to jellyfish. The diversity of these living, pulsating coelenterates is stunning. So is the subtle beauty of these creatures that are almost all water, almost transparent. The Hatfield Marine Science Center, on Yaquina Bay, is named after Senator Mark Hatfield, a good environmentalist who died much too young. It is devoted more to practical science than to public display, but it is worth a visit.

Newport's Yaquina Bay beach is also a star attraction. I love beaches: on the North Atlantic, on Cape Cod, bay and ocean; on the South Atlantic, in the Florida Keys; on the Pacific in Southern California; and on the great inland oceans, Lake Michigan and Lake Erie. I've never seen a beach quite like this. It's raw, like Newport. There are signs everywhere, warning people not to play with snags, huge floating logs that can kill you if you try to ride them. Trees grow right up to the edge of the ocean and often fall in, hence the temptation and the danger. At low tide, the tidal pools are rich with life. Live starfish cling to the rocks, and gobies swim in tiny puddles waiting for Mother Ocean to return twice a day. She always does. It's rich and yeasty and exciting.

the end of the road : here is god's plenty

Just above Newport's beach is a plinth, a memorial to twenty-two Newport citizens killed on military duty in Viet Nam, far across the ocean that begins just below the plinth. There is a spiral walkway from it down to the beach. This honoring of American heroism on the brink of the vast ocean is a perfect, quiet way to end this look at America, here at its western edge. There's no place left to go. We must make the best of what we have, which is plenteous and magnificent. There's room for us all, all three hundred million of us, for our economic and recreational and spiritual needs, if we just don't get too greedy and screw it all up. It's the only continent in town, and the most vibrant country on the planet. The Great Road is a magnificent way to see some of the best of it. I do hope you will. Happy Trails.

notes

introduction

1. The elusive five-hundred-year-old dream of a Northwest Passage may soon be realized in a way few will welcome. Global warming is creating a passage through the ocean north of the Canadian mainland by melting the North Polar ice.

2. An amusing confirmation of this prejudice appeared in 2007 on the revised oral exam that is given to prospective U.S. citizens. The new exam was touted as a great improvement over the empty, stuffy questions of the old one. One of the 140 new questions to be asked at random was "Q: What is the longest river in the US?" "A: The Mississippi." Except that it's not. Oops. An Immigration and Naturalization spokesperson admitted the error, acknowledged that the Missouri was indeed longer, but said, "We're accepting both answers." I don't know what this sort of info has to do with citizenship, but I'd think they'd either require the correct answer or cut the question (National Public Radio, "Morning Edition," February 16, 2007). Both the Ohio and the Mississippi have greater water volume than the Missouri, as they drain wetter areas; but the old Missouri was two hundred miles longer than the Mississippi (2,520 to 2,320). Even after modern dredging and straightening, it is reckoned at 2,341 miles, and that doesn't count its parent stream, the Jefferson, which is 207 miles long (American Rivers Web site).

3. The old Lincoln Highway actually ran along US 20 for a few miles in South Bend, Indiana.

4. Buffalo is actually a pleasant and liveable city, with a lot more to brag on than chicken wings, hard winters, President McKinley's assassination, four straight Super Bowl losses, and a running back named Simpson. Buffalo has lost much of its industrial base and almost half of its population in the past century, but that means affordable housing and easy commutes. Lake Erie is much cleaner than it was thirty years ago. Buffalo has a distinguished architectural heritage, with beautiful old churches and art deco theatres, especially the sumptuous Shea's. It has signature buildings by all the early modern greats: H. H. Richardson, Louis Sullivan, Frank Lloyd Wright, and Eliel and Eero Saarinen. Sullivan's classic Guaranty Building was recently saved from demolition

by a civic-minded law firm, Hodgson Russ. Bless them, and their leader on this issue and others, Dianne Bennett. Only Chicago, the birthplace of modern architecture, can boast a richer architectural history. Buffalo has a lovely park system, courtesy of Frederick Law Olmsted; an excellent symphony orchestra; and a world-class modernist art museum, the Albright-Knox. It has a vibrant international neighbor, Ontario, just across the Niagara River. Niagara Falls, natural grandeur and cheap hydropower, is seventeen miles away.

Buffalo has a great theatrical tradition. George Abbott was born in Forestville, New York, in 1887 and, after a sojourn in Wyoming, graduated from high school in suburban Hamburg. "Mister Abbott" was Broadway's legendary show doctor for nearly seventy of his one hundred and seven years. Glamorous actress Katherine Cornell grew up in Buffalo, and now has a theatre at SUNY Buffalo named after her. Dancer, choreographer, and director Michael Bennett, the creator of *A Chorus Line*, was born Michael DiFiglia in Buffalo in 1943. He moved to New York City to dance, changing his name to that of his Buffalo high school. Half a dozen Buffalo theatre companies present strong seasons, and Shakespeare in Delaware Park is a warm outdoor summer treat. (Saul Elkin says that his King Lear's "Blow, winds, and crack your cheeks" soliloquy in that Olmsted park was once counterpointed by not-very-distant thunder and lightning.)

Buffalo has nurtured three first-rate playwrights of different generations, all still going strong: my fellow unionist Manny Fried, ninety-three and acting in a play as I write this, union organizer and firebrand; A. R. ("Pete") Gurney, chronicler of the troubled but funny Eastern upper middle class; and Elizabeth Swados, creator of intensely theatrical musicals and plays. Writers from the Buffalo area include Joyce Carol Oates, raised in Lockport; and Robert Creeley, John Logan, John Barth, and Leslie Fiedler, all of whom taught in the English Department at SUNY-Buffalo. Poets Lucille Clifton and Ishmael Reed once called Buffalo home. Ani DiFranco is one of the most interesting of modern rockers; she runs her Righteous Babe Records out of the historic Buffalo Asbury Methodist Church building, which she helped save from destruction.

Buffalo's summers are moderate and lovely, and its winters are getting milder as the globe warms. Buffalo might turn the skeletal brownfield remains of its defunct steel industry into a public lakefront that could rival Chicago's. (Olmsted's Buffalo park plans had included a parkway to Niagara Falls connecting with a Buffalo lakeshore park. Bethlehem Steel won that political struggle and occupied the lakeshore instead. *Buffalo News*, November 12, 2006.) Several Frank Lloyd Wright plans that were either never built, or became derelict, or were destroyed—a mausoleum, a boathouse, a period gas station, outbuildings of the great Darwin Martin House, and the Martins' summer house Graycliff, southwest along the Lake Erie shore—are in various stages of realization.

Yet, given Buffalo's record of mediocre political leadership, I am more hopeful than confident about its future. Buffalo is currently aping seedy downtown Niagara Falls in seeking to establish a Seneca casino. Legalized gambling is often the last refuge of desperate pols who want quick jobs and revenue, never mind the social costs. *The New York Times* is, like me, cautiously optimistic: "There is a sense that just maybe Buffalo's losing streak is coming to an end" ("After Half a Century of Decline, Signs of Better Times in Buffalo," September 18, 2006). Wouldn't you know that a freak early ice storm, the "October Surprise," would topple thousands of trees and electric lines, and paralyze the city in October 2006 on Friday the 13th? Buffalo's losing streak may not be over just yet. Go Bills. Go Sabres. Go Bisons. Go Buffalo.

5. Moving old American houses a great deal more historic than mine is a growing phenomenon, though it's a lot harder and more expensive than it was in Stuart Dean's day. It may be the only way to preserve structures that are in the way of encroaching development. Preservationists at groups such as the National Trust for Historic Preservation, though they prefer structures to remain at their original sites, "have also come to believe that relocation, done right, need not necessarily destroy the fabric of a neighborhood" ("Saving History? Take it Away," *New York Times*, February 1, 2007, D5).

6. I am grateful for the research of my neighbor, Brenda Beehler, who owns and occupies the Stuart Dean House: "Timothy Judson built a house on the property in 1834. . . . The East Barn is said to have been built in 1840. It was during this period that the barn served as a horse change. . . . In 1852 the malls and stages were withdrawn when the Buffalo and State Line railroad commenced. Ultimately Mr. Judson's house was moved one quarter mile east of its original suite. The barn remained." The Beehlers are restoring the old barns handsomely. Fredonia art historian Jewel Helen Conover described the barn as "originally a stable paved with bricks, where a change of horses was made on the stagecoach run" (*Nineteenth Century Houses in Western New York*, State University of New York Press, Albany, New York, 1966, 91).

7. I am not alone in my affection for Twenty. John Elwood, now a biology professor in West Chester, Pennsylvania, bicycled across the US in 1991 with a friend named Scott. They did a lot of miles on Twenty, especially in New York and Idaho. He had eighteen flat tires on the trip, six of them in Idaho. The last Idaho flat occurred on Twenty "within sight of the Oregon state line. Taking the hint, I walked my bike into Oregon." George Armstrong Custer's soldiers had a rueful nickname for their inexhaustible commander who would often make them spend all day in the saddle: "Old Iron Butt." I hereby award John Elwood (and Scott) the coveted US Twenty Old Iron Butt Award. Ron Stone and his wife plan to travel Twenty west from central New York to the Pacific on a motorcycle, then head back east to the Atlantic on US 2, and complete the trip by returning to Canandaigua, New York on Twenty. When they finish, they will be shoo-ins for the next Old Iron Butt ceremony. Michael Czarnecki traveled the entire road in one trip and wrote a nice book about it: *Twenty Days on Route 20.* And in 2007, Alborz Munjazeb, 24, was completing his hike across the USA on Twenty. He thinks of the trip as "part meditation and part adventure." (*Berkshire Evening Eagle*, November 24, 2007). Whew. It's good to know that others share my obsession.

chapter one / the power of the word along the great road

1. The Merriam brothers, booksellers from Springfield, Massachusetts, acquired the rights to Noah Webster's dictionary when Webster died in 1843. The corporation that grew from their bookstore, G. & C. Merriam Co., still publishes what is probably America's most authoritative and most controversial dictionary in Springfield, on the Great Road.

2. Springfield honored its distinguished poetic history in 2002 by building a downtown park dedicated to its hugely popular poet son, Theodor Seuss Geisel (1904–1991). The Dr. Seuss National Memorial Sculpture Garden is filled with bumptious bronze statues of his charming characters, made by his stepdaughter. You can frolic here with Horton, Yertle, the Grinch, the Lorax, Things One and Two, and more. Kids seem to like it; so did I.

3. Anne's daughter, Linda Gray Sexton, wrote that "Maxine was the affectionate big sister Mother felt she never had, a calming influence with whom she could share everything from craft to love affairs and from whom she could learn about poetry until she felt powerful enough to sally forth on her own" (Linda Gray Sexton, *Searching for Mercy Street*, Boston: Little Brown, 1994). Sexton and Kumin had a private telephone line installed just for their daily conversations and workshopping. They lived very near each other, but when one of them was off on a gig or a visiting professorship, they kept close this way. Maxine Kumin told me that she was always happy to hear the phone ring in the late afternoon, because she knew it would be Anne.

4. Philip Roth comically titled one of his fictions *The Great American Novel* (1973). At least I think Roth was joking. Asked why he chose baseball as the mythic venue for his farcical account of ancient gods and heroes in modern athletic dress, he replied, "Whaling's been done" (quoted in *Buffalo News*, November 12, 2006). The greatest modern American authors can't help looking back over their shoulders at Melville, even if they try to dismiss him with a funny quip. Actually, baseball had been done, too: very well, mythically, and on the Great Road. Bernard Malamud published *The Natural* in 1962 after living and teaching on Twenty in Oregon (see chapter 8). After Roth published his *Novel*, William Kinsella set parts of *Shoeless Joe* (1982) on the Great Road in Iowa. *Field of Dreams* was filmed from it there (see chapter 4). Maybe Roth should have tried whaling again. Or NASCAR. The verbal gags in *The Great American Novel* are fiendishly clever: "Gil Gamesh" is one star player. Roth one-ups Bill Veeck by using not one midget, but two. Funny as it sometimes is, the book is hard going, not one of Roth's best, and the title remains a joke.

Herman Melville and Norman Rockwell have attained fiscal deification in the Berkshires. Businesses in Berkshire County have created a local currency—"Berkshares"—specific to and cashable only there. Melville is on the twenties, Rockwell on

Dr Seuss Memorial in Springfield, Massachusetts, with the text of "Oh the places you'll go" with Gertrude McFuzz on the right.

the fifties. W. E. B. DuBois, born and raised in Great Barrington, is on the tens (*New York Times*, February 25, 2007).

5. I audited Whit Stoddard's Intro to Art course, in which he used the then groundbreaking method of showing and discussing slides of works of art. He shaped, much for the better, the way I look at the world. As Gulley Jimson says of Cezanne in Joyce Cary's wonderful novel *The Horse's Mouth*, "He skinned my eyes for me." I sang in an opera with Bill Pierson. Williams is a powerful place, putting students in close creative contact with strong minds and ideas. My debt to Williams music professor Bob Barrow is even greater. That I achieved less with his tutelage than did Stephen Sondheim just shows my limitations.

chapter two / the great road to justice and freedom

1. The rich cultural heritage of the Seneca nation and the Iroquois Confederacy is celebrated at Ganondagan State Historical Site, seven miles south of the Great Road in Victor, New York. Ganondagan ("Ga-NON-da-gon") was a thriving Indian community until it was attacked and destroyed by a French army in 1687. The most impressive thing there today is a frame and bark long house, rebuilt to show the communal living style of Ganondagan's seventeenth-century inhabitants. The supposed tree bark of the walls is actually molded plastic, so that the long house won't have to be rebuilt every year or two, but it looks and feels real enough. Each long house would have been home to several families. A few miles to the southeast are Canandaigua Lake and Clark's Gully, the place of the emergence myth of the Seneca, the Keepers of the Western Door for the Iroquois Confederacy. The Seneca call this place *kanandague*, "the chosen spot" (*New York Times*, October 1, 2006). These sites recall the contributions the Iroquois made to modern America, not least to the U.S. Constitution and to women's rights, entirely in keeping with the progressive, egalitarian spirit of the Great Road.

2. Cooperstown's name comes from the family that produced America's first best-selling novelist, James Fenimore Cooper, whose stilted visions of the frontier and frontiersmen such as Leatherstocking Natty Bumppo thrilled the Western world. Beautiful Otsego Lake is the original of Cooper's "Glimmerglass." The excellent summer opera company there goes by the same lyrical name. Cooperstown's diverse museums are first-rate.

Marginal and/or cheesy roadside attractions once grew in profusion along the tourist-busy Great Road in central New York, from Cobleskill west to Cardiff. Now that the New York Thruway has made this section of Twenty sleepy and quiet, only a dwindling few remain, but their names still have nostalgic power: "Secret Caverns." "Petrified Creatures." "The Tepee." The "Upstate Auto Museum" is gone, as is the "Musical Museum"

(antique musical machines); both faded away in the 1990s. Most of the survivors seem perpetually For Sale, with no takers. When I saw the Nelson Inn on Twenty in Nelson, New York in 2002, it was closed and for sale. It probably had the only bar for at least five miles around. Such an opportunity may not occur again. Could a Nelson turn that down?? Yes.

3. Chautauqua County's southern reaches have their own sociohistorical importance, even starry celebrity. Three famous twentieth-century Americans were born and raised in or near Jamestown, New York, and institutions there memorialize them. Roger Tory Peterson taught Americans how to observe and love birds. The Roger Tory Peterson Institute is north of his native Jamestown; it holds his papers and exhibits many of his beautiful bird paintings. Lucille Ball of "I Love Lucy" and "Desilu" was born in Jamestown and raised in suburban Celoron. She did her first acting in school plays in Jamestown, and is celebrated in the Lucy-Desi Museum there, where you can buy a bottle of Vitameatavegamin. Lucy's ashes lie in Jamestown's beautiful Lake View Cemetery.

Robert H. Jackson was born just south of the New York State border in Pennsylvania, and grew up in Frewsburg, New York, five miles southeast of Jamestown. He got his law degree in Albany, on the Great Road, and set up a law practice in Jamestown. He became U.S. Attorney General, and was appointed to the Supreme Court by FDR in 1941; he became one of its most distinguished justices. He took a leave from the Court in 1945 to lead the prosecution in the Nuremberg war crimes trials. His legal opinions, such as *West Virginia Board of Education v Barnette*, an assertion of individual rights in a flag salute case, are greatly respected and often cited. The respect for freedom and justice fostered by the culture of the Great Road is manifest in his distinguished career. The Jackson Center has been established in Jamestown "to preserve the life and legacy of Robert H. Jackson." He is buried in Frewsburg.

4. Oberlin also holds one quirky, noteworthy "last." Oberlin deemphasized athletics and suffered horrendous football losing streaks in the 1990s, but it remains the last Ohio team to defeat that football juggernaut, Ohio State. The year was 1921, the place Columbus, and the score was Oberlin 7, Ohio State 6. In 1892, an Oberlin football team coached by John Heisman (Really! The Trophy guy!) defeated Ohio State twice and Michigan once on the way to a 7–0 season. Go, Yeomen!

5. There is yet another great story of gender equity on the Great Road. Because it doesn't fit neatly into the political context of this chapter, I have demoted it to a footnote, but it was momentous. Though she was born and died in England, Elizabeth Blackwell (1821–1910) attended medical school in Geneva, New York, on what became Twenty. Refused admission by more famous medical schools, she was accepted at Geneva Medical College, and graduated at the head of her class in January 1849. She was completing her medical education as the Seneca Falls delegates were meeting in July 1848, eleven miles to the east. What a dynamic place and time! Blackwell became the first modern female physician *anywhere*, and went on to a long and distinguished career in both England and America. It is said that those who voted to admit her may have thought the whole thing a preposterous joke. Perhaps. But admit her they did, and she survived and excelled. Here on the Great Road another huge barrier to full equality for women was demolished.

6. The village of Fredonia, New York, is where I work, on the Great Road, at the State University of New York, College at Fredonia. The name "Fredonia" is a coinage, perhaps meaning something like "free gifts," a reference to the richness of this new land. A dubious etymology suggests it might come from an old word for a feudal price

a rebel paid to clear his name, but I can find no trace of such a word either in Anglo-Saxon or Middle English. A comically abortive attempt to establish part of Texas as "The Republic of Fredonia" failed in 1827. Whether or not it referred to American rebels, the name "Fredonia" clearly was linked to the idea of "Freedom." Samuel Latham Mitchill (1764–1831), a New York scientist and politician, advocated this Latinate coinage for the name of the new nation, but it was never likely that the United States of America would become "Fredonia." (Groucho Marx would have approved of it: as Rufus T. Firefly, he rules the dinky mythic country of "Freedonia" in *Duck Soup* [1933]. "Hail, Freedonia!!") This village liked the name, as did ten communities in the United States, from New York to Arizona.

My college was founded in 1826 as the Fredonia Academy. The New Englanders who came into these wild western lands in the 1820s valued education highly, and my excellent college is a tribute to them. Fredonia is just another pretty little western New York village, yet its early citizens imbibed the creative atmosphere and made significant contributions to the experimental ferment of the Great Road. Fredonia was the site of the first underground natural gas well, dug twenty-seven feet deep in 1821. As "the birthplace of underground natural gas" in the United States, its streets were very early lit by gas lamps—in time for the 1825 visit of the aged Marquis de Lafayette, a hero of the Revolutionary War half a century earlier.

Mark Twain rode a train from his home in Buffalo to Dunkirk, New York, and then a horse car to Fredonia in January 1870 to speak at the Fredonia Normal School, which would become my college (*Dunkirk Observer*, November 5, 2006). His mother, Jane Clemens, lived in Fredonia while he edited a newspaper, *The Buffalo Express*, from 1869 to 1871. ("My mother had a great deal of trouble with me, but I think she enjoyed it.") He often visited her here, at the beginning of his greatest creative period. His late, dark short story, "The Man Who Corrupted Hadleyburg" (1899), is thought by locals to have been inspired by bad Fredonia behavior. ("Hadleyburg" is more likely drawn from Hannibal, Twain's home town.) His Fredonia great-niece, Jean Webster, wrote the oft-filmed coming-of-age novel *Daddy-Long-Legs*. Fredonia's most famous and successful author was Grace Richmond (1866–1959), author of twenty-seven popular novels, many about the character "Red Pepper Burns." Her handsome house, built in 1847, stands on East Main Street—US 20. She is buried in Fredonia's beautiful Forest Hill Cemetery.

Fredonians claim that two important national institutions were founded in the village. Both still exist, though neither has much oomph today. The impressive hall erected on US 20 in Fredonia in 1915 by the Patrons of Husbandry (better known as The Grange) has inscriptions stating "Grange No. 1" and "founded April 16, 1868." The Grange was a powerful political and economic force in support of the nation's farmers, and had enough clout to swing some nineteenth-century elections. The organization's official creation myth does not mention Fredonia, preferring Minnesota and 1867. It may be that this Fredonia Grange was only one of the first to be incorporated. I encountered a delightfully noisy gaggle of kids in Grangers T-shirts at a BLM Oregon Trail museum while researching this book. It looked more like a fun outing than anything serious, and, indeed, the Grange now bills itself as "America's Family Fraternity," and is nonpartisan in politics.

The Woman's Christian Temperance Union was founded in 1873 in (among other places) the Fredonia Baptist Church; that building stands today on Church Street, a block from 20. Other Christian women's groups elsewhere were doing very similar organizing and activism, but the WCTU's web site gives Fredonia's women the honor of primacy:

"The women of Fredonia, New York are credited with being the first of the women's groups to visit the saloons, under the leadership of Mrs. Esther McNeil. Subsequently, on December 22, 1873, they were the first local organization to adopt the name Woman's Christian Temperance Union." In the same year, eight miles to the west, in my village of Brocton, Thomas Lake Harris's Brotherhood of the New Life was turning out twenty thousand gallons of wine, wine that Harris claimed was Godly: one more instance of battling moralities on the Great Road. In 1874, the temperance movement became a national organization. The WCTU grew mighty enough to spearhead the passage of the Eighteenth Amendment in 1919, and to begin that failed "noble experiment," Prohibition. Concord Grapes, already the region's main crop, would be cultivated to the exclusion of wine grapes; jelly and juice would trump cabernet. My friend, the exemplary New York State Assemblyman Bill Parment, has had our county declared a "Concord Grape Heritage Region," and that's certainly true.

Prohibition did significantly reduce the consumption of alcohol in the United States, as intended. Yet, sadly, its most enduring legacies—unintended consequences that are still with us—were to encourage criminal syndicates and breed contempt for law and social engineering. Our species has sought altered consciousness for as long as it has existed. No law, however well-meaning or strongly enforced, can change human physiology. Our nation's thirty-plus-year "War on Drugs" is and always will be a preposterous, hypocritical, wasteful farce. Many of today's local Concord grapes, "Heritage Region" or not, become Manischewitz or Mogen David wine, not Welch's jelly or juice. Long before the Twenty-first Amendment (1933) repealed the Eighteenth, the WCTU had established its headquarters in the prim, alcohol-free suburb of Evanston, Illinois, just north of US 20. It remains there to this day, though Evanston ceased to be a "dry" town in 1972.

chapter three / power and empire on the great road

1. This trend continues. The Census Bureau, working with statistics from the period July 1, 2005, to July 1, 2006, lists the ten states that are growing fastest. Only one of them, Idaho, is in the northern half of the country, and it's in the West. Colorado and South Carolina displaced Delaware and Oregon in the top ten of growth. Texas gained more people than any other state. New York posted its first loss in population since the 1970s, though state officials said that undercounting had caused it, and that it would be corrected. North Carolina has supplanted New Jersey as the tenth most populous state. "The entire Northeast grew by only 62,000 people. The West grew fastest, followed by the South" (*New York Times*, December 22, 2006). Phoenix, arid and mercilessly hot, has recently replaced temperate Philadelphia as the nation's fifth-largest city.

2. Nothing is permanent in American politics. The federal civil service system worked admirably through the twentieth century. In the twenty-first century, it is being undercut by political appointees in charge of agencies, and by "outsourcing" to "private contractors." Paul Krugman reports that fewer than half of those contracts are now open to competitive bidding ("The Green-zoning of America," *New York Times*, February 5, 2006; see also the *New York Times*, February 4, 2006). The new formula sees to be: "To the campaign contributors belong the spoils."

3. The assassin, anarchist Leon Czolgosz, was quickly tried, convicted, and electro-

cuted in the best modern way: in the new electric chair, the first in the world, in the state prison in Auburn, New York. Thus, his horrible crime and his horrible death both occurred on the Great Road. Isn't it sad that so many American leaders have been murdered, and so many more shot at? And isn't it absurd to think that the best way to teach people not to kill people is to kill people?

4. Wealth and political power are linked in our nation in complex ways. Despite great ambition, high intelligence, a warm, flamboyant personality, and enormous wealth, John D.'s grandson, Nelson Rockefeller, never achieved the presidency. Generations to come may well wonder whatever the phrase "Liberal Republican" can have meant. Nelson Rockefeller was just such a walking oxymoron. Booed, taunted, and drowned out by his fellow Republicans in the wee small hours at the 1964 Republican convention, he was thrashed for the presidential nomination by Barry Goldwater, who was in his turn thrashed in the election by President Lyndon Johnson. Rockefeller later remarked privately that joining the Republican party was a mistake he could never overcome. His progressive tenure in Albany as governor of New York includes some great triumphs, including the creation of the university where I work. He became vice-president when he was appointed to the post by Gerald Ford in the wake of Watergate in 1974, but he never participated in any important administration decisions. A hollow, figurehead vice-presidency, to which he was appointed by an appointee, was as high as he could climb.

chapter four / westering

1. Erie, Pennsylvania celebrates its nautical military history with a bayfront maritime museum, and a handsome, seaworthy replica of the brig *Niagara*, the ship in which Commander Oliver Hazard Perry won the Battle of Lake Erie in the War of 1812.

2. Though not all unnecessary wars are disasters, most are, certainly most of those inspired or justified by some form of Manifest Destiny. A good book on American foreign policy says: "Manifest Destiny was the bumper sticker sentiment that asserted the civilizing impulse of Anglo-European culture and the innate supremacy of its practices." Mexico, Hawaii, the Philippines, Viet Nam, Latin America, Iraq; so it goes. Quoted from Stefan Halper and Jonathan Clarke, *The Silence of the Rational Center*, reviewed in *New York Times*, February 20, 2007.

3. I think that John Gast must have seen a reproduction of Eugene Delacroix's "Liberty Leading the People," painted in 1830–1831. Indeed, one Web source that lists the Gast uses the Delacroix as its logo, and calls Gast's lady "Liberty," like Delacroix's, not "Columbia" or "America." The postures of the iconic figures are similar, though Gast's lacks the energy and artistry of the French original, a mythic representation of the Revolution of 1830. Gast's female is bosomy but definitely *not* bare-breasted, as Delacroix's so flamboyantly is. Frederic Bartholdi's Statue of Liberty is even more clearly an offspring of Delacroix's heroic revolutionary.

4. Charles Guiteau was a young bank clerk in his native town of Freeport, Illinois, in 1858. He was interested in politics. I can't believe he would have missed such a historic debate, though that is just my conjecture. If he attended, he did not do so to kill. He waited until 1881 to make his terrible mark on American history. See chapter 3.

5. There's a lovely irony in this upscale coffin business for the monks of New Melleray. Like all Trappists, they are sworn to poverty. When a Trappist dies, he is laid in a clean robe in a plain pine box without a lid. The brothers sit vigil over the body in the chapel. I've watched that moving ritual. When the dead brother is buried, his face is covered with a white cloth, the box is lowered into the grave, and all the brothers assist in shoveling dirt onto the body. Dust thou art, and to dust thou shalt return. In a plain, uncovered box.

chapter five / soldiers and indians

1. In the Northeast, that is. Actually, the Indian Wars can be said to have begun in Jamestown, Virginia, shortly after the Jacobean colonists began their experiment in 1607. Jamestown was at first a terrible flop. Before King James had Sir Walter Raleigh beheaded in 1618, Raleigh had made two important contributions to his age and ours: a wonderful body of poetry, and the practice of smoking tobacco. It was the cultivation and export of tobacco, and the consequent importing of African slaves (from 1619), that made the colony and the region economically viable. Hark, what discord followed.

2. Twenty-two miles south of Twenty, in the other direction from Hat Creek, is Agate Fossil Beds National Monument. A small treasure in an out-of-the-way location, it offers a superb display of Miocene fossils, and rancher James Cook's excellent collection of Lakota art and artifacts. The Niobrara River, life-giver of the Sandhills, flows through open range land rich with native plants and animals. Agate Fossil Beds is well worth a detour.

3. "Counting coup" was a remarkable war practice of the Plains Indians. Death, destruction, and conquest were not the main goal of most of their fights; displaying courage and prowess was. Thus, if a courageous warrior got close enough to an enemy to touch him with a coup stick ("coup" means "blow, strike" in French), he gained greater glory than if he had killed him. Subsequent coups and wounding the enemy also conferred great merit, but none so much as the first touch. This attitude toward war as a glorious display of courage made it difficult for Plains Indians to organize and defeat a more disciplined opponent. Only the greatest leaders, such as Crazy Horse, could convince the warriors to keep disciplined order for very long; and even he led by example, not by birth, rank, or command.

4. The Battle of the Rosebud was an inconclusive but significant encounter in south central Montana between the forces of U.S. Army General George Crook ("Three Stars" to the Indians, who respected him) and a large force of Lakota and their Cheyenne allies. It took place on June 17, 1876, eight days before and thirty miles southeast of the battle of the Little Big Horn. Crook was heading north from Fort Fetterman, Wyoming, as the southern salient of a three-pronged Army plan to trap and kill or disarm and imprison the free Lakota. Crook and his men were met, stopped, and given a very hot fight by Indians led by Crazy Horse. The Indians eventually withdrew, and Crook could claim a technical victory, but he was forced to withdraw to the south to reorganize and resupply. This took his forces out of the coming struggle, and contributed to the destruction of Custer and his Seventh Cavalry. Crook later said that "the hardest thing is to go and fight those

whom [*sic*] you know are in the right" (*The Spirit of Crazy Horse*, 11). The Rosebud battlefield today is marked but not signed or developed. It is a peaceful sea of tall grass in the summer. Just north of it is the old trail that Custer and his men took west to their doom. Farther north down Rosebud Creek is the site where Sitting Bull stoically endured the sacrificial cutting of one hundred small pieces of his arm flesh, and had his vision of "enemy soldiers falling into camp," which seemed to predict Custer's attack and defeat. The Rosebud then flows north into the Northern Cheyenne Reservation, at last the home of a people, after their breakout from Camp Robinson, and their epic, fighting trek to Montana (see Mari Sandoz, *Cheyenne Autumn*).

5. Larry McMurtry calls this oceanic prison "claustrophobic" in his book *Oh What a Slaughter: Massacres in the American West 1846–1890* (Simon and Schuster, 2005). I've been there and I don't quite agree. It's open and airy enough. But it was isolated, dry, unhealthy, and utterly unlike anything Plains Indians had ever known. Crazy Horse would have been miserable there. Escape would have been impossible. It's three hours west of Key West by high speed modern ferry. It was reserved for the hardest of hard cases, such as Dr. Samuel Mudd, who treated John Wilkes Booth's broken leg after Booth assassinated Abraham Lincoln. In a lovely historical irony, Dry Tortugas has gone from a place of close confinement to a place of opportunity and liberation. From 2004 through 2006, 1,700 Cubans have landed there and been accepted as legal permanent residents of the United States. Citizenship usually follows.

6. There are several such buffalo kill sites in the West. To see one fully developed as a tourist attraction, go to Head-Smashed-In Buffalo Jump, near Fort Macleod, in Southern Alberta, Canada. The interpretive center is handsomely constructed and well

Road into Rosebud Battlefield, Montana

run by the Blackfoot Nation. As Dave Barry wrote, they really do answer the phone, "Head-Smashed-In, How may I help you?" The gift shop sells mugs and baseball caps with a falling buffalo logo. I think they're a hoot.

7. The Springfield Armory in Massachusetts no longer makes guns, as it did from 1794 to 1968. At its peak, in 1864, it was turning out one thousand guns a day for use in the Civil War. The Springfield Armory National Historic Site covers fifty-five acres, and has the largest collection of firearms in the United States: sort of an American Tower of London. It is still a major tourist attraction; school kids get bussed in to hear lengthy lectures on guns. I know. I heard one.

chapter six / the best idea

1. Ferdinand Hayden's is another distinguished Great Road life, from New England to the Rockies. Born in Westfield, Massachusetts, he was educated at Oberlin College and Albany Medical College. All three sites are on the Great Road. He explored the West and rose to become head of the United States Geological Survey.

2. One hundred and thirty years later, poaching is still a serious problem in the wild lands of the West, especially in and near Yellowstone National Park. Unscrupulous hunters and guides eager for trophy heads will "bait," scatter food, near the park's boundaries, and shoot elk or bighorns who come to eat it. A Montana poaching ring was prosecuted for this in 2006, and its leader was sentenced to a year in federal prison. But local courts often give very light sentences to illegal hunters, and the criminal practice continues. In 2007, two Wyoming hunters plea bargained and pled guilty to three crimes, including poaching a bull elk in the park in November 2006, and illegally carrying firearms in the park. One was sentenced to probation, a fine and jail time of "time served:" five days. Can you say "Slap on the wrist"?? The other got a fine, probation, and thirty days, apparently more for possession of marijuana than for killing protected elk (National Park Service "Morning Report," February 20, 2007). The problem is much the same as the one Harry Yount encountered in 1880—too many acres to cover, too few wardens. Hunters say they are almost never stopped and asked to show their permits. (I was quite surprised when a boating ranger asked to see my camping permit in the backcountry wilderness of Yellowstone Lake.) The National Park Service states that poaching has contributed to the decline of twenty-nine wildlife species in the 390 areas it supervises (*New York Times*, "Poachers Feed Big Egos With Big Antlers," December 9, 2006). On other federal lands, poachers often misuse the roads created for oil and gas exploration (*USA Today*, February 16, 2007, 4A).

3. Don't drop too many tears for Mr. Child. He swiftly adapted to the age of the automobile, shifting to cars and buses. He and his family continued to profit handsomely from the tourist trade in Yellowstone until they sold their business in 1966.

4. One of my Yellowstone Loon friends once posted a hilarious photo of a bison standing quietly on the deck of a park bathroom building, his (or her) head near the entrance to the women's room. A woman could be seen dimly, just inside the door, wondering what the hell to do. The caption: "There's always a line at the women's restroom."

chapter seven / the great road to wilderness

1. The Bush administration's Budget Proposal for 2008 also included $230 million for the national parks, and suggested that *ten billion* dollars should be devoted to them by the time of the Park Service centennial in 2016. Unfortunately, the proposal includes lots of hypothetical private dollars, and seems more smoke and mirrors than cash commitment. The parks have been underfunded for many years, and their staff and their infrastructure are in sore need of a major infusion of cash. A thousand new rangers might be hired if this recommendation ever bears fruit. Gosh, maybe we could even go back to the good old days of ranger-guided hikes?

2. Other statistical sources show a much darker picture of wolf predation. "Wolves in the Northern Rockies killed 344 sheep, 170 cows, two llamas, a horse, a mule and eight dogs last year [2006]. As a consequence, 152 wolves were killed, which is legal if the wolf threatens life or property despite its status as an endangered species" (*High Country News*, February 19, 2007, 3).

3. David Quammen quotes similar stats for Glacier National Park. In Glacier's first ninety years, nine people were killed by grizzlies. In the same time period, forty-eight drowned, twenty-three fell from cliffs and died, and twenty-six were killed in car crashes (*Monster of God*, New York: W.W. Norton, 2003, 306).

chapter eight/ ocian in view

1. Wallace Stegner was born not far off the Great Road, in Lake Mills, Iowa, in 1909. I'd be happy to claim him as a Great Road writer, had not his doomed, super-restless father taken his family to twenty places in Stegner's first twenty years. In "At Home in the Fields of the Lord," he wrote that "my hometown held me six weeks." (See also *The Big Rock Candy Mountain*, 1943, and *Wolf Willow*, 1955.) Stegner finally found a home and acceptance as an undersized adolescent in Salt Lake City. In "At Home" and in *Mormon Country* (1942), he gives a lovely account of how the Mormons, bless their good hearts, welcomed a lonely boy. I know of no other Gentile narrative of the Latter Day Saints that is so warm and positive.

2. LDS organization and enthusiasm still produces strange and improbable events. On a morning run from a motel in Vernal, Utah, in July 2005, I passed a large, impressive LDS Temple at 6:40 a.m. Thirty-one (I counted) adolescent Mormon girls in sweat suits, nymphettes, teeny-boppers, you name it, were shakily wheeling out of the temple grounds on unicycles onto the street I was running on. Many rode in threes and fours, reaching out to support one another. They were squealingly, wobblingly adorable, though I don't think they knew that they were. Why? What were they training for? Some LDS pageant? *Unicycling to Zion? Teetering to Deseret? Wheeling to Shibboleth?* I'll never know. Have you ever seen that many unicyclists at one time? Me neither, till then. It was wondrous strange. And therefore, as a stranger, I gave it welcome. That's Utah.

3. Poet Gary Snyder was a proud Forest Service employee in 1952–1953, helping to spot and put out fires from his lookout in the Washington Cascades. Realizing now that this was not helpful but probably detrimental to forest health, he writes, "The joke's on

me 50 years later." Snyder quotes forest ecologist Jerry Franklin on the Biscuit Fire recovery plan: "Salvage logging of large snags and down boles does not contribute to the recovery of late-successional forest habitat . . . none of the snags and logs of decay resistant species can be judged as being in excess of those needed for natural recovery . . . large, slowly reforesting disturbed areas are important hot spots of regional biodiversity" ("Lifetimes with Fire," *Sierra*, March/April 2007, 58–60).

4. There is no logical reason why, after US 20 runs north of US 30 for two thousand, five hundred miles, the roads should meet and cross in Oregon and give the Columbia Gorge and Lewis and Clark's Fort Clatsop to US 30. Fond as I am of Newport, Oregon, I feel a bit cheated. US 20 was originally planned to terminate farther north at Astoria, Oregon, north of US 30, but political considerations and pressure from the Lincoln Highway Association changed the plans. US 20 was halted at Yellowstone from 1927 to 1938, while US 30 took the northern Oregon route that was originally planned for Twenty. Thus, though it is not quite a proper part of a book on Twenty, I'd like to add a few brief observations on the highlights of US 30 from the Oregon coast along the Columbia and down to Ontario, Oregon. It really should be the route of my road, and it is, I feel, part of the Great Road.

—Volcano Country: I suppose if you live here you get used to it. After all, they don't often blow. Try not to think of Mount St. Helen's. For me, driving in northern Oregon and western Washington was a little like dancing through a long abandoned minefield. Those big cones in the distance, often more than one in view at a time—wow, they're volcanoes! I like the feeling. Sorta.

—Fort Clatsop: Until it was destroyed by fire in October 2005, there was a reconstruction near Astoria, Oregon, of this fort where the Corps of Discovery spent a miserable 106 days in the cold, wet winter of 1805–1806. The exact site is not known; the placement of the reconstruction was an educated guess. In the winter of 1806, the rain almost never stopped. The local Chinook Indians were subtly hostile, and, unlike many Indians the Corps had encountered, were quite experienced at dealing with white men. (Ships of several nations had been sailing, and sailors landing, along the Pacific Coast for years.) The Indians were happy to steal what they could or fornicate for a price. Archeologists looking for the precise site of the fort are searching for traces of mercury, a deadly main ingredient of of the Corps' medication for venereal disease. Most of the men of the Corps died very young. Historians speculate that these poisonous medications may have contributed to their early deaths.

Game was scarce and winter-lean, and provisions were low. The Corps of Discovery made their own salt, boiling down seawater with a constant great fire. The "joy" of reaching and seeing the Pacific Ocean soon turned to miserable monotony. The elk they shot were hungry and depleted, so there was little fat, little food value, in their meat. Morale sank to the lowest of the trip. The sodden winter was as sore a test as grizzly bears or hostile Indians. Western Oregon is indeed very wet and gray in the winter. In 1778, Captain James Cook christened the first landmark he saw on the North American Pacific coast "Cape Foulweather." It's at Depoe Bay, just north of Newport. Searching for a new state slogan in 2006, Oregon got some very funny (and surely unwelcome) suggestions. My favorite: "Oregon: Where Lewis and Clark Discovered Seasonal Affective Disorder."

—"Roll On, Columbia, Roll On," as Woody Guthrie sang. (He wrote that in 1941 while he was subsidized by the Bonneville Power Authority dam builders.) The Columbia River valley is several different landscapes. West of the Bonneville and Dalles dams it is green and lovely. Farther east, the land gets browner because the dams are for power and irrigation downstream. (Some of those dams may soon be gone in order to preserve the local salmon, whose spawning runs have been all but destroyed. Good.) More dams, and more, and it's very quiet country, almost wild land for thirty miles. Then, at Hood River, there are suddenly towns, mills, stores. For most of the way, the Washington (north) side of the river is almost empty—just a very nice quiet road. In Ontario, in eastern Oregon, US 20 and US 30 cross back to their proper relative positions again.

works cited

(and other important books)

Abbey, Edward. *Desert Solitaire: A Season in the Wilderness*. New York: McGraw-Hill, 1968.

Albright, Horace M. As told to Robert Cahn. *The Birth of the National Park Service: The Founding Years, 1913–1933*. Salt Lake City: Howe Brothers, 1985.

———. *Oh, Ranger! A Book About the National Parks*. New York: Dodd, Mead, 1934.

Ambrose, Stephen. *Crazy Horse and Custer: The Parallel Lives of Two American Warriors*. New York: Anchor Books, 1996.

———. *Undaunted Courage: Meriwether Lewis, Thomas Jefferson, and The Opening of the American West*. New York: Simon and Schuster, 1997.

Bach, Orville E. Jr. *Exploring the Yellowstone Backcountry*. San Francisco: Sierra Club Books, 1991.

———. *Tracking the Spirit of Yellowstone*. Blue Willow Press/Yellowstone Association, 2005.

Berry, Wendell. *Home Economics*. San Francisco: North Point Press, 1987.

Cahill, Tim. *Lost in My Own Back Yard: A Walk in Yellowstone National Park*. New York: Crown, 2004.

Cantor, George. *Where the Old Roads Go: Driving the First Federal Highways of the Northeast*. New York: Harper Collins, 1989.

Carmer, Carl. "New York." In *American Panorama*. Philadelphia: Curtis Publishing Co., 1960.

Carr, Ethan. *Wilderness by Design: Landscape Architecture and the National Park Service*. Lincoln and London: University of Nebraska Press, 1998.

Chapple, Janet. *Yellowstone Treasures: The Traveler's Companion to the National Park*. 2nd ed. Providence, RI: Granite Peak Publications, 2002, 2005.

Chittenden, Hiram M. *The Yellowstone National Park*. Norman: University of Oklahoma Press, 1973.

Cross, Whitney R. *The Burned-Over District*. Ithaca: Cornell University Press, 1950.

Cromie, Alice. *Restored America*. New York: American Legacy Press, 1984.

Czarnecki, Michael. *Twenty Days on Route 20*. Kanona, NY: Foothills Publishing, 1997.

DeVoto, Bernard, ed. *The Journals of Lewis and Clark*. Boston: Houghton Mifflin, 1997.

Duncan, Dayton. *Lewis and Clark: The Journey of the Corps of Discovery*. New York: Knopf, 1997.

———. *Miles from Nowhere: Tales From America's Contemporary Frontier*. New York: Viking, 1993.

———. *Out West: A Journey Through Lewis and Clark's America*. Lincoln: University of Nebraska Press, 2003.

Ferguson, Gary. *Hawk's Rest: A Season in the Remote Heart of Yellowstone*. Washington, DC: National Geographic Society, 2003.

Frome, Michael. *National Park Guide*. New York: Prentice-Hall/Simon and Schuster, 1989.

Genovese, Peter. *The Great American Road Trip: US 1, Maine to Florida*. New Brunswick: Rutgers University Press, 2003.

Gooodwin, Doris Kearns. *Team of Rivals:The Political Genius of Abraham Lincoln*. New York: Simon and Schuster, 2005.

Halfpenny, James C. *Yellowstone Wolves In the Wild*. Helena: Riverbend Publishing, 2003.

Hardorff, Richard G. *The Death of Crazy Horse*. Lincoln: University of Nebraska Press, 1998.

Hughes, Ted. *Birthday Letters*. New York: Farrar, Strauss, Giroux, 1998.

Janetski, Joel C. *Indians in Yellowstone National Park*. Salt Lake City: University of Utah Press, 2002.

Jeffers, H. P. *An Honest President*. New York: William Morrow, 2000.

Jemison, G. Peter, and Anna M. Schein. *The Treaty of Canandaigua, 1794: 200 Years of Treaty Relations between the Iroquois Confederacy and the United States*. Santa Fe: Clear Light Publishers, 2000.

Kaszynski, William. *The American Highway*. Jefferson, NC: McFarland and Co., 2000.

Least Heat Moon, William. *Blue Highways: A Journey into America*. New York: Ballantine Books, 1984.

———. *PrairyErth. (a deep map)*. Boston: Houghton Mifflin, 1991.

———. *River Horse: The Logbook of a Boat Across America*. Boston: Houghton Mifflin, 1999.

Leopold, Aldo. *A Sand County Almanac*. New York and Oxford: Oxford University Press, 1949, 1987.

Matthews, Anne. *Where the Buffalo Roam*. Chicago: University of Chicago Press, 2002.

Matthiessen, Peter. *In The Spirit of Crazy Horse.* New York: Penguin Books, 1992.

McPhee, John. *Rising from The Plains.* New York: Farrar, Strauss, Giroux, 1986.

McAllister, Catherine. *The Brotherhood of the New Life.* Fredonia, NY, 1995.

McIntyre, Rick. *A Society of Wolves.* Osceola, WI: Voyageur Press, 1996.

McMurtry, Larry. *Road: Driving America's Great Highways.* New York: Simon and Schuster, 2001.

———. *Sacagawea's Nickname.* New York: New York Review Books, 2004.

McNamee, Thomas. *The Return of the Wolf to Yellowstone.* New York: Owl Books, 1998.

Mech, L. David. *The Way of the Wolf.* Osceola, WI: Voyageur Press, 1991.

Nabhan, Gary Paul. *Cultures of Habitat.* Washington, DC: Counterpoint, 1997.

Neihardt, John G., ed. *Black Elk Speaks.* New York: Simon and Schuster, 1972.

Nelson, Don. *Paddling Yellowstone and Grand Teton National Parks.* Helena: Falcon Books, 1999.

Pollan, Michael. *The Omnivore's Dilemma: A Natural History of Four Meals.* New York: Penguin, 2006.

———. *The Botany of Desire.* New York: Random House, 2001.

Raitz, Karl, ed. *The National Road.* Baltimore and London: The Johns Hopkins University Press, 1996.

Ridge, Alice A., and John Wm. *Introducing The Yellowstone Trail: A Good Road from Plymouth Rock to Puget Sound.* Altoona, WI: Yellowstone Trail Publishers, 2000.

Salisbury, Albert and Jane. *Two Captains West.* Seattle: Superior Publishing Co., 1960.

Sandoz, Mari. *Old Jules.* Boston: Little, Brown, 1935.

———. *Crazy Horse: The Strange Man of the Oglalas.* New York: Knopf, 1942.

———. *The Battle of the Little Big Horn.* Philadelphia: Lippincott, 1966.

———. *Cheyenne Autumn.* New York: McGraw-Hill, 1953.

———. "Nebraska." In *American Panorama.* Philadelphia: Curtis Publishing Co., 1960.

Schullery, Paul. *Mountain Time.* New York: Fireside reprint, 1988.

———. *Searching For Yellowstone. Ecology and Wonder in the Last Wilderness.* New York: Houghton Mifflin, 1997.

Sellars, Richard West. *Preserving Nature in the National Parks.* New Haven and London: Yale University Press, 1997.

Sexton, Anne. *Anne Sexton: A Self-Portrait in Letters.* Boston: Houghton Mifflin, 1977.

Sexton, Linda Gray. *Searching for Mercy Street.* Boston: Little, Brown, 1994.

Sholly, Dan R. *Guardians of Yellowstone.* New York: William Morrow, 1991.

Smoak, Gregory E. *Ghost Dances and Identity*. Berkeley: University of California Press, 2006.

Smith, Curt. *Windows on the White House*. South Bend: Diamond Communications, 1997.

Smith, Douglas W., and Gary Ferguson. *Decade of the Wolf: Returning the Wild to Yellowstone*. Boston: The Lyons Press, 2005.

Snyder, Tom. *Route 66 Traveler's Guide and Roadside Companion*. New York: St. Martin's Griffin, 2000.

Stegner, Wallace. *The Sound of Mountain Water*. New York: E. P. Dutton, 1980.

———. *Beyond the Hundredth Meridian*. New York: Penguin Books, 1992.

———. *Mormon Country*. Lincoln: University of Nebraska Press, 1982.

Stewart, George. *US 40: Cross Section of the United States of America*. Boston: Houghton Mifflin, 1953.

Taylor, Dr. H. C. *Memorial Sketches of the Town of Portland*. Portland, NY: 1873.

Thoreau, Henry David. "Walking." In *The Heath Anthology of American Literature*. 2nd. Ed. Lexington, MA: D. C. Heath, 1994.

———. *Cape Cod*. Orleans, MA: Parnassus Imprints, 1984.

Turner, Erin H. *It Happened in Yellowstone*. Helena: Falcon Books, 2001.

Utley, Robert M., and Wilcomb E. Washburn. *Indian Wars*. Boston: American Heritage/Houghton Mifflin, 1987.

index

Abbey of Our Lady of the Genesee (NY), 61–63
Addams, Jane, 107–108
African American celebrities, 59
African American writers, 23
Albright, Horace M.., 169, 184
American Civil Liberties Union (ACLU), 108
American Mission movement, 96
American Prairie Foundation, 126
American roads, mythic, xvi
Amish farmers, 61
Anderson, Sherwood, 23
Apple River Fort (IL), 109
Arapaho Indians, 156
Arthur Bowring Sandhills Ranch State Historical Park (NE), 128
Arts and Crafts movement, 45–46
Atheneum Hotel at Chautauqua Institution, 47–48
atomic power, 277–278
automobiles and the need for good roads, xiv

"Back Country Byways" (BLM), 151–152
Baird, Gordon, 266
Bannock Indians, 279
Bannock War, 180, 284–285
baseball in Chicago, 59–60
Battle of Fallen Timbers, 99
Battle of Warbonnet (Hat) Creek, 140

bears in captivity, 262–265
Bedell, Grace, 107
beef cattle, 125
beer and Indians, 126–128
Birthday Letters (Hughes), 12, 185
"Birthplace of Television," 276
bison population in U.S., 220–223
Black Hills (SD), 144–145
The Book of Mormon, 37
Bowring, Arthur, 128
Bozeman Trail, 141
Bradford, William, 218
Bridger, Jim, 172, 174–175
Bridger Trail, 162
Brotherhood of Sleeping Car Porters (BSCP), 58–59
Brotherhood of the New Life, 50–54
brucellosis, fear of, 222
Buffalo Bill Cody, 162–164, 170
Buffalo Bill Cody's Wild West [Show], 140
Buffalo Bill Historical Center, 163–164
Buffalo Commons, 124–125, 131
Buffalo Horn, 180, 285
Bureau of Land Management (BLM), 150–152
Burned-Over District (NY), 27–63

"The Camas Prairie War," 279
Cape Cod National Seashore, 218
Capital City (Sandoz), 138

Cardiff Giant, 35–37
  in Iowa, 116
Carhenge, 136
Carrier, Willis, 71
cattle grazing and feedlots, 151
Chadron State College, 136–137
Charbonneau, Baptiste, 159–160
Chautauqua Institution, 46–50
Chautauqua Literary and Scientific
  Circle, 49–50
"Chautauquas," 49–50
Cheyenne Indians, 140
Chief Joseph, 178–179
Church of Jesus Christ of Latter Day
  Saints, 37–39, 164, 273–275
"Civil Disobedience" (Thoreau), 102
civil service, federal, 74–76
Clark, William, 118–119, 158–160
Clark Art Institute, Robert Sterling and
  Francine, 20–21
Clemens, Samuel Langhorne, 111–112
Cleveland, [Stephen] Grover, 87–90
coast-to-coast highways, xxiii
Cody, William F. ("Buffalo Bill"),
  162–164, 170
Colter, John, 171–172
"Colter's Hell Hot Springs," 172
Compromise of 1850, 75
conservation
  and tourism in the west, 217
  of Yellowstone, 184
corn prices and ethanol, 124
Corps of Discovery (Lewis and Clark),
  118–119, 158–160
Cowan, Emma, 178
cowboys and settlers, 128
Coyote Woman, 257
"Craftsman style," 45
Craighead, Frank and John, 187
Craters of the Moon National Monument
  and Preserve (ID), 278
Crazy Horse, 142–143
  Memorial, 145–146
Crazy Horse: The Strange Man of the
  Oglalas (Sandoz), 142
Custer, George Armstrong, 78–81, 139
Custer, payback for, 140–141
"Custer's Last Stand," 81

"Declaration of Sentiments," 68–70
Defenders of Wildlife, 237
Deschutes National Forest, 287
Deschutes River, water diverted, 287–288
deWalt, Roy, 228
Dickinson, Emily, 5–10
  and religion, 28
Dodge, Grenville, 174–175
Douglas, Paul, 101
Douglas, Stephen A., 106–107
Duncan, Dayton, 123

EBR-1 nuclear power plant (ID), 277–278
Eisenhower, Dwight D., xiv
Emerson, Ralph Waldo, 102
energy scandals, 152–153
energy sources, exploration for, 151–152
entertainment, intellectual, 49–50
equality for all, 68–70
Erie (PA), 301
Erie Canal, xi–xii, 73
Everts, Truman C., 175

Farnsworth, Philo T., 276
Federal Land Policy and Management
  Act (FLPMA), 151
feedlots and cattle, 119–120
Fetterman, William J., 148–149
Field of Dreams, 113
"The 59th Bear" (Hughes), 185
"The Fighting 442nd," 166
Fillmore, Millard, 74–76
Finger Lakes (NY) National Forest, 224
Finney, Charles Grandison, 63–65
fire policy in National Forests, 269–270
"First Encounter Beach," 139
"Fishing Bridge" (Hughes), 185
Florence Hotel, Pullman (IL), 55, 57–58
Ford, Henry, xiv
forest fires, statistics, 270
forest fires in Yellowstone (1988), 214–216
Fort Fetterman State Historic Site (WY),
  148
Fort Robinson (NE), 143
Frederick Law Olmsted National His-
  toric Site (MA), 3
Freeport Doctrine, 107
French, Daniel Chester, 22

Frontier, concept of, 100–101
Fundamentalist Church of Jesus Christ of
    Latter Day Saints, 38

Gallatin National Forest (MT), 266
gambling casinos, 284
Gardipee, Flo, 221
Garfield, James A., 83–86
Gast, John, 103–104
geodes, 281
ghost town
    Heart Mountain (WY), 164–166
    Jireh, WY, 147–148
giveaways as memorial (Plains Indians),
    157–158
Grand Teton National Park (WY), 217,
    271–272
Grant, [Hiram] Ulysses S., 109–110
    legislation to create first national park,
    177
Greater Yellowstone Coalition (GYC),
    212, 262
Great Plains
    economic woes, 124–126
    possible futures for, 125–126
Grizzly and Wolf Discovery Center
    (WY), 262–265
Guardians of Yellowstone (Sholly), 214–215
Guiteau, Charles J., 84

Haddox, John, 158
Hall, John, 11
Hanna, Mark, 87, 90, 93
Harriman State Park (ID), 270–271
Harris, Thomas Lake, 50–54
"Harry Yount Award," 181
Hawthorne, Nathaniel, 16
Hay, John, 87
Hayden, Ferdinand V., 174–177
Hayes, Rutherford B., 76–78, 81–83
    and Southern states, 82
Hayes Presidential Library, 81–82
Hicks, Edward, 196–197
High Desert Museum (OR), 287
highway names, xxxii–xxxiii
Hill Cumorah (NY), 41–42
homesteaders, 285
Hopkins, Mark, 96

hot springs, 155
Houdini, Harry, 32
Hubbard, Elbert, 44–46
Hughes, Ted, 11–12
    in Yellowstone, 185–186
Hull, George, 35–37

Idaho, 267–281
    Boise, 280–281
    Idaho Falls, 276–277
    Rexburg, 273–276
Idaho National Engineering and
    Environmental Laboratory (INEEL),
    277
Illinois
    Cedarville, 107
    Chicago, 24–26, 100
    DeKalb County, 105
    Dixon, 93
    Elizabeth, 109
    Freeport, 106
    Galena, 109–110
    Genoa, 105
    Highland Park, xvi–xx
    Nauvoo, 37
    Pullman, 55–58
    Riverside, 104
imperialism, U.S., 91–92
Indian
    dance competitions, 157–158
    fights and forts, 148–149
    policy, U. S., 79
    wars, 139–166, 285
Indiana, 100–101
Indiana Dunes National Lakeshore, 101
"Indian Time," 157
internment camp for Japanese, 164–166
Interstate Highway System, xiv
Iowa, 113–118
    Dubuque, 111–113
    Dyersville, 113
    Fort Dodge, 116
    Grinnell, xxii
    New Melleray, 113–115
    Parkersburg, 115–116

Jackalope, 148
Jireh (WY), 147

Kennedy, John Fitzgerald, 3
Kingman, Daniel, 180–181
Know Nothing Party, 75–76

Lakota Indians, 140, 141, 144–145
land use in the West, 119–120, 124, 151,
    283
Latter-Day Saints, 37–39, 164, 273–275
lava flow, 276–279, 283
Least Heat-Moon, William, xxiv
Leopold, Aldo, 198, 202, 218, 259, 269
Lewis and Clark Corps of Discovery,
    117–119
Life on the Mississippi (Twain), 112
Limerick, Patty Nelson, 100
Lincoln, Abraham, 106–110
Lincoln, Land of, 106–109
Little Big Horn, Battle of, 78–81, 139
Little Turtle, 99
logging industry, 268–269, 287, 289–290
Louisiana Purchase, 117–118
Love sheep ranch, 153–154
Lowell, Amy, 3–4

manifest destiny, empire, and resistance,
    102–104
manifest destiny as art, 103–104
Mari Sandoz High Plains Heritage
    [Research] Center, 136
Massachusetts
    artistic overview of US 20, 3–4
    the Berkshires, 18–19
    Boston and the Word, 1
    Brookline, 3–4
    Concord, world of Thoreau, 2
    religions in, 28
    Williamstown, 19–22
Massachusetts Museum of Contemporary
    Art, 20
Mather, Stephen Tyng, 184
McClellan, George, 110
McKenzie Pass–Santiam Pass Scenic
    Byway, 288
McKinley, William, 90–92
McPhee, John, 153–154, 156
Melville, Herman, 14–16
Mesa Falls Scenic Byway (ID), 271
"A Message to Garcia," 44

methane exploration, 152
Midgely, Mary, 260
Miles from Nowhere (Duncan), 123
Miller, William, 31–32
mineral rights in the West, 152
Model T Ford, xiv
Montana
    Targhee Pass, 267
    West Yellowstone, 261–265
Montana Department of Livestock,
    222
Mormons, 37–39, 164, 273–275
Mount Rushmore National Memorial
    (SD), 146–147
museum directors and Williams College,
    20–21
museums, automobile
    in Indiana, 100

National Forest, first, established, 89
National Forest Service, 268–269
National Forests near Yellowstone,
    212
National Mississippi River Museum and
    Aquarium (IA), 112
National Park Rangers, 181
National Park Service
    Act (1916), 184
    mission statement, 184
natural gas exploration, 152, 160
Nature Conservancy, 126
Nebraska, 118–147
    Alliance, 135–136
    Crookston, 121–122
    Gordon, 135
    population decline in, 123–125
Nelson, Harold (Red), 59, 105
Nelson, Kay, 105
Nelson, Mac
    and home on Route 20, xxiv–xxvii,
        xxxi, 60–61
    and Illinois boyhood, xvi–xx
    and roads east/west, xx–xxii
    and roads north/south, xvi–xx
Nelson, Ruth, 105
Newberry National Volcanic Monument
    (OR), 287
New England Wilderness Act, 225

New Melleray Abbey (IA), 113–115
New West, 286–287
   change and the, 217
New York
   Angola, 71
   Auburn, 65–67
   Brocton, 50–55, 60–61
   Canandaigua, 107
   Cardiff, 35–37
   Cayuga County, 74
   Chautauqua, 46–50
   Chautauqua County, 32–35
   East Aurora, 44–46, 74
   Fredonia, xxiv–xxv, 49, 281, 287, 295, 298–300
   Lily Dale, 33–35
   Palmyra, 37–39
   Piffard, 61–63
   Seneca Falls, 68–70
   Syracuse, 45
   Utica, 52
Nez Perce Indians, 178–179
ninety-eighth meridian, 120–123
Norman Rockwell Museum (MA), 22
Noyes, John Humphrey, 43–44

Oberlin College, 63–65
Oh, Ranger! (Albright), 169
Ohio
   Camden, 23
   Clyde, 23–24
   Fremont, 81
   Hiram, 83
   Kirtland, 37
   Maumee, 99–100
   Menton, 85–86
   Niles, 90
   Oberlin, 63
oil exploration, 152
Old Jules (Sandoz), 128–129
Olmsted, Frederick Law, 2–3
   and Riverside, IL, 104
Oneida Community, 43–44, 84
Oregon, 281–292
   Corvallis, 288
   Newport, 290–291
Oregon Coast Aquarium, 291
Oregon desert, 281–282

Oregon State University, 289
Oregon Trail visitor center, 281

Paiute Indian reservation (OR), 284–285
paradise regained, illusion of, 199–202
Parment, William, 54
The Peaceable Kingdom, 196–197
Plains Indians
   and alcohol problems, 126–128
   and bison, 220
   and vision quests, 260
Plath, Sylvia, 4, 10–13
   in Yellowstone, 185
political power in the U.S., 71–78
polygamy, 38, 40–41, 275
Pony Express, xiii
Popper, Frank and Deborah, 124–125, 131
presidents with Route 20 ties, 72–78
Protestant Christianity, 27–28
Pullman, George M., 55–58

Quake Lake (MT), 266

railroads and the West, 261–262
"ranchettes," 286–287
Reagan, Ronald, 93–94
Red Cloud, 140–141
Red Rock Lakes National Wildlife Refuge (MT), 266–267
religions along the Great Road, 27–44
   Amish, 61
   Indian, 28
   Seventh Day Adventists, 32
   Shakers, 29–31
   Spiritualism, 32–35
   Strangites, 42
   Trappists, 61–63, 113–115
Republican Party, 65
Ricks College, 273–275
Rising from the Plains (McPhee), 153–154, 156
river travel, xii–xiii
roads, need for improved, xiv
Rockefeller, John D., 94–97
   burial place, 87
   legacy, 96–97
Rockwell, Norman, 22
rodeos in the West, 157

Roosevelt, Theodore, 92
Ross, Araminta. *See* Tubman, Harriet
Route 5, 87
Route 6, xxi–xxii
Route 20
    the last great road, xxiv
    major cities on, 105–106
    mileage of, xxxii–xxxiii
    other names of, xxxiii
    in Yellowstone National Park, 170
Route 30, xxiii
Route 41, xviii–xx
Roycroft Community, 45–46
Runte, Alfred, 177, 226

Sacagawea, 158–159
Sandburg, Carl, xxx, 101
A Sand Country Almanac (Leopold), 202
Sandhills of Nebraska, 131, 133–135
Sandoz, Caroline, 131, 133, 136
Sandoz, Jules
    family history, 128–131
Sandoz, Mari, 128–129, 132–133, 137–138
    and Crazy Horse, 145–146
Sandoz country, 128–129
Schullery, Paul, 176
scientific research in the wilderness, 259
Searching for Yellowstone (Schullery), 176
Second Great Awakening, 28
"semi-ghost" towns in Nebraska,
    122–123
Seneca Indians, 28
Seventh Day Adventists, 32
Seward, William H., 65–66
Sexton, Anne, 4, 13–14
Shaker religion, 29–31
sheep ranches, 153–154
Sheridan, General Phil, 290
Sholly, Dan, 214–215
Shoshone Cavern National Monument
    (WY), 169–170
Shoshone Days, 157
Shoshone Indians, 277, 279
Sioux Indians, 140
Sitting Bull, 141–142
Slogum House (Sandoz), 132
Smith, Joseph, 37
snowstorm in June, 161–162

soldiers and indians, 139–166
The Sound of Mountain Water (Stegner),
    271
South Pass City Hotel, xxix–xxx
Spiritualism, 32–35
spoils system, 73–74, 76
Stegner, Wallace, 260, 271
Stickley, Gustave, 45
Strang, James Jesse, 42–43
Strangites, 42
SUNY-Fredonia, ix, x, 23, 49, 266, 275,
    298–299, 300

Tarbell, Ida M., 94–95
Teapot Dome, 152–153
Teton Dam collapse (1976), 275
theatre in Massachusetts, 19–22
"Thinking Like a Mountain" (Leopold),
    198
Thoreau, Henry David, 244, 291
    about wildness, 220
    and Cape Cod, 218
    jailed, 102
    and roads west, xv
    and travel west, 2
Thundereggs, 281
Tilden, Samuel J., 77–78
"Trail Town" (WY), 168
Trappist monasteries, 61–63, 113–115
travel, Americans' love of, xi, xv
Tubman, Harriet, 66–67
Turner, Frederick Jackson, 100
Twain, Mark, 111–112

Underwood, Gilbert Stanley, 262
Union Pacific R.R., 262
unions
    and George M. Pullman, 56

van Buren, Martin, 72–74
Vidler's 5 & 10, 46
"Vine Cliff," 50–51

Walden (Thoreau), 244
"Walking" (Thoreau), 2
Washakie, Chief (Shoshone), 155–156
Washburn-Langford-Doane party, 175
water and the modern west, 282–283

Wayne, "Mad Anthony," 99–100
West, signs of the, 120–123
westward migration of Americans, xxx
westward to Indiana and beyond, 99–138
Wharton, Edith, 16–18
"Whigs," 75
wilderness
    American, 220–224
    defined, 224
    official minimum size, 224
    reasons to preserve, 258–259
    what is it for?, 258–260
Wilderness Letter (Stegner), 260
Wilderness Society, 224
wildlife preservation, 259–260
wildness and wilderness, 224–226
Wilkinson, Jemima, 31
Willamette National Forest (OR), 288
Williams College, 19–20, 83
    and museum directors, 20–21
    Museum of Art, 21–22
Williamstown Theatre Festival, 19–20
Wind River Reservation (WY), 156
Winesburg, Ohio, 23–24
wolves in captivity, 262
Woman's Christian Temperance Union
    (WCTU), 78
women's movement, 68–70
Women's Rights Historical Park, 68
Wounded Knee, 127–128
writers from Chicago, 25–26
writers from Massachusetts, 1–2, 4–10
Wyoming, 147–166, 167–216
    Casper, 150
    Cody, 161–164, 167–170
    Fort Washakie, 156
    Heart Mountain, 164–166
    Jireh, 147
    South Pass City Hotel, xxix–xxx
    Thermopolis, 154–156
Wyoming Dinosaur Center, 156
Wyoming Pioneer Memorial Museum,
    148

Yaquina Bay (OR), 290–292
Yellowstone National Park, 167–218,
    219–260
    Agate Creek wolf pack, 256–258

altitude, acclimate to, 230
animal sightings, 209–210
approaches to, 167
backcountry permit, 238
bears, diet of, 199–200
bears, garbage feeding of, 185–187
bears and tourists, 185
bear watching, 239–240
bear watching (1955–2007), 187–190
Bechler Ranger Station, 267
birdwatching, 249
camping, 211–212
campsite selection, 228–229
by canoe to wilderness, 226–230
canoe trip, cost of, 251
canoe trip, second, 252–253
and cars, 191
cars and horses, 193
cars on dirt/gravel roads, 214
"Colter's Hell," 169
coyotes, 257
dirt roads for horses/wagons, 181
Druid wolfpack, 230–235
Echinus Geyser, 204–205
established as National Park, 177
explorers, 172–176
and fire of 1988, 214–216
fishing restrictions, 213
Grand Canyon of the Yellowstone,
    Lower Falls, 208
Grand Prismatic Spring, 207
Grizzly bear family life, 233
Hayden Valley, 209
hiking suggestions, 213
Indian visitors, early, 171
information websites, 203
Lamar River Valley, 209
Mammoth Hot Springs, 207–208
map of, 227
moose population, 230
Mud Volcano, 208
non-thermal features, 208–209
Norris Geyser Basin, 204–207
Old Faithful Geyser, 204
Old Faithful Inn, 193, 211
as the Peaceable Kingdom, 196–197
planning your visit, 202–203
predator and prey, 197–198

(Yellowstone National Park, *continued*)
and railroads, 191
Ranger programs, 209
Shoshone Geyser Basin, 255
Shoshone Lake canoe trip, 255–256
Slough Creek and campground,
230–232
snowmobiles in, 265
and stagecoaches, 192
Steamboat Geyser, 207
thermal features, 203–208
tourist injuries, 200–202, 240
tourists, 192–195
tourists, early, 178
traffic jams, 210
tree-fire-seed-tree cycle, 216
Upper Falls of the Yellowstone River,
208–209
U.S. Army on duty in, 180–183
wilderness, not an official, 225

wilderness canoe trip, 226–230
wolf population, 235
wolf watching, 209, 230–231, 256–258
wolves, economic impact, 237–238
and wolves, original gray, 197–198
wolves in, 197–198, 233–238
wolves outside the park, 236–237
wolves reintroduced, 233–234
Yellowstone Lake, 209, 228
Yellowstone Lake canoe trip, 240–250
Yellowstone River, 249–250
Yellowstone Park Transportation Company, 192–193
Yellowstone wilderness, travel by water,
212
Yosemite National Park, 177
Young, Brigham, 37–40, 42, 52, 65
Yount, Harry, 181

Ziolkowski, Korczak, 145–146